IRON AGE HILLFORTS IN BRITAIN AND BEYOND

Iron Age Hillforts in Britain and Beyond

D. W. HARDING

OXFORD
UNIVERSITY PRESS

OXFORD
UNIVERSITY PRESS

Great Clarendon Street, Oxford, OX2 6DP,
United Kingdom

Oxford University Press is a department of the University of Oxford.
It furthers the University's objective of excellence in research, scholarship,
and education by publishing worldwide. Oxford is a registered trade mark of
Oxford University Press in the UK and in certain other countries

© D. W. Harding 2012

The moral rights of the author have been asserted

First Edition published in 2012

Impression: 1

All rights reserved. No part of this publication may be reproduced, stored in
a retrieval system, or transmitted, in any form or by any means, without the
prior permission in writing of Oxford University Press, or as expressly permitted
by law, by licence or under terms agreed with the appropriate reprographics
rights organization. Enquiries concerning reproduction outside the scope of the
above should be sent to the Rights Department, Oxford University Press, at the
address above

You must not circulate this work in any other form
and you must impose this same condition on any acquirer

British Library Cataloguing in Publication Data
Data available

Library of Congress Cataloging in Publication Data
Data available

ISBN 978–0–19–969524–9

Printed in Great Britain by
MPG Books Group, Bodmin and King's Lynn

Preface

The purpose of the present study is a critical review of the current state of hillfort research in Britain and Ireland in the wider context of the European Iron Age. Hillforts are a dominant field monument in Britain from the later Bronze Age to the post-Roman Iron Age. With the diversity of sites generally included under the umbrella heading of hillforts, no single explanation of their function or social significance could satisfy all situations. The older conventional view of hillforts as defensive strongholds and regional centres of social elites has been challenged by current fashion in favour of their symbolic and cosmological significance. Even within Britain there are marked regional imbalances in hillfort distribution, raising the question of what functions did hillforts serve that in non-hillfort communities could be served by other means? Changing attitudes to field research are critically reviewed, and future problems and prospects are identified in the light of current priorities in public archaeology. The book is intended primarily for academic and professional readership, but in the current absence of a synthesis covering Britain as a whole through the first millennia BC and AD, it is hoped that it may also provide an introduction to hillforts for students of archaeology at all levels.

Hillforts have been a life-long interest for someone who grew up within cycling distance of some of the major Dorset hillforts, like Badbury Rings and Maiden Castle, and who has schoolboy recollections of Ian Richmond's excavations at Hod Hill. As a teenager I worked as a volunteer digger at Dinas Powys with Leslie Alcock, who applied his mentor Sir Mortimer Wheeler's standards of excavation and recording that were by no means universally practised in the 1950s. On excavations in Wales, I worked with senior students who subsequently came to prominence in British professional archaeology, and with whom I enjoyed a reunion after more than fifty years at the Hillfort Studies Group's spring meeting in 2011 in Pembrokeshire. As a postgraduate at the Oxford Institute of Archaeology and as a young lecturer in Durham, I visited sites and excavations in Britain and abroad in the inspirational and sometimes demanding company of Christopher Hawkes, from whom I learned the importance of seeing the British Iron Age from a wider European perspective, and in whose company I met some of the leading European practitioners of the time.

The late 1960s was a key period in hillfort studies, with the launch of the Danebury project finally offering the prospect of uncovering a substantial proportion of a hillfort's interior, an ambition that had been beyond the resources that most excavators were able to muster. At the same time the

Cadbury Castle excavations prompted controversy for the apparent emphasis on Arthurian connections, at least on the part of the project's fund-raisers and publicists. My own trial excavation at Blewburton Hill was funded only for a single season, but was memorable for the good company of an excellent team, lodged in the Rev. Derwas Chitty's rambling Upton Rectory in the summer of *San Francisco* and *Whiter Shade of Pale*.

Ireland I visited periodically since the 1960s, and during two terms as Extern Examiner to the NUI, I explored key sites in the authoritative company of Barry Raftery, who took me to Rathgall and Dún Ailinne, Michael Herity, with whom I visited Rathcroghan, and Etienne Rynne, with whom I several times visited stone forts in the Burren and the Aran Islands. I am especially obliged to George Eogan, however, for his and Fiona's hospitality, and for numerous informative visits to the Boyne Valley. After the late 1970s, visiting sites in the North was hardly practical, and it was therefore a particular pleasure earlier this summer to be able to visit Emain Macha, belatedly for the first time, during the course of the International Congress of Celtic Studies in Maynooth.

Interim results of important new hillfort excavations, together with reassessments of some older investigations, were assembled in a volume of essays published in 1976 under the title *Hillforts: Later Prehistoric Earthworks in Britain and Ireland*. In that volume, Michael Avery contributed an authoritative introduction that became a student's guide to the topic for a generation. My biggest regret was that I did not contribute a final chapter, summarizing the issues and current state of research. In retrospect, had I done so, its limitations would now doubtless have been a source of embarrassment, not just because of the accumulation of new data, but because approaches to hillfort interpretation have undergone radical change. Older conventional ideas are not necessarily redundant or wrong, but in the face of legitimate challenge they require more rigorous justification if they are to be sustained.

With my appointment in Edinburgh in 1977, my attention turned to northern hillforts, to field walking and air-photographic survey in the Borders, and when opportunity permitted, in the Northern and Western Isles. Few hillforts in Scotland were built on the scale of the Wessex hillforts, though their location can be visually impressive. But the smaller forts of Atlantic Scotland (and Ireland) can command breathtaking topography and architecture in stone that provides another dimension altogether from the Wessex model.

I acknowledge with pleasure my debt to colleagues and old friends who have provided illustrations, notably Michael Avery and Philip Dixon, and those other societies and agencies that are acknowledged in the captions. I am indebted to Ian Blake for comments and suggestions on the text, and to Alun Martin, CUCAP Librarian at the Department of Geography, University of Cambridge, for tracking down the Hambledon Hill air photograph. Once again I am indebted to Avril Stevens and colleagues in the Gullane public library for use of photocopying facilities. Finally I should again record my debt to Carole for her patience and forbearance.

D. W. Harding

Gullane, East Lothian,
Christmas, 2011.

Contents

List of Illustrations — xii
Abbreviations — xvi

1. Defining Issues — 1
   - Earthworks and enclosure — 5
   - Size and distribution — 8
   - Enclosure morphology — 11
   - Topography and location — 15
   - The 'pacification of prehistory' and the 'Celtic' paradigm — 18
   - Hillfort interiors: buildings and their use — 20
   - Resources and social implications — 22
   - The function of hillforts — 27

2. History of Hillfort Studies — 29
   - Early field survey and site description — 30
   - Pioneers of hillfort survey and excavation — 31
   - Hillfort excavation in Central and Western Europe — 35
   - Defensive sequence and chronology — 37
   - Wheeler and the historical paradigm — 39
   - The 'new archaeology' and after — 43
   - Hillfort research since Danebury — 45
   - Publication — 47
   - The future of hillfort studies — 50

3. Anatomy of Hillfort Enclosure — 53
   - Palisaded or stockaded enclosures — 54
   - Ramparts — 58
   - Ditches — 74
   - Entrances — 75
   - 'Unfinished' hillforts — 87
   - Conclusions — 88

4. Inside and Outside of Hillforts — 91
   - Hillfort interiors — 95
   - Extramural settlement — 113

5. Hillforts in the Landscape — 119
   - Hillfort environs: case studies — 120
   - *Oppida* — 130
   - Landscapes without hillforts — 139

6. Chronology	151
Neolithic camps and fortified sites	151
Bronze Age antecedents	154
Roman period occupation of hillforts	158
Post-Roman hillforts in Wales and the west	162
Early historic hillforts in northern Britain	165
Irish ringforts	172
7. Function 1: Defence	177
Warfare in prehistory	178
'War cemeteries' and massacre sites	179
Evidence of destruction	185
'Vitrified forts' and burnt ramparts	188
Chevaux-de-frise	190
Weaponry and sling-stone hoards	192
Ritualized warfare	196
Conclusions	198
8. Function 2: Social, Economic, Ritual	201
Permanent, periodic, or seasonal occupation?	201
Central places, storage, redistribution, and status	203
Burial and funerary rituals	208
Excarnation and 'normative' burial	215
Other ritual or ceremonial roles	217
Currency bar hoards and metalworking	223
Conclusions	225
9. Documentary Sources	227
Caesar, Tacitus, and classical sources	228
Irish literary sources	240
Early historic northern Britain	242
Conclusions	246
10. Ethnographic Models	249
Pā sites of New Zealand	250
North American palisaded settlements	257
West African fortified villages and towns	262
Conclusions	268
11. Conclusion: A Sense of Place	269
Artefacts as symbols	269
Hillforts and defence	271
Landmarks and the legacy of the past	273
Wessex divided	275
'Developed' hillforts	276

Social and economic roles 278
Ceremonial, ritual, and burial 282
Hillforts and social hierarchies 285
Change through time 288
Epilogue 290

Bibliography 293
Index 323

List of Illustrations

LIST OF PLATES

1. St David's promontory fort, Pembrokeshire: (a) view from south-east, (b) stone roundhouses in inner fort.
2. Crickley Hill, Gloucestershire: (a) Period 3 rampart, (b) Period 3 entrance.
3. Irish royal sites: (a) Tara, Co Meath, ditch and bank of the Ráith na Ríg; (b) Dún Ailinne, Co. Wicklow, view from east.
4. Continental hillforts 1: (a) Mont Lassois, Châtillon-sur-Seine, general view across upper Seine, (b) Entremont, Aix-en-Provence, wall with bastion.
5. Shetland blockhouses: (a) Clickhimin, mainland Shetland, (b) Ness of Burgi, mainland Shetland.
6. Northern Scottish forts: (a) Tap o' Noth, Aberdeenshire, from south, (b) Cnoc an Duin (Dun Goll), Ross-shire, inner wall.
7. Hownam Law, Roxburghshire: (a) air view with house platforms under snow, (b) view from south-west.
8. Pennine forts: (a) Ingleborough, Yorkshire, view from west, (b) Mam Tor, Derbyshire, view from south.
9. Tre'r Ceiri, Caernarvonshire: (a) air view, (b) houses within hillfort.
10. Navan fort, Co. Armagh: (a) Professor J. Mallory beside site B restored mound, (b) ditch and bank.
11. Late Iron Age hillforts in north Britain: (a) Mote of Mark overlooking Urr estuary, Colvend, Dumfriesshire, (b) Dundurn, Perthshire.
12. Dunagoil, Bute: (a) general view from east, (b) vitrified wall at north end of citadel.
13. Irish south-western stone forts: (a) Ballykinvarga, Co. Clare, fort wall with *chevaux-de-frise*, (b) Dun Dubh Cathair, Inishmore, Co. Galway, general view.
14. Pembrokeshire hillforts from the air: (a) Carn Alw, (b) Foel Trigarn.
15. Continental hillforts 2: (a) Plateau de Merdogne, traditional location of Gergovia, (b) Citânia de Santa Luzia, Viana do Castelo, Portugal.
16. Hillforts and triple hills: (a) Tre'r Ceiri and Yr Eifl, Caernarvonshire, from north, (b) Eildon Hills, Roxburghshire, from south-east.

List of Illustrations xiii

LIST OF FIGURES

1.1	Distribution of hillforts under 1.2 ha (3 acres) enclosed.	2
1.2	Distribution of hillforts 1.2 ha–6 ha (3–15 acres) enclosed.	3
1.3	Distribution of hillforts over 6 ha (15 acres) enclosed.	4
1.4	Maiden Castle, Dorset, air photograph.	7
1.5	Hillforts in the Roxburghshire Cheviots.	10
1.6	Hod Hill, Dorset, air photograph.	12
1.7	Hambledon Hill, Dorset, air photograph.	13
1.8a	Borders hillforts: Eye Water, Berwickshire, paired cliff-edge forts.	18
1.8b	Borders hillforts: Brough Law, Northumberland, inner rampart.	19
1.9a	Archaeological reconstructions: Biskupin, Poland, marsh fort reconstruction.	23
1.9b	Archaeological reconstructions: Roman siegeworks from Alesia reconstruction.	23
1.10	Hillfort entrance plans: (A) St Catharine's Hill, Winchester, Hampshire, phase 1, (B) Danebury, Hampshire, east entrance, phase 2a, (C) Moel Hiraddug, Clwyd (Flintshire), inner entrance, (D) Dinorben, Clwyd (Denbighshire), south-east entrance.	26
2.1a	Antiquarian images of hillforts: William Stukeley's Prospect of Camalet Castle, 15 August, 1723.	32
2.1b	Antiquarian images of hillforts: General William Roy's plan of Burghead, Morayshire.	32
2.2a	Maiden Castle, Dorset, 1934–7: area excavation of eastern entrance.	40
2.2b	Maiden Castle, Dorset, 1934–7: inner rampart cutting E from the north-west.	41
2.3	Quarley Hill, Hampshire: Hawkes' map of the later prehistoric landscape.	45
3.1a	Palisaded settlements: Gibbs Hill, Dumfriesshire.	56
3.1b	Palisaded settlements: Craik Moor, Morebattle, Roxburghshire.	56
3.2a	Blewburton Hill, Oxfordshire (Berkshire), timber-framed rampart-cavities of horizontal timbers in rampart face.	60
3.2b	Blewburton Hill, Oxfordshire (Berkshire), timber-framed rampart-timber stains of horizontals and vertical posthole cavity from above.	61
3.3	Rampart reconstructions: (A) Blewburton Hill, Oxfordshire (Berkshire), timber-framed rampart: (B) timber and stone faced rampart (*Pfostenschlitzmauer*).	62
3.4	Rainsborough Camp, Northants, tiered inner face of main rampart.	66
3.5a	Abernethy, Perthshire: reconstruction of rampart.	68
3.5b	Abernethy, Perthshire: wall-face exposed by excavation *c*.1898.	69
3.6a	Dun Aengus, Inishmore, Co. Galway: tiered inner rampart.	71

3.6b	Dun Aengus, Inishmore, Co. Galway: ramparts with *chevaux-de-frise* beyond.	71
3.7	Cherbury Camp, Oxfordshire (Berkshire), air photograph.	74
3.8	Causewayed fort plans: (A) Brown Caterthun, Angus, (B) Barmekin of Echt, Aberdeenshire, (C) Arbory Hill, Lanarkshire, (D) Springfield Lyons, Essex.	76
3.9	Hillfort entrance plans: (A) Blewburton Hill, Oxfordshire (Berkshire), (B) Rainsborough Camp, Northamptonshire.	79
3.10a	Crickley Hill, Gloucestershire entrance reconstructions: Period 2.	80
3.10b	Crickley Hill, Gloucestershire entrance reconstructions: Period 3b.	80
3.11	Dual portal eastern entrance, Maiden Castle, Dorset.	82
3.12	Complex hillfort entrances: (A) Danebury, Hampshire, east entrance, (B) Hod Hill, Dorset, Stepleton gateway, (C) Maiden Castle, Dorset, west entrance.	85
3.13	Ladle Hill, Hampshire, unfinished hillfort.	88
4.1a	Woden Law, Hownam, Roxburghshire: from *c.*2500 feet.	92
4.1b	Woden Law, Hownam, Roxburghshire: from *c.*500 feet.	93
4.2a	Cheviot hillforts: Hayhope Knowe, Morebattle, Roxburghshire.	97
4.2b	Cheviot hillforts: Camp Tops, Morebattle, Roxburghshire.	97
4.3	Hut Knowe, Hownam, Roxburghshire, hillfort with fields and cord-rig agriculture.	99
4.4	Four-post structures from hillfort interiors: (A) Ffridd Faldwyn, Montgomery, Powys, (B) Croft Ambrey, Herefordshire, (C) Midsummer Hill, Herefordshire, (D) Danebury, Hampshire, south-western sector.	103
4.5a	Hillforts with external settlement: Castle Hill, Little Wittenham, Oxfordshire.	114
4.5b	Hillforts with external settlement: Battlesbury Camp, Wiltshire.	115
5.1	Hillfort territories in north Wiltshire compared with *Fürstensitze* territories in west central Europe.	122
5.2a	Hillforts of the East Lothian plain: Chesters, Drem.	126
5.2b	Hillforts of the East Lothian plain: Kae Heughs, Barney Mains, Drem.	127
5.3a	Hillforts in upper Eskdale, Dumfriesshire: Castle O'er.	128
5.3b	Hillforts in upper Eskdale, Dumfriesshire: Bailiehill.	129
5.4	Iron Age and early Roman Colchester (*Camulodunum*): outline plan.	132
5.5	Dyke Hills, Dorchester-on-Thames, Oxfordshire, air photograph.	136
5.6a	North Oxfordshire Grim's Ditch: ditch showing as a soil mark west of Ditchley Park.	137
5.6b	North Oxfordshire Grim's Ditch: bank and ditch in Ditchley Park.	137
5.7	Flodden, Northumberland, multi-period ring-work.	141

5.8a	Shetland promontory forts: Burland fort and broch.	146
5.8b	Shetland promontory forts: Hog Island eroded former promontory fort.	146
6.1	Crickley Hill, Gloucestershire, distribution of Neolithic leaf-shaped arrowheads around Neolithic defences.	152
6.2a	Burnswark, Dumfriesshire: view of hillfort from the south.	160
6.2b	Burnswark, Dumfriesshire: air photograph showing Roman camps and siegeworks.	161
6.3a	Late Iron Age hillforts in northern Britain: air photograph of Rubers Law, Cavers, Roxburghshire.	166
6.3b	Late Iron Age hillforts in northern Britain: Dunadd, mid-Argyll.	167
7.1a	'War cemetery' and 'massacre' sites: Maiden Castle, Dorset, burial P7A with iron spear-bolt in spine.	180
7.1b	'War cemetery' and 'massacre' sites: Sutton Walls, Herefordshire, skeletons in ditch by west entrance.	181
8.1	Special function enclosures: (A) Sutton Common, South Yorkshire, (B) Zeijen 1, northern Netherlands.	205
8.2	Hillfort cemeteries: (A) Broxmouth, East Lothian, (B) Maiden Castle, Dorset, eastern entrance.	209
8.3a	'Special sites' in remote locations: Carrock Fell, Cumbria.	218
8.3b	'Special sites' in remote locations: Burgi Geos, Shetland.	219
8.4a	Dun Aengus, Inishmore, Co. Galway: Professor E. Rynne on platform at cliff-edge.	220
8.4b	Dun Aengus, Inishmore, Co. Galway: view from cliff-edge.	220
10.1	Taniwha *pā*, Lower Waikato, New Zealand, plan.	255
10.2	Oyo Ile, Nigeria, town walls and entrances.	264
11.1	Uffington Castle and White Horse, Oxfordshire, air photograph.	274

Abbreviations

AA4	*Archaeologia Aeliana*, 4th series
AAAL	*Annals of Archaeology and Anthropology, University of Liverpool*
AAnt	*American Antiquity*
AAnth	*American Anthropology*
AArch	*American Archaeology*
AI	*Archaeology Ireland*
Ant. J.	*Antiquaries Journal*
ARC	*Archaeological Review from Cambridge*
Arch. Camb.	*Archaeologia Cambrensis*
Arch. J.	*Archaeological Journal*
Arch. Roz.	*Archeologické Rozledy*
BAR	British Archaeological Reports
BAJ	*Berkshire Archaeological Journal*
BBCS	*Bulletin of the Board of Celtic Studies*
BLUIA	*Bulletin of the London University Institute of Archaeology*
BRGK	*Bericht der Römisch-Germanischen Kommission*
CA	*Current Archaeology*
C.Anth.	*Current Anthropology*
CBA	Council for British Archaeology
dBG	Caesar, *de Bello Gallico*
DES	*Discovery and Excavation in Scotland*
GAJ	*Glasgow Archaeological Journal*
EJA	*European Journal of Archaeology*
HFC	*Proceedings of the Hampshire Field Club and Archaeological Society*
HR	*Historical Review*
ICCS	International Congress of Celtic Studies
JAA	*Journal of Anthropological Archaeology*
JESL	*Journal of the Ethnological Society of London*
JFHS	*Journal of the Flintshire Historical Society*
JIA	*Journal of Irish Archaeology*
JMH	*Journal of Medieval History*
JRA	*Journal of Roman Archaeology*

JRGZM	Jahrbuch des Römisch-Germanischen Zentralmuseums
JRIC	Journal of the Royal Institute of Cornwall
JRSAI	Journal of the Royal Society of Antiquaries of Ireland
JRSNZ	Journal of the Royal Society of New Zealand
JWP	Journal of World Prehistory
MA	Medieval Archaeology
MCV	Mélanges de la Casa de Velázquez
NA	Northamptonshire Archaeology
NMAJ	North Munster Antiquarian Journal
NZAAN	New Zealand Archaeological Association Newsletter
OJA	Oxford Journal of Archaeology
PASJ	Pictish Arts Society Journal
PCAS	Proceedings of the Cambridge Antiquarian Society
PDAES	Proceedings of the Devon Archaeological Exploration Society
PPS	Proceedings of the Prehistoric Society
PRIA	Proceedings of the Royal Irish Academy
PSAS	Proceedings of the Society of Antiquaries of Scotland
PSANHS	Proceedings of the Somerset Archaeological and Natural History Society
RAC	Revue Archéologique du Centre
RCAHMS	Royal Commission on the Ancient and Historical Monuments of Scotland
RCAHMWM	Royal Commission on the Ancient and Historical Monuments in Wales and Monmouthshire
RCHM(Eng)	Royal Commission on Historical Monuments (England)
RGF	Römisch-Germanische Forschungen
SAF	Scottish Archaeological Forum
SAIR	Scottish Archaeology Internet Reports
SAL	Society of Antiquaries of London
SAR	Scottish Archaeological Review
STAR	Scottish Trust for Archaeological Research
SxAC	Sussex Archaeological Collections
TAFAJ	Tayside and Fife Archaeological Journal
TBGAS	Transactions of the Bristol and Gloucester Archaeological Society
TBNHS	Transactions of the Buteshire Natural History Society
TCWAS	Transactions of the Cumberland and Westmorland Archaeological Society

TDGNHAS	*Transactions of the Dumfriesshire and Galloway Natural History and Antiquarian Society*
UISPP	Union International des Sciences Préhistoriques et Protohistoriques, International Union of Prehistoric and Protohistoric Sciences (IUPPS)
UJA	*Ulster Journal of Archaeology*
WA	*World Archaeology*
WAJA	*West African Journal of Archaeology*
WAM	*Wiltshire Archaeological and Natural History Magazine*

1

Defining Issues

'Hillfort' is a term of convenience. It is widely recognized that the monuments in question are not restricted topographically to hills, and that their role may not have been primarily, and certainly not exclusively, for military defence. Nor are they restricted chronologically to the Iron Age, though during that period they are particularly prominent. The term came into general currency following the publication in 1931 of Christopher Hawkes' paper, simply entitled 'Hillforts', in *Antiquity*, which also established their predominantly Iron Age date in Britain. Prior to that, Christison (1898) in Scotland had discussed 'fortifications', and Hadrian Allcroft (1908) for England had classified 'earthwork', both extending their studies into the Medieval period. But 'hillfort' for all its limitations has remained in general usage in Britain. Chronologically, this study is concerned with the 'long Iron Age'; that is, including the post-Roman Iron Age in northern Britain especially, and with later Bronze Age antecedents. Geographically it is concerned with regional groups throughout Britain, but with further reference to Ireland, and in the wider context of relevant sites and developments in continental Europe.

The key element of the sites under consideration is enclosure, physically or conceptually demarcating an area to which access is restricted or controlled. This may be achieved by rampart and ditch, stockade or fence, or by the incorporation of topographical and natural features such as cliff-edge or marsh. The scale of enclosing works may range from a relatively modest barrier to massive earthworks that reshape the landscape, and in structural morphology, from single palisade or bank to multiple lines, variously disposed. Topographically they may be located around hilltop contours, on cliff-edge, ridge, or promontory, on spurs or hill slopes, in wetlands or spanning river bends, or across variable terrain. In area enclosed they may range from well under a hectare to 20 ha and more (Figures 1.1–1.3), with the *territorial* or *terrain oppida* of the late pre-Roman Iron Age attaining 300 ha or more. From size alone, therefore, we may infer a great diversity in the practical, social, and symbolic purposes that they may have served. At the smaller end of the scale, the distinction between hillforts and other enclosed settlements is sometimes a matter of subjective assessment, but otherwise their size and scale suggests that

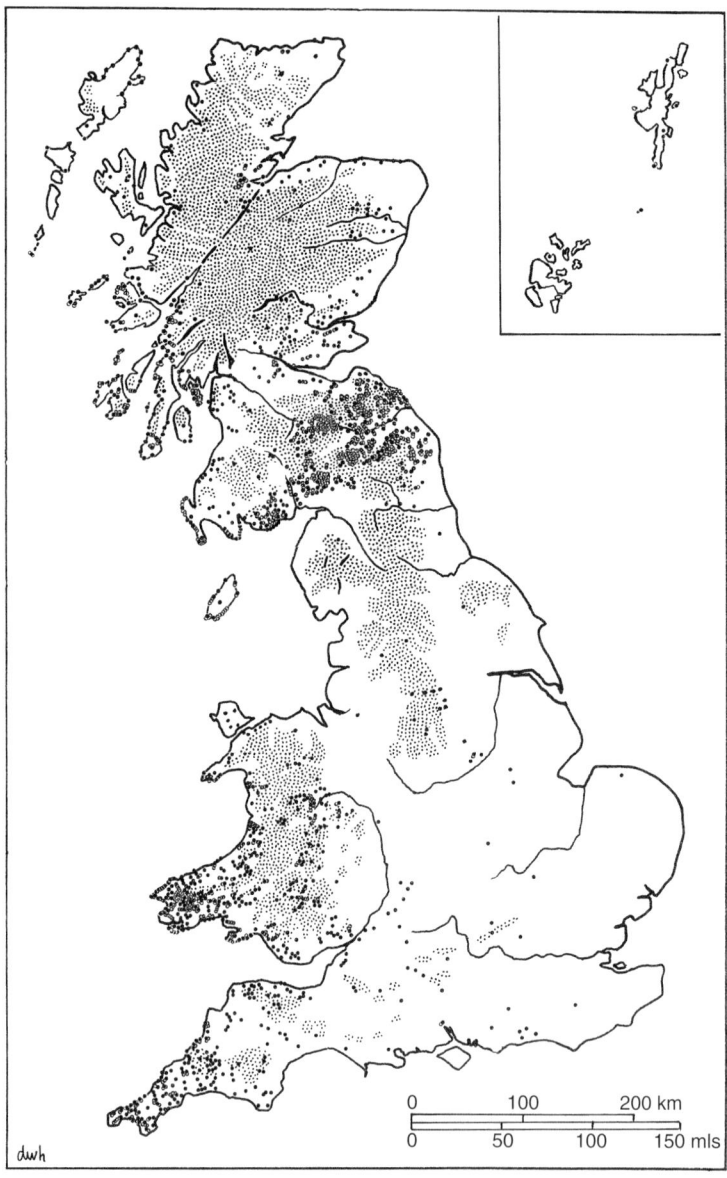

Figure 1.1. Distribution of hillforts under 1.2 ha (3 acres) enclosed. Drawing by D. W. Harding, adapted from OS 1962, IGS 1966, Ritchie 1997: Figure 7.1, with additions.

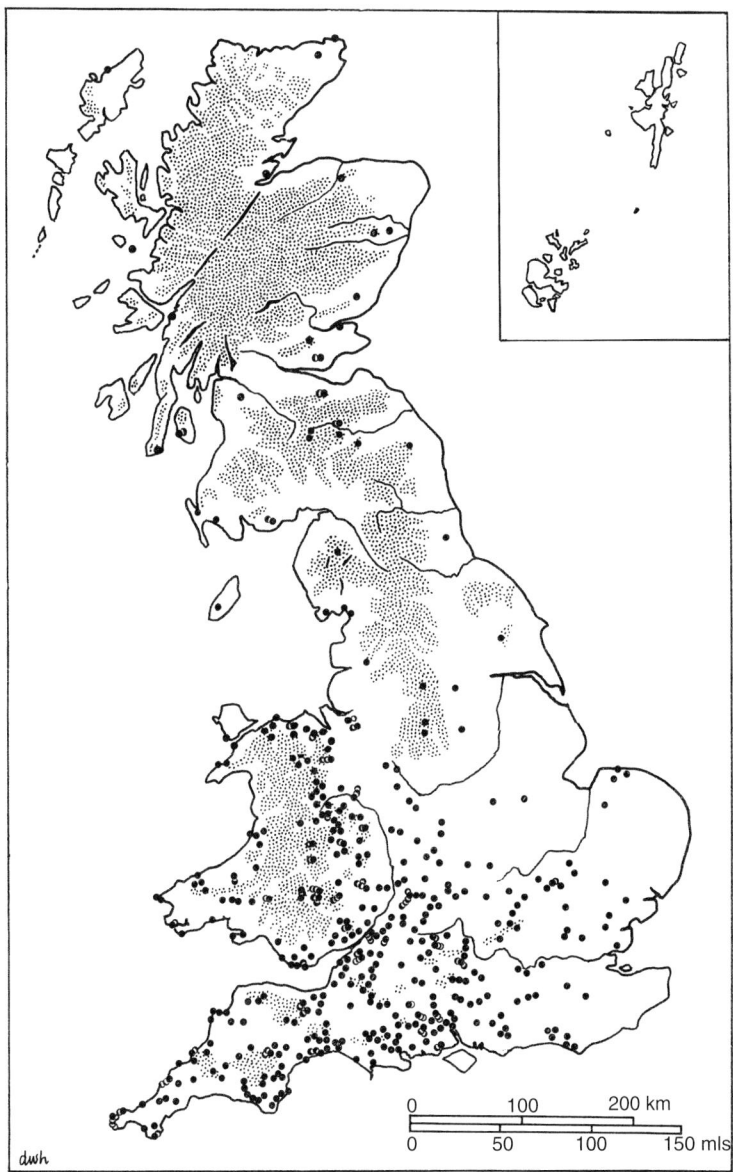

Figure 1.2. Distribution of hillforts 1.2 ha–6 ha (3–15 acres) enclosed. Drawing by D. W. Harding, adapted from OS 1962, IGS 1966, with additions.

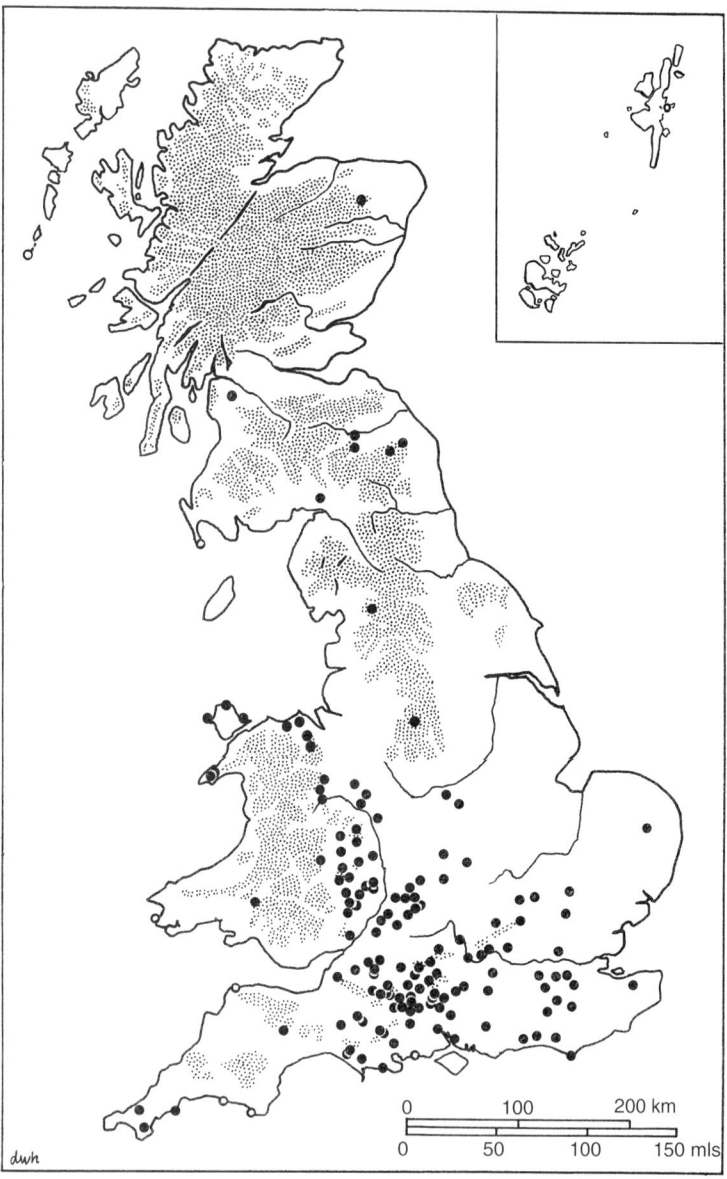

Figure 1.3. Distribution of hillforts over 6 ha (15 acres) enclosed. Drawing by D. W. Harding, adapted from OS 1962, with additions.

they were community sites, serving a social unit larger than a single family or household.

The issue of the defensive role of hillforts will be considered at greater length below. Though this function may on occasions have been subordinated to other requirements, the potential for defensibility in hillforts is generally inferred from the proportions of their enclosure works. On occasions, hillforts appear not to have been sited topographically with defensive advantage as a paramount consideration, and in some instances the sheer size of enclosure would have made controlling the perimeter problematic. But providing protection for family and community is as fundamental a response of humankind as a sense of group identity, and to deny a defensive dimension in the role of hillforts would be to neglect that basic necessity.

If therefore the term hillfort seems inappropriate, then let it be understood that each time it is used, we are mentally hyphenating the qualifications and diversities expressed in the previous paragraphs in front of the term 'enclosure', and substituting 'hillfort' as shorthand in its place.

EARTHWORKS AND ENCLOSURE

Enclosure is one facet of prehistoric settlement that archaeologically is most visible, and conventionally has formed a principal basis of site classification. Whether by means of a stockade or by rampart and ditch, enclosure defines space, segregating and even screening from view activities that take place within from the wider landscape outside. Enclosure may articulate a sense of identity of the community within, in contrast to the wider world without, a relationship that has often been presented as a division between 'us' and 'them'. In the first millennium BC, enclosure may have been encouraged by agricultural intensification and the need to reinforce territorial rights (Thomas 1997). Access to the enclosure is generally strictly controlled, and the elaborate entrances of hillforts may as plausibly be regarded as a means of exercising social control over visitors as a way of strengthening the weakest point in the defensive circuit, or as a means of checking traffic in order to extract dues. Beyond the gates themselves, outworks and 'façade schemes' (Driver 2007) sometimes dictate the direction of access, not just for reasons of tactical advantage in a defensive sense, but doubtless also in order to establish the relationship between 'residents' and 'visitors', and to reinforce the terms on which access is permitted. Enclosure, however, is not just an expression of distinctive identity; it also serves to reinforce that sense of difference. As Connah (2000: 45) wrote in the context of West African Hausa and Yoruba communities, 'the act of enclosure had the capacity to produce a different sort of community, physically, psychologically, and socially, or to confirm and reinforce pre-existing differences.' Life in an open settlement, especially a shifting one, was different from that of an enclosed community.

Enclosed settlements are more readily detected than open settlements, not least because ditched enclosures that have been levelled by agriculture are more amenable to detection by air photography. This bias, as we shall see, may have seriously distorted our understanding of the relationship between open and enclosed settlement, even in well-researched regions like Wessex. Defining an open settlement remains problematic, however, since the absence of physical boundaries that are detectable archaeologically does not mean that none existed. They may well have been of transient construction such as 'dead hedges' or naturally grown barriers like thorn hedges, neither of which would leave more than minimal trace, or they may simply have been well-known limits, the river or the forest edge, beyond which one transgressed into another's territory. The apparently open settlements of the Upper Thames gravels may well have had boundaries of this kind, every bit as binding as rampart and ditch.

The conventional assumption therefore is that enclosure was to define or segregate space, and to afford physical or spiritual protection for whomever or whatever was enclosed from the outside world. The purpose of enclosure, however, may have been less to underline the distinction between 'them' and 'us' than to define or emphasize what is 'special to us'. From late Neolithic henge monuments to the monastic vallum enclosures of early historic times, there is a long tradition of earthworks defining restricted or sacred space. What distinguishes these from most hillforts is that their topographical location, scale or layout is not overtly defensive, though they may have afforded an equally potent barrier against intrusion for the communities that built them. The distinction between ritual enclosures and secular enclosures may not have been as clear-cut as archaeological classification might suggest. Yet cemeteries of the later Bronze Age and Iron Age in Britain conspicuously are not enclosed, other than by individual graves ditches like those of the Arras group in eastern Yorkshire (Stead 1965, 1979, 1991).

Substantial enclosure, by the construction of bank and ditch, of course, has the disadvantage of limiting the space available within the perimeter so that organic expansion is inhibited, unless or until the need for expansion becomes paramount and requires extramural extensions or even the redefinition of the enclosure by the creation of a larger perimeter. One impact of enclosure therefore may be to induce greater order in the spatial layout of internal activities to maximize the available space. This constraint might simulate incipient town planning, but purely pragmatic factors could dictate the regular layout of a site like the wetland fortification at Biskupin in Poland, or even in the inferred layout of four-post structures in some of the Welsh Marcher hillforts in Britain. Not all activities, of course, will have been performed within the enclosure. Some, like metalworking, may have been excluded

Figure 1.4. Maiden Castle, Dorset, air photograph by Major G. W. G. Allen. Reproduced by kind permission of the Ashmolean Museum, University of Oxford.

because of hazards posed by fire and noxious fumes, or, if ethnographic analogy is indicative, because of deliberate social distancing of metalworkers and their alien arts (Brown 1995).

There are indeed instances of hillforts that have expanded beyond the initial limits of enclosure, as is evident from surface indications at Maiden Castle in Dorset (Figure 1.4), but there are equally examples where the enclosed area has been reduced. In northern Britain the later phases of occupational sequence in the stone forts of Argyll, for example, are often smaller than the earliest. In the case of Maiden Castle, the area of the developed hillfort encloses more than double that of the univallate hillfort, but the greatly enhanced complexity of the earthworks, eventually occupying an area as large again as that enclosed, is surely not just about enclosure but about redesigning the landscape and making a monumental statement about the identity of the controlling community. Thomas Hardy was evidently aware of Maiden Castle's presence in the landscape when he referred in *A Changed Man and Other Tales* (1913) to its 'obtrusive personality that compels the senses to regard it', and to its prominent profile that he likened to 'an enormous many-limbed organism of an antediluvian time'.

Boundaries are evidently fundamental and endemic in the later prehistoric landscape, and hillfort enclosures are just one manifestation of this preoccupation, but the significance of 'us:them', 'inclusion:exclusion' should not be exaggerated. Where settlements, open or enclosed, occur around hillforts in a density that might reasonably imply some degree of contemporaneity with the occupation or use of the hillfort, the occupants of the hillfort and the adjacent settlements should surely be regarded as part of the same community. Nor need it follow that the external settlements were necessarily dependent on or subordinate to the hillfort: the occupants of the former may simply have interacted with the latter as required, depending upon their respective roles in the life of the community. In effect, the occupants or users of the hillfort and the surrounding settlements may have been the selfsame people. In all probability there would have been varying degrees of exclusivity between and within communities, and the permitted limits would surely have been well known to the social groups themselves. 'Boundedness' is therefore not necessarily a matter of inclusion or exclusion, but of the regulation of movement and access within certain socially prescribed limits.

One of the problems in understanding archaeological sites arises from the fact that there can be several stages of enclosure from outer territorial or agricultural boundaries to the inner earthworks, whether simple or complex, of the hillfort itself. An example of this is the promontory fort on St David's Head, Pembrokeshire (Plate 1a), where the promontory fort itself encloses just over 3 ha, but beyond which there is an outer wall across the peninsula enclosing a total of 24 ha. No obvious prehistoric features lie within this area, but immediately beyond is an extensive system of field boundaries and cultivation ridges (Murphy 2001). The issue here is what we define as the 'site'; whether or not dating evidence can confirm contemporaneous use, it seems improbable that the earthworks enclosing the hut-circles at the tip of the peninsula (Plate 1b) represent more than the focus of a larger settlement system. Equally it would be absurd to treat the small hillforts at Hut Knowe, Hownam (Figure 4.3 in Harding 2004a: Figure 3.16), or Tamshiel Rig, Southdean, Roxburghshire (RCAHMS 1956: Figure 566), as defined by their enclosure walls, other than in the most limited sense of enclosure morphology. It seems reasonable to suppose, therefore, that there would have been levels of accessibility, with strictest control of the hillfort nucleus itself, and perhaps specific areas beyond the enclosure walls, such as sacred places or water sources, violation of any of which might have triggered inter-community conflict.

SIZE AND DISTRIBUTION

We have already noted that the area enclosed by hillforts or related earthworks can range from under a hectare to more than 300 ha, though the larger *territorial oppida*, for which the term *terrain oppida* is preferred here, might be regarded as a separate class of field monument. Hillforts of the more conventional type seldom exceed 20 ha in area, and 6 ha (15 acres) was chosen as the lower threshold for large hillforts in the Ordnance Survey classification for the *Map of Southern Britain in the Iron Age* of 1962. Even here caution must be exercised. Several promontory forts from south-west England to western Scotland enclose more than 6 ha, but, as a proxy measure of status in terms of size of community or scale of resources involved, their limited earthworks would hardly compare with the major hillforts of central southern England and the Welsh Marches. The smallest sites enclose under 1.2 ha (3 acres), though these actually constitute more than half the total number in Britain. For England and Wales alone, Forde-Johnston (1976: 12) calculated that 'out of every 10 Iron Age forts 1 is Large, 3 are Medium, and 6 are Small'. Identifying a meaningful distinction at the interface of small hillfort and protected homestead is plainly problematic in regions like the Scottish Borders or in south-west England and west Wales, and can often only be achieved subjectively on the basis of scale of enclosing earthworks, which sometimes seem disproportionately elaborate for the size of enclosure. In social terms it must be self-evident that hillforts in the 'small' category cannot have functioned in the same way as 'large' hillforts. In the parishes of Hownam and Morebattle, where the majority seldom exceeds a hectare in area enclosed, hillforts can be sited within a kilometre of each other (Figure 1.5), compared to, say, 5–10 km on Salisbury Plain (Cunliffe 1971: Figure 14), where none is in the smallest category and several are in the largest. This must reflect the relatively fragmented character of Border communities compared to a greater degree of social cohesion in Iron Age Wessex. In continental Europe, only in the *castros* zone of the peninsular north-west are hillforts so densely distributed (Queiroga 2003). In terms of landscape archaeology, the Border uplands are particularly productive, since here the 'zone of survival' has preserved even the fugitive traces of palisaded enclosures and cord-rig agriculture. For this reason, though the region is comparatively well-researched, Cunliffe's (2000: 14) arguments for concentrating on areas already fairly intensively studied could equally be applied here in the hope of recovering something closer to a complete later prehistoric landscape.

Given the variety of topography in Britain, it is hardly surprising that the overall distribution of hillforts should be uneven, but the extent of imbalance is plainly not immediately explicable through environmental factors, and requires further analysis and comment. Forde-Johnston (1976) noted that the great majority of sites in England and Wales lay south and west of a line from the Mersey to the Thames estuary, in marked contrast to Fox's (1932) Highland/Lowland axis along the Jurassic ridge from the Severn to the Wash. In fact, the combined distribution of medium and large hillforts (Cunliffe 2005: Figure 15.1; Brown 2009: Figure 2b), using the same OS classification, obscures a paucity of larger hillforts west of a line from west Dorset through the Wye Valley to the Vale of Clywd; medium-sized hillforts by contrast

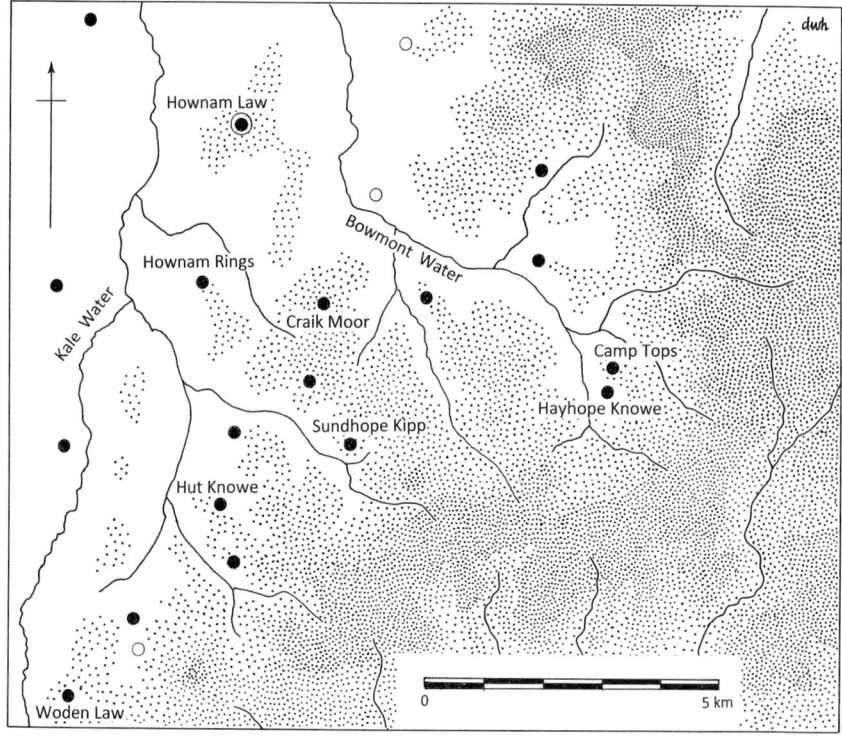

Figure 1.5. Hillforts in the Roxburghshire Cheviots. Drawing by D. W. Harding.

extend more generally beyond this boundary. The smallest hillforts are concentrated in the English/Scottish Borders as well as in the south-west peninsula and west Wales. In eastern England, and in northern England from the southern Pennines to the Tyne, by contrast, there is a notable scarcity of hillforts, an absence that cannot be attributed to lack of suitable topographic locations. In East Anglia and Lincolnshire topography may have been a factor, though even here relatively low eminences can dominate extensive landscapes. Even at Stonea Camp, Cambridgeshire (Malim 1992; Jackson and Potter 1996) at a maximum of 5 m OD the 9.6 ha (24 acre) enclosure follows the contours of a fen-edge island that is a locally prominent feature. The fact that the Pennines and, for example, the spinal range of mid-Wales are largely devoid of hillforts makes the point that hillforts could not exist in a vacuum, and that their location is not divorced from the environment that their builders wished to exploit.

The overall distribution of hillforts, therefore, shows some broad regional contrasts. Hillforts certainly occur in eastern Scotland, the focus of Gordon Childe's (1935a, 1946) 'Gallic' forts, but not in the same density of distribution as elsewhere. In Argyll the class of smaller stone-walled forts is not so clearly distinguished from the broader category of dun enclosures (Harding 1997), while throughout northern and western Scotland it is still unclear how promontory forts related to the smaller Atlantic roundhouses or brochs that served as 'stronghouses' for households in quite widely dispersed communities. Eastern and northern England are by no means devoid of hillforts, but are certainly not typical hillfort zones. Eastern Yorkshire, especially, where the local population of the mid- to later pre-Roman Iron Age is distinctively represented by its square-ditched barrow cemeteries, is not distinguished by hillforts after the later Bronze Age. This being the case, the question arises, what served instead the functions elsewhere accorded to hillforts? Other classes of field monuments, including those grouped under the heading of 'ringforts' have come into focus in the past twenty years, but the answer may not simply lie in the identification of 'hillfort substitutes', but in recognizing the way in which different local communities functioned and what fulfilled the equivalent role of hillforts.

ENCLOSURE MORPHOLOGY

Hillfort enclosure may be achieved by single or multiple circuits of construction. In most southern British examples the rampart is built from material quarried from a ditch immediately in front of it to form a combined barrier, presenting the maximum height from bottom of ditch to crest of bank to the outside world. In some instances, such as Hod Hill, Dorset (Richmond 1968), additional rampart height was gained by using material from internal quarry scoops, the irregular and discontinuous line of which does not suggest that they served any other purpose (Figure 1.6). In some upland situations, where solid rock is close to the surface or where loose scree afforded a ready source of building material, the ditch may be minimal or non-existent. Nevertheless, for many hillforts the ditch may have had a significant role as part of the defining boundary of the enclosure, and has too often in the past been relatively neglected by excavators on the assumption that its only purpose was as a quarry for the all-important rampart, the construction techniques of which have commanded greater attention. Externally, a low counter-scarp bank may simply be the product of periodic clearing of silt from the ditch, though in situations where the ramparts are built on steep hill slopes, like Cadbury Castle, Somerset (Alcock 1972; Barrett *et al.* 2000), downward construction may have been a practical expedient (Rivet 1961: Figure 8).

Bivallate or multivallate construction, involving two or more circuits of rampart and ditch, closely set with little or no intervening berm, may in some instances have been part of the initial design, but more frequently resulted from secondary additions to an originally univallate enclosure. The purpose of

Figure 1.6. Hod Hill, Dorset, air photograph by O. G. S. Crawford. Reproduced from Crawford and Keiller 1928, by permission of Oxford University Press.

such elaboration has been much debated. For Wheeler, multivallate ramparts of the kind that he excavated at Maiden Castle (Wheeler 1943) represented 'defence in depth', linked to the effective range of a sling. It has never really been clear, however, how multiple ramparts could have been defended, since once the outermost line had been ceded, the retreating defenders, without the aid of retractable bridges, would have been equally vulnerable as their attackers. Wheeler believed that multivallation at Maiden Castle was introduced from the south-west, an interpretation that was abandoned with the demise of diffusionism. It is true that multivallation is common in south-western forts, and especially in promontory forts, where the fact that only a narrow neck of

Defining issues

Figure 1.7. Hambledon Hill, Dorset, air photograph by Dr J. K. St Joseph, Cambridge University Collection of Aerial Photography reg. no. AY20, June 29, 1948. Reproduced by kind permission of University of Cambridge. Crown copyright material is reproduced under Class Licence Number C2006000011 with the permission of OPSI and the Queen's Printer for Scotland.

land required a defensive barrier made it feasible to multiply that barrier in depth. It is worth remarking, therefore, that multivallation is not an essential feature of 'developed' hillforts of central southern England, and, contrary to the image that might be gained from the prominence given to Maiden Castle in hillfort studies, it is not the invariable or inevitable culmination of hillfort development.

An alternative view therefore would regard multivallation as a monumental expression of status, designed to impress rather than for its defensive utility, though massive investment in military deterrence, of course, need not invariably accord with realistic defensive utility. Most surprising are smaller multivallate forts, like those from southern and eastern Scotland, where the multivallate earthworks occupy an area as great as or greater than that enclosed (Harding 2004a: Figures 3.6, 4.5). Without excavation, of course, we cannot be certain that all functioned simultaneously as part of a unitary system of enclosure. At Broxmouth, East Lothian (Hill 1982a: Figure 3; Armit and McKenzie, in prep.), for example, no more than two of the four lines of earthwork on the hillfort's western circuit were apparently in use at any one time.

The wide-spaced, multivallate forts of south-western England represent a different phenomenon altogether, since the space between the circuits is sufficient to have provided a separate area, segregated from the citadel but still within the outer circuit, that could have been designated for different purposes. Corralling stock has been the popular option, but insufficient excavation has been undertaken to determine the nature of activity or occupation.

Classification of hillforts by enclosure morphology might imply a greater regularity of design and function than was ever intended or realized, and might lead to the assumption that hillfort construction was planned and carried out in completed phases, with periods of occupation during which the enclosing works may have been maintained but not substantially changed. By contrast, Sharples (2010: 120, 296) maintained that, at Maiden Castle and elsewhere during the early and middle Iron Age, rampart construction was a more or less continuous, if seasonal, process in which communities competed to display their capacity for conspicuous resource consumption, in this case of construction materials and human labour. At Danebury, Hampshire (Cunliffe 1984a: 18–19, Figure 3.4) there was certainly evidence for periodic clearing out of the ditch, with the effect of creating a low counterscarp, but this could be regarded as routine maintenance, even if it was carried out seasonally and accompanied by acts of ceremonial symbolism.

What Mercer (2006: 69) suggested in the context of Neolithic causewayed enclosures was even more fundamental, namely that it was the process of constructing the enclosure that was more important than the achievement of the outcome. Much the same idea was floated by Woolf in the context of European Iron Age *oppida*, when he said that it may have been 'the action of fortifying, rather than the end product, which was of greater social significance' (1993: 232). This might be a tenable explanation where the cumulative plan displays a markedly irregular outline, as in some Neolithic causewayed enclosures or in discontinuous earthworks of terrain *oppida* in south-eastern Britain. Assessing unity of conception is a highly subjective matter, but unity of execution can reasonably be inferred where, for example, the size and profile of the ditch or the method of construction of the rampart are broadly the same throughout the circuit. The problem is, of course, that multiple sections through extensive earthworks to validate this presumption are seldom undertaken, either for reasons of limited resources or because within the prevailing climate in favour of non-intrusive investigation duplicating excavation has not seemed justifiable.

As the evidence stands, it seems probable that most hillforts were intended to be built as unitary constructions, even if they were subject to changes of circumstance and plan in the process, otherwise there would surely be more examples of patently 'unfinished' hillforts among the 1500 or more known in Britain. If they were designed in any measure to protect or to exclude, then it would have been vital to complete a basic circuit. But, like cathedrals of a later age, the major 'developed' hillforts may have taken many generations to bring to completion, and their design may have undergone radical changes in the process. Major episodes of reconstruction, such as the addition of multivallate enclosures or the rebuilding of a collapsed wall rampart as a dump or *glacis* rampart, may have modified the original plan. Maintenance and repair, on the other hand, may well have been seasonal and perhaps linked to some other festive traditions involving the community as a whole.

TOPOGRAPHY AND LOCATION

Hillforts may be sited tactically in relation to topography, to take advantage of locations that offered natural defence, that commanded outlook over important routes of access or that were in proximity to good agricultural land or pastures. Some hillforts occupy prominent landmarks perhaps with the express intention of making a statement through high visibility; others seem to be designed with the opposite objective of merging into the natural landscape. Some 'hillforts' are at relatively low level, yet may still command a good prospect. At 25 m OD, the Broxmouth hillfort in East Lothian hardly dominated a commanding position, yet it had a clear prospect of the coastal plain eastwards to Berwickshire and west to Traprain Law as well as across the Firth of Forth to the Fife coast. In some instances inter-visibility might imply a network of sites in contemporary use as part of a larger political, social, or economic design. Others are located in apparent isolation from any obvious surviving associations.

Forde-Johnston (1976) adopted a conventional classification of hillforts based on topographical location, dividing them into contour forts and promontory forts with sub-groups of hill-slope forts and plateau forts. Promontory forts plainly take maximum advantage of topography, requiring only minimal earthworks, where precipitous cliffs afforded natural protection around the remaining circuit, so it would be easy to conclude that the choice of promontories was dictated by considerations of defence with economy of resources. Some precipitous cliff-edge locations, nevertheless, must have presented severe problems for safe occupation, and in the event of attack may have left no way out if the defences were breached. So their interpretation as defensive strongholds is far from conclusive, and alternatives that took advantage of their awe-inspiring locations, such as ceremonial sites for inauguration rituals might be more persuasive. Not all promontories are quite so inaccessible from the sea. Clawadd y Milwyr on St David's Head, Pembrokeshire, has a lower tongue at its seaward end (Plate 1a) which, though rugged and wave-beaten, was used in early modern times to load cargoes of stone on to ships, so that access would certainly have been possible if necessary. Excavation at Trevelgue Head in Cornwall (Nowakowski and Quinnell 2011) indicated iron-working as a major activity, so that the site, adjacent to one of the safest anchorages along the north Cornish coast, may have been a centre for coastal trading and exchange. Inland promontories like Crickley Hill, Gloucestershire (Dixon 1994), are generally less precipitous, though at 1 in 3 gradient, this is still sufficient to afford good natural defence. The neck of the promontory, not eroded into a peninsula by the sea, required a broader line of earthworks, behind which the enclosed interior would thus have been well screened. The same economy of enclosure can be achieved by cutting off a bend in a river, as at Dyke Hills, Dorchester on Thames, though without any advantage of height, so that internal activity would have been visible from the opposite bank.

Adapting hilltop contours plainly would allow the construction of an enclosure with equal defensive strength and outlook around the entire circuit, and some hillforts do indeed conform broadly to this pattern. Some hillforts like Scratchbury, Wiltshire, however, appear to have been deliberately 'tilted' in a particular direction, as if to allow activities in their interior to be visible from below (Brown 2009: 196). More surprising is the slavish adherence to the contours in the 'developed' hillfort at Hambledon Hill, Dorset (Figure 1.7), resulting in a total length of rampart greater than that of its neighbour on Hod Hill, yet enclosing only three-fifths of the latter's area (RCHME 1970: 83). Ridge forts are a variant within the contour class, the contours on two sides coinciding with the perimeter works of the fort, with entrances sited facing the level ground of the ridge, as in the case of some small stone forts in Argyll.

Plateau forts represent a small minority of sites, whose disregard of contours might argue against a primarily defensive role. Hill-slope forts, notably concentrated in south-west England and in south Wales (Fox 1952), plainly are not sited with defensive considerations at the fore. Tregeare Rounds in Cornwall exemplifies the type, straddling the contours a couple of hundred metres below the crest of the hill, and with the entrances through its triple earthworks all facing downhill. Tactically, it is plainly vulnerable to attack from over the blind summit. A similar tactical weakness applies to Archwood Hill in Dumfriesshire (RCAHMS 1997: Figure 133), which, simultaneously or cumulatively, boasted no less than four lines of enclosure, so that once again substantial effort was expended on the enclosure works, but apparently not to maximize defensive advantage.

If we accept that the layout of promontory forts and contour forts was essentially determined by topography, then it would follow that there was no standard 'plan' for a hillfort, in the way that henge monuments in Britain or the 'rondels' of eastern central Europe conformed to a general pattern (Podborský and Kovárník 2006). One exception to this is the 'oblong forts' of eastern Scotland (Harding 2004a: Figure 4.2), characterized by their elongated oblong-with-rounded-corners shape, which again often ignores the tactical advantages of following the contour. Their apparent lack of an entrance through the main rampart certainly eliminates a defensive weak point, but would have inhibited normal domestic or agricultural activities such as driving wagons or herds into the enclosure. This group apart, there are no obviously planned square or rectangular hillforts, though occasionally, as at Hod Hill, Martinsell in Wiltshire or Uley Bury in Gloucestershire, the site contours encouraged a sub-rectangular outline. Equally, however, there are relatively few circular hillforts, and where they do occur, as in the 'ring-works' or 'mini-hillforts' of eastern England, they are sufficiently distinctive to warrant separate consideration. Though Forde-Johnston (1976: Figure 146) included simple and bivallate circular hillforts as part of his 'western tradition', in reality few of the south-west sites, including Cornish 'rounds', are quite as regularly circular in plan as his model.

Hillforts are commonly thought of a serving or controlling a territory as central places, and therefore spatially separated. Occasionally, however, they occur in relatively close proximity, like Hod Hill and Hambledon Hill, raising questions whether some 'developed' hillforts may have served not as central places but as 'peripheral places', marking the bounds of the territory of adjacent communities (Harding 1979: 11). Occasionally in the Borders they can occur within very close proximity, as at Eye Water, Berwickshire (Figure 1.8a), where two multivallate, scarp-edge forts are separated by less than 100 m. Even more striking is Newhall Hill, Dumfriesshire (RCAHMS 1997: Figure 139), where two substantially ditched enclosures are within 10 metres of each other, the one occupying the hill crest with the other on its steeper eastern slope. In such cases it seems possible that dual control of land by kin groups of equal status might be indicated. For Yeavering Bell Oswald and Pearson (2005) posited a social 'bi-archy', perhaps originating in twin summit enclosures and perpetuated in the enlarged fort by the siting, in relation to the eastern and western concentrations of roundhouses, of two larger 'elite' roundhouses facing the southern entrance (Oswald *et al.* 2006: Figure 6.18).

One aspect of hillfort location that is frequently remarked on by general observers but generally ignored by professional archaeologists is proximity to water supply. Very few hillforts are like Mam Tor in Derbyshire in having springs within their enclosing walls, though in a number of cases like Crickley Hill in the Cotswolds and Midsummer Hill in the Malverns (Stanford 1981), springs are available on the slopes below the ramparts within relatively easy reach. In some cases like Cadbury Castle there could have been wells, and in others artificial ponds like the Breiddin in Powys (Musson 1991). It is generally argued that in a period in which siege warfare was not practised, the absence of a reliable water supply within the hillfort would not have been a crucial disadvantage. Whilst this may be true, it would certainly have made permanent residence for a sizeable community more onerous if daily supplies of drinking water had to be carried from streams or springs some distance from the hillfort.

(a)

Figure 1.8. Borders hillforts: (a) Eye Water, Berwickshire, paired cliff-edge forts, (b) (opposite) Brough Law, Northumberland, inner rampart. Roger Mercer is squatting on the inner wall face behind the outer face. Photographs by D. W. Harding.

THE 'PACIFICATION OF PREHISTORY' AND THE 'CELTIC' PARADIGM

Since the 1980s there has been a trend in later British prehistory to play down the role of warfare and to imagine instead egalitarian communities of peaceable farmers free from conflict that hierarchical societies generate. It would be easy to assume that this reflected simply a generational shift of interpretation, but as Haselgrove and Moore (2007b: 11) have reminded us, this is an especially British perspective, and not one that is widely shared in continental Europe. The 'pacified Iron Age' in Britain was particularly espoused by J. D. Hill (1984, 1989, 1995b; see also Finney 2006) in a series of influential papers, the thrust of which was to reject the older 'Celtic' paradigm of hierarchical societies in which the warrior ethic was dominant, which had been based largely on classical accounts of Iron Age society, leavened with inferences drawn from early Irish sources. The new dogma challenged the assumption that hillforts had any significant defensive role, still less that they were the central places of a warrior elite, arguing instead that the great majority of the Iron Age population of Britain was made up of peaceable farmers. In sum, the British Iron Age was seen as not only pacified but also decidedly egalitarian, with society

(b)

even in Wessex based essentially on small-scale, autonomous household units. Simon James (2007: 161) quite rightly questioned the 'highly contentious implication' that farmers were universally peaceable, but his more incisive critique of the new orthodoxy struck at the heart of the matter when he recognized that it pandered to current political and social fashions just as plainly as the 'Celtic' paradigm and the 'invasion hypothesis' of the 1930s to 1950s reflected the political and social climate of earlier generations.

Most recently Lock (2011) has argued against 'endemic warfare' in the Iron Age, and that hillforts had a more significant role in mediating 'endemic insecurity' and a fear of 'disruption of internal social harmony' (ibid. 357). According to this view, threats to social equilibrium like hatred or jealousy could have been attributed to malevolent cosmic forces, and communal activities such as building and maintaining hillforts could have been part of the remedial process. He was anxious to dispel any caricature of rampart construction as 'prehistoric anger management therapy' (ibid. 359), though that may well prove to be a phrase that is cited in undergraduate examination questions for the next generation.

It is certainly true that an older conventional view of the Iron Age too readily accepted caricatures such as Strabo's (*Geography* IV, iv, 2) of swaggering, drunken, and aggressive Celts as representing, perhaps with some embellishment, the reality of Iron Age society. A warning note should have been sounded by the fact that the documentary sources were far from explicit on the role of hillforts in 'Celtic' warfare (Harding 1979: 1), perhaps a clue to the possibility that this was a formulaic image rather than practical reality. Since the late 1980s the idea that Britain (or Ireland) in the Iron Age was in any meaningful sense 'Celtic' has also been challenged (James 1999; Collis 2003; but see also Karl 2008), and so has Jackson's (1964) long-standing view that the Irish tales of the Ulster Cycle through oral tradition might afford a 'window on the Iron Age' in terms of social conventions including interpersonal conflict and warfare (Aitchison 1987).

A second issue that has been raised is the apparent paucity of weaponry in the early-middle Iron Age of southern Britain (around which the debate has essentially revolved), by comparison with a greater number of finds from the Late Bronze Age and late pre-Roman Iron Age. Once again, James (2007) has pointed out that military equipment is not alone in being under-represented in the earlier Iron Age, and that all metalwork, including utilitarian types, are less evident in the archaeological record, not as a result of any decline in production, but more probably as a result of a shift in the practice of deliberate deposition. Viewed in this light, the early-middle Iron Age situation might be regarded as the norm, and the Late Bronze Age especially as the exception. Unless weapons are buried in graves, as they are in various regions of continental Europe in the Hallstatt and Early and Middle La Tène Iron Age, or deposited in supposedly votive contexts such as rivers or lakes, they are likely to have been carefully treasured over several generations, and even when no longer practically serviceable, prized artefacts like scabbards with ornamental embellishments are likely to have been recycled for other purposes. But the very fact that we have prestige artefacts like the Witham and Battersea shields and a significant number of swords with ornamented scabbards surely indicates a high regard for the trappings of the warrior, whether or not the custodian of such items ever wielded them in anger. The probability is that most interpersonal or inter-group violence in the Iron Age was conducted with weapons far less grand than those that survive in the archaeological record.

HILLFORT INTERIORS: BUILDINGS AND THEIR USE

It is facile to assume that stripping of hillfort interiors will clarify their function and social use unless we are able to interpret what excavation uncovers. In some cases excavation may uncover very little, but even where structures are found, our interpretation of them has generally been formulaic rather than critically informed.

The dominant structural type that has generally been regarded as distinctive of the later Bronze Age and Iron Age in Britain is the 'roundhouse', a term applied to circular buildings of quite disparate size and construction (Harding 2009) that constitute a major structural component of domestic or agricultural settlements throughout Britain, and certainly not exclusively in hillforts. Their use as domestic dwellings is usually inferred from the presence of hearths and from a range of domestic utensils in the associated material assemblage, though in many instances the absence of the former and the poverty of the latter might leave the issue open to doubt. Their function cannot generally be inferred from their structure or ground-plan alone, though the layout of some variants, like the ring-ditch houses of northern Britain, may suggest their use as byre-houses. At High Knowes, Alnham, Northumberland (Jobey and Tait 1966), two large ring-ditch houses are accompanied by two smaller roundhouses, apparently as paired units. Assuming a functional distinction, it would be easy to presume that the larger buildings were residential and that the smaller were ancillary buildings like barns, when the reverse might have been more likely in an agricultural settlement. In the Atlantic north and west, broch towers almost certainly served not just as dwellings for extended family groups but as strongholds for communal storage of produce, given the additional capacity of their multi-storied construction. Ethnographic evidence might suggest that separate roundhouses could have been allocated to women or non-kin dependants, but if so this would be hard to detect archaeologically. Social distinctions of rank are not obviously reflected in differences in size or structure within contemporary groups of buildings, though this possibility should not be excluded. The period 3 layout at Crickley Hill, Gloucestershire, has a series of smaller roundhouses seemingly clustered around the dominant, large, central roundhouse (Dixon and Borne 1977: Figure 3), and two large roundhouses at Yeavering Bell have been cited above as candidates for elite residences. But these are currently exceptions, and for much of the British Iron Age it would be hard to adduce evidence that status was reflected in size or layout of buildings.

Size and construction technique must nevertheless reflect use. The floor area of a roundhouse 7 m in diameter, which Reynolds reckoned, for example, was the maximum span for a stake-wall roundhouse that could be roofed, is less than a quarter of that of a roundhouse 15 m in diameter. The large roundhouses of Little Woodbury–Pimperne type, therefore, must have been *inclusive* in the sense of accommodating a range of activities and functions, whereas settlements with multiple smaller roundhouses perhaps reflect the beginnings of functional segregation of space. The choice of different construction techniques for roundhouses of broadly the same size—successively post-ring to stake-wall at Moel y Gaer, for example—must reflect differences in intended usage, one possible implication perhaps being that stake-wall houses reflect seasonal occupation. The multiple replacements of stake circles at Cadbury Castle or Danebury certainly would be consistent with repeated seasonal construction.

Grain storage is the one function to which specialist structures may have been dedicated, in the form of underground pit-silos and upstanding, four-post granaries. Even these may have been incorporated within roundhouses, unless or until agricultural intensification resulted in the need for bulk storage and storage of surpluses. The larger roundhouses of the earlier Iron Age in Wessex would certainly have had a considerable storage capacity in their high-pitched roof space, whilst in western and northern Britain the incorporation of souterrains into houses suggests that integral storage was a norm. The central four-poster at Little Woodbury, Wiltshire, House 1 (Bersu 1940), could have stored the domestic supply, forming a natural focus of the household, perhaps even incorporating a shrine dedicated to the household spirits. Within the framework of a substantial roundhouse these would not have needed earth-fast foundations, so that Little Woodbury may be an exception in that regard. But externally as free-standing structures these four-posters of course would have required proper foundations.

Pits and four-posters both occur in hillforts, sometimes in concentrated numbers indicating storage on a communal scale, assuming that this was their primary purpose. With a structure as basic as the timber four-poster—including those variants that have six or even five posts—other possible functions such as excarnation platforms should not be excluded, but collective storage certainly seems to have been an important role of hillforts in southern Britain. Pits likewise could have been used for other forms of dedicated deposition, but grain storage in pits has been shown empirically to have been viable (Reynolds 1974). Pit storage was not universal in the British Iron Age, and for practical and ecological reasons was practised mainly south-east of a line from the Severn to the Wash. Chronologically, the greatest density of storage pits is found in the middle pre-Roman Iron Age. Four-posters likewise have a distribution mainly in southern and south-eastern Britain. This, of course, does not mean that the rest of Britain was dedicated exclusively to pastoralism, as Piggott (1958a) rather simplistically proposed, but it does suggest that agricultural production in southern England especially by the middle pre-Roman Iron Age was capable of significant surpluses.

RESOURCES AND SOCIAL IMPLICATIONS

The resource implications in terms of materials and labour involved in constructing a hillfort on the scale of Maiden Castle are self-evident but are nevertheless not easy to quantify. Estimates can be made as to the volume of core materials needed to build a rampart of specified height and width (Hogg 1975: 56), and estimates might even be advanced for the amount of timber required for a timber-framed rampart, assuming that its design could be inferred with sufficient accuracy from excavation. Where structural foundations have been well-preserved in waterlogged conditions, as at the lake-edge fort at Biskupin in Poland (Figure 1.9a), the technique of construction and

Defining issues 23

(a)

(b)

Figure 1.9. Archaeological reconstructions: (a) Biskupin, Poland, marsh fort reconstruction, (b) Roman siegeworks from Alesia reconstruction at the Archéodrome, A6 services near Beaune. Photographs by D. W. Harding.

material quantities required might be calculated with greater reliability, but the evidence for timber-framed ramparts in Britain is seldom so well preserved. In the case of late La Tène continental fortifications employing the *murus Gallicus* technique with iron nails or spikes at the intersections of the timber baulks, as at the Mont Beuvray in Burgundy, an estimate could be made of the volume of iron required, which would unquestionably have been on a massive industrial scale. Much more difficult, however, are the social issues involved; who carried out the labour of construction and who exercised the authority to muster the materials and workforce?

That woodland management in prehistory would have been necessary to supply and to regenerate the quantities of timber required in enclosure construction is now widely accepted. Even for the construction of a single large Iron Age roundhouse, the number of trees and stools required is formidable (Reynolds 1993), and this for a building the lifespan of which may have been as little as a couple of generations though potentially much longer. The quantities involved in providing timber for the front and rear revetment and internal bracing of a timber-framed rampart would be prodigious by comparison, to the extent that we may question whether the shift to dump rampart construction in the middle pre-Roman Iron Age in southern Britain was not in part occasioned by the depletion of timber supplies despite best efforts at management. Timber is predominant in the construction of hillforts based on the chalklands of southern England, though occasionally, as in phase 2 of the eastern entrance at Maiden Castle, limestone was imported to the site to enhance the grandeur of the entrance passage. If the limestone facing provided the icing on the cake, the conspicuous consumption of resource was nevertheless in the investment of timber in the rampart. The lifespan of a timber-framed rampart is difficult to assess and probably easy to underestimate. Assuming that oak was the preferred timber, with its innate durability and resistance to fungal decay, the basic framework could have endured for a century or more provided that, on the same principle as a roundhouse wall was kept dry by overhanging eaves, the rampart was kept dry by decking on the parapet. The front face, where it was exposed to the elements, would have been more vulnerable, though the vertical and longitudinal timbers could have been replaced on a piecemeal basis where pressure from the rampart core had induced collapse. Replacing the internal cross-members, of course, would have been an altogether more difficult task.

Stone construction not surprisingly reflects the local geology. In some igneous and metamorphic environments suitable material may well have been available on the surface, thus obviating the need for quarrying a ditch in intractable bedrock. Even so, the labour of collecting surface stone in the required quantities should not be underestimated. On limestone it would generally have been necessary to quarry for building material, as at Crickley Hill, where the principal source was the main ditch, supplemented in period 3 by shallower quarry-pits along the inner edge of the wall (Dixon 1994). Crickley certainly showed evidence of gang or team construction, and some of the architectural devices in the period 3 gateway, for example (Figure 1.9b), suggest the presence of skilled masons experienced in using relatively small stone slabs. By contrast, the northern blockhouses, for example, used much larger stone blocks, with techniques such as partial corbelling and slab capping for their intramural galleries, devices that would have required temporary scaffolding and hoisting equipment during construction, and must surely have involved specialist masons and engineers.

There remains, therefore, the question of technical expertise, whether in practice hillfort construction was a traditional community skill or whether specialist architectural or engineering expertise was available to the builders. We may infer from roundhouse construction that joinery skills such as using a range of joints and preparing planks would have been locally available. Technical similarity in plan, as for example in the entrances at Danebury and St Catharine's Hill (Figure 1.10A, B) or in the rebuilding of entrances with guard-rooms at Moel Hiraddug and Dinorben in north Wales (Figure 1.10C, D), on the other hand, might imply the influence of a specialist architect or engineer, though there is nothing in British hillfort design as novel as the introduction of mud-brick wall-construction at the Heuneburg in Baden-Württemberg. A first requirement of hillfort construction would surely be a calculation of the resources needed, by the equivalent of a modern quantity surveyor. This implies the existence of standard units of measurement for length and volume, which need not have been very much more complex than would be required in daily transactions such as measuring quantities of grain. A basic knowledge of geometry is certainly implicit in the ground-plans of Iron Age roundhouses in southern and northern Britain. There also remains the question of the labour force, whether the entire community was involved in one capacity or another or whether selected gangs of joiners and semi-skilled labourers were recruited to undertake the work as part of the dispersed community's obligations to the ruling hierarchy. It is also possible, of course, that slave labour was involved, as may have been the case for other burdensome or dangerous tasks such as quarrying or mining.

Who exercised control over these resources is a matter of debate. The older hierarchical model, in which the hillfort would have been the central place of a chief and his tribal elite, as we have noted, has been challenged, the hierarchical nature of Iron Age society in the immediately pre-Roman period in southern Britain being seen as a late development. As a concession to the 'democratization' of the earlier Iron Age, Cunliffe supposed that Danebury could have been as much 'a symbol of social cohesion and of power' of 'the social group as a whole' as of 'a more narrow sector of the elite' (1995: 92). Nevertheless he retained the concept of a 'coercive power' that would have

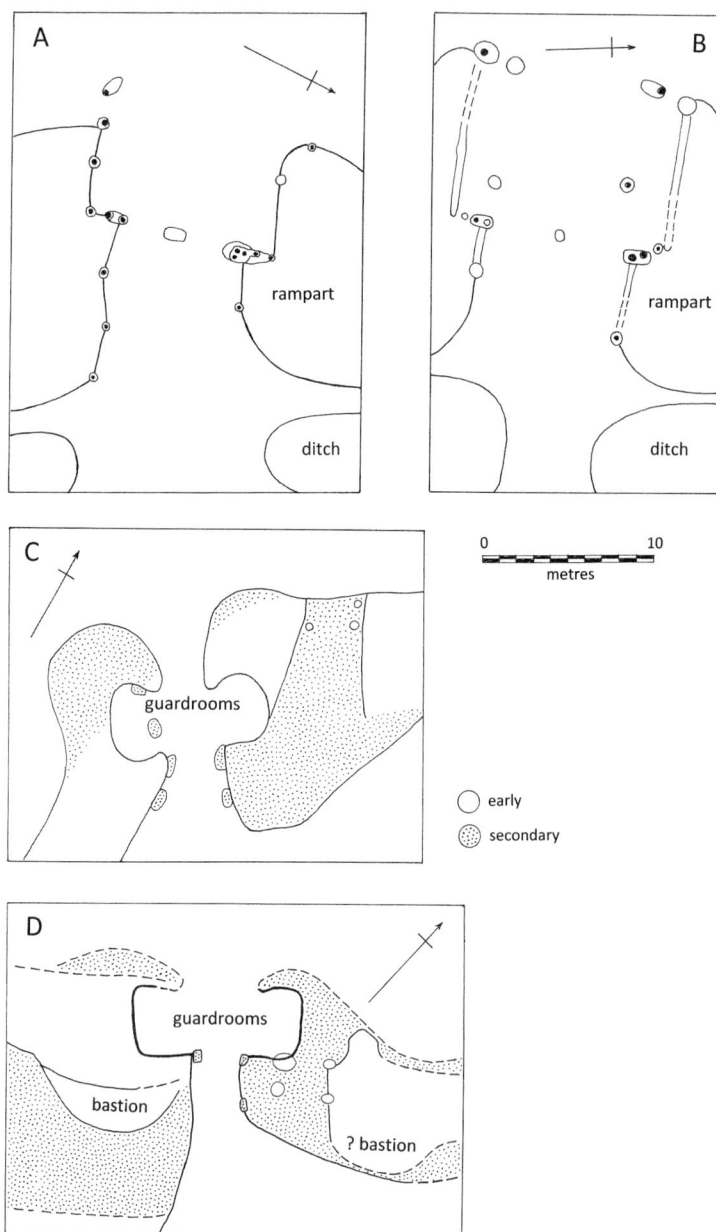

Figure 1.10. Hillfort entrance plans: (A) St Catharine's Hill, Winchester, Hampshire, phase 1, (B) Danebury, Hampshire, east entrance, phase 2a, (C) Moel Hiraddug, Clwyd (Flintshire), inner entrance, (D) Dinorben, Clwyd (Denbighshire), south-east entrance. Drawings by D. W. Harding adapted from Hawkes *et al.* 1930, Cunliffe, 2005, Guilbert, 1979b from a drawing by J. L. Davies, and Gardner and Savory, 1964.

exercised authority in the construction of such monumental works, whether by a 'democratic' council of elders or by a single, dominant lineage, as in a chiefdom. He finally opted for the latter, with 'a chieftain who, by the late period at least, may well have resided for much if not all of the year within the fort' (ibid. 93). In contrast to the major Wessex hillforts the smaller, hamlet-scale hillforts of the Scottish Borders or west Wales would not have required anything like the same quantities of materials, though the same question arises as to who exercised authority over their management and use. Even if this was a hierarchical overlord, however, there is no reason to suppose that within a system of reciprocal obligations, these resources would not have been made available to a local community.

THE FUNCTION OF HILLFORTS

These issues are all clearly fundamental to an interpretation of the role of hillforts in Iron Age society, and the assumption that defence was a priority as the 'default' interpretation should certainly be re-examined. Given the diversity of sites and the time span under consideration, it is self-evident that different hillforts in different circumstances will have fulfilled a variety of different roles, and likely even that individual sites will have changed over time. Nevertheless, this diversity may usefully be categorized under three headings, adopting and perhaps adapting Neustupný's triple criteria for classifying the function of artefacts in general and enclosures and fortifications in particular (2006, with earlier references). He distinguished *practical* function, *social* function, and *symbolic* significance or function. In the case of a hillfort, the physical barrier of rampart and ditch might well have a practical function in keeping enemies at bay, preventing livestock from straying or predators from getting in. In considering the social function of hillforts, Neustupný cited their potential as military defences and as trading centres, which illustrates the problem of distinguishing practical and social roles. A principal social role of hillforts might be to articulate the identity of the community that it represents, whether resident or dispersed, and to provide that community with a permanent sense of place with which to identify. Yet this role is inextricably bound up with the site as symbol in its role of communicating these meanings to others, particularly in seasonal or periodic gatherings or festivals and a variety of intra- and inter-community activities. The symbolic significance of a hillfort could be quite different from its overt, practical function, and could acquire enhanced significance over time. By the later fourth century AD, when a Romano-Celtic temple was built within the derelict ramparts of Maiden Castle, the site's symbolic function was surely different from that prevailing at the height of its occupation. Neustupný placed greatest emphasis on communication of ideas through an artefact's symbolic significance. Integral though symbolism might be, it is hard to see how it could be expressed other than as an adjunct to a structure designed to fulfil a practical or social role. Few Iron Age monuments, other perhaps than funerary monuments, are likely to have been built primarily as symbols, and even burials served the practical role of disposal of the dead. It is conceivable, of course, that an artefact or structure might embody a symbolic meaning to an external observer that was not consciously intended by its designer. Neustupný is evidently cautious in the use of 'ethnohistoric parallels' and the current fashion for the 'empathy' approach to social and cognitive reconstruction. It is not difficult to infer a role for hillforts in ritual and ceremonial activities, but whether the hillfort simply provided the locale or embodied some other symbolic attributes is impossible to prove archaeologically. Part of the problem, as Neustupný stressed, is that these three functions are not divisible, the social and symbolic roles especially being mutually embedded.

If we were to update Hawkes' (1954) 'ladder of inference' model, and consider hillforts under the headings 'technological', 'economic', 'social', and 'symbolic or cognitive', there would be little doubt that the role of the first two by now, for some reasonably well-investigated sites at least, would be relatively straightforward to reconstruct. The latter two roles were always going to be more difficult to infer, though prospectively perhaps more rewarding. To evaluate social and cognitive aspects nevertheless requires reliable data, the rigorous re-assessment of which can sometimes prove laborious, but without which any archaeological reconstruction is founded on quicksand. Above all the current fashion for asserting what prehistoric societies thought or believed, based on nothing more secure than 'empathy' with the past, is the province not of serious scholarship but of creative fiction.

2

History of Hillfort Studies

Popular perception polarizes opinions, and archaeology is no exception. Instead of complexities and paradoxes, we instinctively prefer simplification and certainties, even if this distorts the truth, except, of course, where academic compromise affords the comfort zone of indecision. Accordingly, Stukeley and the early antiquarians are regarded as eccentrics, concerned only with druids and ancient Britons painted with woad, whilst General Pitt-Rivers has been portrayed as the pioneer of modern, scientific archaeology in an era of dilettante barrow diggers. In Scotland, Daniel Wilson has been acclaimed for his first use in English of the term 'prehistoric', yet as far as hillforts were concerned he was scathingly dismissive of their significance. David Christison is widely cited as the excavator whose work at Dunadd on behalf of the Society of Antiquaries of Scotland so appalled Lord Abercromby that he misguidedly transferred his bequest, originally in favour of the Society, to the University of Edinburgh for the foundation of the Abercromby Chair of Prehistoric Archaeology. Yet Christison's *Early Fortifications in Scotland* of 1898 was an authoritative survey of hillforts that was acknowledged as a model in Hadrian Allcroft's *Earthwork of England* (1908). Every generation likes to imagine that it has advanced the frontiers of knowledge to a degree that allows it to look upon earlier achievements with the benefit of better informed if slightly self-satisfied hindsight, but progress is seldom without its setbacks and sidetracks. Each generation hopefully builds upon the advances of its predecessors, and the questions posed by pioneers will necessarily appear facile to later researchers. Early antiquarian investigations had to address fundamental issues of basic site identification and dating, and it is salutary to recall that even Pitt-Rivers' initial investigation of Sussex hillforts (Lane–Fox 1869) was primarily designed to advance the case for their being pre-Roman. We might also note that he was in no doubt that their function was as defensive sites, against one alternative view, current even then, that they were used for ritual purposes.

EARLY FIELD SURVEY AND SITE DESCRIPTION

Serious study of hillforts, notwithstanding the dilettantish curiosity evinced by landed gentry or leisured clerics, began effectively with the topographic descriptions and surveys of sixteenth-century antiquaries like William Camden, whose *Britannia* was published in 1586. This monumental work was revised and re-issued in several editions over a period of two hundred years, and was notably extended in Gough's edition of 1789. It was in the 1600 edition that the hillfort at Maiden Castle in Dorset was first recorded in print. The earliest reference to the fortifications at Stanwick in North Yorkshire was in the *Itinerary* of Camden's contemporary John Leyland. It was Leyland who, in his description of Cadbury Castle in Somerset, may have been responsible for the notion that the hillfort was Camelot of Arthurian myth (Alcock 1972: 12), a tradition that was rejected by Camden, who believed Cadbury to be Roman on the basis of Roman coins that had been recovered from the site. These early topographic archives began a long-lasting tradition of non-intrusive field archaeology, which deserves to be recognized in a period which is better remembered for the eccentricities of Romantic antiquarianism. It is hardly surprising that the main focus of early antiquarian interest was on burial mounds and stone circles, among which John Aubrey's surveys and investigations of the mid-later seventeenth century at Stonehenge and Avebury are prime examples. Even so, hillforts were major monuments in the landscape, and though wrongly if understandably attributed to Romans, Saxons, or Danes, their antiquity was never in doubt any more than was their defensive function.

William Stukeley (1687–1765) is perhaps the most enigmatic of the early antiquaries, not least because his studies divided so remarkably between his earlier surveys and recording of buildings and standing monuments and his later obsession with the druids, Avebury, and Stonehenge. Stuart Piggott described the 'two periods in Stukeley's intellectual life, the first, to 1725, reliable and objective, and the second, from his ordination to his death, speculative and fantastic' (1985: 153). He characterized Stukeley as 'a pioneer of scientific field research and the founding father of the lunatic fringe', ending his life immersed in the excesses of druid mania (Piggott 1985: dust-jacket). Whatever triggered this extraordinary transformation, it coincided with his unexpected marriage, leaving London, and his ordination into the Church of England.

Stukeley's later eccentricity, however, should not be allowed to detract from the value of his earlier fieldwork. This was concerned with architecture and buildings rather more than archaeological field monuments, and hillforts were not especially prominent among his interests. He nevertheless was capable of astute observation of individual sites, and at Ogbury, Wiltshire, was perhaps the first to recognize what subsequently became known as 'Celtic' fields. He made a distinction between hillforts that he believed mistakenly to be Roman camps and some that he rightly recognized as 'British' and therefore presumably pre-Roman. The basis for this is generally unclear, though in the case of Wilbury, Hertfordshire, he assigned it to the 'British' category because the Roman road, the Icknield Way or 'Icening street', cut through its outer entrenchment. His fullest description, however, was of Cadbury Castle, which was

> very steep and high. there are three or four ditches quite round, sometimes more. the area within is twenty acres at least, rising in the middle. its figure is squarish, but conforms to the shape of the hill.... the rampart is large and high, made chiefly of stones cover'd with earth... here is only one entrance from the east. 'tis not unlikely there were buildings erected in later british times, being of so great strength, and a perfect watch-tower, surveying the countryside around to an incredible distance. In this camp they find many pebble stones exactly round.... they suppose 'em stones to sling withal.... Roman coins in great plenty have been found here... the entrance is guarded with six or seven ditches. on the north side in the fourth ditch is a never-failing spring called K. Arthur's well....
> (Stukeley 1724: 142)

The details in this description, including the internal acreage and numbers of Roman coins suggests that Stukeley may have been familiar with Camden's earlier account. He illustrated the multivallate defences of Cadbury with a drawing of the site from a distance, labelled 'Prospect of Camalet Castle 15 August 1723' (Figure 2.1a), suggesting that he was at least prepared to entertain the Arthurian associations of the site.

PIONEERS OF HILLFORT SURVEY AND EXCAVATION

One of the most remarkable contributions to field survey of the mid-nineteenth century was that of Henry MacLauchlan in Northumberland. Yeavering Bell had already attracted the attention of eighteenth-century antiquaries like John Horsley and William Hutchinson, but from 1850 MacLauchlan, who trained as a military surveyor, was employed by the Duke of Northumberland to survey first Hadrian's Wall, then Roman and prehistoric sites on the line of Dere Street through Northumberland to the Cheviots, including especially 'Celtic camps'. Some of these, including Yeavering, were then investigated by George Tate in the early 1860s, again sponsored by the fourth Duke. At Brough Law Tate exposed the stone rampart that Jobey (1971) subsequently showed was of double-faced or semi-*murus duplex* construction (Figure 1.8b). Among MacLauchlan's other achievements was the survey of

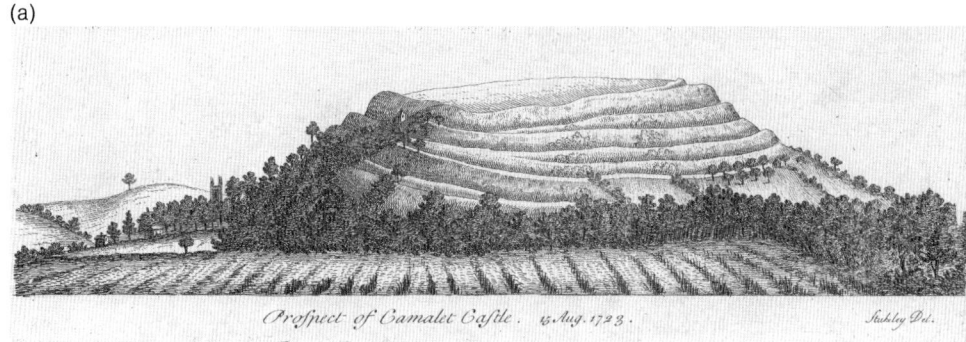

Figure 2.1. Antiquarian images of hillforts: (a) William Stukeley's Prospect of Camalet Castle, 15 August, 1723, (b) General William Roy's plan of Burghead, Morayshire, from Roy 1793. Images courtesy of the Centre for Research Collections, University of Edinburgh Library.

the Stanwick fortifications in north Yorkshire (Wheeler 1954: Plate II). In southern England, from 1853–8 Edwin Martin-Atkins was excavating at Uffington Castle to a standard of observation that was certainly more acute than most of his contemporaries. Though not published until 1904, Martin-Atkins' notes make it clear that he not only recognized the parallel post-rows that supported a timber-framed rampart, but he also rightly concluded from an examination of the associated pottery that the fort had been built before the Roman conquest. Another early pioneer of non-barrow excavation was Stephen Stone in Oxfordshire, who planned ditches and pits exposed by gravel quarrying at Standlake, and made scale models to illustrate his lectures on his findings, but who did not devote his attentions to hillforts.

Despite this pioneer work, the beginnings of modern hillfort research is still often equated with the investigations of the late 1860s in Sussex of Lt-Colonel Lane-Fox, whose major achievement as General Pitt-Rivers was the monumental and lavishly produced publication of his *Excavations in Cranborne Chase* (1887–98). His reputation was enhanced by Hawkes' (1947) re-interpretation of the settlement excavations at Woodcuts and Rotherley, and by Sir Mortimer Wheeler's elevation of Pitt-Rivers to founding-father status in British field archaeology, to which subsequent generations have duly paid homage. Pitt-Rivers' contribution was unquestionably important, not least in diverting attention towards fortifications and settlements and away from barrows, which had been the preoccupation of his mentor, Canon Greenwell and his forebears. But Pitt-Rivers' early investigations were no more scientific than those of most of his contemporaries. His excavations of raths and promontory forts in southern Ireland in the early 1860s were certainly not notable for their methodological rigour. By the late 1860s it is clear that Col. Lane-Fox was capable of recognizing stratigraphy in sections. Even in his later excavations, however, he did not record finds stratigraphically, not least because his workmen dug in spits, clearing sites regardless of stratigraphy in exactly the same way that his predecessors had done and some of his successors continued to do into the twentieth century.

By the time he inherited the Cranborne Chase estate, Pitt-Rivers had developed a more systematic method of recording finds, but he still delegated supervision to his assistants, 'visiting the excavations at least three times a day, and arranging to be sent for whenever anything of importance was found' (Pitt-Rivers 1887: xviii; 1888: xiv). In his excavations at Winkelbury, Wiltshire, his focus was on the defensive earthworks, but it is significant that, despite his reputed concern for stratigraphy, he did not detect any construction episodes in section, nor did he elaborate upon the stake-holes that he apparently observed in the rampart sections. His subsequent investigations of Bronze Age camps like South Lodge and Martin Down opened trenches in the interior, but still the emphasis was on accurate recording of 'pottery and other relics' (Pitt-Rivers 1898: 186), and apart from pits he does not appear to have recognized structural features whatsoever. Re-excavation has shown that his labourers also missed considerable numbers of artefacts (Bowden 1991: 156). In sum, Pitt-Rivers was not a particularly outstanding excavator, and the excavation records of work on Cranborne Chase were themselves of variable quality, depending upon which of his assistants was principally responsible. Pitt-Rivers was a polymath, for whom the study of ancient settlements and material culture, together with ethnology and physical anthropology, was a means of demonstrating the Darwinian principles of evolution. His scientific approach was developed selectively to that end, rather than to serve the advancement of archaeology as a discipline. He was still largely preoccupied with artefacts, albeit to his credit not simply valuable relics for their own sake, but with the classification of everyday artefacts that he rightly recognized as more representative of everyday culture. His contribution to field archaeology was substantial, and deserves recognition, but Pitt-Rivers' reputation nevertheless has benefited from a good press.

In Scotland, an outstanding early landmark in the recording of field monuments was General Roy's *The Military Antiquities of the Romans in Britain* (1793), but Roy's account generally only included hillforts such as Burnswark, where there was a direct relationship to Roman works, or where he wrongly attributed native sites to the Romans. George Chalmers, in his first volume of *Caledonia* (1807), recognized that the defences at Burnswark were designed to afford protection from native attack and not just in anticipation of Roman invaders (1807: 87–8). His selection of hillforts nevertheless is somewhat arbitrary and his summary descriptions are introduced in random order. But his footnotes are more perceptive, remarking on groups of hillforts, in which some were possibly subordinate to major sites like the Caterthuns, and sometimes with intervisibility as an apparent factor in their location. He was aware of the phenomenon of vitrification, and of the presence of 'subterraneous buildings' comparable to those of Cornwall and Ireland. In his account of Dunsinane, he summarized the results of excavation findings, but was still more fixated by the site's historical and literary associations.

Field research in Scotland began much later, with David Christison's survey of hillforts in the decade preceding his Rhind lectures of 1894. Christison recognized the ambiguity of the term 'hillfort', and was hesitant in describing them as 'prehistoric' on the grounds that defining the beginnings of history in Scotland was itself debateable. The study of hillforts he regarded as neglected by antiquaries in favour of classical antiquities, in which bias he held Daniel Wilson to have been culpable. *The Archaeology and Prehistoric Annals of Scotland* (1851) pays scant attention to hillforts, with the notable exception of vitrified forts, which had already prompted debate on their character and purpose. According to Wilson,

a very slight review of the more simple class of British hill-forts will suffice, since we fortunately possess, in many of the contemporary records already described (*i.e. Roman texts*), more precise and definite history than they can now yield.... Their lofty sites having secured them from the inroads of the agriculturalist, while his aggressive ploughshare has obliterated all traces of the far more skilfully constructed Roman camp and military road that once occupied the neighbouring valleys... These are obviously the outposts of the hardy Caledonian, from whence he watched his opportunity for some sudden foray or midnight surprise of the garrisons occupying the stations along the wall.
(Wilson 1851: 409–10, my parenthesis)

He acknowledged that, in the classical world, architecture and sculpture might complement the primary authority of written sources. But in selecting a handful of examples of Scottish hillforts for brief description of their earthworks, he ruefully observes that the 'Caterthun is no Athenian Acropolis' (ibid. 409), and that he has little worth recording to add to Chalmers' account.

Christison's survey was a landmark in British hillfort studies. Not even for Wessex had there been a dedicated synthesis of hillforts and related monuments, and it is sad indeed that the author's subsequent fieldwork at Dunadd should have tarnished his reputation for later generations. The counterpart to Christison's pioneer work, which it acknowledged in its Preface, was Hadrian Allcroft's *Earthwork of England* of 1908, which despite its parochial title includes some of the important Welsh hillforts and makes occasional reference across the Scottish border. Among the Welsh hillforts Allcroft noted the work of the Rev. S. Baring-Gould at Tre'r Ceiri, who in 1903 had cleared several stone houses, carefully recording the finds, but with no apparent reference to any possible stratigraphy. Though a native of Devonshire, where he had worked on Dartmoor with the Rev. W. C. Lukis, Baring-Gould had also excavated in Pembrokeshire at Foel Trigarn and the promontory fort on St David's Head. He was a man of extraordinarily wide interests, ranging from theology to folklore and folk music, but he is perhaps best remembered for his composition among others of the hymn *Onward Christian Soldiers* whilst a curate in Yorkshire.

HILLFORT EXCAVATION IN CENTRAL AND WESTERN EUROPE

The most extraordinary contribution to European Iron Age hillfort studies of the nineteenth century was the programme of investigation of sites of the Gallic War period initiated by Napoleon III, which resulted in his *Histoire de Jules César* and its *Atlas* of 1866. Napoleon III initiated excavations on a number of sites that had been identified as those that featured in the campaigns, including Bibracte, Gergovia, and notably Alesia, where both native defences and Roman siegeworks (Figure 1.9b) were studied in detail. From the surviving documentation it is clear that the fieldwork was conducted and recorded for the most part with great care by standards of the day. At the Mont Beuvray, supervision of the excavations was eventually taken over by Joseph Déchelette, whose *Manuel d'Archéologie* of 1908 was incomplete when he was killed in the trenches in the first few months of the First World War. Napoleon III's motivation was nationalistic pride in the Gaulish resistance to Rome, and an affinity with the military achievements of Caesar. Accordingly he commemorated himself as well as Vercingetorix in the monument that he had erected at the site of Alesia, Alise-Ste-Reine. As one French archaeologist once chauvinistically observed, Vercingetorix was defeated by the *second* greatest general in history.

In south-western Europe in the nineteenth century, the interest of antiquarians and place-name scholars had been focused on the Celtiberians and their documented resistance to Roman expansion. The 1860s also saw early investigations of the Celtiberian town of Numantia, destroyed following the siege by Scipio Aemilianus in 133 BC. Further excavations were undertaken in the decade before the First World War by a German expedition under Adolf Schulten. Meantime in Portugal, the *castros* of the peninsular north-west had attracted the interest of Martins Sarmento, who between 1875 and 1884 conducted excavations at the major settlement near Guimarães known as the Citânia de Briteiros, which was close to his family estate, following up this campaign with further excavations at the nearby Castro of Sabrosa, where Christopher Hawkes (1958, 1984) was to carry out more controlled stratigraphic investigations in the 1950s. Martins Sarmento was a man of means, who had qualified as a lawyer but never practised. He dedicated his later life to regional archaeology, but was nevertheless widely known and respected in western Europe, and the Sociedade Martins Sarmento museum in Guimarães, founded in his honour in 1882, houses his collections.

Among the foremost fieldworkers of the earlier twentieth century was Gerhard Bersu, whose excavations included notable campaigns at the Goldberg in Baden-Württemberg and at the Wittnauer Horn in Switzerland (Bersu 1945). In Britain he is noted for his groundbreaking excavations at Little Woodbury, Wiltshire, in the immediately pre-war years (Bersu 1940), for his excavations on the Isle of Man as an internee (Bersu 1977), and after the war, in Scotland at Traprain Law and elsewhere. In fact, the technique of area stripping that he applied at Little Woodbury, involving the successive uncovering of adjacent strips of ground, he had first developed at the Goldberg on the eve of the First World War (Maria Bersu, personal communication), long before the age of blitz-and-clean area excavation. Bersu's interpretations of the structures at the Goldberg *Herrenhof*, nevertheless, are open to question; likewise, his interpretation of the rectangular structures at the Wittnauer

Horn, apparently arranged around the steep-sided perimeter of the promontory fort, with the interior largely left open, has been challenged in detail (Berger *et al.* 1996).

The German contribution to hillfort studies was especially important in the 1950s, with the launch of a programme of research excavation of the princely stronghold (*Fürstensitz*) at the Heuneburg on the upper Danube in Baden-Württemberg, and of the associated burials (*Fürstengräber*) at the Hohmichele. On the basis of this, Kimmig (1969) proposed his hierarchy of fortifications in the west Hallstatt zone, at the top of which the *Fürstensitze* reinforced their dominance by controlling long-distance trade with the Mediterranean world. The publication of the series of volumes since 1962, *Heuneburgstudien* by the Römisch-Germanische Kommission, has been an achievement unprecedented in hillfort studies. Of equal importance was the rescue excavation on a massive scale in advance of development of the former Luftwaffe airfield within the later La Tène fortifications at Manching in Bavaria, where Krämer for the first time used machinery to open several kilometres of trial trenches in order to define the area of occupation (Krämer and Schubert 1970).

DEFENSIVE SEQUENCE AND CHRONOLOGY

Establishing the date of hillforts was an understandable priority from the earliest period of hillfort investigation. Early pioneers, even into the 1930s, would hardly have seen the need for a formal research strategy in tackling a hillfort excavation; their purpose was to date the site and to establish something of its character, objectives that seemed self-evident. Before the advent of radiocarbon sampling, dating was dependent entirely on material artefacts, especially pottery, which occurred in relative abundance in southern England, and among which early, middle, and late Iron Age assemblages were already well recognized by the 1930s, though their assessment in absolute terms was somewhat compressed within the last few pre-Roman centuries. In large parts of northern England and lowland Scotland, however, Iron Age settlements were virtually aceramic, inducing an even more conservative chronology, because 'parallels' had to be sought from further south, with what was deemed to be appropriate 'time-lag'. One way of establishing the broad parameters of a hillfort's occupation is to examine and hopefully to date through associated artefacts the structural sequence of its defences, though this of course need not mirror exactly the occupational sequence of its interior. As an objective attainable with limited resources, and before radiocarbon dating, a section through the rampart, or accumulated occupation in the lee of the rampart, afforded in principle the best prospects of stratigraphic and chronological clarification.

With limited time and resources (Hawkes had just three weeks and eight workmen at Quarley Hill, Hampshire, in 1938), it is scarcely surprising that the trenches through the ramparts were woefully inadequate. The main cutting at Quarley Hill cannot have been more than three feet wide through a rampart and ditch more than twice that in maximum height and depth, not only compromising health and safety, but rendering any structural framework within the rampart or any secondary usage of the ditch extremely hard to detect. Had the rampart been faced with a stone wall, it is possible that some surviving courses might have been found within these narrow trenches, but if the rampart had been timber-framed, with uprights spaced at intervals, then the chances of their being missed or misinterpreted must have been very high. Well into the 1960s, rampart cuttings were constrained by resources to narrow sections; even at Danebury the rampart sections were not qualitatively different in design or execution from those that had characterized hillfort excavation in the 1930s. At Blewburton Hill in 1967 (Harding 1976b) an attempt was made to combat this problem by sectioning the rampart with two parallel trenches, each 4 metres wide and separated by a 3 metre baulk, which established that the main, earth-fast uprights were as much as 4 metres apart. The only possibility for more extensive area-stripping of a hillfort's defences was when those earthworks had been eroded to their foundations, as at Grimthorpe in Yorkshire, where in 1961–2 Ian Stead (1968) was able to open a swathe of rampart foundations some 86 metres in extent with the aid of mechanical stripping. Likewise at Ivinghoe Beacon, Buckinghamshire (Cotton and Frere 1968) the earthworks had been almost completely denuded, so that the excavators were able to strip some 12 metres of former rampart to expose just four pairs of irregularly spaced post-holes of a timber-framed rampart. For surviving earthworks, it was not until the 1970s in Wales that a new era of rampart excavation began, with the stripping of the defences at the Breiddin (Musson 1991) and at Moel y Gaer (Guilbert 1975a) on a scale that permitted the detection of constructional features over 30 or 40 metres. By the end of the decade, Philip Dixon's 10 metre-wide cutting across the defences at Crickley Hill probably represents as complex an exposure of successive ramparts in depth as has been achieved anywhere in Britain.

In northern Britain, the primary objective of hillfort excavation in the early post-war period was likewise the clarification of the defensive sequence. Mrs Piggott's (1948) excavation at Hownam Rings became the model, with the expectation that the progressive complexity of enclosure, from palisade through univallate to multivallate earthworks, would be widely replicated as a reflection of cultural development. The final phase at Hownam Rings, when a settlement of scooped house platforms extended over the defunct defences, together with the innovation of stone-built roundhouses, was attributed to the imposition of the *pax Romana*. The 'trend towards enclosure' remained an implicit assumption for a generation or more (Harding 1982: 189–94), though the universal applicability of the 'Hownam model' was challenged by Peter Hill as a result of his excavations at Broxmouth. Here not only had he adduced evidence for the appearance of stone-built 'Votadinian' houses well before the conquest, but he had also argued that the structural sequence was more complex than the Hownam model implied (Hill 1982a, 1982b). Such models were encouraged by the problems of independent dating without cross-reference to other site sequences. With the routine availability of radiocarbon dating, new approaches became possible (Armit 1999) in which defensive sequence was less dominant. With the full publication of Broxmouth (Armit and McKenzie forthcoming), the pre-Roman appearance of stone-built houses will be confirmed, but the site progression from unenclosed settlement through various stages of enclosure to a final, post-enclosure occupation may seem not so far removed from the Hownam model.

WHEELER AND THE HISTORICAL PARADIGM

The hillfort excavation par excellence of the 1930s, of course, was Wheeler's four-year campaign at Maiden Castle, Dorset. In his report (Wheeler 1943) he offers both 'reasons' and 'objectives' for the research programme. His reasons hardly amount to a research strategy in modern terms. Firstly, he tackled it because, like Everest, it was there; if 'not the largest in area of British earthworks (*he was to excavate that after the War*) . . . the most imposing of their class' (my parenthesis). Second, this part of Wessex, between Hengistbury Head and Hembury, he regarded as comparatively neglected hitherto. Reading the sub-text, it is clear that he regarded Maiden Castle, identified with Ptolemy's *Dunion*, as probably the foremost among the twenty *oppida* that Suetonius (*Divus Vespasianus*, 4) claimed were captured by Vespasian's Second Augustan legion. Tying archaeological interpretation to documentary history was not simply a matter of disciplinary inclination; it also afforded a chronological context for the site. Thus it was not just the conquest that provided a chronological horizon; the late dating of the introduction of multivallation was also linked to the historical horizon of the Gallic Wars and to the influence of Venetic refugees (Wheeler 1943: 382–3).

The Maiden Castle excavation was also a major landmark in the popularization of archaeology, long before the advent of television archaeologists. Wheeler foresaw the need for public funding of archaeology and therefore recognized the benefit of public interest and involvement in archaeological discoveries. In his publications and newspaper briefings he presented his results in a way that tried to satisfy scholarly accuracy whilst at the same time appealing to a wider audience. As with his later campaign at Stanwick in north Yorkshire, Wheeler's objective was to illuminate the pages of history through his excavations, and graphically he did it in his reconstruction of the Roman assault on the east gateway at Maiden Castle. The report was written in 1941 and there can be no mistaking the Churchillian cadences of his narrative:

> The whole war cemetery as it lay exposed before us was eloquent of mingled piety and distraction; of weariness, of dread, of darkness, but not yet of complete forgetfulness. (Wheeler 1943: 63)

The principal objective of the Maiden Castle excavation, following conventional practice, was to 'investigate the structural history of the great fortifications' and its associated material culture. In his secondary target of 'recovering some part of the town-plan' Wheeler was frustrated, not apparently by the sheer scale of the task, as might have been anticipated, but by the palimpsest of superimposed episodes of activity which, hardly surprisingly, he claimed defied clarification. The Iron Age occupation of the hill, of course, was not his only concern; he investigated the Neolithic Long Mound and re-examined the Roman buildings that had first been identified in the later nineteenth century. His Iron Age excavations concentrated principally on establishing the structural sequence of the defences through broad rampart sections and of the eastern entrance of the developed hillfort by use of his innovative 'grid' system of area excavation (Figures 2.2a and b). Interior occupation with examined only in the lee of the rampart in the south-west corner, and in the vicinity of

(a)

Figure 2.2. Maiden Castle, Dorset, 1934–7: (a) area excavation of eastern entrance, (b) (opposite) inner rampart cutting E from the north-west. Reproduced by kind permission of the Society of Antiquaries of London from Wheeler 1943, © reserved.

the Roman temple, where a focus of Iron Age settlement was linked to the eastern gateway by a metalled street.

A comparison of the claimed objectives and strategies of Wheeler's campaign at Maiden Castle in the 1930s and Sharples' programme of the mid-1980s (Sharples 1991a, 1991b) reflects the changes in archaeological theory and practice in the half-century that divided them. Wheeler's approach was essentially that of an historical archaeologist, and one for whom the diffusionist view was implicit. His subsequent campaign in northern France, abruptly interrupted by the imminent outbreak of war, was prompted by the assumption that structural features like multivallation and material types such as bead-rim pottery were both introduced from the continent, especially by Venetic refugees fleeing from Caesar's campaigns of 56 BC. He did not doubt the military purpose of the earthworks, multivallation being linked to sling warfare and the notion of 'defence in depth'. Much of this had gone out of fashion by the 1980s. Diffusionism as an explanation for culture change became unacceptable from the later 1960s, while the hillfort's massive earthworks were in Sharples' vision of Maiden Castle an expression of status and prestige rather than primarily defensive.

The principal differences in approach, however, lay in the emphasis placed on the landscape context and environment of the hillfort by the later research

(b)

programme. An extensive tract of landscape around the hillfort was surveyed, soils were sampled geochemically, material artefacts were collected and their distributions plotted, air-photographic features were mapped and documentary sources for former land use were studied. Within the hillfort itself the interior was surveyed geophysically, and for phosphate and magnetic susceptibility, revealing hitherto-unrecorded detail of structural features. Excavation was limited to half a dozen trenches located contiguously to Wheeler's and designed to check specific aspects of stratigraphy and to clarify chronology through radiocarbon dating; to this extent it reflected a growing antipathy among professional archaeologists to intrusive investigation in circumstances other than where a site is threatened with destruction. So the key issue of the nature of the site's internal occupation or overall function was in no way advanced and Wheeler's optimistic objective of 'recovering some part of the town-plan' remains as elusive as ever.

Wheeler's interpretation of Stanwick in north Yorkshire was even more emphatically dictated by historical evidence, in this case Tacitus' accounts of events of the first century AD. Whilst the archaeological evidence recovered from within the area of the Tofts certainly indicated occupation at that time, sections through the various ramparts of the extensive earthwork complex yielded no dateable material whatsoever. The rationale behind the dating of the largest, southern earthworks, Phase III in the Wheeler sequence, stretched the available evidence well beyond breaking point. The ramparts on the southern circuit showed a dog-leg, which had been accentuated by its use for access by modern farm traffic. Assuming this to be an original entrance, Wheeler excavated Site H to expose it, with Leslie Alcock as supervisor. Oddly for an entrance, the ditch proved to be continuous, but odder still was the absence of gate-posts or flanking support for the entrance passage, a framework that should have been in place before the ditch was quarried for material to fill the rampart core. Whilst this might have sowed doubts in more modest minds, for Wheeler it only confirmed his conviction:

> The inference from all this is scarcely in doubt. During the cutting and building of the principal surviving entrance ... a sudden alarm stopped the work. As an emergency measure, the causeway was cut away, so that the ends of the unfinished ditches were joined up, thus isolating the intended gateway and turning it into a defensive strong-point.... Not a single potsherd was recovered from the whole site; no appreciable traffic had ever passed this way to or from the great enclosure. The picture of frustration is complete.... We can almost see the tribesmen toiling vainly at their gate, almost hear the Ninth Legion tramping up from its new fortress at York to one of its rare victories.   (Wheeler 1954: 15–16, 23)

A non-existent entrance without a single potsherd as dating evidence could nevertheless be assigned to the campaigns of Petillius Cerialis and the Ninth Legion between AD 70–74. The whole historical tableau was predicated on the belief that Stanwick was the headquarters of Venutius and Brigantian resistance to Rome after his estranged queen Cartimandua had sought refuge with the Romans. More recent excavations at Stanwick, of course, have cast a rather different light on Stanwick as a centre that was engaged in amicable and productive exchange in Roman goods with southern neighbours. A full re-evaluation of Stanwick must plainly await the final publication of the settlement excavations of 1981-9, and even then it seems likely that some issues will remain unresolved.

THE 'NEW ARCHAEOLOGY' AND AFTER

By the 1970s, British prehistorians were in the grip of the so-called 'New Archaeology', which notably challenged the older diffusionist approach that had seen each major advance or cultural innovation in European prehistory as originating in a single 'cradle of civilization' somewhere in the Middle East. From the adoption of agriculture to the beginnings of metallurgy and the emergence of urbanized state societies, all these innovations in north-western Europe had been seen as deriving ultimately from more advanced civilizations of the Mediterranean and Middle East. In the 1960s no-one would have been surprised at the notion that the Amesbury archer might have come from somewhere in continental Europe. Colin Renfrew's *Before Civilization* (1973) challenged some of the sacred cows of European prehistory, such as the belief that European megaliths and even Stonehenge owed their genesis to Mycenaean influences, harnessing radiocarbon dates for the first time to reinforce the case for independent developments in Atlantic Europe and Britain.

But the 'New Archaeology' was not just concerned with diffusionism. It embraced a wide range of theoretical and methodological approaches adopted from other disciplines in an attempt to create a broader theoretical basis for archaeology beyond the prevailing historical paradigm. Among the foremost exponents of the 'New Archaeology' was David Clarke, whose *Analytical Archaeology* (1968) was rapidly followed by an edited volume of essays, *Models in Archaeology* (1972a). In this volume Clarke himself advanced a reinterpretation of the Glastonbury 'lake village' (1972b), which has since been roundly discredited (Coles and Minnitt 1995), basically for taking liberties with the archaeological evidence, but also for its social reconstruction (Clarke 1972b: 839) that went far beyond what could reasonably have been inferred, even if the basic data had been reliable. The application of these models unfortunately was always prone to jargon or verbosity, even in the articulation of basic concepts. In the absence of excavated evidence, there was no means of knowing that the hillforts surrounding the Somerset levels were in contemporary occupation, but for Clarke this need not inhibit the construction of a Thiessen polygon mosaic of the 'Glastonbury territory', because,

> Although the hill forts may not be exactly contemporary, they nevertheless are the man-hour insignia for considerable populations who both pre-existed and post-existed their construction. (Clarke 1972b: 843)

As an aid to spatial analysis, Thiessen polygons were very fashionable in hillfort studies, with the implicit assumption that hillforts were 'central places' with a 'catchment area'. Cunliffe used them to plot hillforts in central Wiltshire (Cunliffe 1971), A. H. A. Hogg (1971) at the same conference used 'weighted' ones to analyse hillforts south of the Thames, and Collis (1977b) applied the technique to hillforts in central Hampshire. But by the end of the 1970s they had disappeared without trace, and in the fourth edition of *Iron Age Communities* (Cunliffe 2005: Figure 15.27) there is just a single survivor of that icon of an earlier generation. More enduring than the gimmicks and verbal gymnastics of the 'New Archaeology', however, was the fact that the demise of the 'invasion hypothesis' as an explanation for the appearance of hillforts allowed alternative models of indigenous development, social and economic, to be explored (Bradley 1971; Cunliffe 1971).

The 1970s also saw the launch of the most sustained programme of hillfort excavation ever conducted in Britain, at Danebury in Hampshire (Cunliffe 1984a, 1984b; 1995; Cunliffe and Poole 1991a, 1991b). The project was distinguished not only by the fact that a sizeable proportion of the interior was stripped and excavated, but also for its Danebury Environs Programme which tackled the crucial issue of the hillfort's context in the Iron Age landscape. Though the scale of interior excavation was much greater than on any previous research excavation, methodologically the Danebury excavation itself followed conventional archaeological objectives. The rampart cuttings remained narrow sections designed to establish the basic sequence, the entrance was a focal point of interest, and the stripping of the interior to assess the 'town plan', the objective in which Wheeler had been frustrated by the depth of stratigraphy at Maiden Castle, was achievable by mechanically stripping the shallow topsoil over chalk (Cunliffe 1983: 29). Conceptually, the hillfort excavation looked back to Wheeler; only in tackling the hillfort in its landscape context was the project achieving the vision that Hawkes had imagined for Quarley Hill in the 1930s (Figure 2.3). Interestingly, the chronological sequence was based essentially upon *ceramic styles*, rather than upon absolute dates, which would have been dependent upon too many crucial contexts containing suitable material for sampling. Pottery is ubiquitous in the southern English Iron Age, so if it can be ordered into sequence, it has almost universal applicability. The sequence of styles and style zones was essentially based upon the excavator's doctoral research of the early 1960s, which

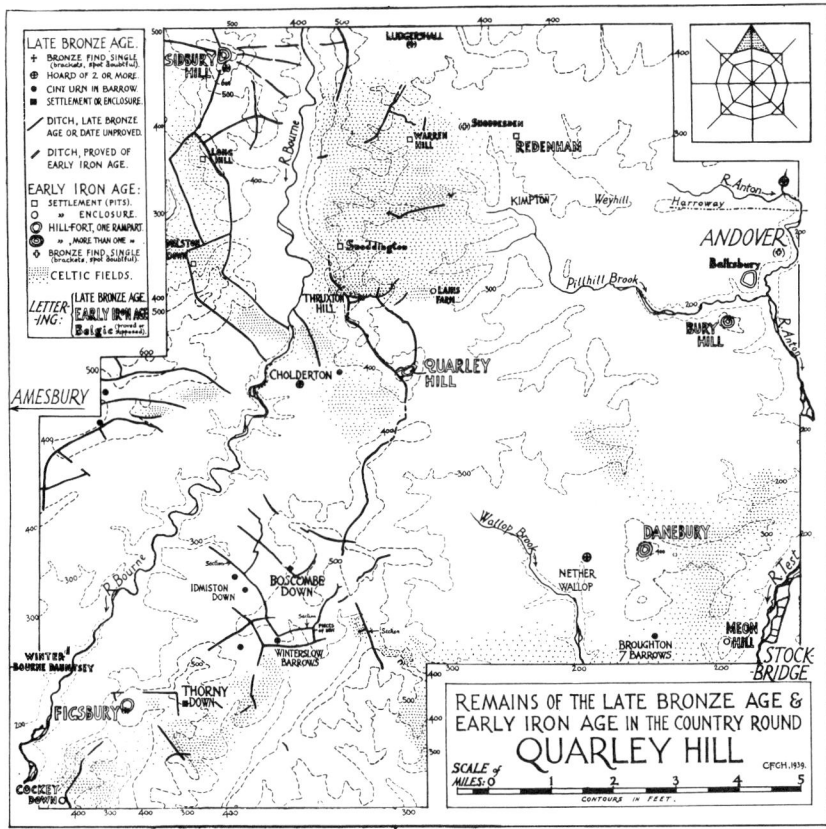

Figure 2.3. Quarley Hill, Hampshire: Hawkes' map of the later prehistoric landscape. Reproduced from *Proceedings of the Hampshire Field Club and Archaeological Society*, Vol. XIV, pt. 2, 1940, Figure 1, by kind permission of the Society.

inevitably required revision over the ensuing thirty years. Problems of residuality were also highlighted in the course of re-evaluation.

HILLFORT RESEARCH SINCE DANEBURY

By the late 1980s a much more fundamental shift was taking place in the interpretation of hillforts. The new orthodoxy represented a reaction to the Danebury model, which saw the hillfort essentially as a central place within the landscape controlled by an elite dominating a hierarchical society. In fact, Collis (1981) had already challenged the idea that hillforts were controlled by aristocratic rulers of a stratified society, and that they had a centralized role in regional administration, and in particular in the redistribution of resources. To these two targets was added a third: the belief that hillforts served any defensive or military role, or that conflict was endemic in Iron Age society (Bowden and McOmish 1987, 1989). These views were vigorously ventilated in the controversial but short-lived *Scottish Archaeological Review*, which devoted several issues in the 1980s to the insular Iron Age. The 'different' Iron Age (Hill and Cumberpatch 1995; Hill 1995b) that has found widespread favour in the past fifteen years is one in which southern Britain especially was regarded as populated by egalitarian farming communities living a much more pacified life than was envisaged by the older conventional image of warlike 'Celtic' society. Indeed, the traditional notion of a 'Celtic' Iron Age was itself subject to deconstruction on the basis that no classical source ever referred to Britain as being inhabited by Celts, and that any correlation between speakers of what subsequently became known as Celtic languages and the archaeological cultures of Hallstatt and La Tène, though long assumed, was totally unproven (James 1999; Collis 2003; for an alternative view see Harding and Gillies 2005; Karl 2008). 'Ritual' explanations were favoured over the simplistically practical, so that orientation of roundhouse doorways towards the east or south-east was not to take advantage of morning sunlight and to avoid facing the prevailing wind, but in response to Iron Age cosmological beliefs. Equally, material found in pits that was formerly assumed to be rubbish and farmyard sweepings were now to be regarded as 'structured deposits' with ritual or symbolic overtones (Hill 1995a). As for the stratified Iron Age societies that seemed to be implicit in Roman accounts of contemporary Iron Age communities, these were now seen, together with coinage inscribed with the names of tribal dynasts and wealthy burials in the south-east of England, as an innovation of the late pre-Roman Iron Age rather than a long-standing tradition. These reflections of the Marxist paradigm have, of course, wider implications for Iron Age studies than for hillforts alone, but if true would be fundamental in the context of hillforts' functions.

The conclusion of the Danebury excavation also marked the end of an era in fieldwork. Though the project had been prompted by the need for a management programme for the site, it had essentially been conducted as a research excavation. By the end of the 1980s, most archaeological fieldwork in Britain was dictated either by commercial development or by considerations of site management and public presentation. There was also an increasing consensus that non-intrusive methods of investigation were preferable to excavation, resulting in major survey programmes like the Wessex Hillforts Project, carried out by the Centre for Archaeology of English Heritage (Payne *et al.* 2006). Limited excavation was undertaken on a selective basis, as at Uffington Castle and neighbouring sites through the 1990s by the Hillforts of the Ridgeway Project, based in Oxford (Miles *et al.* 2003; Lock *et al.* 2005). Where excavation was permitted, as at Maiden Castle, it tended to be focused on clarification of previous investigation, clearing or extending trenches where the site's integrity had already been compromised. More recently, the Cheshire Habitats and Hillforts project has adopted a similar strategy in re-investigating earlier excavations at Helsby and Eddisbury. The ascendancy of developer-funded field archaeology induced a widening gulf between professional and amateur fieldworkers, and the budgetary demands of the prevailing regime made it increasingly difficult to sustain research excavations that were not funded through government agencies. In consequence, even long-term projects like Crickley Hill were brought to a premature conclusion by the mid-1990s.

Ironically, at the very moment when hillfort studies in Britain had reached a watershed, the challenge was taken up in Ireland with the launch of a major new initiative in 1991 by the Discovery Programme, set up by the Taoiseach, Charles Haughey, under the chairmanship of George Eogan, himself the director of the long-term excavations at Knowth in the Boyne Valley that exceeded the scale and vision even of Danebury. Key among the sites selected for investigation were the Western Stone Forts, notably the spectacular cliff-edge fort at Dun Aengus on the Aran Islands, where no serious investigation had taken place since its restoration by the Board of Works in 1886–8. A second regional focus was north Munster, where the massive stone fort at Mooghaun was selected for excavation (Grogan 1995, 1996, 2005a, 2005b). Finally, the programme could hardly fail to investigate Tara, sponsoring renewed investigation of Ó Ríordáin's sections of the Ráith na Ríg to complement the planned publication of his excavations of the 1950s at the Mound of the Hostages and the Rath of the Synods (Grogan 2008).

In the north, meanwhile, progress had been made on the publication of Waterman's important excavations at Navan Fort, Armagh, which had taken place between 1961 and 1971, but progress on which had stalled with his premature death in 1979 (Waterman and Lynn 1997). Continuing excavations at Navan have since revealed an even greater complexity of internal structures, whilst sampling excavation and survey at nearby Haughey's Fort has indicated that the importance of the complex is probably much greater than the sum of its individual parts. The concept of a secular and ritual landscape involving several related *foci* may prove to be one of the more enduring contributions to hillfort archaeology in Britain and beyond.

PUBLICATION

For Sir Mortimer Wheeler, excavation without prompt publication was tantamount to destruction. This laudable sentiment, however, was not nearly so easily achieved in the days when there was no automatic provision for a post-excavation budget, and specialist reports, for example, could only be accomplished as individuals and resources became available to undertake the work. A further issue was how much of the evidence from excavation needed to be included in the published report, and how much could be safely relegated to the archive for anyone determined to evaluate it for themselves? Most postgraduate researchers engaged in a field-based topic will have encountered published reports that fail to answer issues of retrospective concern, and will equally have discovered that extracting satisfactory answers from the archive can be no less frustrating.

The Maiden Castle report exemplified the problems of publication of an excavation on this scale, and whether it was logistically possible to include even all the basic data that would be necessary for the reader to make an independent evaluation of the evidence without recourse to the archive. A major limitation of the report is that finds were not attributed to explicit stratigraphic context, being instead assigned to relative positions in an interpretative sequence such as 'a late A level'. Any possibility of reinterpretation based upon associations and stratigraphic relationships is therefore denied, which seems extraordinary from the foremost twentieth-century exponent of stratigraphic excavation. Other limitations perhaps should be attributed to the circumstances in which the report was written. 'The wreckage of the present has in these days been more instant to my mind than the wreckage of the past,' wrote Wheeler (1943: xvii) in his artillery battery, 'and *inter arma* I have no heart for studentship.'

The problem of necessary selectivity is endemic to large excavations yielding immense quantities of material, as the Danebury reports demonstrate. Even assuming access to microfiche readers (and disc records are now of course more accessible), there is a limit to how much information can be presented. Essentially, though the recording and storage of the finds was by stratigraphic context, the presentation of the pottery is by fabric and form in an interpretative sequence of nine ceramic phases, which forms the fundamental framework for dating. This certainly could not be challenged on the basis of the published account, which raises doubts as to whether the report therefore satisfies Mercer's (2002: 359–60) criteria for a 'print-published report'. Nevertheless, the Danebury volumes are presented in a clear and logical sequence of basic data, specialist reports and evaluation and synthesis that makes the selected material accessible and comprehensible.

The report on the later prehistoric enclosure and occupation of Cadbury Castle (Barrett *et al.* 2000), by contrast, was presented in an innovative and rather idiosyncratic format that purported to promote understanding over simple description. Accurate and clear description in archaeology should not be denigrated, however, since without it interpretation is liable to be based on insecure foundations. This is not simply passing the buck by hoping that some truth will fortuitously present itself from the process of observation and description; still less is it an argument for not having a cogent research strategy, and presenting the results of excavation in the context of that strategy. That modern perceptions and perspectives will differ radically from those of Iron Age communities is one of the inevitable frustrations of archaeological interpretation. Much as we might wish for insights into the mindset of prehistoric communities, however, it is hard to fathom how excavated data can provide us with such information, other than by extending the limits of inference into the realm of creative fiction:

> The tension between individual experience and a community identity was resolved because the practices of an individual's life appeared to subsume within it some portion of the larger body of communal values. These larger values outlived the life of the individual and expressed the ideological coherence of the group; they were one way in which individuals might recognize a resonance between their own lives and the timeless order governing the world. It was these values which gave life its fullest meaning. (Barrett *et al.* 2000: 321)

If this paragraph means anything at all, it could be applicable in any society at any time, and whilst such experiences and values will undoubtedly have had an impact on the archaeological record, attributing outcome to cause archaeologically can only ever be speculative. Because a question is incapable of being answered definitively from archaeological evidence, of course, does not mean that it is not worth asking, but at least we should acknowledge when we are at or beyond the limits of archaeological inference. The current fashion for asserting what prehistoric communities believed has more to do with fairground clairvoyance than with serious scholarship.

A major problem posed by research excavations in the past was lack of funding for post-excavation processing of results leading to publication. From the late 1970s a massive increase in the number of rescue excavations undertaken by commercial units also led to a backlog in publication which has taken some years to redress. Still, there are important excavations, in which substantial public funds were invested, both for the fieldwork itself and for post-excavation work, which remain unpublished after more than thirty years. Part of the problem is that too many senior academic archaeologists seem to be systemically incapable of meeting publication deadlines, a problem that universities through staff appraisal schemes and professional associations through codes of practice seem impotent to address. Even book reviews, including those that appear online to avoid the delay of an annual journal, commonly take two years or more to appear.

With excavations now yielding ever-increasing quantities of data, not just structural and artefactual but palaeo-environmental, as a result of ever more sophisticated sampling and analytical techniques, the question again arises: what form should archaeological publication take? Not only can conventional publication no longer cope with the volume of data, but with the development of digital technology, a whole new suite of options has become available for storing and disseminating data in a way that makes it more accessible than conventional methods. A serious consequence of the prevailing environment of developer-funded archaeology, however, has been the growth of 'grey' literature, reporting of excavation results to clients and sponsoring agencies without full and prompt publication through conventional archaeological channels that are accessible to all. North of the Border, *Discovery and Excavation in Scotland*, published by the Council for Scottish Archaeology, at least provides summary information, but elsewhere one is reminded of Wheeler's dictum, by which he assuredly meant publication in the sense of making results of fieldwork accessible without restriction.

THE FUTURE OF HILLFORT STUDIES

The Danebury excavation with the Danebury Environs Programme remains a landmark in twentieth-century field archaeology; its planning, execution, and reporting representing the highest standards of the time. The Environs Programme of the early 1990s, sponsored by English Heritage, nevertheless reflects the direction in which field archaeology has been taken in recent years. Its second and third proclaimed objectives, namely to promote knowledge of the Iron Age landscape and how it had been affected by subsequent land use, are still mainstream concerns of archaeology as an academic discipline. The primary objective, however, was directed at archaeological site-management and the recreational potential of key sites (Cunliffe 2000: 13–14). Assuming this was not simply a formula for circumventing the current antipathy to any excavation that is not prompted by commercial development, then it represents a substantial swing from simple acceptance that public funding requires public accountability to the public interest setting the agenda.

With archaeology increasingly regarded, and indeed funded, not as an academic discipline but as 'community archaeology' we must be reconciled to the fact that advances in knowledge will be the incidental by-product of site management in the public interest. Equally, in the field of developer-funded archaeology, new discoveries will result not from a planned research strategy but as the arbitrary consequence of commercial or public development. What began as 'Rescue archaeology', the emergency response to the threat of site destruction, has become the normal *modus operandi* of 'professional' archaeology, in which meeting commercial schedules is the priority. The mechanical digger, once the very symbol of destruction on the *Rescue* poster of the 1970s, and an instrument of last resort in the face of impending destruction, has become the instrument of first resort for television archaeology and 'developer-led' archaeology (a term so much more revealing than 'rescue' or 'salvage').

Despite their size, even hillforts are not immune to the threat of destruction. A series of sites in Scotland, not excluding Traprain Law, has been damaged or obliterated by quarrying. Now that threat has extended to one of the largest hillforts in Britain, at Ham Hill in Somerset. But in general hillforts are recognized publicly as local landmarks, and as such are more likely to feature in community archaeology projects. Research excavation of the older conventional kind is now effectively a thing of the past. In the prevailing climate of league tables for 'international' research, universities are more likely to promote spurious field survey in Timbuktu than a programme of fieldwork in Britain. 'Amateur' archaeological societies that were pioneers of hillfort research between the Wars, like the Hampshire Field Club and the Surrey and Sussex Archaeological Societies, or, further north, the Newcastle Antiquaries and the Cumberland and Westmorland Society, are unlikely to be in a position to invest the necessary funding that even a modest research excavation would require, even if permission could be obtained for what would probably be regarded as unwarranted intrusive investigation. In the brave new world of field archaeology, it seems that it is not *Time Team* that is out of step but conventional research excavation and indeed archaeology as an academic discipline, even though television archaeology of that kind will probably one day be regarded as laughably reprehensible, in the same league as nineteenth-century barrow-digging. Furthermore, when Government ministers, knowing no better, commend metal-detecting as legitimate archaeology and are allowed to do so virtually unchallenged by the very scholars who should be upholding the highest and most rigorous academic research standards, *et tu Brute* seems to be the only appropriate comment.

So what is the future of archaeology as a discipline? Has it developed a more rigorous methodology founded on a clearer theoretical framework, or is it suffering from the universal disease of 'dumbing down'? The 'empathy' approach seemingly permits special insights without the demands of traditional scholarship, as illustrated in a recent study of Maiden Castle and Wessex hillforts:

> The hill that rises from the chalk plain was not a neutral place. As people moved across the landscape, feeling stones push through the leather of their shoes or soles of their feet, waiting for cattle to finish grazing, or watching clouds bring rain from across the Channel, they would build up complex understandings of place.   (Toase 2008: 28)

In its naïve form, Neo-Romanticism may be harmless enough in popular publications, but systematically exceeding the limits of reasoned archaeological inference could undermine the academic credibility of archaeology as a discipline among peers for a generation or more. We must ask what physicists or medical specialists, let alone philosophers and historians, would make of a recent explanation of the role of hillforts:

> Through communal building and repairing, including ritual actions and deposits, threats to sociality and conviviality are mediated at the boundaries and actions that take place within the enclosure are protected and purified. Hillforts become a defence against cosmological threats and thus metaphors for social cohesion, where bad emotions are transformed to the good life and emotional stability.
>
> (Lock 2011: 359)

It is hard to credit that, in just half a century, the language and interpretation of archaeology could be so transformed that it would have become incomprehensible to Wheeler or Kenyon.

3

Anatomy of Hillfort Enclosure

The most conspicuous element of a hillfort is generally its perimeter works, whether rubble wall or degraded bank and ditch. Their excavation in cross-section is a means of disclosing the structural sequence, which need not correspond to the occupational sequence of the site. The next most notable feature of the enclosure is its entrance, marked by a gap or inturn in the wall or bank, and a natural causeway across the ditch.

Many hillforts are the product of a complex structural sequence, reflecting successive periods of occupation and building activity. Their perimeter works may range from relatively simple palisaded enclosures to more elaborate double or multiple earthworks that may occupy as great an area as that enclosed. Though a succession of occupational phases may result in progressive enhancement of the enclosing earthworks in both scale and complexity, it would be facile to assume a progression through time from the simplest form of construction to the most elaborate. There is no *a priori* reason why any given configuration, univallate rampart, bivallate, or multivallate, or method of construction, palisade, wall rampart, dump rampart, could not have been chosen at any given stage of a site's use.

Though there are instances where a palisaded enclosure has been superseded by a timber-framed box rampart fronted by a ditch and subsequently by a dump rampart created by enlarging and deepening the ditch, in principle there is no reason why simple dump or *glacis* ramparts should not have been as early as or earlier than more elaborately constructed timber-framed ramparts, being less demanding of resources and requiring no greater manpower or effort to build. In practice, however, it would be difficult to replace a dump rampart, or a timber-framed rampart that had fallen into disrepair, with a timber-framed structure without labour-intensive clearance, because of the problems presented by the horizontal ties. This doubtless accounts for the apparent absence of horizontals from rampart B at Cadbury Castle (Alcock 1972), as a result of which the structure was fatally weakened. The only practical option would be to clear out and enlarge the ditch to create a heightened dump over the debris of the earlier wall.

Hillfort excavation has invariably given priority to examination of the structure of the ramparts rather than to the ditch, which has generally been seen as little more than a quarry for the rubble core or stone facing of the bank. This assumption can certainly be challenged; where the ditch has been excavated by more than a narrow section, it has sometimes yielded finds that may be regarded as structured rather than casual.

PALISADED OR STOCKADED ENCLOSURES

Palisaded enclosures are not a chronologically or culturally diagnostic form of settlement, though they are common in the earlier first millennium BC, especially in northern England and the Scottish Borders. An exception to this generalization is the Anglian-period polygonal palisade at Doon Hill, East Lothian (Hope-Taylor 1980; Reynolds 1980) and related types of enclosure, which do not strictly fall within the compass of the present study. In recent years the restricted distribution of palisaded enclosures in the Scottish Borders (Ritchie 1970), in part conditioned by the circumstances of upland survival (RCAHMS 1997: 121), has been supplemented significantly by air-photographic survey (e.g. RCAHMS 1994: 50). In some instances, residual upcast may form a very slight bank on the lip of the trench, and in the case of double palisades this can create a low bank between the two palisade trenches (Piggott 1949). Feachem's excavation at Harehope, Peeblesshire (Feachem 1960) added a further variant of *embanked palisade* in which the twin palisades are embedded in low banks created by scraping a shallow ditch from the area between.

A timber stockade was a resource-intensive form of enclosure. At Staple Howe, Yorkshire (Brewster 1963), an enclosure containing just three or four houses had a perimeter in the order of 172 metres in length. On the basis of the excavator's estimate of posts with a girth of 30 cms (1 foot), the continuous stockade would have required no less than 573 such posts, not including possible bracing posts, each requiring a mature tree. If the timbers were half that diameter, the total would have exceeded a thousand trees, indicating the scale of managed resource that a relatively modest enclosure might demand. The size of enclosure, therefore, must have mattered. Resource consumption on this scale cannot have been incurred arbitrarily, and the enclosed space must have been required by need or accepted on the basis of status. Scarcity of resource would probably have encouraged frugal management. Fence posts rot and snap at the interface between soil and air, but otherwise are reusable, though shorter, a consideration which could have important implications for the use of radiocarbon dating. Double palisades like those employed at West Brandon, Co. Durham (Jobey 1962), High Knowes,

Alnham, Northumberland (Jobey and Tait 1966), or Gibbs Hill, Dumfriesshire, would have been even more demanding of timber, though as protective enclosures they were doubtless more effective against wild predators as well as human intruders. Once an animal had leapt over the outer fence, the confined space within would have inhibited attempts to leap the inner palisade, and it is possible that furze, brambles, or other entwining material may have been stacked into the intervening space to snare any intruder, human or animal. At Hayhope Knowe, Roxburghshire, the excavator detected traces of individual postholes in the palisade trenches, indicating that the upright posts had been between 20–25 cms in diameter and spaced at intervals a little over 30 cms (Piggott 1949: Plates XIII–XV). She calculated that the entire enclosure would have required no less than 1,600 upright posts. Given the size of uprights and their close spacing, it seems unlikely that hurdles could have been integrally woven around the uprights, though panels of hurdling could have been attached to them. From carbon samples, willow and alder appeared to have been the two principal species of building timber, perhaps suggesting two separate components.

Gibbs Hill has no less than six phases of palisaded enclosure (Figure 3.1a; RCAHMS 1997: 122–4). The chronological span of the site has not been established, but palisaded enclosures continued to be occupied in south-western Scotland until the later pre-Roman period, so that longevity of occupation, perhaps intermittent, may well account for the site's structural complexity. The sequence, confirmed by the complex intersection of upcast from the trenches rather than of the trenches themselves, is certainly not one of progressive complexity. The first two and last two phases are single palisades, whilst the third and fourth are double. The largest in area enclosed is the second, which also apparently was enhanced by a length of earthwork on its north-west circuit, the direction of easiest access to the settlement, in contrast to the sequence at Hayhope Knowe, where the earthworks represent a later addition. The lesson is certainly clear, that unilinear progression from simple to complex was not an invariable reality. In the south-eastern Borders the series of palisades, single, double, single and boulder-revetted at Craik Moor, Morebattle, Roxburghshire (Figure 3.1b) almost certainly represents a sequence of timber barriers, culminating in a stone wall that cut off the hilltop spur, presenting a monumental façade, but without an obvious entrance or surviving walls along its flanks.

Mrs Piggott regarded the double palisade as anticipating a timber-framed wall rampart. She recognized that there was no evidence at Hayhope Knowe for an earth and rubble core, but suggested an infilling of heather or brushwood as an alternative. We certainly should not dismiss the possibility that a timber-framed box rampart might have been constructed without an infilled core, though it would have been more vulnerable to firing in the event of

(a)

(b)

Figure 3.1. Palisaded settlements: (a) Gibbs Hill, Dumfriesshire, (b) Craik Moor, Morebattle, Roxburghshire. Air photographs by D. W. Harding.

hostile activity than a solid-cored rampart. This interpretation was certainly considered by Halliday and others for the twin palisaded phases at Gibbs Hill and elsewhere (RCAHMS 1997: 126–9). In upland environments, shallow soils and intractable brash may preclude the ready construction of a ditch from which the core material was normally derived, and scraping scree from a wider area may have been an unduly labour-intensive activity. Elsewhere, a good candidate for such a timber-framed rampart would be the early phase at Ffridd Faldwyn (O'Neil 1942: period II), where the posts of the so-called 'double palisade' were more widely spaced and matched in front and rear alignments than might be expected of simple palisading. Avery (1993 Vol. II: 157) rightly accepted the evidence that these posts cannot have supported a solid-core wall, so that a hollow timber-framed rampart seems a viable alternative. Likewise, the twin post-rows 1107 and 1108 of the Late Bronze Age enclosure at Taplow Court, Buckinghamshire (Allen *et al.* 2009: 35–41, 193), which the excavators acknowledged could have been two successive palisades, they preferred to believe supported a hollow timber-framed wall with walkway above.

In southern Britain, palisaded enclosures not infrequently preceded the construction of more substantial earthworks, though it is not always clear from older excavations like Hembury, Devon (Liddell 1930, 1931, 1932, 1935; Todd 1984a), whether the palisade trench supported a free-standing timber stockade or whether it constituted the front face of the earthen rampart. At Bindon Hill, Dorset (Wheeler 1953), the 'palisade trench' most probably supported a free-standing stockade, but an inner alignment of posts, just behind the 'marking out bank', was probably correctly interpreted as the front face of the earthen rampart. At Hollingbury, Sussex (Curwen 1932) and at Blewburton Hill, Oxfordshire (Collins 1947, 1953; Collins and Collins 1959; Harding 1976b), the palisaded enclosure was certainly earlier than the hillfort, occupying a smaller area than its successor. At Moel y Gaer, Rhosesmor, Clwyd (Guilbert 1975a), two lines of palisade were located outside the main rampart and ditch of the hillfort. One was an embanked palisade with postholes set at 0.5–1.0 m intervals, the second comprised a continuous palisade trench with uprights around 1.20 m apart, so that both could have supported woven hurdling. The latter was demonstrably earlier than the former, and the implication is that one or both may have represented pre-hillfort phases of enclosure. Whilst it may be true that 'large palisaded enclosures can therefore be seen generally to precede hillforts' (Cunliffe 2005: 349), there are inevitably examples that prove the exception. One of these is Dinorben, Clwyd (Guilbert 1979a, 1980), where at least one of the five lengths of palisade trench (trench d) cut through an earlier ditch feature (ditch 1).

RAMPARTS

Timber-framed and timber-faced wall-ramparts

Wall ramparts may use virtually any combination of timber, stone, or turf to revet the front and rear faces of the wall, or to stabilize the core material internally. Essentially the objective is to increase the height-to-width ratio of the wall and thereby to present a steeper, taller, and more impressive obstacle than would be provided by piling earth or rubble at its natural angle of rest. Whether the rampart provided a fighting platform for defence, or simply a vantage point from which the approaches to the enclosure could be observed, its summit presumably had a walkway with breastwork along the parapet, from which guards would have had a considerable height advantage in spotting and repelling any assault. That height advantage may be increased by tactical use of contours, and of course by the construction in front of the rampart of a ditch, the material from which also provided a solid core for the rampart. The ditch was logically outside the rampart, in order to present the maximum salient to a potential intruder. Earthworks in which the ditch was on the inside, like henge monuments of the late Neolithic or the Irish 'royal sites' of later prehistory, were presumably not designed with defence primarily in mind, though additional 'quarry ditches', often intermittently aligned along the inside of the bank, are known on a number of sites, like Hod Hill in Dorset.

    The principal limitation of the wall-rampart was that the weight of the wall-core inevitably put pressure upon the retaining revetments front and back, and their eventual collapse must have been very difficult to repair without effectively deconstructing and rebuilding the rampart. To limit this risk, the structure was strengthened by having horizontal bracing between front and rear revetments, and in some variants, longitudinal bracing or internal compartmentalization in order to reduce stress on the vertical faces. Collapse of the front face would evidently be accelerated if it was undermined by erosion of the inner lip of the ditch, and accordingly the rampart was generally set back from the ditch edge, to leave a *berm* between ditch and wall, even though this might afford an intruder a foothold once the ditch had been crossed. In some instances the berm seems to have been unnecessarily broad for this purpose, up to 4 metres or more as at Grimthorpe, Yorkshire (Stead 1968), so that we may wonder whether it also served some additional purpose, external to the rampart but within the enclosure ditch. A second disadvantage of wall-ramparts with timber facing may have been their vulnerability to firing, though in practice in the British climate this must have been difficult to achieve, especially under defensive fire. In Gaul, wall-ramparts proved to be vulnerable to Roman assault towers, which, once the ditch had been bridged, could be rolled against the ramparts to engage defenders on an equal footing.

It is possible that turf cladding could have been stacked against the vertical face to buttress against collapse and to inhibit firing, which might account for the extra width of the berm in front of the revetment. At the back of the rampart, some means of access by the defending force would have been essential, if not by ladder or timber steps then by grading the tail of the rampart into a ramp or series of terraces. In these circumstances, the vertical revetments would have been effectively internal reinforcement. All of these factors, of course, assume greater significance if defence was a major element in rampart design. If conspicuous display was a key consideration, then practical considerations may have been subordinated to more impressive architectural effect.

There are so many variations in rampart design that virtually every site could be designated a distinctive type. Among those in which timber is the predominant material for creating the framework and revetment, Avery (1993) distinguished between timber-framed and timber-walled ramparts, the former having quite widely spaced uprights, generally paired front and back, with the implication that they were tied by transverse timbers through the core of the rampart to create a rigid framework. The latter had more closely spaced and often more substantial timbers in the front face forming the main retaining wall. In some instances, the rear revetment timbers were less firmly bedded into subsoil or bedrock, since the horizontal ties were held effectively by the body of the rampart, and in others they appear to have been dispensed with altogether, so that the rampart was effectively a timber-faced dump. Even where the framework was based on more widely spaced uprights, we must presume that additional planks or half-split timbers were laid between the uprights along the face to prevent spillage and erosion of the rampart core.

Classic examples of the timber-framed variant include Hollingbury, Sussex (Curwen 1932) and Grimthorpe, though both these examples were narrower than many, with an average transverse width from front to rear revetment of around two metres. In the same league was the period 1 rampart at Uffington (Miles *et al.* 2003), though the dump backing in this case must have been as wide again. Almost as narrow was the earliest rampart at Danebury (Cunliffe 1984a), though it too apparently had a substantial dump behind it from the outset. Its front row of timbers survived on the very lip of the ditch, which must presumably have been deepened, widened, or eroded to this point subsequent to construction of the timber-framed rampart. Rather wider was the period 1 rampart at Maiden Castle, Dorset (Wheeler 1943: Plate XI), based upon a section through the southern inner portal of the eastern entrance (though see Avery's 1993 comprehensive review of Wheeler's excavation, with previously unpublished material). Here both front and rear revetments appeared to have a markedly backward-sloping profile, and the rear face was evidently concealed in part by an earthen *talus*. A similar sloping *talus* backed the rear face at Blewburton Hill (Harding 1976b).

The Blewburton timber framework, with earth-fast timbers set 4 metres apart, longitudinally and transversely, is exceptional in having its main uprights quite so far apart, though elsewhere similar structures could easily have been missed by rampart cuttings that were simply too narrow to detect the pattern. By contrast, a series of horizontal cavities, which had evidently compacted around the transverse timbers in the wall core, and within which traces of charcoal indicated their former presence (Figure 3.2a), were spaced at much closer intervals. These had not invariably survived, and were easily destroyed in the normal process of stratigraphic excavation. Despite distortion, they suggested that transverse timbers on at least two levels had braced the structure at horizontal and vertical intervals of around half a metre, a density of construction that not only would have been extraordinarily profligate in timber, but which might seem incompatible with uprights at 4 metre intervals. In fact, there *was* archaeological evidence for intermediate uprights, though not apparently earth-fast, between the front and rear revetments in cutting 2 (north). At the inner end of the stain of a transverse horizontal, a vertical post had been encased in chalk, revealing its squared cross-section

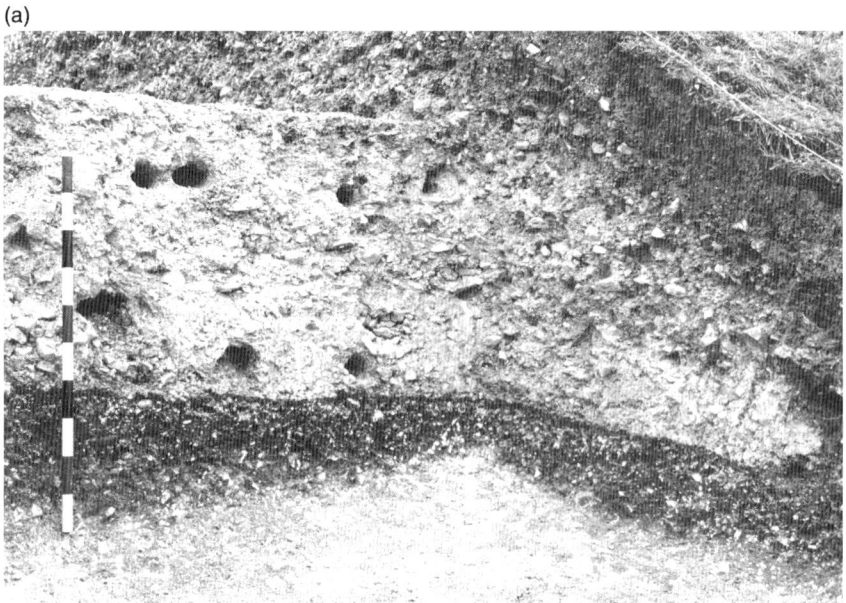

Figure 3.2. Blewburton Hill, Oxfordshire (Berkshire), timber-framed rampart: (a) cavities of horizontal timbers in rampart face, (b) (opposite) timber stains of horizontals and vertical posthole cavity from above. Photographs by A. D. Phillips and D. W. Harding; (a) reproduced by permission of Oxford University Press.

as measuring 18 by 14 cms (Figure 3.2b). There may have been other major uprights bracing horizontals both longitudinally and transversely, though no evidence in the form of post-holes penetrating bedrock was found, so that they would have been difficult to detect once the core of the chalk rampart had compressed the cavities left after their decay. In this same cutting there was also evidence for horizontals of slighter scantling, closely set, not unlike brushwood filling noted elsewhere. Having earth-fast posts at limited intervals would hardly reduce the structure's stability, and might perhaps indicate assembly of the timber framework in prefabricated sections; the structure may thus have been more complex that the earth-fast excavate plan indicated (Figure 3.3A).

A similar spacing between the horizontal bracing timbers is suggested by the burnt timbers in the rampart at Leckhampton, Gloucestershire (Champion 1971, 1976), while at the Caburn in Sussex the horizontal tie-holes located by Wilson (1938: 176, Figure 3 and Plate II) were around 75 cm apart. The same order of spacing separated the transverse timbers of the Period 2 rampart at Crickley Hill (Dixon 1976: Figure 4). Two levels of horizontals were traced within the surviving height of the rampart at the Caburn, and likewise at Ranscombe Camp, Sussex (Burstow and Holleyman 1964). Assuming that all these ramparts stood a minimum of 2 or 3 metres high, as is indicated by the size of their accompanying ditches (and hence the volume of infill they would need to accommodate), and assuming that the construction of the rampart was uniform around the circuit, which is rather less certain, the quantities of

(b)

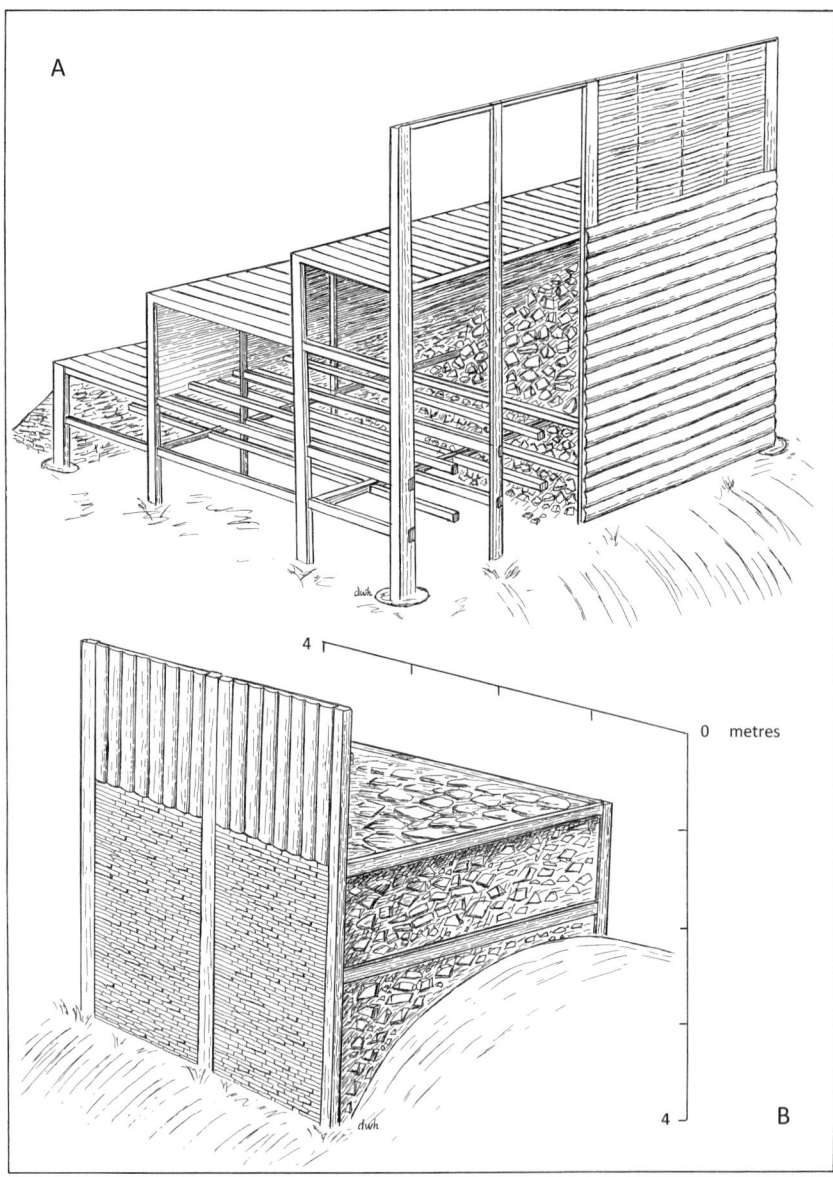

Figure 3.3. Rampart reconstructions: (A) Blewburton Hill, Oxfordshire (Berkshire), timber-framed rampart; cut-away drawing does not reflect sequence of construction, (B) timber and stone faced rampart (*Pfostenschlitzmauer*), wall-face and proportions based on Rampart B, Cutting D, Cadbury Castle, Somerset, where no evidence was recovered for essential horizontal transverse timbers. Drawings by D. W. Harding; (B) adapted from Alcock 1972 and Barrett *et al.* 2000.

timber required would have been prodigious. Even with woodland management, the likelihood of serious resource depletion could well account for the fact that so many hillforts were refurbished with dump ramparts.

Brushwood appears to be a component of several hillfort ramparts. Irregular branches characterized the inner bank at Rainsborough (Avery *et al.* 1967: Plate XVIIIA, cutting A), and 'bundles or spreads of brushwood or timbers of very small scantling' were found in the lower levels of the Period 2 rampart at Crickley Hill (Dixon 1994: 181). Apart from disposing of offcuts from the preparation of timber on site, the purpose of incorporating brushwood, which might have invited subsequent settlement and distortion of the wall core, remains unclear. One reason might have been to facilitate drainage, since a sodden earthen or rubble core would have imposed a far greater weight on the revetments than a dry one; settlement by comparison may have posed a lesser threat to the integrity of the wall.

The timber-faced dump wall variant is best illustrated by Poundbury, Dorset (Richardson 1940), where the postholes of the front revetment were spaced at around 0.75m intervals, behind which the successive layers of rampart 1 had been tipped at a natural angle of slope. Another probable example is Hod Hill (Richmond 1968), where the postholes interpreted by the excavator as the rear alignment of a box framework, as Avery (1993) recognized, were more probably the front revetment of a secondary rampart bedded in the tail of the earlier earthwork. A timber-faced dump was also adopted for the second phase of rampart at Moel y Gaer, and for the third phase at Wandlebury, Cambridgeshire (Hartley 1957), reinforcing the impression that dump ramparts were a later development generally.

Stone-faced timber-framed ramparts

There are several variants of stone-faced rampart that nevertheless incorporate a timber framework within the core of the rampart for the purpose of stabilizing the wall-core. Without some such device, external revetments, even in stone and even if battered at an angle of 20–30 degrees, would still be vulnerable. In some cases internal reinforcement was achieved by creating subdivisions in stone. In northern Britain many stone-faced wall ramparts must have had an internal timber framework, though excavation in the past has not always detected its fugitive traces unless the rampart had been subject to firing. Integrating the two components nevertheless must have required some technical skill on the part of the builders, and perhaps was not always successfully achieved. One method was to alternate vertical timbers in the wall-face with horizontal stone coursing, as at Maiden Castle or in rampart B at Cadbury Castle (Barrett *et al.* 2000), the continental counterpart of which is the *Pfostenschlitzmauer* type of wall rampart (Figure 3.3B). Vertical timbers in front and rear faces must have been jointed to transverse timbers, as in their all-timber counterparts, to form a rigid framework, though no horizontals were actually traced at Cadbury. The stone facing would thus be used simply to infill the spaces between verticals in lieu of planks or split timbers, perhaps offset to form an inward batter or with courses canted inward in the manner of broch construction. In the case of Cadbury, the small lias slabs, imported specially to the site, were plainly more for display than for effective retention of the wall core (Alcock 1972: 130). An alternative style of wall construction omitted the vertical timbers, having instead a series of square holes in the wall facing, as in the period 2 rampart at Crickley Hill, into which the transverse timbers were bedded. It seems unlikely that the transverse timbers were bonded into the stonework, since this would have required something like a fantail joint in the beam-holes for which there is no evidence. Front and rear walls would still have afforded support and separation for an internal timber framework if both transverse and longitudinal timbers were used, as in the classic *murus Gallicus* format. In a third variant there is no external evidence that the timbers were bonded into the front and rear walls, simply resting on their irregular inner stonework, as appears to have been the case at Leckhampton (Champion 1976). The same may have been true of the inner rampart at Maiden Castle, Bickerton, Cheshire (Varley 1935, 1936), though the schematic nature of the published sections makes assessment uncertain. In some cases the horizontals may have been supported on lines of stones, but for the most part, the timber lacing was apparently introduced level by level as the rubble core was raised. Whichever method was used, structural rigidity depended essentially on the core framework rather than on the revetment walls, which may have been little more than an ornamental façade.

Stone facing of wall ramparts, not surprisingly, is uncommon in the chalklands of Wessex and Sussex, and the limestone of the facing walls of the Period 2 ramparts and twin carriageways at the eastern entrance at Maiden Castle was probably imported from a source a few miles towards the coast, where Chalbury Camp (Whitley 1943), which used a similar style of stone revetment, is located on oolitic limestone. The use of stonework for architectural effect is clearly visible in rampart A at Moel y Gaer (Guilbert 1975a), where the 'pillars' of horizontal coursing between the front upright timbers are often based on an edge-set slab. This is a combination that characterizes some later Iron Age buildings in Atlantic Scotland, and is only feasible when used as a facing against a rubble backing. It has no obvious merit in preference to drystone coursing *simpliciter* and we may infer that display of technical skill was not an insignificant consideration in hillfort construction. Essentially this is still a timber-framed rampart, the core of which is retained by parallel lines of posts set around 5.75 metres apart. The front row of posts was much more substantial than those of the inner row, being on average 30 cms across and set in holes up to 70 cms deep, compared to an average depth of just 25 cms in the rear alignment. With the rampart sited on a slope, the front revetment clearly was expected to bear the main weight of the core. The tail of the rampart sloped downwards to a height of no more than 50 cms at its rear face, presumably for ease of access to the parapet. Some 3 metres inside the front revetment was a further intermittent alignment of widely spaced postholes, which the excavator suggested may have been surviving evidence of a more frequently spaced series of posts without rock-cut foundations, as proposed above for Blewburton Hill. There was some evidence at Moel y Gaer low in the rampart core for transverse horizontals tying front and rear revetments, although because of the intermittent space of the surviving uprights of the intermediate row, some of these would have had no apparent internal support. In view of the fugitive nature of the upright posts, longitudinal horizontals bracing the whole into a rigid framework could equally have failed to survive. Within the core of the rampart the excavator detected distinct breaks in tip-lines between 1.3 and 2.0 metres apart, perhaps indicating cellular divisions separated by wicker hurdles. This technique of construction, generally more evident in stone-filled ramparts, was presumably a deliberate device for reducing the effects of slippage.

Perhaps the best-documented example of a stone-faced rampart with horizontal beam holes rather than vertical timbers is the period 2 rampart at Crickley Hill, which also provides an unprecedented insight into the construction sequence (Dixon 1976, 1994: 177–81). Once again the central framework of the rampart was based on two parallel rows of posts around 2.5 metres apart, of which the individual posts were between 25–35 cms in diameter and set about the same depth into bedrock. Where the front revetment wall survived to a height of 1.8 metres, socket holes were visible for three tiers of horizontal lacing. A number of these timbers survived as charcoal traces as a result of later burning of the rampart, sufficient to indicate that they had extended through the core from front to back. From slight traces within the core material, the excavator speculated that there may have been longitudinal timbers linking the uprights of the framework on which these intermediate transverse timbers could have rested.

In the front revetment of the rampart, which had been built using stone coursing of differential sizes, there was clear evidence of 'gang breaks' in the wall face. Adjacent to the entrance, the rampart had been built in lengths just short of 6 metres up to a height of 40 cms, at which point a level of horizontal timber lacing would have been introduced, the process being repeated at 1.20 metres. At the rear of the rampart the revetment wall was not so well preserved, but it is possible that here the levels of horizontal timbers coincided with insetting of the rampart to facilitate access in tiers to the parapet. This was certainly the case at Rainsborough Camp, Northamptonshire (Avery *et al.* 1967), where three 'steps' around 70 cms high gave access to the wall head from within the hillfort (Figure 3.4). The effect would thus have been similar

Figure 3.4. Rainsborough Camp, Northamptonshire, tiered inner face of main rampart. Photograph by kind permission of Michael Avery.

to the inner terraces of stone-walled forts, of which those of the Aran Islands and south-western Ireland are outstanding examples.

If the period 2 rampart at Crickley Hill had longitudinal as well as transverse timbers in its internal framework, then its front face and core would essentially have complied with the normal criteria of a *murus Gallicus* type of rampart, only the stepped inside revetment differing from the norm. Of similar design was the drystone revetted timber-laced rampart of period 3 at Castle Hill, Almondbury, Yorkshire (Challis and Harding 1975: 116–21, and Figures 60–64). The section drawings of the 1970 rampart cutting, supervised and recorded by Aidan Challis, are the most reliable basis for interpretation available, in preference to the schematic sections published by the excavator (Varley 1976). These show a collapsed wall of shale at the front and slumped walling some 4 metres behind it, between which Challis recorded both transverse and longitudinal timbers, all heavily charred by intense burning that must represent a catastrophic episode similar to the deliberate destruction of the vitrified forts of Scotland. What is not certain at Castle Hill is whether the transverse timbers originally projected into the facing walls, though from the section drawings this certainly seems possible. The slabbed revetment at the base of the sections could indeed have been from an earlier phase, though the combination of slabbed facing with drystone construction, as we have seen from Moel y Gaer, would not be unique.

In Scotland (Cotton 1954), Childe's 'Gallic fort' rampart type, based on Castle Law, Abernethy, Perthshire (Christison and Anderson 1899), but possibly replicated at Castle Law, Forgandenny (Christison 1900), had open sockets in the front face for transverse timbers and longitudinal timbers creating a lattice of timber lacing within the rampart core (Figure 3.5a). As with Crickley Hill, however, associated material evidence points to occupation several centuries earlier than the period of the Gallic War, as Childe recognized, and equally a related type of fortification may have been current on the continent well before Caesar observed it at Avaricum.

For many years, Burghead in Morayshire was regarded as the closest example in Britain to a wall of Iron Age *murus Gallicus* type, based upon reports of nineteenth-century excavations of the promontory fort's ramparts (Cotton 1957). These suggested not only a framework of transverse and longitudinal timbers within the drystone wall faces, but also the use of iron nails to secure the timber lacing. Excavation in the later 1960s (Small 1969) of the surviving western defences of the upper compound at Burghead confirmed the presence of substantial stone-faced walls with internal timber lacing, but yielded radiocarbon dates indicating construction in the fourth to sixth centuries AD. Subsequent excavation at the promontory fort at Green Castle, Portknockie (Ralston 1980; 1987) again demonstrated that the timber-framed rampart, likewise comprising transverse and longitudinal timbers, belonged to the second half of the first millennium AD. Quite clearly, the construction of timber-framed wall ramparts continued, or was revived, in northern Britain, even if it gave way in Wessex to other types of defensive enclosure.

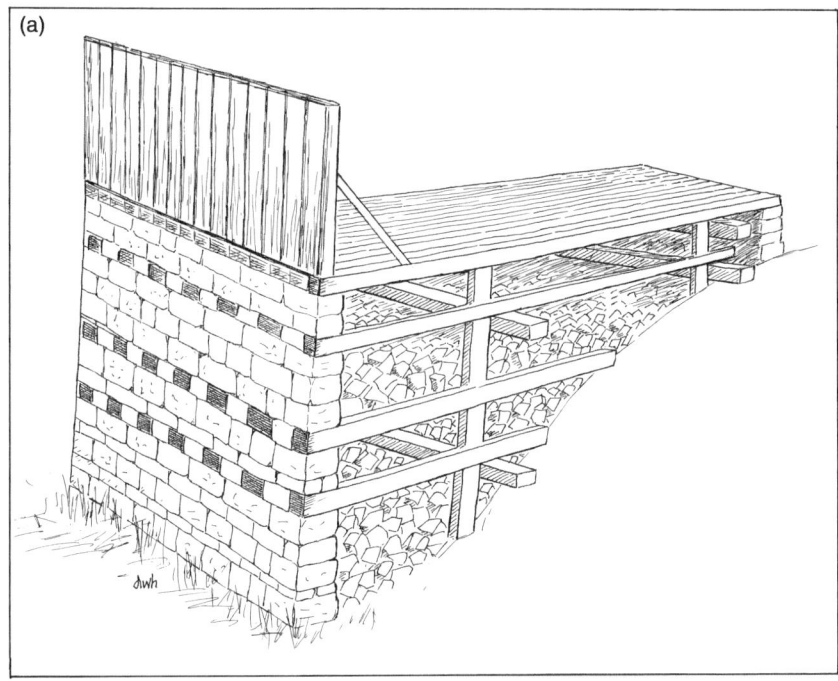

Figure 3.5. Abernethy, Perthshire: (a) reconstruction of rampart, drawing by D. W. Harding; (b) (opposite) wall-face exposed by excavation c.1898 image Crown Copyright Royal Commission on the Ancient and Historical Monuments of Scotland, reproduced under Class License Number C2006000011 with the permission of OPSI and the Queen's Printer for Scotland. We are grateful to the Society of Antiquaries of Scotland for permission to reproduce Plate 1 from Christison and Anderson 1899.

Stone-faced and stone-built walls without timber lacing

As with timber-faced ramparts, the simplest version is one in which the front face, of drystone construction, is revetted into a rubble-dump backing. This is effectively the stone equivalent of the Poundbury type of rampart, of which one of the most impressive examples is the period 2 rampart on Site A at Stanwick (Wheeler 1954), where a front facing of limestone blocks retained a core of boulder clay and rubble without any apparent rear wall. The front wall may have had a more pronounced batter, however (Avery 1993), than the Ministry of Works' reconstruction suggested (Wheeler 1954: Plates XI, XII). The wall-rampart variant is represented at Chalbury Camp, Dorset, where front and rear walls were not regularly coursed, and where the front revetment on site A was founded on large orthostats. There was,

(b)

however, no evidence of timber uprights, nor for horizontal lacing in the core of the rampart, despite a wider than average cutting, so that the rampart represents the basic standard of stone-walled, non-timber laced, rubble construction.

The period 3b rampart at Crickley Hill showed greater complexity. First, its front stone revetment wall was founded in the ditch, which was widened in compensation. The effort involved demonstrates graphically the problems of refurbishing a wall rampart other than by converting it into a simple dump. In a 10 metre-wide cutting south of the entrance this wall survived to a height of more than 3 metres (Plate 2a), revetting a rubble core on the original berm in front of the period 3a wall that represented the initial refurbishing of the older period 2 rampart. The core of the extended rampart was divided internally by transverse walls, creating a series of infilled casemates to strengthen the rampart. The final effect was therefore a two-tiered frontage, with possibly a stepped wall on the rear face.

The division of a stone-filled rampart by means of transverse partitions is well illustrated in the rampart of Britain's highest hillfort, at Ingleborough in the Yorkshire Pennines (King 1987; Bowden et al. 1989). Here the partitions, spaced at a little over 2-metre intervals, comprise sizeable edge-set slabs; the same technique of construction is used to revet the inside face of the wall, whereas the outer wall face is built in coursed gritstone. The dating of the defences at Ingleborough remains uncertain; Roman finds from the stone huts within the interior are not necessarily a reliable guide to the span of interior occupation, still less to the date of the defences. Given its location at over 720m OD (2350ft), King not unreasonably suggested that it may have been built in the late sub-Boreal later Bronze Age–Iron Age transition.

Unless a solid, stone-faced wall had some internal compartmentalization or internal wall faces, it would inevitably be prone to slumping, even if its external face was significantly battered. Secondary re-facing or buttressing may represent an attempt at repair. It is not clear whether the complex cross-sections inferred by the nineteenth-century investigators at Worlebury, Somerset (Dymond 1902), was the product of original design or secondary repair. The tiered effect may well have enabled the builders to attain greater height, which seems from Caesar's brief allusion to the double wall or *murus duplex* of the Aduatuci (*dBG* II, 29), to have been the point of the exercise. Tiered stone walls are found mainly in western Britain, the example from Gurnard's Head, Cornwall (Gordon 1940), having two rear steps of drystone construction, with substantial headers bonded into the rubble core. A good example was excavated by Wainwright (1971) at Tower Point, Pembrokeshire, where unusually the *murus duplex* represents the second phase of construction, being built into the collapse of an earlier stone-faced dump rampart. 'Back-terracing' (Savory 1976) is also a feature of the north Welsh stone forts on Conway Mountain, at Tre'r Ceiri and elsewhere. Brough Law in the Breamish valley of Northumberland is unusual in having double walls only at the front of the rampart (Figure 1.8b), which Jobey (1971) nevertheless believed were integral to the original build rather than the result of secondary buttressing.

A similar technique is implied in the so-called *median wall faces* of forts in Argyll, some of which may result from secondary buttressing. In the only reliably excavated instance, the early historic galleried dun at Kildonan (Fairhurst 1939), secondary activity was demonstrable. At Ranachan Hill in Kintyre (RCAHMS 1971: No. 173) an internal revetment is visible at three points in the innermost wall, two facing inwards and one facing outwards, but in all cases seemingly integral to the original construction. In Atlantic Scotland there is the added complication that, where the wall thickness is sufficient, 'median wall faces' may be the residual surviving traces of intramural cells or galleries rather than of tiered construction.

The most spectacular examples of tiered construction, of course, are the stone forts of the Aran Islands, of which Dun Aengus is the finest

Anatomy of hillfort enclosure 71

(a)

(b)

Figure 3.6. Dun Aengus, Inishmore, Co. Galway: (a) tiered inner rampart, (b) ramparts with *chevaux-de-frise* beyond. Photographs by D. W. Harding.

(Figures 3.6a,b). Once again it is not always clear whether tiered construction was original or the result of secondary buttressing. This problem is compounded at Dun Aengus (Westropp 1910a; Cotter 1993, 1995, 1996) by the comprehensive renovation of the walls by the Board of Works in 1886–8, though records survive from the previous half century, latterly including photographs, indicating the pre-restoration state of the walls. Dun Aengus plainly underwent substantial and repeated alteration, but stone walls of the height of Wall 1, which survives to 4.90m, would surely have required buttressing from the outset, and the presence of tiered walls elsewhere in south-western and northern Ireland suggests that this could have been an integral element of their design. If defence was a primary purpose, then the internal tiers would have given easy access to the parapet. But the stone forts of western Ireland look to have been much more than defensive enclosures, and the tiered effect gives them an inward-looking aspect like a stadium or theatre. An equivalent in timber is the triple-ringed enclosure of the 'rose' phase at Dún Ailinne (Wailes 1976; Johnston and Wailes 2007), which, because of the graded depths of its postholes from innermost to outermost the excavator interpreted as a grandstand or similar place of assembly, an interpretation which would also be consistent with the converging avenue that led to its entrance. The stone forts may be more monumental in construction, but their inward-looking aspect may reflect similar roles.

Dump ramparts

The dump or *glacis* type of rampart differs fundamentally from wall construction in abandoning the principle of presenting a vertical face to an assailant. At the same time, it dispenses with a berm, since the outer face of the rampart and the inner face of the ditch effectively form a single continuous slope. If this seems like an inferior defensive barrier, one has only to attempt to climb the now degraded ramparts of a site like Maiden Castle, Dorset, to appreciate that even these under fire would have presented a formidable obstacle. In the context of the Roman conquest of Gaul, massive dump ramparts were less vulnerable to Roman siege techniques and machinery than were wall ramparts, though it is doubtful whether knowledge of Roman military tactics had any immediate bearing upon the origins of *glacis* fortification.

Cunliffe argued (2005: 355) that the shift to dump construction in the fourth or third century BC in southern Britain was the result of 'basic flaws in design' of wall ramparts; namely the inevitability that timber revetments would rot and that ditch edges would erode, resulting in collapse. Stone faces, as we have seen, might also be prone to collapse. These problems were certainly overcome by dump construction. The disadvantage, however, was that a salient of 30–45 degrees, even of loose rubble, could be climbed with difficulty, and natural erosion and weathering would have necessitated regular cleaning out of the ditch if the rampart's defensive capability was to be maintained. This material may have been used to heighten the main rampart, or it could be more easily thrown forward to create a counterscarp bank. At Danebury, Cunliffe (1984a: 18–19, and Figure 3.4) calculated a minimum of fourteen such episodes of clearance from the tip lines in the counterscarp bank. It is nevertheless hard to regard the dump rampart as a structural improvement on wall-ramparts; its principal advantage was surely speed of construction and economy of resources in not requiring massive quantities of timber.

In major site sequences, like Maiden Castle, Hod Hill, Danebury, Blewburton, and elsewhere, dump ramparts replace wall ramparts, but dump ramparts were not universally later than wall ramparts. At Rams Hill, a dump rampart was apparently the earliest in the defensive sequence (Bradley and Ellison 1975), and likewise a dump rampart was inferred as part of the earthwork defence of the later Bronze Age enclosure at Taplow Court (Allen *et al.* 2009). Nevertheless, there was undoubtedly an increase in the number of dump ramparts in southern Britain in the later pre-Roman Iron Age. Avery (1993) argued that there was a fundamental difference between wall-ramparts and dump ramparts in terms of fighting tactics, the dump being adapted particularly to the use of 'stoning', not necessarily with the aid of a sling. Dump ramparts, of course, need not have dispensed entirely with structural reinforcement. The crest of the earthwork could still have held a breastwork to protect defenders and impede assailants, like the stone wall of the dump rampart at Hod Hill or the period 6 palisade at Maiden Castle (Wheeler 1943: 102, 104–5, and Plate X).

Avery (1993) divided dump ramparts on the basis of their size and profile, into Low and High, with Extra High. Height, of course, in some measure reflects the length of time that an enclosure was in use and the number of times that its perimeter earthworks were reinforced or enlarged. One variant, with massive dump rampart and broader, shallower ditch was highlighted by Wheeler's excavation at Fécamp in Seine-Inférieure (Wheeler and Richardson 1957), from which the type took its name. Evoking Caesar's description of Noviodunum of the Suessiones, which he was unable to take by storm 'because of the breadth of its ditch and the height of its rampart' (*dBG* II, 12), this type of rampart was formerly regarded as typical of 'Belgic' Gaul, with tentative examples in south-eastern England at Oldbury in Kent (Ward-Perkins 1944) and elsewhere. Dump ramparts of this kind are now known to have a distribution much wider than the territory, however defined, of 'Belgic' Gaul, and need not be constrained by historical associations.

DITCHES

Hillfort ditches have seldom been excavated over any great length, even to the limited extent that ramparts have been, in order to determine whether they contained material other than casual detritus. Just occasionally, however, by chance rather than by research design, some further clue to the supplementary role of ditches may be uncovered. The ditch was generally interrupted only at the entrance, where a solid causeway gave access to the gates. It was normally maintained in a dry state, unless the local geology lent itself to water retention, as at Stanwick (Wheeler 1954), or at Cherbury Camp, Oxfordshire (Berkshire) (Figure 3.7), where the marshy location of the site was key to its defensive location. Ethnographic analogy, however, suggests that ditches may have contained other obstacles, if not embedded stakes then thorny material that would impede intruders.

Ditches can be of varying profiles, those associated with wall ramparts often being steeply V- or U-shaped, some dump ramparts, as we have seen, being fronted by broader, shallower ditches. It is possible that material quarried from different depths in the ditch was used selectively, as the evidence from the period 2 rampart at Crickley Hill suggests. At Uffington

Figure 3.7. Cherbury Camp, Oxfordshire (Berkshire), air photograph by Major G. W. G. Allen. Reproduced by kind permission of the Ashmolean Museum, University of Oxford.

(Miles *et al.* 2003: 83), material from the ditch may have been stockpiled in the interior rather than thrown directly into the timber-framed rampart, particularly where blocks of different sizes were required for constructing the wall faces. In other circumstances, the effort of deep quarrying may not have been justified if material nearer the surface was adequate for the job, especially in many upland locations, where quarrying a ditch would have been impractical. It is debatable whether ditches were kept clean or allowed to silt up naturally. The Danebury evidence certainly suggests periodic maintenance, which may have involved communal effort, perhaps with ritualized overtones. In other instances, however, deliberate deposits, including human remains, within hillfort ditches suggest ritual usage that seems to negate the idea that they were maintained in defensive readiness.

ENTRANCES

Michael Avery (1993, I: 90) declared unequivocally that 'the study of entrances is basically the study of the tactics of attack and defence'. Whilst this may be true at one level, entrances were also important in controlling traffic in and out of the enclosure, and elaboration of the entrance may have had equal significance as part of the 'rites of passage' from the outside world to the community within. Entrances range from relatively simple to ostentatiously elaborate. At its most basic, the requirement was for some form of revetment, in timber or stone, of the sides of the entrance passage, in order that gates could be suspended without leaving gaps in the frontage. The number of entrances is generally limited to one or two for convenient access, depending on local topography. In Wessex it has been observed (Payne *et al.* 2006: 138–9) that several univallate hillforts originally had two entrances, commonly on opposite sides of the enclosure, one of which had been blocked in a secondary phase of activity. Liddington Castle in Wiltshire (*op. cit.* Figures 2.54–6) and Danebury are conspicuous examples. No reason has yet been convincingly adduced to explain this phenomenon, nor yet whether it was for local reasons or as a result of mutually shared pressures on a regional scale.

Forde-Johnston (1976) distinguished simple entrances, represented by the great majority of sites in England and Wales, from those with in-turned or out-turned, looped or overlapping ramparts. From excavation it is clear that the more complicated outworks, like those at Danebury or Maiden Castle, were developments of the later pre-Roman Iron Age, but there is no invariable rule of thumb that indicates that all simple entrances were early. In northern Britain most hillfort entrances fall into the simple category, though in the case of multivallate enclosures like Broxmouth, East Lothian (Hill 1982a; Armit and McKenzie forthcoming) this may entail an elongated passageway.

In total contrast, a small group of 'causewayed forts' (Harding 2004a: 91–3) in Angus and Aberdeenshire is exceptional in having multiple entrances through more than one enclosing circuit (Figure 3.8). Although the eastern Scottish examples are especially distinctive, they are not unique in having multiple entrances. Arbory Hill, a high altitude fort at 429 metres OD (1394 ft) in Lanarkshire (RCAHMS 1978: No. 213), has five entrances through its bivallate enclosure, which would be quite enough to compromise a primarily defensive role. Excavation at the Brown Caterthun (Dunwell and Strachan 2007) has shown that the enclosures were cumulative and of different

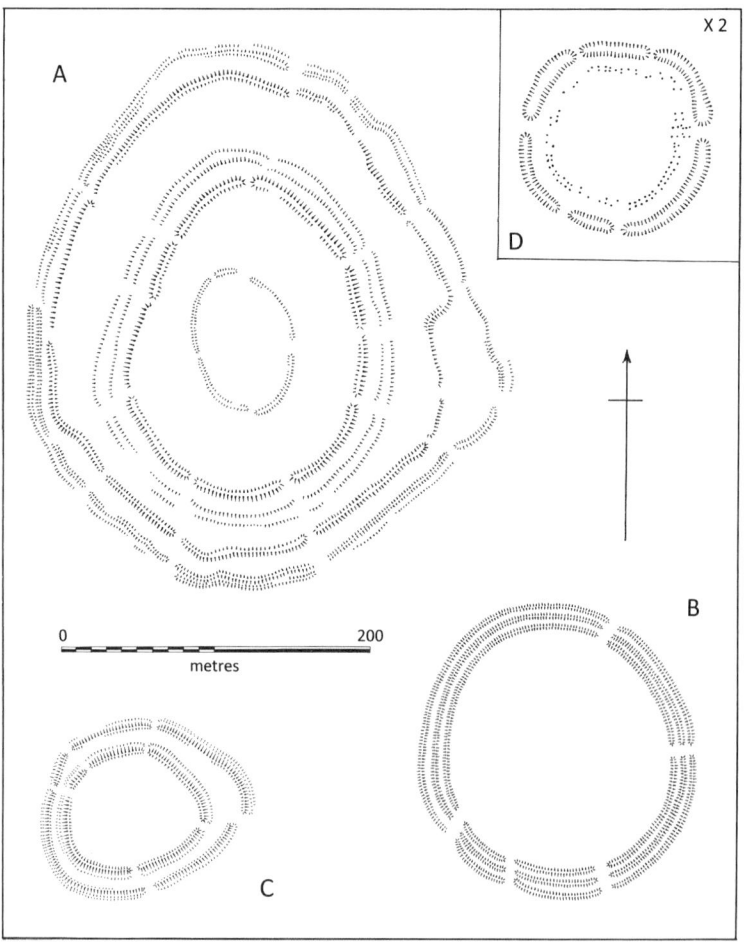

Figure 3.8. Causewayed fort plans: (A) Brown Caterthun, Angus, (B) Barmekin of Echt, Aberdeenshire, (C) Arbory Hill, Lanarkshire, (D) Springfield Lyons, Essex. Later phase walls omitted from (B) and (C). Drawings by D. W. Harding adapted from Dunwell and Strachan 2007; Feachem 1966; RCAHMS 1978; and Buckley and Hedges 1987.

construction, and the excavators concluded that the site more probably served a range of economic, social, and ritual activities than primarily as a defended settlement.

Gates

Of the gates themselves surprisingly little is known from British hillforts. At Biskupin in Poland the main entrance had double-leaved gates which had been preserved in the marshy environment, and it is surely this type of gate that would have been most appropriate for hillfort entrances in temperate Europe. From southern Britain evidence of gate fittings is sparse. Cadbury (Alcock 1972: Pl. 36; Barrett *et al.* 2000) was exceptional, the upright stile on which its gate was suspended having an iron spike driven into its heel with a domed head that rotated on a sill-beam. An iron collar prevented it from splitting. A collection of keys and latch-lifters may not all have belonged to this gate, being lost when the site was sacked in the late pre-Roman Iron Age. Avery (1993) pointed out that the massive earth-fast timbers at Rainsborough could never themselves have been uprights of a moving gate. He suggested alternatively that hillforts may have had piece-gates that could be erected when required. Documentary and ethnographic sources, however, suggest that gates may have had symbolic as well as practical significance, and as such would surely have been massive rather than makeshift structures. Uprights of a swinging gate could have been based on pivot-stones or timber sockets and held at the top in sockets in the cross-bar of the larger framework. Occasionally, as at Crickley Hill period 2, a slot across the entrance passage between major gate-posts probably held a sill-beam. This feature has sometimes been interpreted as a 'drop-slot' for a raised gate, as at Croft Ambrey, Herefordshire (Stanford 1974), though the rationale for this interpretation is not entirely clear. A two-leafed gate, opening outwards, would obviate problems with ground levels rising into the interior and avoid blocking guard chambers or sentry posts within the passageway. The absence of surviving evidence of associated ironmongery is hardly surprising if the gates to the hillfort constituted an important component, both functionally and symbolically. Perhaps the hillfort was consecrated by the formal installation of the gates, which, together with fittings may have been ceremonially removed when it was decommissioned.

In the stone forts of Argyll, on the other hand, entrances are seldom elaborated or extended beyond the width of the wall, and it is certainly possible here that the entrances may have had gates that were simply lifted into position and stacked against the entrance passage when not required (Peltenburg 1982: 153). The door may have rested against a pair of jambs at Ranachan

Hill, or it may have been lodged against a rebate, as at Knock Scalbart (RCAHMS 1971: No. 170), possibly held in placed by a bar on analogy with complex Atlantic roundhouses.

Entrance passages

Excavation of entrance passages in southern Britain has revealed a complexity of structural features in timber and stone that may have been subject to rebuilding or alteration on numerous occasions. At Croft Ambrey, Stanford (1974) identified fourteen successive phases in the south-west gate, based upon re-cut post-holes and superimposed road surfaces in the vertical stratigraphy, which was deeper than on many of the Wessex chalk downs sites. At Midsummer Hill in the Malverns (Stanford 1981), he proposed a sequence of eighteen successive phases of the south entrance, though the evidence for some phases was admittedly limited. Elsewhere, with minimal stratigraphy, as at Ffridd Faldwyn, Powys (O'Neill 1942), or at Blewburton Hill, the major phases of construction can nevertheless be distinguished on the basis of alignments or matching size and depth of post-holes.

Two principal variables reflect the possible functions of entrance passages, their width and their length. For defensive purposes alone, a narrower entrance would be less vulnerable, and a longer passage, with an inner set of gates, would contain a larger number of an attacking force under defensive fire from the ramparts. For access to wheeled traffic, a wider passage would be preferable. In some instances the width of the passage and triple sets of post-holes suggest the possibility of twin carriageways, though never in Britain with the elaborate pattern of post-holes supporting the gatehouse of the east entrance at Manching in the late La Tène (van Endert 1987).

In general, timber-lined passages in southern Britain are earlier than stone-lined passages, as at Blewburton Hill (Figure 3.9A). The postholes here, provisionally interpreted (Harding 1976b: Figure 5) as the earliest entrance, in hindsight were more probably part of the timber framework of the wall-rampart. This would have extended up to the earlier (phase 1) timber passage, comprising two lines of substantial posts, around 4 metres apart, of which the innermost pair was the largest and deepest, and doubtless held the main gate. The central pair of posts, on the alignment of the subsequent phase 2 gate, together with the next outer pair, possibly supported a bridge or timber gatehouse over the passage. The ditch at the inner end of the entrance, into which the post-pits of the phase 3 entrance were dug, now seems more probably to have been part of a Later Bronze Age enclosure like Rams Hill or Castle Hill, Little Wittenham, than an otherwise unparalleled complication of the Iron Age entrance. The period 2 entrance at Crickley Hill (Figure 3.10a) was of similar dimensions to Blewburton, but its flanking revetment incorporated sill-beams into which verticals had evidently been embedded. Its gate was centrally located in the passage in the largest pair of post-pits, inset slightly from the flanking revetment and linked by a beam-slot. Each contained three posts, probably not just replacements, but supports for the gate and its bridging superstructure. At the inner end of the passage a further pair of substantial post-holes may have held a second gate (Dixon 1994). Both of these entrances fall within the single carriageway category.

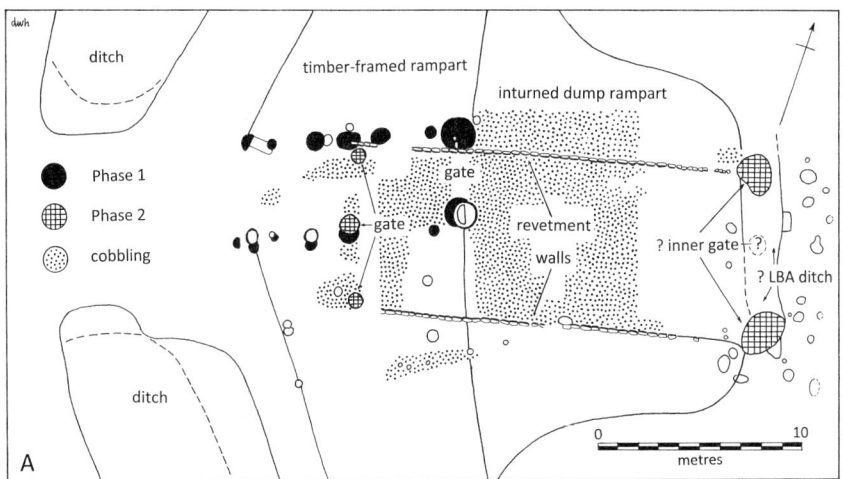

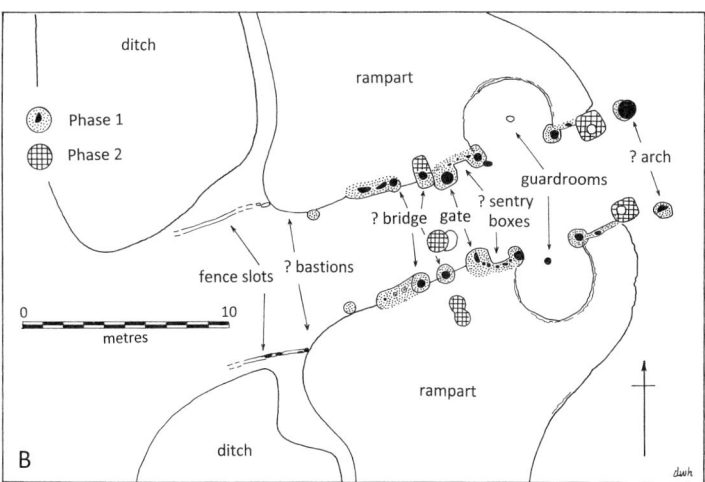

Figure 3.9. Hillfort entrance plans: (A) Blewburton Hill, Oxfordshire (Berkshire), (B) Rainsborough Camp, Northamptonshire. Drawings by D. W. Harding adapted from Harding 1976b and Avery et al. 1967.

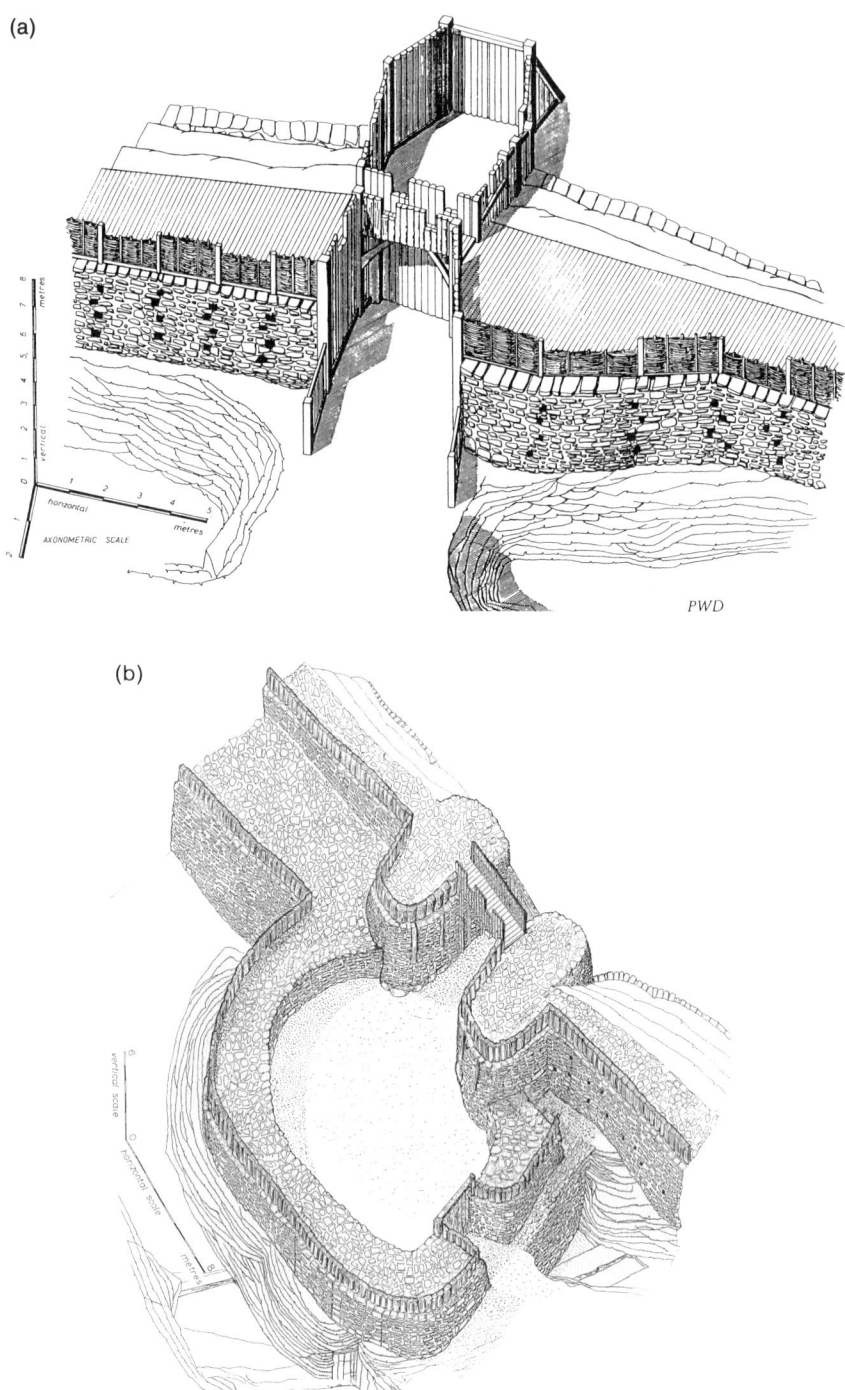

Figure 3.10. Crickley Hill, Gloucestershire entrance reconstructions: (a) Period 2, (b) Period 3b. Drawings by Philip Dixon, reproduced by kind permission.

Twin carriageways in British hillforts have been identified purely on the basis of having a central post between the gates, which generally accompanies a wider passageway. The period 2 inner east entrance at Danebury was around 8.5 metres across (Figure 1.10B), with a rebate immediately behind the gates widening the passage to around 12.5 metres. At St Catharine's Hill, Winchester, barely a dozen miles to the east, an almost identical layout (Figure 1.10A) in period 1 was only marginally smaller, suggesting the possibility that the same designers or engineers may have been responsible for both. The recesses behind the gates were apparently open in both cases, so hardly qualify as guardrooms, though they may nevertheless have provided room for traffic entering and leaving the enclosure to be checked. Double entrances of this kind were not restricted to Wessex; the early phase at Ffridd Faldwyn appears to have been based on the same basic design, though here with a double set of post-holes spanning the carriageways and almost certainly supporting some form of gatehouse superstructure. There is no apparent chronological sequence in the construction of single or twin carriageway entrances; at St Catharine's Hill (Hawkes 1976a: Figure 6; Cunliffe 2005: Figure 15.12), a twin carriageway was reduced in period 2 to a single carriageway and Avery (1993: Figure 35) proposed a similar sequence for Dinorben.

Stone-lined passages tend to be longer than those with timber revetment, whether for defensive or ceremonial purposes. The Blewburton stone-lined passage was nearly 20 metres in length and nearly 8 metres across, though its gates were set within that width so that each portal would have been no more than 3 metres wide. The road surface was cobbled, suggesting regular traffic, but it had no guard rooms or obvious sentry controls. Two large post-pits at the inner end of the passage must have held gate-posts, presumably with some central support unexcavated beneath the intervening baulk. In defending the gates, the tactics would presumably have been to contain an attacking force within the passageway, where it would be most vulnerable to defensive fire. One surprising omission from the plan, perhaps, is any evident provision for a bridge across the passage. Period 6 of the inner entrance at Danebury (Cunliffe 1984a: Figure 3.25) was another long, stone-lined corridor leading to a double gate, again with some form of gatehouse or façade. Its curving passageway was lined with flint revetment over a distance of 46 metres, and together with the contemporary outworks, must have presented a formidable defence. Even so, burning of the main gate-posts convinced the excavator that the gateway had been destroyed by fire in the early first century BC.

The only truly 'dual portal' gateways are those at Maiden Castle, Dorset. The double entrance of the eastern gateway was integral to the design from the earliest Iron Age (Wheeler 1943: Figure 4), acquiring greater complexity with the addition of a barbican and other outworks in subsequent phases

(Figure 3.11). The twin passageways were initially revetted in timber, then with a combination of timber and limestone, but with no evidence of guardrooms. In the final phase 4 (Wheeler 1943: Figure 9), probably around 200 BC (Avery 1993, II: 226), the remodelled outworks certainly look more defensive with their presumed 'fighting platforms', whilst in the inner entrance a hoard

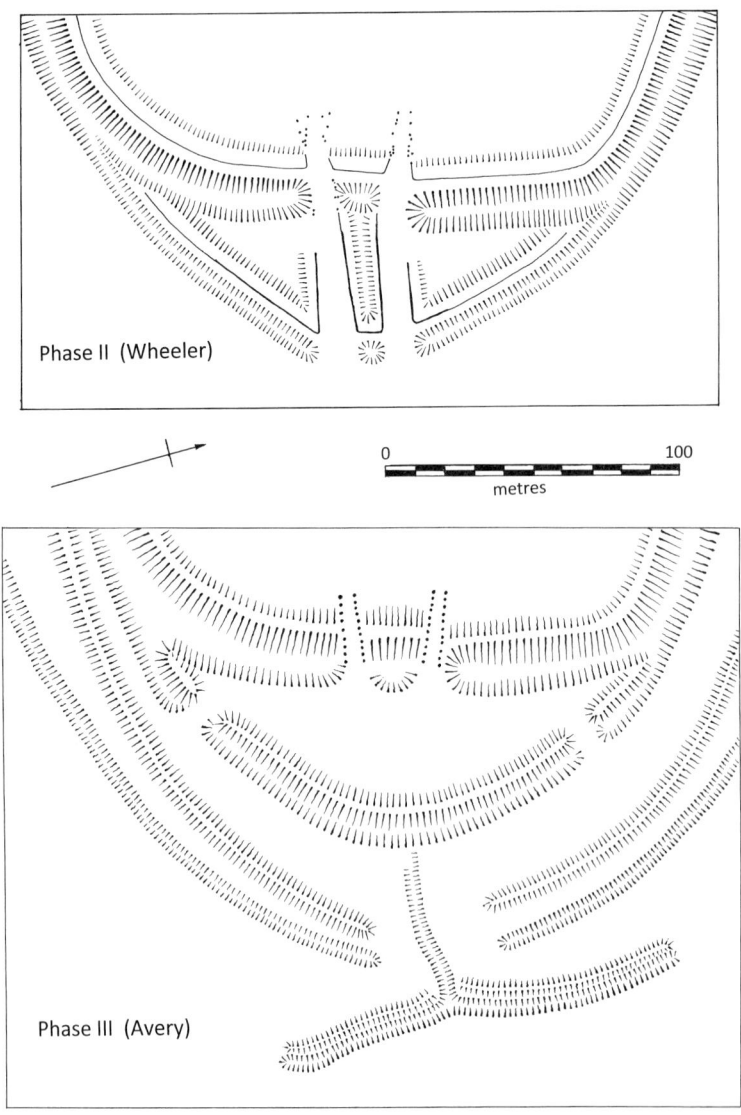

Figure 3.11. Dual portal eastern entrance, Maiden Castle, Dorset. Drawing by D. W. Harding after Wheeler 1943, and Avery 1993.

of more than 22,000 sling-stones was found adjacent to two small stone-built sentry boxes at the rear of the south passage. But in the preceding phases, even in phase 3 with its circuitous approach, the impression is of an extended, ceremonial way into the enclosure, rather than one primarily designed for defence. There is a symmetry in layout, as if left-hand and right-hand columns in winding circuits could process in mirror image from the outside world through the twin portals to the enclosure of the hillfort.

Guard chambers

A distinctive feature of hillfort entrances, from north Wales through the Marches to Somerset and Northamptonshire, is the provision of guard chambers flanking the entrance passage. These are generally constructed of stone, or a combination of timber and stone, but there is some evidence, from Midsummer Hill (Stanford 1981) for example, for all-timber construction. Either rectangular or semi-circular in plan, guard chambers were generally located towards the inner end of the entrance passage, as at Dinorben and at Rainsborough (Figure 3.9B). Accommodating guard chambers required a significant thickening of the rampart terminals, or even a pronounced in-turn, as at Titterstone Clee (O'Neil 1934) and the Wrekin in Shropshire (Kenyon 1942). The remarkable similarity of sequence at Dinorben and Moel Hiraddug, just across the Clywd valley (Guilbert 1979b), suggests not simply contemporary episodes of rebuilding but the possibility that the same architects and engineers may have been responsible for both (Figures 1.10C, D).

Guard chambers presumably housed guards, who could close the gates at the sounding of an alarm and in normal circumstances could control traffic coming into and leaving the hillfort. Their occurrence generally in opposed pairs makes sense, especially in the case of twin carriageway entrances, where there is room for wagons to pass going in and out. As a military feature their utility has been questioned, but this is to misunderstand their purpose. Access from guard chambers to wall head would presumably have been by internal stair or ladder, and hearths like those in the Rainsborough guard chambers suggest that they housed off-duty guards when they were not patrolling the ramparts or controlling traffic in and out of the fort.

The distribution of guard chambers is notably *not* Wessex-oriented. Savory (Gardner and Savory 1964) originally saw them as characteristically Cornovian or Deceanglian, and later (1976) as representative of a wider political alliance in the west Midlands and Welsh Marches. To the south and south-east, Cadbury, Leckhampton, and Rainsborough, and to the north-east Castle Hill, Almondbury, are significant outliers.

Bastions, barbicans, and complex outworks

There are few better examples of the sophistication of structural stone-work than the period 3b gateway at Crickley Hill (Plate 2b; Figure 3.10b). The inner gate was aligned with the highest level of the terraced rampart, and probably comprised a single leaf 2.6 m wide, opening inwards within a framework of horizontal sill and lintel supported by vertical jambs. Immediately in front of the gate, vertical posts were bedded in the stonework flanking the passage, which the excavator believed would have carried a timber bridge over the passage, perhaps even supporting a gatehouse above. At the rampart terminals, two stone bastions were each founded upon massive weathered boulders that had been imported, perhaps from some older monuments whose stones had important symbolic connotations. In Mediterranean Europe, bastions are regularly found spaced along hillfort walls, as at Entremont in Provence (Plate 4b), to provide covering fire along the wall face, but in Britain they are only very occasionally found as a feature of hillfort entrances. Projecting from the Crickley Hill entrance bastions a short inner and longer outer hornwork protected the entrance from direct assault, with an outer gate of comparable size to its inner counterpart. The hornwork showed similar construction breaks as the main ramparts of period 3b. In addition, both outer hornwork and the walls within the northern bastion showed a marked lobed effect, which the excavator speculated may have been designed to stabilize the stonework. The hornworks probably had a timber breastwork (Dixon 1994: 192), essential if the gateway was intended for effective defence and not simply to impress visitors as a monumental façade.

Complex entrances are generally assumed to have been designed for defence. Some, like the Stepleton gate at Hod Hill (Figure 3.12B), are obviously designed to impede a direct assault on the gates by diverting access parallel to the rampart. The eastern entrance at Danebury is more complex (Figure 3.12A). The extended passage outside its inner gates was protected on its north side by a curving hornwork which, as the excavator explained with Wheelerian overtones, formed the 'command post' (Cunliffe 1983: 77) from which the defence of the gateway could be controlled. It had clear line of sight of the outer gates and the double outer hornwork, as well as covering the inner ditches and the passageway to the inner gates. All would have been within a range of around 60 metres, within which slingshots would have been effective. The surprising fact is that, by comparison with the Danebury model, other hillforts with complex entrances are not nearly so readily explicable in terms of tactical defence, generally lacking any obvious 'command post' or system from which defenders could be rapidly withdrawn. The unexcavated western entrance at Maiden Castle (Figure 3.12C) attained a scale of complexity that defies tactical explanation, though it would appear like its eastern counterpart to have had a dual portal.

Anatomy of hillfort enclosure 85

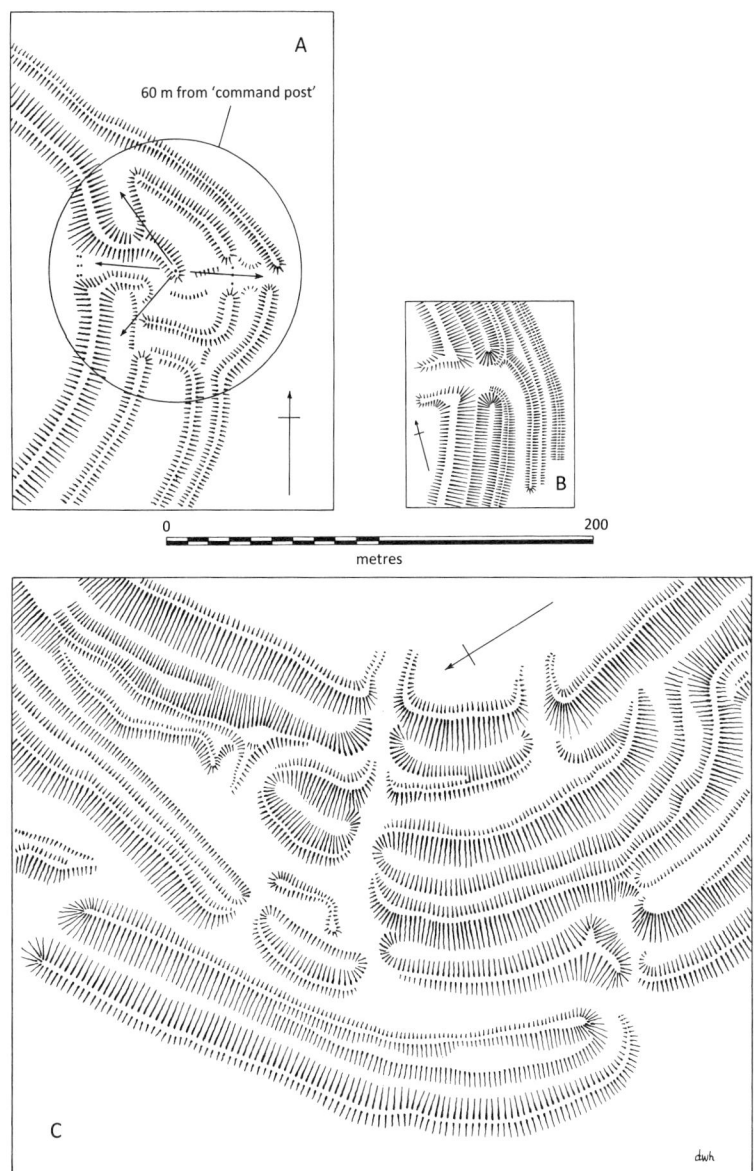

Figure 3.12. Complex hillfort entrances: (A) Danebury, Hampshire, east entrance, (B) Hod Hill, Dorset, Stepleton gateway, (C) Maiden Castle, Dorset, west entrance. Drawings by D. W. Harding adapted from Cunliffe 1971, 1984a; Richmond 1968; Wheeler 1943; RCHME 1970.

Blockhouses or gatehouses

Blockhouses are a particularly distinctive type of entrance forework, known especially from a small group of sites in Shetland, of which Clickhimin (Plate 5a; Hamilton 1968) and Ness of Burgi (Plate 5b; Lamb 1980) are outstanding examples. These drystone constructions incorporate many of the features of broch or complex Atlantic roundhouse architecture, including intramural galleries flanking the entrance passage. The passage itself also may display elements of broch architecture, such as door rebates and bar-holes. At Clickhimin a staircase implies access to an upper storey or to the wall head, and a scarcement on its inner wall face suggests structures backing its inner face.

A major problem with blockhouses is that they are essentially free-standing, rather than being an integral part of a continuing defensive circuit, forming a monumental façade, impressive on approach, but easily negotiated as an obstacle to access. At Clickhimin and at Ness of Burgi, the wall-ends have not simply been robbed away, but display intentionally finished stonework. It has been suggested that at Clickhimin the blockhouse was originally intended to join up with the fort wall, as at the Loch of Huxter (Lamb 1980), though even there it is not actually bonded in to the rest of the circuit. At Ness of Burgi and at Scatness nearby (Carter *et al.* 1995), it is hardly surprising that the blockhouse stopped short of the cliff edges in view of the risk of erosion, perhaps relying on a more ephemeral barrier for the last few metres, but in fact at both sites the blockhouses terminate well short of the cliff edge. We can only conclude that an impressive façade was more important than defensive effectiveness.

Dating of Shetland blockhouses is problematic. The use of 'broch architecture' is not itself a sure guide to an early Iron Age date, since its surviving visibility leaves open the possibility of emulation well into the later Iron Age. At Scatness the radiocarbon dates are from secondary contexts, but it is possible that the blockhouse remained extant well into the first millennium AD. At Clickhimin, however, the position of the blockhouse somewhere within the earlier Iron Age sequence seems reasonably assured (*v. infra* p. 145).

Hillforts without entrances

One group of hillforts in eastern Scotland, distinctive for their rounded oblong enclosure plans, sometimes single, sometimes double, present a particular problem in their apparent lack of an entrance at all (Harding 2004a: 85–90, and Figure 4.2). Typical is Finavon, Angus (Alexander 2002), where Childe (1936: 349) suggested that the original entrance must have been where the modern track cuts through the rampart. Other sites in the same general class, however, like Dunnideer, Strathdon (Cook 2010), or the enclosure on the summit of Tap o' Noth, Aberdeenshire (Plate 6a), have no visible entrance, while Castle Law, Forgandenny, Perthshire (Bell 1893; Christison 1900) has access through the outer enclosure but none through the inner. Two possible solutions were advanced by Alexander (2002: 49), either that access was gained by timber stairs over the wall, or that the entrance was so narrow that the collapsed walls have totally obscured its location. Ralston (2006: 76) pointed to the absence of trackways or hollow ways that might betray the position of a concealed entrance. At Forgandenny, Bell (1893: 18) suggested that the level of the entrance passage may have been higher than the surviving height of the walls, which in places was minimal. A sill across the entrance, like that at Cnoc an Duin, Ross-shire, might well have obscured the entrance altogether, as it would have in the latter case had not the flanking walls on either side of the passageway survived to make it clear. Entrances to stone forts in Scotland certainly can be very narrow, and hence liable to obscuring by collapse; at Dùn Mac Sniachan, Benderloch in Argyll (RCAHMS 1974: No. 136), for instance, the vitrified fort has no surviving trace of an entrance. In most cases, however, it is possible to infer where an entrance may have been on the basis of local topography. The oblong forts of eastern Scotland are a special case, apparently with restricted access that must have inhibited their use as normal domestic and agricultural enclosures.

'UNFINISHED' HILLFORTS

Given the number of hillforts known in Britain and the span of time that they occupied, it is hardly surprising that some show signs of interrupted construction (Feachem 1971). At Hayhope Knowe, it was just the western end of the earthwork that was never completed. At Cnoc an Duin, Ross-shire (Plate 6b), a substantial wall along the north side of the hill has several gaps, though whether these are simply where heather has grown over less substantial stonework is unclear. Just beyond the western entrance, however, the wall terminates abruptly, and is missing along the entire southern edge of the ridge. Its absence is more puzzling because some attempt was made to create a secondary wall or terrace beyond the line of the inner wall. In southern Britain, the classic example of an unfinished fort is Ladle Hill in Hampshire (Figure 3.13; Piggott 1931). Here, Piggott was able to propose a sequence of construction, beginning with a 'marking-out' trench on the inner lip of the ditch that would not normally survive the completion of works. The ditch was then excavated in sections, possibly by separate gangs,

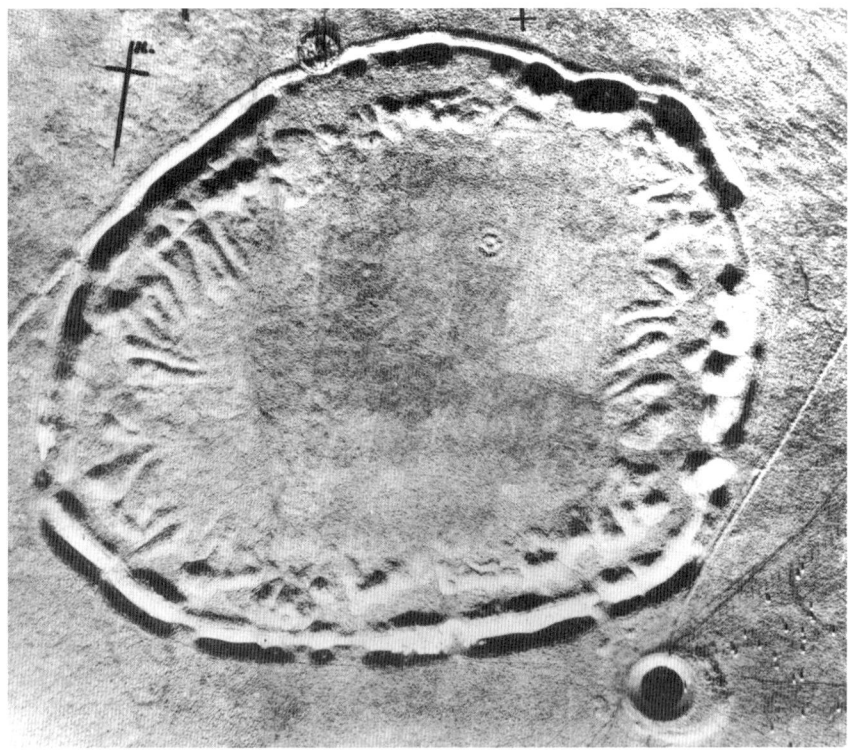

Figure 3.13. Ladle Hill, Hampshire, unfinished hillfort. Air photograph Crown Copyright, reproduced under Class License Number C2006000011 with the permission of OPSI and the Queen's Printer for Scotland.

and the core material dumped within the line of the proposed bank, the building of which was not started until more suitable larger blocks had been quarried from lower in the ditch. Double-handling in order to separate material from the quarry ditch, though labour-intensive, and gang construction would both accord with what has been learned of hillfort construction in recent years.

CONCLUSIONS

If conventional classification of hillfort defences now seems a sterile exercise, a review of excavated evidence nevertheless suggests that we may still be far from understanding how these key structures were actually built. The surviving patterns of earth-fast post-holes may belie a greater complexity of construction, and non-earth-fast timber structures within the core of a rampart may leave minimal trace. An internal row or double row of uprights, as at Crickley Hill or Moel y Gaer, may have been more widespread than excavated ground plans evince, and would surely have been necessary in ramparts up to 4 metres in transverse width. At the same time, the internal framework could have supported a tiered structure at the back of the wall-head and parapet, comparable in timber to the stepped effect of the Rainsborough rampart, making access from the interior easier. The quantities of timber implicit in such constructions make it probable that, notwithstanding resource management regimes, the shift towards dump construction in the later first millennium BC was in no small measure induced by an increasing scarcity of adequate timber supplies.

Evidence for building in sections, reflected in 'construction breaks' in the wall-face as at Crickley Hill or in differential filling of the core as at Moel y Gaer, could well result from different family or kin groups being responsible for lengths of the enclosure, as is also attested ethnographically (*v. infra* Chapter 10). Alternatively it could indicate seasonal construction or sectional repair as particularly exposed or vulnerable lengths of walling required. Greater variability in wall construction has even been detected in the *murus gallicus* at Manching, dating from around 140–120 BC, where in some sectors four longitudinal timbers have been detected, and in others just two (Wendling 2011). The assumption that the construction of hillfort ramparts was uniform around the entire circuit, even if that circuit was conceived as an entity, plainly may be misplaced.

We shall examine later the arguments for and against a defensive role for hillforts, but analysis of the various structural features of hillfort enclosure might indicate a *prima facie* case for a defensive function, whilst recognizing that this was not the only or even the primary consideration. The scale of construction is sometimes monumental to the point where display or statement of identity or status must have been intended and the layout of entrances is such as to suggest that enforcement of the observation of formalities in approach may have been an important factor in hillfort design.

Plainly the construction of enclosing works was expensive in resources and labour. This was presumably a communal effort, even if under the control of a 'coercive power', hierarchical or otherwise. What is less clear is how far there were 'professional' architects and engineers involved, and what mathematical or metrical knowledge was available to them.

The importance of enclosure is self-evident, even if it still requires further clarification. What was enclosed, and what was excluded, will be examined in the next chapter.

4

Inside and Outside of Hillforts

By the 1960s, a greater interest in the social and economic role of hillforts demanded more extensive excavation of their interiors. Whilst fieldwork was still dependent on volunteer labour and limited research funds, the expense of large-scale stripping by hand would have been prohibitive, and only with public funding of 'rescue' or 'salvage' excavation in advance of development was it practical to contemplate large-scale area excavation. Hillforts that were extensively excavated included Balksbury (Wainwright 1969; Wainwright and Davies 1995; Ellis and Rawlings 2001) and Winklebury (Smith 1977; Robertson-Mackay 1977; Fisher 1985) in Hampshire. Whilst large-scale examination of hillfort interiors is plainly essential to an understanding of their economic and social functions, there is a high probability that ephemeral features, the foundations of which did not penetrate into subsoil or bedrock, will be destroyed by mechanical stripping, if they have not already been damaged beyond retrieval by ploughing. So the question remains: how partial and therefore potentially misleading are the surviving plans of hillfort interiors thus exposed?

Hillfort *exteriors*, arguably equally important to an understanding of the role of the enclosure as its interior, have been even more neglected, first because of an implicit assumption that the earthworks defined the area of the 'site', and second, because the logistical problems of excavating outside the limits of the ramparts increased exponentially with distance from the enclosure. The possibility, indeed probability, of activity contemporary with the occupation of the hillfort having extended beyond the limits of the rampart need not necessarily imply a social division between *acropolis* and *polis* on the eastern Mediterranean model. It simply requires a redefinition of the concept of what constituted the 'site' in which the enclosure earthworks are not the definitive criterion. The issue was identified more than thirty years ago (Harding 1979; Hingley 1980), and excavation and survey at Battlesbury Camp, Wiltshire (Ellis and Powell 2008) and Castle Hill, Little Wittenham (Allen *et al.* 2011), has shown its importance for future research.

There are three principal, non-intrusive ways of investigating hillfort interiors and immediate exteriors. The first is by surface survey, not in itself as simple as may appear at first sight, since detecting and meaningfully depicting the highly fugitive traces of prehistoric occupation requires an experienced eye, sensitive to the residual surface signs of constructional activity. One has only to compare an early plan of Hambledon Hill, Dorset (Crawford and Keiller 1928: Figure 5), with the Royal Commission's surveys of the 1960s (RCHME 1970, Child Okeford 22), and 1996 (Mercer and Healy 2008: Figure 3.148) to appreciate the differences that can reflect the effects of season and lighting on topography, and of experience and expectation upon interpretation.

The second non-intrusive technique of investigation is air photography. For many sites, including many on the chalk downs of Wessex and Sussex, where hillfort interiors are commonly uncultivated grassland, air photography may be relatively unproductive. But there are plenty of instances in northern Britain where house foundations are visible within the perimeter earthworks, as at Hownam Law (Plate 7a), or where associated features such as the traces of cord-rig agriculture can be recorded much more easily with the aid of air-photographs, as at Woden Law (Figure 4.1) in the Roxburghshire Borders. In southern Britain, however, air photography has contributed significantly to the discovery of settlement in the immediate vicinity of hillforts, notably where agriculture has encroached hard up against the earthworks (Payne et al. 2006: 139–41.)

Figure 4.1. Woden Law, Hownam, Roxburghshire: (a) from c.2500 feet, (b) (opposite) from c.500 feet. Air photographs by D. W. Harding.

The third non-intrusive means of investigation is by geophysical survey, a range of techniques that likewise require not only the right physical conditions to produce a positive outcome, but also an important element of interpretation to render the raw data readable. Survey of southern English hillforts by proton magnetometer began in the late 1950s and early 1960s with the pioneering work of Martin Aitken and Michael Tite from the Oxford Research Laboratory for Archaeology (Aitken and Tite 1962), initially at Madmarston Camp in Oxfordshire (Fowler 1960), at Conderton Camp, Worcestershire (Thomas 2005), and at Rainsborough Camp in Northamptonshire (Avery et al. 1967). Pits and hearths were readily detected, but post-holes remained elusive (Tite 1967). From the late 1960s, conductivity and magnetometer surveys were undertaken at Cadbury Castle with qualified success (Alcock 1972: 70–2). Further resistivity and gradiometer surveys were conducted across the entire interior in 1992–3, and the results presented in the final report (Barrett et al. 2000: Figures 73, 74). By the mid 1980s geophysical survey had established itself as a standard technique for larger scale investigation. For the field campaign at Maiden Castle, designed to coincide with the occasion of the first World Archaeological Congress of 1986 in Southampton, it still only achieved limited success, in part because the density of magnetic anomalies simply made it hard to distinguish individual features.

More recently, survey by the Wessex Hillforts Project (Payne et al. 2006) has demonstrated the invaluable contribution that non-intrusive survey can

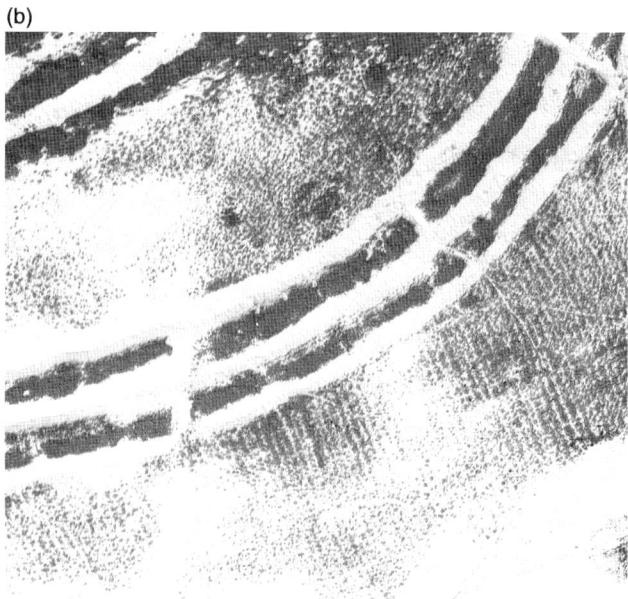

make to the investigation of hillfort interiors and the evaluation of the role of hillforts through the Iron Age. At Bury Hill, Hampshire, for example (ibid. 54–8), it was possible to show that the period 1 fort was virtually devoid of structural evidence of occupation, whereas the subsequent period 2 hillfort contained a density of pits, with a void marking the central road between entrances. Lesser features, however, like structural post-holes still generally elude detection, and the technique is still vulnerable to problems posed by geological factors, as the survey of Walbury, Berkshire, demonstrated (ibid. 44–7). Furthermore, it became apparent that geophysical survey did not necessarily reflect positively features that had been recognized from surface survey, since the technique was responding to different conditions. At Beacon Hill, Burghclere, for example, magnetometer survey detected magnetically enhanced deposits like hearths, pits, or some house ditches, but in general gave an impression of the site less densely occupied than appeared from surface survey (ibid. 47–54).

In Europe, geophysical and ground-penetrating radar surveys have been employed with notable results from a number of sites, including the classic later La Tène site at Manching, where among other discoveries, the latter detected the ditch of a sub-rectangular Late Hallstatt *Herrenhof* on the eastern side of the complex. More recently geomagnetic and ground radar survey of the Celto-Ligurian *oppidum* at Entremont has revealed the concentrated plan of streets and buildings in the 'lower town', dating from around 150 BC until the town's destruction by the Romans in the 120s. The importance of this form of survey is that it can indicate the overall layout of settlement, in this case confirming that there are no distinctive public buildings, though wider and narrower internal divisions between streets do perhaps suggest some differential use of space (Armit 2011a).

Finally, of course, the ultimate option for investigating hillfort interiors is excavation, the only sure way at present of establishing what lies beneath the ground. Excavation, however, is labour-intensive and expensive, the more so since it potentially generates many times its own cost in specialist analysis and reporting. More crucially, it is destructive, and the quality of the results will be determined entirely by the standards of recovery and recording deployed, which at best can only match the prevailing best practice at the time, and cannot anticipate future innovations and improvements. These limitations have encouraged a current reluctance among professional archaeologists and agencies to condone excavation in any circumstance in which the site is not already threatened with destruction by development or by serious degrading by natural forces. The problem with this approach, of course, is that discoveries are determined by non-archaeological factors, which, whilst potentially providing a useful corrective to the prevailing research bias, is hardly a substitute for research planning.

HILLFORT INTERIORS

Walled towns and villages of the eastern Scottish Borders

An initial premise regarding the social function of hillforts might be that they were for community occupation; in effect, that they were walled villages or towns. That view might be encouraged by examples of hillforts in the eastern Borders, large and small, within which circular house foundations survive in some numbers. Eildon Hill North, Roxburghshire, at its maximum 16 ha (39 acres) in enclosed extent, has an estimated 300 house platforms, while Hownam Law (Plates 7a, b), at nearly 9 ha (22 acres) one of Feachem's (1966) 'minor *oppida*', has at least 155. South of the Tweed, the hillfort on Yeavering Bell (Oswald and Pearson 2005) at 400 metres OD (1300 ft) encloses 5.6 ha (13 acres), and contains platforms for some 130 houses, many with surviving ring-grooves confirming their timber construction. Whilst there is no reason to assume that all of these structures were in contemporary occupation, the probability is that there were others that have not survived to be surveyed, and that those that have conflate several structural phases. As to dating, Feachem assumed that Eildon and other major hillfort *oppida* in south-east Scotland represented the culmination of the hillfort sequence on the eve of the Roman conquest. Its concentration of houses was taken as evidence of its status as a proto-urban settlement and tribal 'capital' of the Selgovae. In reality there is remarkably little evidence for early Iron Age occupation at Eildon, whilst radiocarbon dates (Owen 1992: Figure 2.18) make it clear that there was important activity in the Late Bronze Age and in the Roman period. Environmental evidence can be adduced for suspecting that high-altitude forts in northern and western Britain might well have been built and occupied in the later Bronze Age rather than in the late pre-Roman Iron Age. The idea that Traprain Law was a comparable tribal centre of the Votadini in the immediately pre-Roman Iron Age was always controversial in the absence of evidence of more than sporadic occupation at this period, in contrast to the considerable evidence for activity on the site in the later Bronze Age, and again in the Roman period. Traprain was always different in that it lacked the surface evidence of house stances that distinguished Eildon Hill, Hownam Law, and Yeavering Bell, and it should not be bracketed together with the Borders hillforts.

Among the intermediate-sized enclosed sites of the Tweed valley, the White Meldon (3.5 ha) and Cademuir (3 ha) in Peeblesshire also have a considerable number of platforms for timber houses that could well date from the later Bronze Age. Both sites contain thirty or more foundations for timber houses distributed widely over their interiors, suggesting regular seasonal use if not permanent occupation. Halliday (1985: 238) some years ago suggested a possible relationship between high-altitude forts like Hownam Law, standing at nearly 450 metres OD, together with Cademuir (400 metres) and White Meldon (430 metres), with unenclosed platform settlements and cairnfields of the later second millennium BC. There certainly appears to have been extensive use of the uplands in the later second and early first millennia BC, perhaps in preference to the more heavily wooded valleys, and there is no reason to exclude the high-altitude forts from this pattern of activity. Halliday (ibid. 238) went so far as to suggest that, far from culminating in progressively larger hillforts, the sequence may have been from nucleated settlements at a much earlier period to a more dispersed pattern of smaller forts and defended settlements in the Iron Age. Mercer and Tipping (1994: 5) tentatively even suggested a Middle Bronze Age date for Hownam Law, not on the basis of any direct evidence from the Cheviots, but on analogy with high-altitude sites in northern Scotland, like Tap o' Noth, Aberdeenshire, and Ben Griam Beg in Sutherland (Ralston and Smith 1983), the latter located at 580 m OD (1900 ft), the former at 570 m OD (1850 ft), heights which it was argued would have been untenable for settlement after the onset of the sub-Atlantic. A similar argument, of course, could be advanced for high-altitude forts elsewhere in Britain, such as Tre'r Ceiri in the Lleyn peninsula at 480 m OD (1560 ft), and notably for the highest of all, Ingleborough (Plate 8a) in the Yorkshire Pennines at 730 m OD (2370 ft).

There remains, of course, the question whether these high-altitude sites were enclosed from the outset, or whether the surrounding walls were added to what was already a significant open settlement. The latter thesis, which is currently the favoured view of Mam Tor, Derbyshire (Plate 8b), located at 517 m (1700 ft), would gain credibility if we could point to instances of unenclosed hilltop settlement, in the absence of which it seems more likely that concentration of settlement and enclosure went hand in hand. In the case of the larger hillforts in south-eastern Scotland and the Borders, their enclosing walls would seem to define the area of occupation, in that similar house platforms have not been found immediately beyond the walls, as they have at Carn Fadrun in Caernarvonshire, for example. There is also the question whether all these 'house platforms' were indeed for dwellings, and if so, whether they were for permanent or seasonal occupation. What is quite striking is the relative uniformity of the surviving foundations, and the absence of any obvious divisions or patterns in their layout.

At the smaller end of the enclosure size spectrum, there are numerous small hillforts or defended settlements in south-eastern Scotland that can be described as protected villages on the evidence of house foundations within their walls. Hayhope Knowe (Piggott 1949) had ring-ditch and ring-groove houses aligned along a central street that divided the interior between entrances at opposite ends of the enclosure (Figure 4.2a). A similar pattern can be detected at nearby Camp Tops (Figure 4.2b; RCAHMS 1956: No. 653), and in

(a)

(b)

Figure 4.2. Cheviot hillforts: (a) Hayhope Knowe, Morebattle, Roxburghshire: (b) Camp Tops, Morebattle, Roxburghshire. Air photographs by D. W. Harding.

Peeblesshire seven ring-groove houses appear to have flanked a central street at the Black Meldon (RCAHMS 1967: No. 259), while at Richie Ferry in Lanarkshire (RCAHMS 1978: No. 209) the layout shows even more remarkable symmetry with four entrances. It might be pretentious to claim this as anything more than the most basic of internal planning and organization of space, given that the area enclosed is so limited and the axial division is plainly dictated by the position of opposed entrances. It is interesting to note, however, that a very similar pattern was detected by geophysical survey at Conderton Camp, Worcestershire (Thomas 2005), except that there the roundhouses were aligned along one side of the street with storage pits concentrated on the other side. Braidwood in Midlothian (Stevenson 1949a; Piggott 1958b) is more difficult to interpret, since there may have been one or more phases of open settlement in addition to the phases represented by the palisaded and earthwork enclosures (Gannon 1999). Most of these sites are around a quarter hectare in area (*c.* ½–¾ acre), but their enclosing earthworks can occupy almost as much again, as at Sundhope Kip, Hownam (RCAHMS 1956: No. 303), for example, where the settlement is located on the end of a spur, protected on its only easily accessible side by three outer banks in addition to the innermost enclosure.

Not all these Borders sites have surviving evidence of internal occupation, and it is possible that some may have served as stock enclosures and other purposes that only excavation could demonstrate. Those that were for habitation probably served as permanent settlements rather than transhumance camps. Many of the enclosed sites of the Roxburghshire Cheviots are in close proximity to areas in which evidence of cord rig has been recognized from air-photographic and ground survey. This class of narrow rig cultivation was first plotted extensively in the late 1970s and 1980s, and was regularly found in association with palisaded settlements and ring-ditch houses, as at Woden Law East or Scowther Knowe in Roxburghshire, suggesting the possibility of a later Bronze Age or early Iron Age date. Subsequent research has shown that cord-rig agriculture may reflect agricultural practice over much of the first millennium BC, but in the Cheviots it is unlikely to have survived as a viable form of cultivation much beyond the earliest Iron Age. At Hut Knowe North, Hownam, excavated sections showed that the rigs were most likely the product of spade cultivation (Halliday 1993: 71–2), though in some instances it is possible that an ard was used initially in what Peter Reynolds called the 'sod-busting' process. Of particular interest in the present context is the small hillfort at Hut Knowe (Figure 4.3; RCAHMS 1956: No. 312), a two-phase enclosure that might well originally have been of the small protected village class. Hut Knowe is virtually surrounded by cord rig, and in its second phase its southern entrance was approached by a track-way, flanked by a series of fields enclosed by low embankments and containing cord rig. The enclosed fields contrast with alternating blocks of cord rig that surround the hillfort on

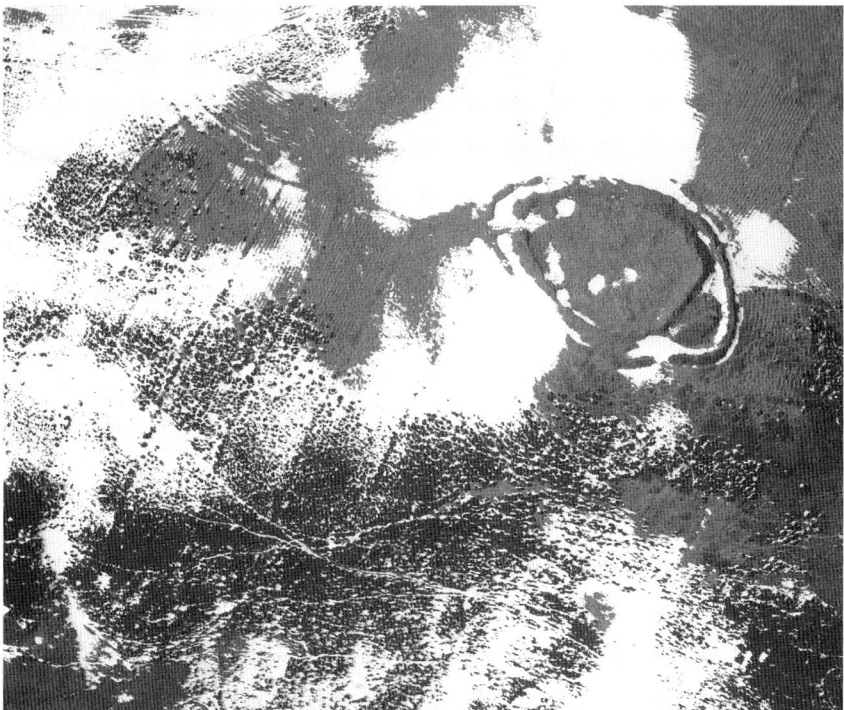

Figure 4.3. Hut Knowe, Hownam, Roxburghshire, hillfort with fields and cord-rig agriculture. Air photograph by D. W. Harding.

its north-west side, suggesting that here may be successive layers of agriculture. There is also an unenclosed or partly-enclosed settlement to the north within the overall complex (Harding 2004a: Figure 3.16), suggesting a possible relationship between the hillfort and lesser dependent settlements. The provision of a track-way through the arable fields is presumably indicative of a mixed agricultural economy, but there can hardly be any doubt that the pattern of cord rig is broadly contemporary with the hillfort. Not all the fields or plots of cord rig need have been worked at any one time: indeed, close inspection of the blocks of rigging, for example at Hut Knowe North, shows that these conceal separate areas of activity on a smaller scale. Nevertheless, if the defended settlement housed half a dozen families, it is possible that each had a separate field or block of land for which it was responsible.

The most challenging issue arising from the Borders evidence is whether nucleation into larger community centres had already taken place by the later Bronze Age, with subsequent abandonment of high-altitude sites in the Iron Age, followed by their re-occupation in the Roman period, as appears to be indicated by admittedly small-scale excavation at Eildon Hill North (Rideout 1992). It remains undemonstrated that the density of 'house platforms' indicates large-scale occupation, and if so, whether this was permanent or seasonal. The consensus view that new platforms would not have been built if existing ones were unoccupied ignores the possibility that space may have been strictly allocated to different social groups. Excavation at Eildon certainly did not suggest that the house platforms of either Late Bronze Age or Romano-British occupations were for substantial buildings, even though they produced evidence for a range of domestic activities.

Caernarvonshire forts

One of the most distinctive groups of hillforts in terms of their evidence of internal occupation is the Caernarvonshire series in north Wales (RCAHMWM 1956, 1960, 1964), principally Carn Fadrun, Garn Boduan, and Tre'r Ceiri in the Lleyn peninsula, but with a notable outlier on Conway Mountain (Castell Caer Seion) to the north-east. Hogg evidently thought of the Lleyn forts as contemporary or overlapping in date, observing that they 'dominate obvious natural units of territory of about 8 or 10 square miles bounded by marshy valleys, and containing no other substantial fort' (Hogg 1960: 24). Tre'r Ceiri (Plate 9a) would certainly rank as a high-altitude hillfort, rising to 480 m OD (1560 ft) at its summit, with Carn Fadrun (370 m OD, 1200 ft) significantly higher than Garn Boduan (270 m OD, 877 ft) and Conway Mountain (240 m OD, 780 ft). In area enclosed, however, Tre'r Ceiri (2.5 ha, 6.25 acres) and Conway Mountain (3 ha, 7 acres) are significantly smaller than Carn Fadrun (5 ha, 12.5 acres), and Garn Boduan enclosed 10 ha (25 acres) before the addition of its secondary extension. Within the latter's circuit some 170 surviving stone-built houses are fairly evenly distributed over the primary enclosure. These were all circular in plan with diameters in the range of 5–8 m. Excavation of four such houses in 1954 failed to yield any dating evidence, but the excavator concluded nevertheless that they should belong to the pre-Roman Iron Age. The size of population at any one time has been a topic of debate, but Alcock (1965) calculated that in both area enclosed and population density, Garn Boduan compared quite closely with Edwardian Conway, and as such might warrant the designation of an Iron Age town. This assessment sits uneasily with his belief that the higher-altitude forts were not for permanent settlement but for shelter and protection of summer pastoralists.

In marked contrast, excavations in the early twentieth century at Tre'r Ceiri (Baring-Gould and Burnard 1904; Hughes 1907) uncovered a good deal of Romano-British material, including some relatively high-status items, though regrettably none from securely recorded or stratified contexts, so that dating of individual components within what was plainly a multi-period sequence remains unproven. Reviewing the evidence from Tre'r Ceiri, Hogg (1960) distinguished the limited number of round house plans from those of sub-rectangular or cellular plan, which he rightly inferred must represent a later style of building. He recognized that in some cases, the cellular arrangement had been achieved simply by subdividing with partition walls buildings that must originally have been circular (Plate 9b). The pottery from the domestic occupation was evidently all Roman, though it was apparently scarcer in the roundhouses, some of which he concluded could have been of pre-Roman origin. These conclusions were largely endorsed by a ten-year programme of consolidation of the defences and internal buildings. Examination of around 150 buildings indicated that the initial layout comprised thirty to forty large roundhouses, of which the majority had been subdivided or further modified by cellular additions (Hopewell 1998). Conservation work also suggested at least two episodes of construction in the south-west entrance, where the bastions appeared to be secondary, and in the main west gateway, where Romano-British pottery was found in the core of secondary wall facing of the entrance passage (Hopewell 1992, 1993). Hogg also noted that the cellular buildings especially used a distinctive form of construction, namely edge-set slabs, sometimes in combination with horizontal coursing, but especially to revet scree, creating in effect a one-sided wall, a construction technique that is particularly characteristic of cellular building in Atlantic Scotland from the second quarter of the first millennium AD. Hogg was therefore doubtless right in believing that the principal period of occupation of the cellular houses was in the early first millennium AD.

The nature of that occupation remains a matter of debate. Hogg thought that a series of scooped terraces around the outside of the fort walls, especially on the west and south sides, were 'hardly explicable save as plots for some form of cultivation' (1975: 94), though he recognized that this could only have been feasible in climatic conditions more favourable than today. Furthermore, Tre'r Ceiri has yielded no querns, which might have been expected even from poorly conducted excavations. Yet the 'ill-recorded burials' (ibid. 93) on the plateau outside the south-west gate suggest that the site was not simply one used by transhuming pastoralists. Gilmour (2000: 253–5) offered a rather different perspective on the site's function. He saw the main enclosure as a series of rising levels, with clusters of cellular buildings on each, which he compared to the hierarchy of levels of early historic 'nuclear' forts of Scotland (Stevenson 1949b). Its summit was dominated by a Bronze Age cairn, seemingly intact despite the massive programme of stone construction that the hillfort plainly necessitated. His conclusion accordingly was that Tre'r Ceiri served some special purpose, perhaps involving inaugurations and ritual activities, in which the ancient cairn and the several springs beyond the walls, as well as the site's obviously commanding location in relation to important western sea-routes, could all have played a significant role.

Carn Fadrun differs from the other three sites in one important respect; namely, that the great majority of surviving roundhouse foundations are on the slopes outside and all around the hillfort, which suggests a larger community settlement and not just a temporary refuge or seasonal gathering point. Within the fort's multi-phase walls, irregular or cellular structures are comparable to those at Tre'r Ceiri, and may be of similar Roman Iron Age date. The summit of Carn Fadrun is occupied by a very small, stone-built citadel, which, on the basis of historical records, has been assigned a twelfth century date. At Garn Boduan too the highest point is occupied by a small fort, which the 1954 excavator assigned to the early historic period. At the south-western end of Conway Mountain there is also an independent enclosure, contiguous with the main fort, but with no access directly to it, which Hogg believed to be contemporary with the larger fort, despite is unusual layout and construction. Without adequate dating evidence, early historic re-use cannot be discounted. The main occupation of the fort, however, must belong to the earlier Iron Age, not only because of the exclusive representation of circular house plans, but also because the finds from limited excavations in 1951–2 (Griffiths and Hogg 1956) found only saddle querns, which should indicate occupation before the 'quern replacement' phase of the later first millennium BC. As to function, the stone-built houses look to be designed for permanent occupation, and the occurrence of sling-stones, more than six hundred in Hut 1, which has the appearance of a guard-house by the main entrance, may indicate a defensive dimension.

A major problem in dating the origin of these hillforts, and indeed of dating later prehistoric roundhouse settlements (Ghey *et al.* 2007), is the absence of a diagnostic material assemblage, especially pottery, for much of the first millennium BC, as in upland regions of northern England where, prior to the widespread application of radiocarbon dating, the presence of scraps of Roman pottery or glass, even from patently secondary contexts, inevitably resulted in a late dating by default (Harding 2004a: 53). This has undoubtedly prejudiced the identification of early hillfort construction and occupation in largely aceramic areas, and has perhaps also obscured the possibility of later post-Roman reoccupation as well.

Hillforts from the Welsh Marches to the Vale of Clwyd

Stanley Stanford's campaigns of hillfort excavation of the 1960s and 1970s, like George Jobey's in Northumberland, were low-budget projects using volunteer labour under the umbrella of university extramural archaeology departments, which nevertheless maintained exemplary standards of fieldwork and publication. Croft Ambrey (Stanford 1974) in particular revealed concentrations of four-post structures, arranged in blocks and with multiple replacements of their post-holes (Figure 4.4, B) that suggested a density of distribution across the summit plateau. Long accepted since Bersu's (1940) excavation at Little Woodbury, Wiltshire, as granaries, Stanford nevertheless insisted that these

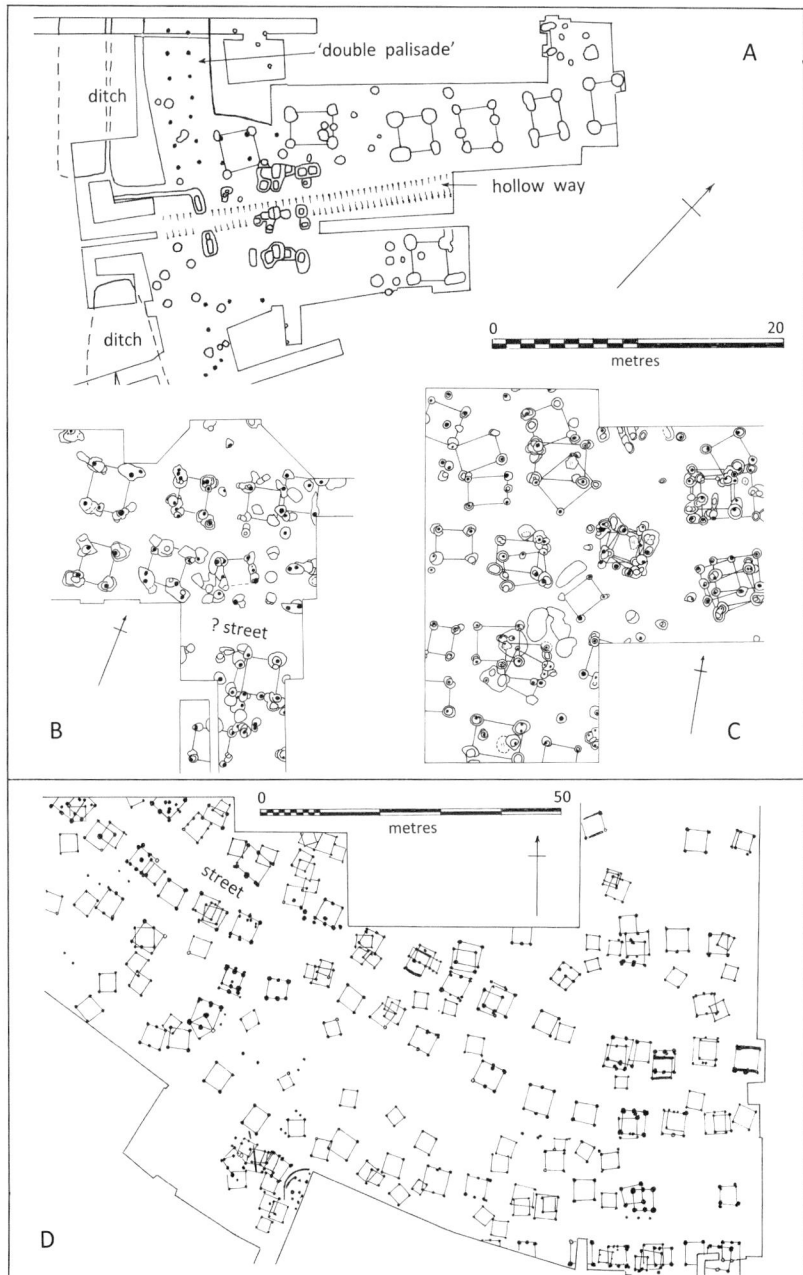

Figure 4.4. Four-post structures from hillfort interiors: (A) Ffridd Faldwyn, Montgomery, Powys, (B) Croft Ambrey, Herefordshire, (C) Midsummer Hill, Herefordshire, (D) Danebury, Hampshire, south-western sector. Drawings by D. W. Harding adapted from O'Neil 1942, Stanford 1974, Stanford 1981, and Cunliffe and Poole 1991a.

were primarily dwellings, even if some were used for storage purposes, presumably because he assumed that there must have been a resident community, and four-posters were the only type of structure that had been uncovered. Sampling of the interior had necessarily been extremely limited, though quite widely spread, so that even allowing for zoning of activities, the absence of other types was striking. Very few pits were located, perhaps, as the excavator suggested, because Croft Ambrey was peripheral to the storage pit distribution in southern Britain. Geophysical survey was deployed over a substantial swathe of the plateau fort, and though the technique was still in its infancy at the time, it should have detected concentrations of pits had they existed. Consequently Stanford's inference that the interior was largely dedicated to orderly lines of four-posters need not appear so fanciful, and might be compared in continental Europe to the interpretation of the interior of the hillfort at the Altburg von Bundenbach in the Hunsrück (Schindler 1977).

The interpretation of four-posters as 'huts', however, still seems improbable. Principally they are too cramped in internal area: those claimed by Stanford (1971) at Credenhill Camp as being large enough at 7 m^2 (72 sq. ft) for dwellings, though at the larger end of the four-poster spectrum, still have no more space than a roundhouse just 3 m in diameter, a size that is virtually unknown archaeologically. In some instances it might be possible to interpret adjacent four posters as longer rectangular buildings, but for all their seeming orderliness, few of the four-posters from hillforts in the Welsh Marches look like candidates for larger composite rectangular buildings. Perhaps the closest is the series aligning the street leading in from the inner southern entrance at Ffridd Faldwyn (Figure 4.4A; O'Neil, 1942: Figure 8), which bears some resemblance to the period 2 layout at Crickley Hill. In several cases at Midsummer Hill within the area of the four-posters (Figure 4.4C), hearths were located, though several are either too larger or too close to the timber uprights to have been contemporary. They may in any event have been part of the grain storage process, so hardly endorse a domestic use. The conclusion therefore must be that the Croft Ambrey and Midsummer Hill four-posters were granaries, and their concentrated and ordered disposition surely argues a special function for the hillforts of the southern Marches. The ritual dimension revealed in the annexe at Croft Ambrey and dated to a phase of Roman activity may be relevant, but in itself reflects a secondary phase of activity.

By contrast to the absence of roundhouses in the hillforts investigated by Stanford, in the northern Marches roundhouses are certainly in evidence. At Moel y Gaer, Rhosesmor (Guilbert 1975b, 1976, 1981b), the second period of occupation, equated by the excavator with the stone and timber wall rampart, was represented by a number of stake-wall roundhouses and four-poster structures, the distribution of which suggested positively that they were elements in a contemporary, planned layout of the interior (Guilbert 1981b: Figure 18). Some of the four-posters were at the larger end of the size spectrum, up to 4 m², and the size and depth of the holes, substantially greater than the post-holes of the period 1 post-built roundhouses, convinced the excavator that they supported taller structures, perhaps granaries with raised floors or storage buildings with more than one floor level. Though a substantial area of the interior was opened (0.3 ha, ¾ acre), the hillfort encloses 2.4 ha (6 acres) in all, and the excavator stressed the possibility that, in an ordered layout, other types of structure, activity areas, and open spaces may well have existed that were not represented in the excavated sample. On the issue of building plans and functions Guilbert subsequently questioned what he called 'any "working hypothesis" quite so trite and unsubstantiated as an equation of the round with dwellings and the rectangular with storage units' (1981b: 107). He argued that in period 1 at Moel y Gaer, contemporary with its palisaded enclosure, the post-ring roundhouses (ibid. Figure 17) were all structurally very similar, and with one notable exception, were all oriented with their doorways to the south-east. The exception, with its doorway facing west towards the enclosure entrance, he concluded may have served as a guard house. Only 11 out of 29 had surviving evidence of hearths, normally regarded as the clearest sign of domestic occupation, and of these nine also had stake and post-holes around the hearth that probably supported some kind of framework associated with it. Whilst it was possible for traces of the hearth itself not to have survived archaeologically in the remaining majority of houses, only one had evidence of these associated stake-holes. The inference, therefore, was that not all the circular buildings functioned as domestic houses. There was a preponderance of hearths in structures over 8 metres in diameter and an absence of hearths in a number of those of smaller size, but the excavator was cautious in drawing conclusions regarding function on the basis of size from a relatively small sample of the entire enclosure. Particularly puzzling is the association of apparently flimsy stake-wall roundhouses with substantial, earth-fast four-posters, in contrast to the preceding phase of post-built roundhouses and the later shift to rectilinear 'floors' and working areas. This major shift in architectural convention is matched only by the change from rectangular buildings in period 2 at Crickley Hill to circular plans in period 3.

Further north in the Clywd valley there are suggestions of 'zoning' of different structural types within the hillfort at Moel Hiraddug (Brassil et al. 1982). At the north end of the western enclosure are clusters of circular structures which sample excavation demonstrated were houses with low stone wall foundations, more akin to those of north-west Wales than of the northern Marches. Within the eastern enclosure were platforms levelled into the slope of the kind that are commonly interpreted as house foundations, but which excavations at Dinorben showed lacked any definitive structural traces to substantiate this. Finally, at two locations within the western enclosure there were visible under favourable conditions grass-marks indicating the positions of four-poster structures. Whether these concentrations of different features really indicate zoning of activities depends also upon whether any of them belonged to the same phase of occupation in what was evidently a complex sequence.

The element of planning detected at Moel y Gaer was evidently not universal. At the Breiddin (Musson 1991), where both roundhouses of various structural forms and four-posters were found in some numbers, it was not possible to distinguish the same orderly arrangement, and though the majority of four-posters belonged to the later pre-Roman Iron Age occupation, the occurrence of roundhouses and four-posters was not at all exclusive. Furthermore, the layout of four-posters was not in regular alignments or clusters in the manner of Croft Ambrey or Ffridd Faldwyn, for example, and the excavator preferred to see the internal layout as reflecting organic growth rather than planned development.

Ireland and 'Royal Sites'

Hillforts in Britain may display quite dense or relatively sparse structural activity, but they seldom include any outstanding focal features. The Irish 'royal sites', by contrast, enclose major structures that demand interpretation as special on account of their size or complexity in comparison to normal domestic settlements. One of the most spectacular of these ritual or ceremonial foci was the massive, multiple post-ring structure on Site B at Navan fort (Waterman and Lynn 1997), which culminated in the creation of a massive cairn that was apparently fired deliberately and covered with an earthen mound (Plate10b) in 95 BC, based on dendrochronological dating of its central totem. This, however, was only one important element in a complex sequence of structures that dominated the hilltop in the second half of the first millennium BC. The earlier structural phases (3ii–iii) were originally interpreted as a secular settlement, though possibly of a high social status community on the basis of the associated material assemblage. More recently, however, the prevailing view has favoured the site's ritual role from the outset of its later prehistoric occupation. Furthermore, geophysical survey and sample excavation has revealed evidence of an extended central complex, notably a circle of triple ring-slots, designated Site C (Lynn 2000, 2002), that proved to be contiguous and contemporary with Site A, thus forming a conjoined figure-of-eight plan, comparable to the phase 3 structures on Site B and to the Rose phase at Dún Ailinne.

Navan was enclosed by an earthwork with external bank and internal ditch, so that Lynn drew a distinction between this type of enclosure, which he rightly regarded as 'illogical from a defensive point of view', and 'true hillforts, which should therefore be seen as sites with a primarily defensive significance'

(Waterman and Lynn 1997: 215). Though the earthworks at the Ráith na Ríg at Tara (Plate 3a) are plainly non-defensive (Dowling 2006), this is less obvious at Navan, where the steep slope of the hill still gives the interior a considerable height advantage over the outer bank (Plate 10b). Until late in the fieldwork programme, the enclosure earthworks had never been excavated, so that the 'hengiform' layout had prompted the suggestion of a much earlier date for its construction (Simpson 1989). Unlike other examples in Ireland of internally-ditched enclosures, like the Ráith na Ríg or even Dún Ailinne, the Navan enclosure was an almost exact circle, so much closer morphologically to the Neolithic class of henge monument. Neolithic pottery and flint artefacts indicated earlier activity on the hilltop, so that the Iron Age ceremonial centre could have been the culmination of a much longer sequence of sanctity. In contrast to the strategy that has underpinned virtually every hillfort excavation in Britain for the past century of sectioning the defences at the outset in order to establish their structural and chronological sequence, investigation of Navan had targeted first the ploughed-out ring-work that constituted Site A, then the mound that was Site B. There were never any plans for investigating the remainder of the 5 ha (12 acres) enclosure beyond the two focal points on the hilltop. More recently, however, the ditch has been sectioned, and dendrochronological dates, notwithstanding the contrary evidence of a radiocarbon assay, strongly points to the earthworks being constructed at the same period as the phase 4 multi-circle on Site B (Mallory 2000). The steeply profiled ditch was no less than 4.5 metres deep below its present level and was plainly intended to be a formidable barrier, whether against human intruders from without or potent spirits from within (Warner 2000).

A key element in understanding the significance of Navan fort, however, is its potential relationship with other sites in the immediate vicinity, notably Haughey's fort, the King's Stables, and Loughnashade. Of these the relationship between Navan fort and Haughey's fort, just 1 kilometre to the west, must be crucial. First recognized as a triple-ditched enclosure from air photography (Hartnell 1991), construction and occupation of Haughey's fort would appear to date to the Late Bronze Age, with radiocarbon dates from the twelfth to eighth centuries BC, thus preceding the main periods of activity at Navan (Mallory 1988, 1991; Mallory et al. 1996). Finds from Haughey's fort included basic Late Bronze Age pottery types, but also bronze and lignite bracelets, a gold stud and bead, and fragments of gold leaf and wire, material indicative of the site's high social status. It could have been contemporary with the enigmatic site at the King's Stables (Lynn 1977), just a couple of hundred metres to the north-east, where a penannular bank enclosed an artificial pond, within which were found Late Bronze Age mould fragments and quantities of animal bone, suggestive of ritual activity at the beginning of the first millennium BC. Just below Navan fort to the north-east lies Loughnashade, where in the late eighteenth century, four bronze horns were retrieved, together with human remains, suggestive of a ritual deposit from the Iron Age. Lynn (Waterman and Lynn 1997: 217) suggested that the relationship between Navan and Loughnashade may have been analogous to that between Haughey's fort and the King's Stables, and it would certainly be attractive to regard the whole complex from Late Bronze Age through the first millennium BC as a high-status ceremonial and ritual landscape, in which only Haughey's fort really resembles a hillfort in the conventional sense.

At Dún Ailinne, Co. Kildare (Plate 3b; Johnston and Wailes 2007) the enclosing earthwork, like Navan with internal ditch, was sectioned, and was found to be of dump construction with no evidence whatsoever of reinforcement. Contrary to the excavator's assertion, however, that there was no sign that the ditch had been recut or that the bank had been remodelled (ibid. 27) the section (ibid. CD Figure 3.1) shows every likelihood that the ditch had been recut, as it appeared to have been in the entrance (ibid. CD Figure 3.2), whilst the multiple tip layers in the bank do not contradict the possibility of more than one episode of ditch cleaning. If the earthwork is indeed contemporary in whole or in part with the multiple phases of the summit occupation, it would be surprising if this were not the case, even allowing for the fact that a symbolic enclosure might not require the regular maintenance of a practical or defensive one. A single radiocarbon date suggested that it was constructed in the Iron Age rather than the Neolithic, though prolific Neolithic material was found in the course of the summit excavations.

The complex sequence of structures exposed on the summit plainly proclaims the site's special status. A ceremonial function seems particularly appropriate for the 'Rose phase', which consists of two circular buildings in figure-of-eight arrangement, the larger of which, with a maximum diameter of 38 m, is considerably in excess of anything that could have been roofed, though the adjoining building may have been. The triple, concentric ring-grooves of the larger enclosure were of graded depth, suggesting that the structure was tiered like a grandstand. From its entrance, an avenue of postholes flanked by palisades suggests a ceremonial approach to the complex, leading eastward towards the principal entrance to the enclosure.

Activity appears to have been concentrated on the summit, and elsewhere across the site, magnetometer and resistivity survey was totally unproductive. Likewise test excavation of several substantial areas on the north side of the hill yielded no structural evidence. These areas were stripped mechanically, on the not unreasonable grounds that features in topsoil would not have survived intensive ploughing, but, as Guilbert (1975b: Figure 4) demonstrated elsewhere, ephemeral structures like stake-wall roundhouses would not have survived in these circumstances. Air photography revealed little additional information regarding the occupation of the enclosure or its immediate environs. The probability is that the site was not intensively occupied other than in its central focus.

If we regard the Irish 'royal sites' as having a ceremonial and ritual aspect, rather than being domestic, even if high-status, settlements, then the faunal assemblages may be interpreted not simply as indicative of economy but potentially as evidence for ritual feasting (McCormick 2009). A comparison between the faunal remains from Navan fort and Dún Ailinne shows a predominance at the former of pig in comparison to cattle at the latter, with a marked preference for veal. Both boar and bull, of course, are potent symbols in La Tène art, including motifs on continental and British coinage.

At Tara the 'hengiform' class of enclosure known as the Ráith na Ríg could have had a ritual or ceremonial context from a much earlier date, with the Neolithic Mound of the Hostages (Dumna na nGiall) notably contained within its circuit. Geophysical survey (Newman 1995) has indicated the possibility that the approach to the enclosure's entrances may have been demarcated by processional 'avenues'. Furthermore, at the north-west entrance the causeway across the ditch evidently resulted from secondary infilling, suggesting a more complicated sequence of enclosure than was formerly appreciated. Excavation in the early 1950s had sectioned the bank and ditch, and established the presence of a palisade trench just inside the ditch. It also recovered evidence for metalworking on the site. All of this was confirmed and amplified by re-excavation of O'Ríordáin's trenches in 1997 (Roche 2002). The metalworking activities were dated to the early fourth century BC, thus pre-dating by some time the construction of the earthworks in the first century BC. The fact that both bronze and iron working, together with glass making, was taking place on the site need not detract from its ritual significance, since smithing was traditionally in later Irish society an activity that had supernatural connotations.

Whilst it is generally agreed that these 'hengiform' enclosures were not defensive in the conventional sense, Warner (2000) has argued persuasively that their earthworks were designed both to keep the uninitiated out—perhaps in some cases using the bank as a vantage point to view proceedings within, rather like a Roman amphitheatre—and to keep the potentially dangerous supernatural forces within their allotted enclosure. The hengiform design of the 'royal sites' is not, therefore, some peculiarly Irish aberration of hillfort but a customized form of enclosure fit for purpose. In effect, it was defensive, but designed to protect the outside world from the other world. The fact that older monuments like the Mound of the Hostages were incorporated within these 'ritual' sites is therefore not coincidental, and Mallory has recently suggested (14 ICCS field visit, August 2011) that the mound on Site B at Navan may have been a deliberate attempt to emulate the great funerary monuments of the past.

Wessex and southern England

We have seen that individual houses within hillforts, even if constructed of timber rather than with more durable stone foundations, can still survive in upland locations. But in Wessex, the intensity of agricultural usage might have been expected to have obliterated surface traces of internal settlement. A notable exception is the 22 ha (55 acres) fort at Hod Hill, where only the western half of the interior had been ploughed up to the Second World War, so that O. G. S. Crawford in 1925 was still able to observe 'perfectly preserved' hut-circles and 'village streets' (Crawford and Keiller 1928: 41). The two roadways are clearly visible on his air photograph (Figure 6), beginning as a single feature leading in from the north-east Stepleton gate before dividing, one branch leading towards the Home gate at the south-east corner of the enclosure, the other leading towards enclosure 36, which Richmond (1968: 23) interpreted as the 'chieftain's hut'. Apart from its compound, there was no great variation in size of houses to indicate any difference in status or function. As Richmond observed, the density of buildings is much sparser towards the western side of the surviving segment, which may indicate a measure of zoning in the use of the interior. Pits were recorded in the extant sector, but in no great profusion and not in concentrations, as at Danebury, for example. Across the Stour valley at Hambledon Hill (Figure 1.7) there was a rather greater range in sizes of house platforms, from less than 5 metres up to nearly 14. Noting that none of the platforms showed evidence of multi-period construction, and working once again on the principle that new platforms would not have been dug if others were unoccupied, Mercer (1986) calculated that Hambledon could have sustained a population of between 1,000 and 2,000 people, in effect a community of town size. The internal plan shows no special evidence of urban planning, though house platforms along the east side of the central section preserve the tiered alignment of earlier terracing, linked to a field system that is also visible outside the north-east defences. It would be tempting to see Hod and Hambledon as twin sentinels of neighbouring communities across the Stour valley, but the dating evidence suggests in fact that Hambledon was occupied in the earlier Iron Age, with Hod Hill being pre-eminent in the later pre-Roman period. The establishment of the Claudian fort at Hod Hill within the confines of the Iron Age fort was surely intended as an unequivocal political statement, reflecting the hillfort's role as a paramount Durotrigian centre.

Among other hillforts in Wessex where later agriculture has not obliterated surface traces of Iron Age occupation, are Chalbury in Dorset and Beacon Hill in Hampshire, both at around 4 ha (10 acres) substantially smaller than Hod and Hambledon. At Chalbury (Whitley 1943) some seventy circular platforms or depressions are spread throughout the interior, some undoubtedly house foundations, while the smaller linear spread towards the northern end of the enclosure probably represents pits. The summit is crowned by two Bronze Age barrows, too prominent for them not to have had some significance for the Iron Age community. Beacon Hill (Eagles 1991) had thirty clear house stances and a similar number that could have been houses or working platforms. The number of pits is once again small in proportion to the number of probable houses. The houses themselves also display a range of construction types and sizes, some of the larger penannular banks with external ditches being well within the range of larger Wessex roundhouses. At the eastern end of the site, the houses appear to be broadly disposed along the contours of the hill, but otherwise there is no obvious sign of a planned layout.

Among those hillforts where geophysical survey has yielded interesting results is Castle Ditches, Tisbury, at the head of the Nadder valley in Wiltshire (Payne *et al.* 2006: 103–7). At least twenty roundhouse foundations are visible, with diameters ranging from 10 to 15 metres, which are provisionally assigned to an earlier Iron Age occupation. To the later occupation are attributed a series of smaller ditched enclosures of irregular outline, but broadly disposed in clusters on either side of a 'roadway' extending from the east to west gateways. Pits are also in evidence, though scattered throughout the enclosure. The multivallate defences and complex entrances would appear to endorse the site's candidature as a 'developed' hillfort, being comparable in plan and scale to Cadbury Castle. The occurrence of clusters of smaller ditched enclosures within the hillfort, apparently representative of its later phase of occupation, is of particular interest, as this is the layout that characterizes later pre-Roman non-fortified Iron Age settlements on Cranborne Chase.

Assuming that these concentrations of roundhouses are indicative of contemporary occupation, there can be little doubt that some Wessex hillforts served a resident community, engaged in a range of activities, domestic, economic and agricultural, and doubtless also ritual and ceremonial. There are, however, also a number of instances in which evidence of residential use is limited or absent, whether in terms of surface remains and geophysical survey or, more definitively, where excavations has taken place. At Balksbury (Wainwright 1969; Wainwright and Davies 1995; Ellis and Rawlings 2001), around 80 per cent of an 18 ha (45 acres) enclosure was stripped between 1967 and 1997 to reveal only very sparse structural remains of its Late Bronze Age and earlier Iron Age occupation, with rather more evidence of activity in the central area late in the pre-Roman Iron Age, when the enclosure earthworks had long fallen into abeyance. In the absence of obvious traces of habitation, the excavators' preferred conclusion was that the site was essentially a stock enclosure, well sited with easy access to a water supply and good pasture, and possibly intended primarily for seasonal use. In these circumstances, we might infer that any houses could have been of the more ephemeral stake-wall construction that would not have survived the site's mechanical stripping.

The topographic location of the enclosure as well as its size militates against a primarily defensive role, which may further explain the fact that the earthworks do not appear to have been maintained in good repair subsequent to the initial phase of usage.

At Winklebury, a smaller but still larger than average enclosure at 7.6 ha (19 acres), nearly 40 per cent was stripped mechanically down to chalk for cleaning and recording (Smith 1977). Stratigraphy had apparently been destroyed by generations of ploughing, and the phasing was therefore dependent upon pottery from individual features. On this basis, the earlier phase of occupation was characterized by post-built roundhouses, some matching in size the major roundhouses of the Wessex later Bronze Age and early Iron Age, and four-posters. The layout showed little evidence of zoning, though there was some clustering of four-posters in the south-east of the area opened. The four-posters interestingly were of two contrasting types, one with large post-pits, the other with regular house-sized post-holes (ibid. Figure 13), the implication presumably being that not all four-posters supported raised floors and heavy superstructure or served a similar function. In the later phase of occupation, the roundhouses appear to have been founded on ring-grooves. Four-posters had evidently been replaced by pits, of which the overwhelming majority belong to the later occupation. An area of 'working hollows' also was assigned to the late phase. Winklebury certainly shows a distinct contrast in structural types between the early and late occupation, which is matched by the shift in rampart construction from early timber-faced wall to glacis-style dump in the later phase (Robertson-Mackay 1977), perhaps with an interlude of abandonment between the two. Despite the paucity of evidence for cereal processing, the density of structural remains and the substantial character of the early houses seems consistent with regular occupation.

We have already seen that the excavation of hillfort interiors was severely constrained by practical considerations until the advent of 'rescue archaeology' provided the opportunity for wholesale stripping of sites in advance of development. Though Danebury was a long-term investigation, excavation of the interior progressed following the felling of dead or dying trees and in advance of replanting. Tree roots and earlier agricultural improvement had damaged the deposits above chalk bedrock to the extent that the overburden was removed mechanically, so that effectively the Danebury interior suffered from the same limitations that apply to other salvage excavations, namely that structures based on ephemeral foundations, like the stake-wall roundhouses that were preserved in the lee of the ramparts, would not have survived in the open interior, though some evidence of ring-groove structures did. After a campaign of twenty years, 57.3 per cent of the interior was cleared, though within this area in the second decade features were only sampled on a selective basis.

The occupation of the Danebury hillfort has been broadly divided into two principal phases; an early occupation assigned to the sixth and fifth centuries BC, and a later dating from around 300 BC. Already in the early phase there was a clear zoning of activity within the enclosure, based essentially on the main east–west axis of the street that led between the two entrances. South of this line, the emphasis was on domestic settlement, represented structurally by houses, storage pits and four-posters, while the northern sector was dominated by a concentration of storage pits, with houses and their associated pits and four-posters adjacent to the ramparts. A network of subsidiary roads contributed to the zoning effect. The density of pits implies a capacity for storage well beyond that of contemporary farm settlements, so that Danebury could have provided storage for the grain surplus of a wider community as a 'territorial focus for processing and storage' and perhaps redistribution (Cunliffe 2005: 427). From the beginning of the third century, Cunliffe argued that Danebury acquired special status as a 'central place'. In the process, its enclosing earthworks were radically reorganized. The south-west gate was blocked and the main east gate was refurbished and made more monumental in scale. The main street continued to serve as the focal divide internally. A subordinate street crossing the southern sector was now lined with four-posters, as was a lesser road just inside the rampart. On the north side of the site, circular houses and pits clustered in the lee of the rampart, while the interior was given over to houses and a scatter of pits, with some four-posters spilling over the road from the southern distribution. Several larger rectilinear structures, centrally located, were interpreted as shrines. The significance of these changes over time were discussed by the excavator (Cunliffe 1995) with the advantage of the outcome of the Danebury Environs Programme, which enabled the local evidence to be considered in the context of its relationship to the wider regional community.

EXTRAMURAL SETTLEMENT

The investigation of extramural settlement in the immediate vicinity of a hillfort, as opposed to settlements in the wider catchment area, has been generally neglected in hillfort research strategies, though chance finds have indicated the possibility of significant occupation of the slopes around the defensive circuit and presumably therefore in some directly dependent relationship to the hillfort. In upland regions, extant remains of house platforms can sometimes be seen outside the defensive enclosure, as at Carn Fadrun on the Llŷn peninsula or at Foel Trigarn in Pembrokeshire (Plate 14b), as recent air photography has confirmed. The problem remains, of course, that these houses need not have been contemporary with the occupation of the hillfort, though equally there is no reason to exclude that possibility.

In southern England, two hillforts in particular have long been known for having external settlement in close proximity, Castle Hill, Little Wittenham, Oxfordshire (Figure 4.5a), and Battlesbury Camp, Wiltshire (Figure 4.5b). The external settlement at Castle Hill, Little Wittenham, occupies a substantial swathe of land extending 500 metres or more on the south-west side of the hillfort (Allen *et al.* 2011). The earliest investigation (Rhodes 1948) yielded material remains suggesting a date in the later Bronze Age–earliest Iron Age transition, and an early date for the external settlement was reinforced by Rutland's rescue excavations in 1970 (Hingley 1980). This might have suggested occupation before the construction and use of the hillfort defences, though Hingley's assessment of casual finds of pottery from the hillfort in Reading Museum and the Ashmolean (he might have added from the British Museum too, catalogued under Brightwell) suggested that external and internal settlements could have been contemporary. More recently, geophysical survey and test excavation within the hillfort has indicated a smaller, ditched enclosure on the summit, apparently dating to the later Bronze Age (Allen and

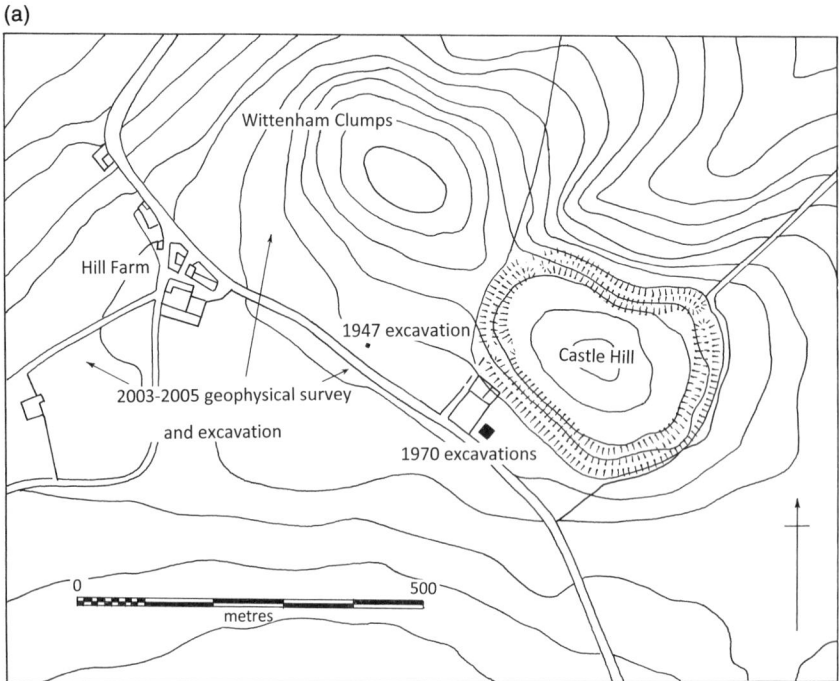

Figure 4.5. Hillforts with external settlement: (a) Castle Hill, Little Wittenham, Oxfordshire, (b) (opposite) Battlesbury Camp, Wiltshire. Drawing and photograph by D. W. Harding.

Lamdin-Whymark 2005: 69–71), though the primary rampart of the hillfort itself, for which there was inadequate dating evidence, may have been built not long after. As to the external settlement, test excavation in the vicinity of Hill Farm showed an extensive area of occupation successively spanning the early and middle Iron Ages, and represented by ditched enclosures, circular gullies, probably associated with roundhouses, as well as pits and possible four-post structures (ibid. 77–82). Where an external settlement is contemporary or later than the internal occupation it would be feasible to think of population expansion or endemic growth resulting in secondary spread of activity beyond the hillfort enclosure. But with external occupation apparently from the outset, it would be tempting to develop Hingley's suggestion that the earliest enclosure was designed as 'the citadel and acropolis of an extensive undefended settlement' (1980: 54). The more recent excavators considered various options, including the external occupation as a 'satellite settlement of lower status' as well as the separation spatially of functionally-different activities (Allen *et al.* 2009: 197–8).

At Battlesbury, traces of external settlement were recorded by Mrs Cunnington (1924) and again by Sonia Chadwick (Hawkes) (Chadwick and Thompson 1956). More recently at Battlesbury Bowl (Ellis and Powell 2008), a strip 440 metres long was excavated along a ridge to the north and north-east of the hillfort, which, together with air-photographic evidence, suggested a regulated landscape around the hillfort, including areas designated

(b)

for occupation within ditched boundaries. The structural evidence included post-built roundhouses, pit clusters, and groups of four- or six-poster buildings. As at Little Wittenham, there is evidence of occupation from the Late Bronze Age–Early Iron Age transition, but an intensification of activity in the middle pre-Roman Iron Age. While the inadequacy of information regarding the use and occupation of the hillfort itself precludes a reliable assessment of the relationship between the two, it seems improbable that a hillfort of the structural complexity of Battlesbury was not at some stage in contemporary occupation with the external settlement. Equally challenging is its relationship to Scratchbury, less than 2 kilometres to the south-east. It has been remarked that Scratchbury is hardly located to best advantage in terms of defence, its interior being visible from the valley floor (Bowden and McOmish 1989). Battlesbury and Scratchbury are inter-visible, with Middle Hill, devoid of known occupation other than a Bronze Age barrow, between them, a relationship that may be compared to hillfort landscapes elsewhere.

The evidence from Battlesbury (Cunnington 1924) and from Broxmouth (Hill 1982a) raises the possibility that cemeteries may have been located in proximity to hillforts. The fact that hillfort excavation has seldom extended beyond the perimeter earthworks might thus have contributed to the apparent paucity of formal cemeteries in the archaeological record for much of the British Iron Age. In continental Europe by contrast, the association of cemeteries with hillforts is not uncommon from the Late Bronze Age onwards, as at the Cayla de Mailhac in Languedoc with its associated cemeteries of Le Moulin and Le Grand Bassin (Louis *et al.* 1955, 1958, 1960), or in the classic *Fürstensitze* and *Fürstengräber* of late Hallstatt Europe from the Heuneburg in Baden-Württemberg to Stična in Slovenia. The existence of external settlement (*Aussensiedlung*) has been long established at the Heuneburg (Kurz 2000), though it should be noted that the evidence recovered beneath the Giessübel-Talhau tumuli was some 450 m from the hillfort walls, raising issues of definition as to what constitutes an extended site and what distinguishes it from a cluster of separate if dependent sites.

At Rathgall in Co. Wicklow (Raftery 1976), occupation certainly extended beyond the confines of the hillfort enclosure. Rathgall was one of the first hillforts in Ireland to yield evidence of Late Bronze Age activity, but the excavator was faced with the same problem that had confronted hillfort studies in Britain in the 1970s, and in south-west Ireland more recently, how to demonstrate in the absence of diagnostic finds or radiocarbon dates from definitive contexts whether the defences were contemporary with the internal occupation. There were three broadly concentric circuits of enclosure at Rathgall—the innermost was patently later—two inner ramparts closely spaced with a third outermost rampart enclosing a total of 7 ha (18 acres). Raftery adopted the rationale that the construction of the enclosures most probably corresponded to the preponderance of material evidence from the site, dating to the later Bronze Age, including Dowris-phase gold- and bronzework. If so, however, the enclosures did not constrain the later Bronze Age activities on the hilltop, for he also uncovered quite extensive evidence for settlement on the slopes outside the hillfort. If the ramparts were indeed contemporary, therefore, we are bound to ask what distinguished the internal occupation from external, whether there was a dependent community occupying the immediate environs of this high-status centre, or whether the threefold ramparts segregated groups progressively from those who had access to the innermost enclave. The focus of activity within the central area was concentrated on two circular features defined by ring trenches, one probably a house (Raftery 1976: Figure 2), though containing a ritual pit deposit, the other enclosing three cremation burials and more pits containing Late Bronze Age bronzes (Raftery 1981: Figure 30). The implication therefore is certainly that the inner occupation had a ritual dimension, and that the Rathgall hillfort was not simply a defended domestic and agricultural settlement.

The important conclusion is that we should break out of the preconception of hillforts as defined and constrained by their earthworks and instead consider the immediate environs of the enclosure, with extramural settlement, watersources, stock areas, and perhaps even some arable as integral to the 'site'. This is a perspective that has been neglected for too long (Harding 1979: 12) in favour of the (perfectly legitimate) landscape approach to the context of hillforts, which we shall examine next.

5

Hillforts in the Landscape

Landscape in common usage refers to the physical landforms of hills, valleys, rivers, and lakes, together with vegetational cover that may have changed significantly over the centuries depending upon environmental factors as well as the impact of human settlement. It may also refer to the man-made landscape of buildings and settlements, roads and boundaries made by human occupation over the centuries. Although field archaeologists tend to focus their attention upon 'sites', it has long been recognized that individual settlements cannot have functioned in isolation from their environment, nor from their neighbours in the landscape. Equally important, although at the limits of archaeological inference, is how later prehistoric people viewed their own environment, which can hardly have been a matter of ignorance or indifference. The fact that a Neolithic long barrow extends down the spine of the hillfort at Hambledon Hill, or that a causewayed enclosure lies concentrically within the circuit at the Trundle in Sussex, may not have determined the hillfort's location, but it is hardly likely that Iron Age builders were unaware of their antiquity and significance.

Landscape archaeology is often wrongly regarded as a recent contribution to field archaeology. Following the long-term excavations at Danebury of the 1970s and 1980s, the Danebury Environs Project still stands as one of the most significant advances in hillfort studies, together with landscape surveys around Maiden Castle, Dorset, and Cadbury Castle among others. A pioneer in this field was Christopher Hawkes, encouraged from the 1920s by O. G. S. Crawford. In the St Catharine's Hill report, Hawkes had stated explicitly that his purpose was to show 'the place occupied by the hill settlement in the life of the contemporary countryside' (Hawkes *et al.* 1930: 6), and in his Hampshire hillfort excavations of the 1930s he demonstrated this principle, notably at Quarley Hill (Hawkes 1939), where his excavation was designed to elucidate the relationship between hillfort and those linear features that physically linked it to its surrounding landscape (Figure 2.3).

HILLFORT ENVIRONS: CASE STUDIES

The Danebury Environs Programme

The Danebury excavation was the ultimate sequel to Hawkes' Hampshire hillfort campaign, and with its Environs Programme, extended the study of the hillfort in its landscape context on a scale never previously practicable. This entailed a study of documentary sources and air photographs as well as field survey with selective excavation. The region chosen was a tract of chalkland between the flood plain of the river Test and the Bourne valley, though the core area was centred on Danebury within an arc formed by the neighbouring hillforts of Woolbury, Bury Hill, and Quarley Hill (Cunliffe 2000). Implicit in this approach is the idea that the hillort was in some meaningful sense, politically, socially, or economically, a *central place* in the Iron Age landscape, a fundamental tenet that survived to Cunliffe's final synthesis. Subsequently he also entertained the possibility that some hillforts had performed a peripheral rather than central role (see also Harding 1979), noting that 'hilltop fortifications of comparable size were being erected at Figsbury, Quarley and Woolbury either as the foci of rival polities or possibly as boundary markers' (Cunliffe 2000: 177), the latter role being one that came to prominence in the early historic period. Much of the subsequent criticism of Cunliffe's interpretation of Danebury stems from the central place concept, and more particularly from the consequential inference that the hillfort and its territory were controlled by an elite within a hierarchical social structure. Even in later overviews (Cunliffe 2000), the idea that the hillfort was controlled throughout by a 'paramount' authority exercising 'coercive power' over 'vassals' (ibid. 183) remains the essence of the social reconstruction. Whilst the present writer takes no special issue with this view, the hierarchical model is not universally accepted by those who favour a more egalitarian social interpretation prior to the immediately pre-Roman period.

It is clear that hillforts were constructed within a landscape that had already undergone extensive division and demarcation by the later Bronze Age. When the landscape of prehistoric Britain first became consciously the territory of neighbouring communities, when the distinction between 'our land' and 'their land' became an issue, remains problematic, and may even have preceded the establishment of permanent, sedentary settlement. In central southern Britain, a crucial change from an 'open' to 'enclosed' landscape occurred by the second half of the second millennium BC. Field systems covering extensive tracts of land were apparently laid out in the Middle Bronze Age. At Windy Dido, west of Quarley Hill, coaxial fields covering some 90 ha represent a major investment of effort in a system of cultivation plots. In some cases, as at Quarley Hill or on Stockbridge Down north-east of Woolbury, these were linked to spinal linear earthworks, but in some instances linear earthworks of the later Bronze Age actually cut diagonally across pre-existing field patterns, indicating a continuing process of landscape change. Many of the linear earthworks show evidence of secondary use, perhaps continuing into the earlier Iron Age (Cunliffe 2000: 155–62). At Quarley Hill, the construction of the hillfort is late in the sequence, perhaps early in the fifth century BC, though possibly with an earlier palisaded phase.

Shortly after 300 BC, as we have seen, Danebury underwent a major structural reconfiguration, involving the rebuilding of its eastern gateway with massive external hornworks. The south-west gate was blocked and its causeway across the ditch removed, apparently symbolizing a more fundamental political and economic reorientation of the site, away from the south-western axis with Wessex that had dominated its earlier economic regime in favour of a realignment towards the South Downs economic and cultural zone (ibid. 181). In ceramic terms, this shift is reflected in the distribution of saucepan pottery of the St Catharine's Hill–Worthy Down sub-group (ibid. Figure 4.30). The range of Danebury's internal functions nevertheless continued largely unchanged: 'a massive storage capacity, in the form of rectangular post structures and below-ground silos, was maintained' (ibid. 181) and its role as a central place was seemingly enhanced. Figsbury, Quarley Hill, and probably Woolbury remained 'undeveloped', so that Danebury's territory was extended to a radius of 10 kilometres or more, with its nearest neighbours of comparable status being St Catharine's Hill to the south-east, Sidbury to the north-west, and Yarnbury across the Bourne and Avon to the west. It is worth comparing this to the territories attributed by Härke (1979) and more recently Diepeveen-Jansen (2007) to *Fürstensitze* of the late Hallstatt period in west central Europe, which can be 100 km across and potentially therefore in a totally different league (Figure 5.1).

A major issue in Cunliffe's interpretation arises from the 'virtual absence' of the St Catharine's Hill–Worthy Down ceramic assemblage, found in prolific quantities in the hillfort itself, from the settlements examined in the Environs Programme at Houghton Down, Nettlebank Copse, and Suddern Farm. The obvious inference was that these sites had been abandoned at a time broadly coincident with the refurbishing of Danebury. But the excavator went further, to conclude that the displaced population from these abandoned settlements had moved into the hillfort itself. This 'simple' explanation (ibid. 182, 184) presents two major difficulties. First, there is no evidence of any significant intensification of the residential role of the hillfort at this time, the round-houses being still largely peripheral to the clearly dominant storage function. With just over 5 ha enclosed, Danebury simply did not have the residential capacity of, say, Hod Hill at 20 ha or Maiden Castle with not much less. Second, the consequent suggestion, that land in the Danebury environs was worked from the hillfort and that more distant sources of supply to fill the

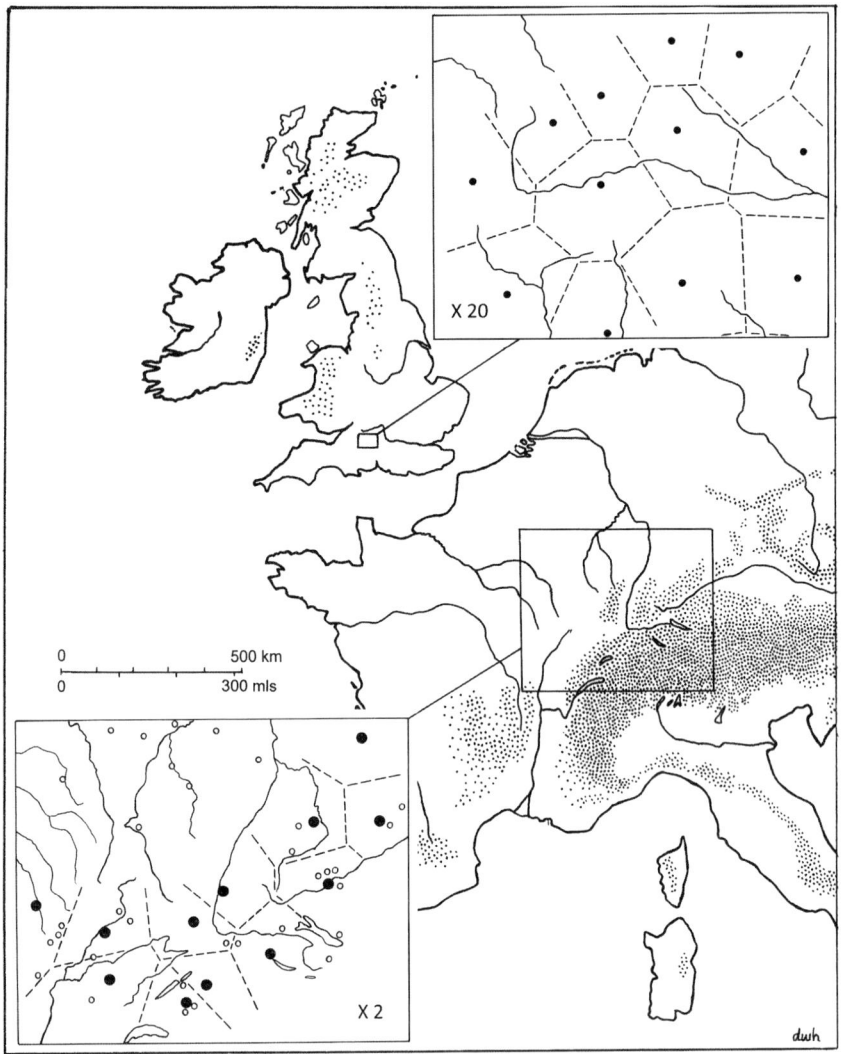

Figure 5.1. Hillfort territories in north Wiltshire compared with *Fürstensitze* territories in west central Europe. Drawing by D. W. Harding adapted from Cunliffe (2005) and Härke (1979).

storage capacity were controlled by unspecified satellites unaffected by whatever crisis had triggered the abandonment of the farmsteads of the inner zone of dependency, hardly carries conviction.

This problem highlights one shortcoming of the Danebury Environs Programme. Intensive as was the air-photographic coverage, it necessarily has an overwhelming bias towards *enclosed* sites. *Unenclosed* settlements are detected by air photography much less frequently because they are only easily spotted under optimum conditions. More commonly, they are uncovered by chance in the course of commercial development involving transects across a landscape, or occasionally as one facet of a multi-period settlement with other more conspicuous components. What might occasion a shift from enclosed to unenclosed settlement is uncertain, but it is perfectly plausible to suggest that unenclosed settlements existed in parallel to enclosed sites throughout the first millennium BC, and that the Danebury Environs evidence is the product of a shift in emphasis between the two that is exaggerated in the archaeological record by circumstances of differential survival or discovery.

An alternative explanation would be to suppose that the displaced communities did move to the hillfort, not as refugees in a destabilizing political environment, but as part of an expansion of the hillfort community to include extramural settlement. The examples of Battlesbury and Castle Hill, Little Wittenham, or Rathgall in Co. Wicklow, as we have seen, have long presented a case for more extensive excavation immediately outside hillforts. In the case of Danebury, earthworks adjacent to the outer rampart on its south side have been interpreted as stock corrals providing a significant area of protected pasture (Cunliffe 2005: 428). This and adjacent areas around the outer earthworks could have been occupied as intensively as the internal sequence.

Cunliffe (2005: 426–8) characterized the agricultural regime of the Early and Middle Iron Age Wessex as dominated by cereal production, with pits and upstanding granaries providing bulk storage, and sheep rearing on a substantial scale, both for meat and for wool and secondary products. In the period of the developed hillforts there was an intensification of arable production. In terms of numbers represented, the faunal assemblage at Danebury suggested an increase in sheep with corresponding decrease in cattle, though Grant (1991) had qualified this by suggesting that the latter were husbanded more intensively and the former less so. It is possible that this shift in economic emphasis prompted the apparent change in the settlement pattern in the Danebury environs. The late pre-Roman phase saw a marked reversal of the balance between cattle and sheep, accompanied seemingly by a decline in the resident population in the fort, though not its total abandonment. In the surrounding countryside the settlement regime included once again significant 'enditched settlements', attributed by Cunliffe to an elite within the social hierarchy, with the lesser orders occupying 'clustered enclosure settlements' of the kind that are widely represented in Wessex in the late pre-Roman Iron Age.

There are plainly many issues that remain to be resolved, notably arising from the possibility that excavation in the immediate external vicinity of the hillfort might cast a very different light on the nature of hillfort occupation, and in relation to the very significant bias in the landscape survey towards enclosed rather than unenclosed sites. This said, there is no doubt that the Danebury programme was the most important single initiative of the third quarter of the twentieth century in British Iron Age studies.

The Traprain Law Environs Project

The Traprain Law Environs Project (TLEP) appears to have been consciously modelled on the Danebury programme, though on a more modest scale. Haselgrove's report (2009) presented the results of excavations of three enclosures with sampling of three more, all sites of later prehistoric date revealed as air-photographic crop marks in the environs of Traprain Law in East Lothian. A principal objective of the exercise was to establish the date of occupation of the satellite settlements in relation to the occupational sequence at Traprain Law itself. In view of the poverty of the material assemblage, the task was inherently more difficult than in the Danebury context, where the assemblage was more prolific and included a broadly credible ceramic sequence. The TLEP coincided with renewed investigation of Traprain itself, initiated by the National Museums of Scotland, and rescue excavations carried out in advance of major upgrading of the A1 between Haddington and Dunbar. Though not designed as a linked programme, all three contributed to an evaluation of the relationship between the hillfort and the sites in its immediate landscape environment.

Superficially, the results of the TLEP excavations hardly look impressive in terms of structural remains or artefactual assemblages. Some of the amorphous scoops or spreads of cobbled paving may seem unconvincing as truncated remains of buildings, but these ephemeral remains are often all that survive. Dating and cultural attribution has always been hampered by the sparse and largely undiagnostic material assemblage, as a result of which fieldwalking has been a generally unrewarding exercise. Despite Fraser Hunter's best efforts, even he has to admit that 'teasing patterns from the material is tricky, as the quantities per site are small' (Hunter 2009: 148), and for the pre-Roman period even that may be an optimistic assessment. Likewise, geomagnetic survey has proved problematic in the past because of the intractable nature of the local geology, and though improved instrumentation has resulted in significant progress, comparison of air photographs and geomagnetic surveys (Haselgrove 2009: Appendix 1) still shows problem areas.

Air-photographic coverage in south-east Scotland has been generally very good, though there are blank areas, probably attributable to soils and land use, which can distort distributions. Ditched settlements as elsewhere are more likely to register as crop-marks than palisaded or unenclosed sites. Whereas the TLEP focused on enclosed sites, sites uncovered by investigations on the line of the new A1 were predominantly open, as at Phantassie and elsewhere, unsurprisingly perhaps since archaeological representations at the planning stage had encouraged the route's avoidance of known enclosures. Enclosed sites with a complex sequence of occupation, of course, may reveal episodes of unenclosed settlement. Particularly common in south-east Scotland are the later 'scooped' settlements like those from Knowes, Standingstone, and Whittingehame Tower in the TLEP area.

The choice of sites for excavation in the TLEP was determined essentially by the air-photographic record, which included both 'curvilinear' and 'rectilinear' enclosures. This basic classification has been long recognized (McMillan 2001), and the assumption that rectilinear plans are characteristic of the later pre-Roman Iron Age seems broadly to be justified. Most ditched enclosures identified by air photography have been conventionally assigned to the Iron Age, for which period ironically the TLEP yielded relatively little evidence for occupation. Several sites produced evidence of later Bronze Age enclosure, broadly contemporary with one period of intensive activity at Traprain itself, though not necessarily with any length of occupation, and there may have been an element of mobility in the settlement pattern. By contrast, investigations on the line of the A1 produced very little evidence of later Bronze Age activity, suggesting perhaps a preference in this period for enclosed settlement. In fact, the A1 transect, like the TLEP settlements, was largely devoid of occupation in the earlier Iron Age too, as was Traprain Law itself, despite the older conventional belief that it was an important Votadinian *oppidum* at this time. This, of course, need not exclude the possibility that the hillfort was enclosed and used for purposes other than permanent settlement. The apparent paucity of evidence for earlier Iron Age occupation in the TLEP area, by contrast to Broxmouth or Dryburn Bridge (Dunwell 2007) and elsewhere in the East Lothian coastal belt, led Haselgrove (2009: 229) to suggest that settlements of the earlier Iron Age may have been fewer but larger and occupied for longer, resulting in a disproportionately sparse representation in the archaeological record. The absence of diagnostic artefacts for the earlier Iron Age, however, imposes undue reliance on radiocarbon determinations, which in some cases could be residual rather than from sealed contexts, and hence not a true indicator of a settlement's span of occupation, as Sharples (2011) argued for Standingstone, so that the paucity of Iron Age sites may prove more apparent than real. In the later pre-Roman Iron Age there was initially a renewed emphasis on enclosure, including more rectilinear plans, before enclosure was generally abandoned in favour of open or 'scooped' settlements, coinciding with the intensive reoccupation of Traprain Law itself.

The conventional interpretation of the occupational sequence at Traprain Law has also undergone reappraisal as a result of the more recent excavations (Armit *et al.* 1999, 2000). Feachem (1956) had proposed a fivefold sequence of enclosure, progressively expanding until its final reduction in a late Roman or post-Roman phase with the construction of the 'Cruden wall', named after an earlier excavator and the only one that is clear and uncontentious today. Recent work has left no doubt, however, that the hill was intensively occupied in the second and third centuries AD, when it is possible that some of the

126 Iron Age Hillforts in Britain and Beyond

rectilinear enclosures identified from air photography in close proximity were also still in use (Armit 1997: 103, Figure 69). For the earlier walls an Iron Age date is possible, but to suggest that the hill was enclosed during its Late Bronze Age use might currently strain the evidence. That important phase of activity is attested to not only by the older finds of Late Bronze Age bronzes, but by a recent series of radiocarbon dates that consistently indicate activity in the ninth century BC.

Upper Eskdale

In south-east Scotland, as a result of relatively intense air-photographic survey, individual hillforts like the Chesters at Drem (Figure 5.2a) and Kae Heughs by Barney Mains (Figure 5.2b) can be related to a wider landscape of pit alignments and lesser enclosures (Harding 2004a: Figure 3.14), while in upland locations the survival of extant earthworks, as at Tamshiel Rig in Roxburghshire (RCAHMS 1956: No. 943; Halliday 1982) affords a comparable landscape context. Less familiar are the sites of the south-western Borders. Despite extensive destruction by afforestation, the landscape surrounding the

(a)

Figure 5.2. Hillforts of the East Lothian plain: (a) Chesters, Drem; (b) (opposite) Kae Heughs, Barney Mains, Drem. Air photographs by D. W. Harding.

confluence of the Black and White Esk in eastern Dumfriesshire (RCAHMS 1997) preserves the relict landscapes of two adjacent domains, dominated by inter-visible hillforts at Castle O'er (Figure 5.3a) and Bailiehill (Figure 5.3b), both occupied in the Iron Age and into the Roman period. That they have a similar occupational history is suggested by the fact that both have inner enclosures densely occupied, with outer annexes in which there is no trace of extant buildings. Both are multi-period, Castle O'er contracting marginally in its second, stone-walled phase, Bailiehill having three periods of inner enclosure of which the latest overlay and largely obscured the earlier earthworks. The interiors of both citadels are densely occupied by circular houses, clearly superimposed in a succession of building episodes, so that it is unclear how many were occupied at any one time. Nevertheless, Castle O'er, with its two opposed entrances and central street, closely resembles the pattern of protected villages in the eastern Borders, so that we might expect six or eight buildings to have been occupied at any one time. Most of these buildings are between 8–10 m in diameter, but one of the latest (ibid. Figure 73, L) has triple ring-grooves with a maximum diameter of 16 m, which is at the upper end of the Iron Age roundhouse range. In both forts there is evidence of roundhouses overlying or cutting into the latest phase of enclosure, from which it would appear that occupation continued after the defences had been allowed to fall into abeyance. In contrast to the trend in the eastern Borders towards stone building, all of these houses appear to have been of timber construction. Dating of the occupation of Castle O'er is indicated broadly by radiocarbon

(b)

dates from contexts relating to the earthworks, which fall mainly within the opening centuries AD, but allow the possibility of occupation continuing into the late Roman period. At Bailiehill the interior ground-plan is not so clear, with house stances even more densely superimposed. Two of these (ibid. Figure 74, H, J) are ring-ditch houses, a type which is current in the Borders and eastern Scotland from at least the mid-first millennium, but which may have survived in some cases rather later. In the absence of excavation, the date of Bailiehill rests solely on its similarities and relationship to the Castle O'er complex.

Castle O'er lies at the centre of a network of linear earthworks radiating from the hillfort along the west side of the White Esk and embracing an area of around 100 ha. Much of the system has been destroyed since it was first recognized in the late eighteenth century by General Roy and plotted in the late nineteenth by the estate owner, Richard Bell, and we cannot be certain that all the earthworks were as early as the hillfort. On the east side of the White Esk, the Deil's Jingle, extending for 4 km along the watershed, is almost certainly Medieval in its present form, but its alignment may well have followed a much earlier boundary. The existence of other lengths of earthwork that loop towards their counterparts on the west side of the river certainly suggests the former inclusion of a more extensive network on the east.

Figure 5.3. Hillforts in upper Eskdale, Dumfriesshire: (a) Castle O'er, (b) (opposite) Bailiehill. Air photographs by D. W. Harding.

Radiocarbon dates from the hillfort annexe suggested that its addition, and therefore in all probability the linear earthwork system itself, was contemporary with the continuing occupation of the fort. The inference, therefore, is that this was a pastoral estate and the linear earthworks were major ranch boundaries and enclosures.

Enclosed settlements of less than hillfort proportions are distributed at variable intervals around 1 km on either side of the White Esk valley, probably together forming a network of dependent settlements contemporary with the hillfort's occupation. Typically such enclosures are dug into the sloping hillside, with ditches of almost defensive proportions, though there is considerable variation in size and scale. From their internal house stances and yards, nevertheless, a common domestic and agricultural function can be inferred. The one exception was at Over Rig, located on the west bank of the White Esk, which had substantially eroded its multiple enclosing earthworks. Not only was the site prone to waterlogging, its earthworks with internal ditch hardly conformed to the normal settlement model. Artefactual remains indicated activity in the first century AD, though radiocarbon dates suggested a wider span. Internally there was some evidence for timber buildings, but also a unique, very slightly trapezoidal setting of stones, the purpose of which was unclear. In view of the site's unusual setting and layout, and in the absence of normal traces of domestic occupation, the excavator concluded that its function was ritual or ceremonial, for which its location in a natural amphitheatre would have been well suited.

(b)

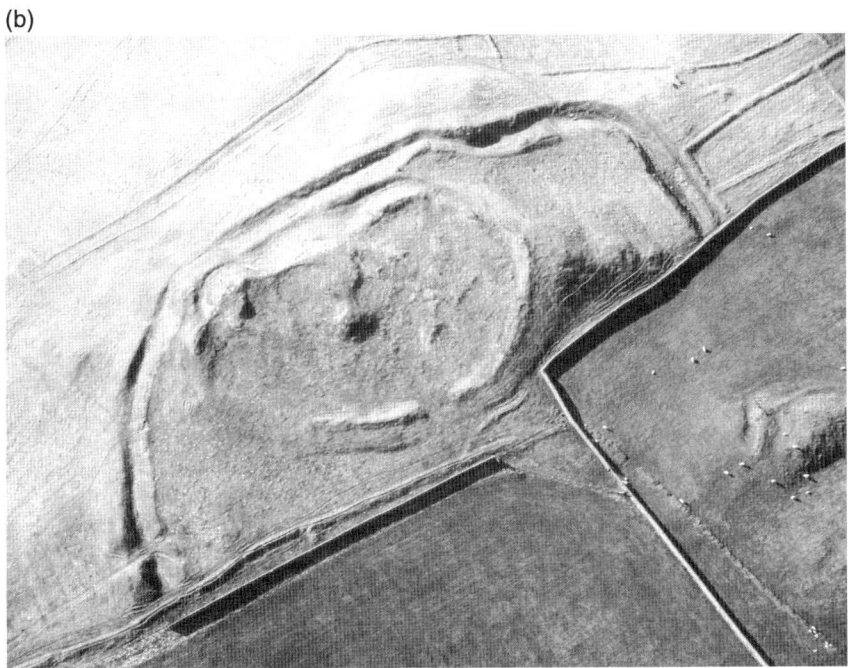

The Castle O'er complex is of particular interest because it was evidently flourishing in the early centuries AD, when Eskdale would have been under Roman jurisdiction or within a northern 'buffer zone', so that its continuing existence as a thriving ranching community must have resulted from an accommodation with the Roman military authorities. This in itself need occasion no surprise, since the history of Roman occupation shows numerous examples of pro-Roman alliances, often linked to commercial or economic benefit as well as political expediency. What is surprising at Castle O'er is that the defences seem to have been maintained into the Roman period, the houses only extending over their limits in the late Roman period. Where other lesser hillforts went into abeyance, Castle O'er and Bailiehill evidently thrived, apparently controlling an expanding estate in upper Eskdale and perhaps reflecting local power struggles (RCAHMS 1997: 164) in which diplomatic liaison with Rome may have proved a crucial factor. In fact, contrary to the older view of hillforts articulating native resistance to the Roman military advance, current evidence suggests that many in the Borders had already been abandoned before the end of the first millennium BC, with extensive landscape clearance and the widespread establishment of small farming settlements (ibid. 184). The Castle O'er complex may have acquired special status under Roman occupation, therefore, but it was doubtless already in the ascendant in the later pre-Roman period.

OPPIDA

From the examples illustrated above it is clear that many hillforts not only functioned within a landscape context, but were also physically integrated into that landscape, with linear boundaries, track-ways, or field enclosures radiating from them like a spider's web. On the eve of the conquest in south-eastern England the territorial or terrain *oppida* like Camulodunum or the Chichester dykes might be seen as the ultimate integration of the hillfort concept into the landscape. For the late pre-Roman Iron Age in southern Britain, Cunliffe (2005: 159) distinguished three classes of *oppida*, enclosed *oppida*, nucleated *oppida*, and territorial *oppida*. Sites like Camulodunum were classified as territorial *oppida*, but the term 'terrain *oppida*' is here preferred, because that is what they are: dyke systems that extend over considerable tracts of land, incorporating natural features of local topography in their circuit. Some nucleated sites like Wheathampstead, Verulamium, or Silchester are indeed linked to linear earthworks that may have been territorial boundaries or land divisions, just as hillforts like Danebury or Quarley Hill were linked to wider systems earlier in the Iron Age, but the territorial role of terrain *oppida* requires further definition.

In the older conventional view, *oppida* of the late pre-Roman Iron Age were seen as the penultimate stage in a progression from hillforts to towns, and the evidence of coinage, imported goods, and craft specialization were all regarded as consistent with incipient urbanization. In continental Europe, this was seen as one aspect of the process of state formation, despite the fact that evidence for permanent settlement before the Roman period in the Gaulish *oppida* that came to prominence in Caesar's Gallic campaign was relatively sparse until recent years. In the past twenty years, this view of proto-urban *oppida* has been widely challenged (Woolf 1993), even for Gaulish sites like Villeneuve-Saint-Germain and Condé-sur-Suippes in the Aisne, where an ordered layout of streets and buildings accorded with the expectation of an urban settlement (Haselgrove 1995). Even the unique site of Manching in Bavaria (Sievers 2003), for long regarded as a model of late Iron Age urbanization, within its later second-century 360 ha enclosure perhaps hardly surprisingly has areas that are less densely occupied than the central zone. Some sectors are virtually devoid of structural occupation, perhaps suggesting that tracts of enclosed land were designated for purposes other than urban occupation. Manching's 'urban' characteristics, of course, including craft specialization, minting of coins, and exotic imports, originate in La Tène C1 and therefore antedate the enclosure walls by more than a century. There was considerable expansion from the central La Tène C1/C2 focus to east and south in La Tène D1, and some variation in the size of buildings has been detected through time (Wendling 2011). Nevertheless, the ordered arrangement of streets and enclosures containing rectangular buildings might reasonably be regarded as one trait of urbanization. Sites like Manching, located on relatively level terrain, may have been more amenable to town planning than hill *oppida* like the Mont Beuvray or those of Bohemia and Moravia, where topography perhaps precluded such a regular zoning of activities (Fichtl 2000: 97).

Among terrain *oppida* in south-east Britain, the site of Camulodunum at Colchester (Figure 5.4) occupies a triangular plateau at the confluence of the Colne and the Roman River, 'a site of great natural advantages' (Hawkes and Hull 1947: 3). The pre-Roman dykes extended broadly across the western side of this peninsula, thus enclosing potentially an area of around 30 square kilometres. The *oppidum* was seemingly unrelated to the earlier Iron Age hillfort at Pitchbury, which lies nearly 3 km north of the Colne. The sequence of construction is complex, the earliest dykes probably dating from the mid-first century BC and the latest a generation or so after the Roman conquest. Various schemes have been proposed (Rodwell 1976; Hawkes and Crummy 1995), and continuing research will inevitably result in further revisions. The earliest of the dykes embrace concentrations of activity around Sheepen, Lexden, and Gosbecks, notably the Heath Farm Dyke (Crummy 2007). Further east across the plateau, the east-facing Berechurch dyke may also be pre-Roman, and its dating has sometimes been associated with the threat of

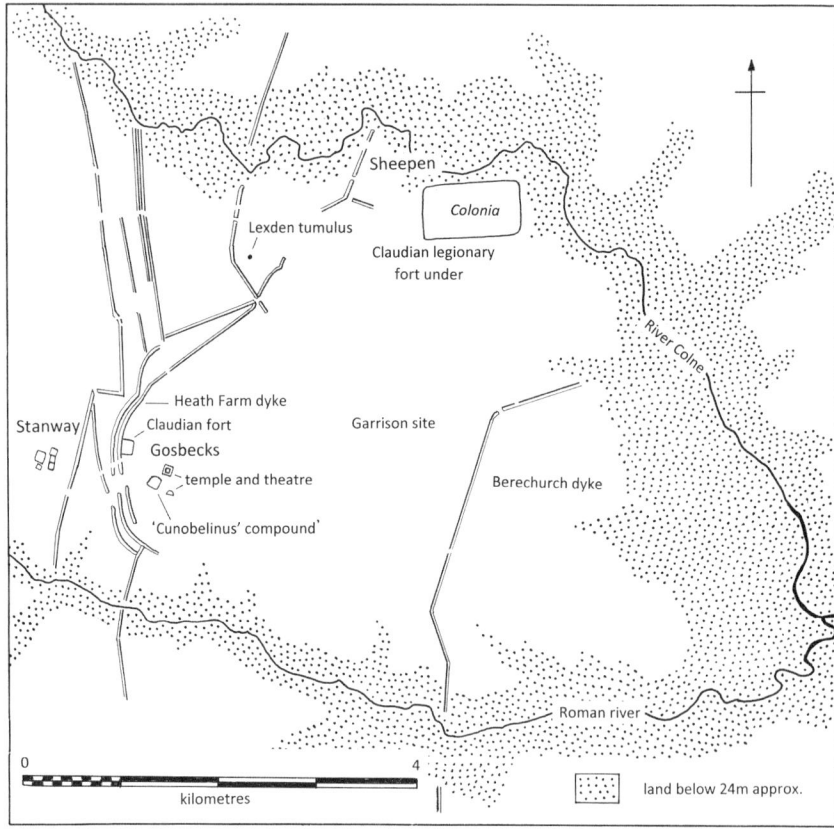

Figure 5.4. Iron Age and early Roman Colchester (*Camulodunum*): outline plan. Drawing by D. W. Harding adapted from Hawkes and Crummy (1995) and Crummy (2007).

Roman attack from the coast at the time of Caligula (AD 37–41). That dykes continued to be built into the Roman occupation is testimony to the site's pivotal importance politically in the first century AD, when defensive additions may have been prompted by the risk of native rebellion, as in the Boudiccan uprising.

Camulodunum, of course, was identified by Dio as the royal residence of Cunobelinus (Cassius Dio, *History*: lx, 21, 4). In the immediately pre-Roman period, one major focus of settlement was in the vicinity of Gosbecks, where air photography has revealed a complex network of fields, enclosures, and track-ways, concentrated around a polygonal ditched enclosure that inevitably has been identified as the likely residence of Cunobelinus. The site lies within the western dyke system, but may in part have pre-dated its construction. That this site was endowed with some special and enduring sense of place is indicated by the concentration of Roman-period buildings, including a temple and theatre, in close proximity to the polygonal enclosure. More recently (Crummy 2007), further east on the plateau, the extensive Garrison site has exposed a drove-way and field enclosures, suggesting that Camulodunum in the immediately pre-Roman period was an important farming estate, in which stock-raising was a major component of the agricultural economy. Its status is underlined by the richly furnished late Iron Age tombs in the immediate vicinity, not only the Lexden tumulus (Laver 1927), but the even more spectacular series from Stanway (Crummy et al. 2007), located just outside the western dykes and a kilometre west of the Gosbecks settlement.

Structural evidence for the immediately pre-Roman occupation is nevertheless sparse. The narrow exploratory trenches of Hawkes' and Hull's excavations may not have been conducive to the recovery of coherent plans of timber buildings, but even from more recent area excavation it is hard to distinguish convincing plans, circular or rectangular (Hawkes and Crummy 1995: Figure 6.20). One reason for this could be that changes in domestic building in south-eastern England introduced techniques of construction that did not leave the conventional pattern of earth-fast post-holes (Harding 2009). A notable exception, therefore, is a large roundhouse of ring-groove and post-hole construction which was the dominant feature of an earlier first-century BC enclosure within the Garrison complex. At the Stanway site the earliest and smallest polygonal enclosure may have contained a roundhouse of middle Iron Age date, whilst a kilometre or so further west again, the Abbotstone settlement too produced evidence of roundhouse settlement from the middle Iron Age. Both these latter sites reflect a measure of local continuity into the Roman period, but there seems to be a fundamental change in the second half of the first century BC from these individual, enclosed sites to the dyked *oppidum*. The historical record and the coin evidence point to the conclusion that Camulodunum in the half-century before the conquest was a major Catuvellaunian centre in territory that had formerly been held by the Trinovantes (Hawkes and Crummy 1995: 172–8). The imposition of a Roman legionary fortress and subsequent *colonia* is indicative of the fact that anti-Roman feeling was deeply entrenched and perhaps aggravated by the Trinovantes' pro-Roman sympathies from the time of Caesar's raids. Irrespective of individual attributions, there can be little doubt that Camulodunum was a major royal centre of the late pre-Roman Iron Age with economic assets that warranted defensive works in a politically volatile environment.

Equally important though rather less coherent is the St Albans–Wheathampstead group of sites in Hertfordshire (Bryant and Niblett 1997), between which the alignments of the Beech Bottom Dyke extending north-east from the Verulamium complex, and the Devil's Dyke, which putatively formed one side of Wheeler's Wheathampstead enclosed *oppidum* (Wheeler and Wheeler 1936), suggest a link between the two. Doubt has since been cast on the integrity of Wheeler's *oppidum*; the Slad, which he included as part of the enclosed circuit, is probably natural, and evidence for occupation of the plateau is not extensive. By contrast, subsequent investigations have revealed late pre-Roman Iron Age activity outside Wheeler's site on either side of the Lea Valley. Bryant's (2007) alternative suggestion that these dykes may have served as a track-way leading towards a ceremonial or ritual complex seems persuasive, not least because of an increasing awareness of the role of ritual activities in the context of continental *oppida*, notably and exceptionally Gournay-sur-Aronde in the Oise (Brunaux *et al.* 1985; Brunaux and Rapin 1994; Lejars 1994), but not excluding Manching. This need not preclude the traditional view of the Beech Bottom Dyke as a territorial boundary; indeed, the territorial interface may have encouraged the area's role as a focus among neighbouring communities for special functions, whether economic and commercial, or ceremonial and ritual.

The Verulamium complex seems to have become important late in the pre-Roman period, with various activity areas apparently segregated by a series of dykes or enclosures. There is little evidence for settlement of the middle Iron Age in the vicinity to underline its traditional importance, and its emergence may have been triggered by agricultural extensification (Haselgrove and Millett 1997: 283). The pattern appears to be of separated farmsteads with enclosures, paddocks, and track-ways, rather than one of nucleated concentration as might be expected of a proto-urban development. Settlements show a preference for the higher ground of the plateau edge, as at Gorhambury or Prae Wood, though evidence for earlier occupation has also been found in the valley beneath the early Roman town, which may therefore obscure an important pre-Roman focus of activity. That these settlements were nevertheless high-status sites is implicit in the minting of coins, including those of Tasciovanus with the mint mark for Verulamium. As elsewhere there is evidence of zoning of activities, with separate areas designated for ritual, burial, and perhaps for metalworking in the late pre-Roman Iron Age. Even so, they hardly conform to any urban model, and Haselgrove (2000: 105; Haselgrove and Millett 1997: 286) preferred to described them as 'polyfocal settlements'. He has argued persuasively for their origin as sacred sites that were not initially settled permanently, but were used as periodic, neutral centres, only subsequently acquiring their political and economic status, a model that might equally be applicable to some of the continental *oppida* (Haselgrove 2000: 106–7).

An interesting contrast to these sites is provided by the pre-Roman settlement at Silchester, where excavations beneath the basilica of the town of Calleva Atrebatum have uncovered occupation from the later first century BC into the first century AD. Here in the forum-basilica excavations (Fulford 1987; Fulford and Timby 2000) unusually there is evidence for the transition from roundhouses in the earlier phase of occupation to rectilinear buildings in the later phase, when the layout of the settlement was organized more regularly on the basis of a grid of streets. By this time, an area of 32 ha (80 acres) was enclosed by the Inner Earthwork, so that its layout conforms more closely than most south-eastern *oppida* to a proto-urban model. Haselgrove (2000: 105) compared the site to northern Gaulish *oppida*, and in its planned layout, it displays potentially urban characteristics, though as yet without evidence for public buildings or segregated zones of activity. The material assemblage would be consistent with this interpretation, including continental imports, amphorae from Spain and Italy, together with southern Gaulish samian, central Gaulish wares, and Gallo-Belgic pottery. Coins confirm the site's status as a dynastic centre, possibly from the time of Commius and certainly by Augustan times under his son or grandson Tincomarus. Excavations since the mid-1990s in Insula IX of the Roman town have also uncovered evidence for the pre-Roman layout, and have raised the possibility that even under Roman occupation, the north-west/south-east orientation of the pre-Roman plan may have been reverted to in defiance of the orthodox Roman grid as a gesture of political independence (Fulford and Clarke 2011).

The Upper Thames region includes two very different variants of late pre-Roman Iron Age *oppida*. The riverside enclosed *oppida* at Dyke Hills, Dorchester (Figure 5.5), and at Abingdon were both intensively occupied, though not with any obvious zoning or planned layout. Abingdon was occupied from the later pre-Roman Iron Age into the Roman period, and eventually beyond the Iron Age ditches to develop as a small Roman town. The Dyke Hills settlement remains unexcavated, though Pitt-Rivers sectioned its ramparts (Lane-Fox 1870). The crop marks, however, are not unlike those from Linch Hill, Stanton Harcourt, in Oxfordshire (Grimes 1944) and would be consistent with later pre-Roman Iron Age occupation. The other class of terrain *oppida* is represented more enigmatically in the North Oxfordshire Grim's Ditch (Figure 5.6a, b; Crawford 1930; Lambrick and Robinson 2009: Figure 9.24), originally supposed by Crawford to be late Roman but shown from various sections to belong to the immediately pre-Roman period (Harding 1972: 56–9). The Grim's Ditch *oppidum*, if it ever functioned as a unitary system, is vast, encircling an area of around 50 square kilometres from the river Glyme to south-west of the Evenlode. It is an enigma because, although it encloses some known Iron Age sites, there is no obvious settlement focus. Furthermore, although subsequently a number of villa estates clustered within its circuit, they do not show overt continuity from a pre-Roman pattern of agricultural settlements, and no Roman town was ever established within its limits. Whether its construction was cumulative and never fully realized (Copeland 1988), or whether it was intended to serve some undefined boundary role between the territories of the Catuvellauni and the Dobunni, remains a matter of speculation.

Figure 5.5. Dyke Hills, Dorchester-on-Thames, Oxfordshire, air photograph by Major G. W. G. Allen. Reproduced by kind permission of the Ashmolean Museum, University of Oxford.

The most northerly of the recognized *oppida* in this class is Stanwick, just south of the Tees in north Yorkshire (Wheeler 1954; Haselgrove *et al.* 1990; Welfare *et al.* 1990). It might be related to the terrain *oppida* of the south-east, its linear earthworks at maximum extent enclosing around 300 ha, although the sequence of construction has not been fully resolved. In several places the earthworks have been shown to have lesser banks underlying them, perhaps indicating that their course was in some measure determined by pre-existing land divisions or boundaries. In their final form, nevertheless, these substantial earthworks belong to a relatively short span in the mid-first century AD, and unquestionably are late in relation to a sequence of occupation of the east side of the Tofts, which may have originated a couple of centuries earlier. At present, evidence for occupation, though significant, is restricted to this area of the site, and it is unclear whether other concentrations remain to be discovered. The scale of the earthworks and the resource implications of their construction seems a massive investment if the purpose was largely to contain high-quality arable land and pasture. More probably, they signalled a major change in the site's status, coinciding as they appear to do with the introduction

Hillforts in the landscape

(a)

(b)

Figure 5.6. North Oxfordshire Grim's Ditch: (a) ditch showing as a soil mark west of Ditchley Park; (b) bank and ditch in Ditchley Park. Photographs by R. L. Wilkins and D. W. Harding, reproduced by permission of Oxford University Press.

of Roman imports which the excavator interpreted as diplomatic gifts (Haselgrove 2000: 106). Spanish amphorae for transporting olive oil, Rhodian wine-amphorae, and a wide range of samian types were all imports before the Roman conquest of northern England. Historically this phase of prosperous settlement equates with the dominance of Cartimandua as pro-Roman client ruler of the local Brigantes, as recorded by Tacitus, thus reversing Wheeler's interpretation of the site as the stronghold under Venutius of the anti-Roman political faction. Broadly contemporary with this first-century AD phase of activity is the Melsonby hoard (Fitts *et al.* 1999), for which a range of interpretations has been advanced, including a votive hoard or founder's hoard. One possibility, however, is that the iron hoops that Wheeler (1954) had imagined might have been the tyres from a chariot burial were from a bound bucket of the kind used for late La Tène cremation burials in north-eastern Gaul. Several items in the hoard had apparently been damaged by heat, and it is doubtful that the remains of a funeral pyre would have been detected by the site's nineteenth-century explorers. A richly furnished grave in proximity to the *oppidum* would not be inconsistent with evidence from the south-eastern 'royal' *oppida*.

A more extensive review of sites of the late pre-Roman Iron Age would undoubtedly reinforce the considerable diversity of their location, layout, composition, and probable function. Some are effectively enclosed by earthworks, while others are discontinuous and irregular in their layout, even allowing for the fact that natural features may have been incorporated into their intended circuit. Some *oppida* appear to be an aggregation of functionally discrete units while others display a more nucleated structure. Some display evidence of high status, perhaps royal, occupation, while others, like the Braughing complex, lack such associations. Burial and ritual activity seems to be implicit in all of these sites, and may be fundamental to their initial importance. Any suggestion of urbanization seems to be secondary, and only at Silchester are the characteristics of street planning and other conventional attributes of towns potentially in evidence. Woolf (1993) argued that the issue of urbanization was a red herring, and one that was exacerbated by our preconception of towns as conforming to the classical or Medieval models. The beginnings of urbanization, incipient state societies, market economy, and craft specialization, even if these are applicable to late pre-Roman Iron Age society in north-west Europe, are not our immediate concern here, and if we detach the terrain *oppida* of southern Britain from the presumption of proto-urban status it is possible that their diverse functions might throw light on some of the roles fulfilled earlier in the Iron Age by hillforts. The one factor that distinguishes Stanwick, Camulodunum, the Chichester dykes, or the North Oxfordshire Grim's Ditch among others is the sheer scale of their construction, though it is matched or surpassed by the major *oppida* of central and west-central Europe. That most obvious fact must tell us something about the changes that were taking place within Iron Age society; at the same time it underlines a fundamental continuity, since, massive though the shift in scale may be, it may be one of degree rather than one of kind.

LANDSCAPES WITHOUT HILLFORTS

The fact that hillforts are commonly perceived as iconic of the British Iron Age is a reflection of a Wessex-oriented perspective, since large parts of eastern England from East Anglia to the Tyne are devoid of hillforts, not just in areas where there are no hills, but also in the Lincolnshire and Yorkshire Wolds or the eastern Pennines, where there is no lack of suitable locations. If not totally absent, hillforts are sufficiently few in number to indicate a different political, economic, or social structure from that implicit in Wessex. The questions therefore should be asked, why did the communities in these areas not build hillforts, and what alternatives were there to fulfil the purposes that hillforts served elsewhere?

'Ring-works' of eastern England

Among a number of ditched enclosures from Essex to Yorkshire that over the past thirty years have been shown by radiocarbon dating to belong to the later Bronze Age (Needham 1992), two stand out on account of the circularity of their plans, the orientation of their entrances, and the dominance of a single, central, circular building. Mucking South, Essex (Jones and Bond 1980), located on a 30 m terrace overlooking the Thames estuary, was first identified from air photography, when it appeared to resemble a Class IIA henge monument in the older conventional classification in size and layout (Atkinson *et al*. 1951), with two concentric ditches and diametrically opposed entrances through both circuits. Internally it had a central ring-groove building that showed no obvious entrance gap. Its later Bronze Age date was affirmed by radiocarbon dates and by its post-Deverel-Rimbury 'plain-ware' assemblage. The Mucking North enclosure (Bond 1988) was much smaller, with single ditch, but nevertheless had the same regular, circular outline. Paddock Hill, Thwing (Manby 1980, 2007), on the north-eastern edge of the Yorkshire Wolds, was superficially similar though larger, with an overall diameter around 110 metres. It proved, however, to be of composite construction, though its principal phases belonged within the later Bronze Age. Only the external ring-work wall conformed to normal hillfort conventions, with timber-revetted rampart and external ditch, itself apparently a secondary addition to the inner earthwork, comprising an internal ditch and external bank. The large, central structure, assigned to the final ring-work phase, nevertheless had opposed entrances that maintained the south-east and north-west orientation of the entrances of both inner ring-ditch and outer ring-work ditch.

The most obvious parallel for the bank and ditch arrangement of the inner earthwork at Thwing, classified by Manby (2007) as group 1, of course, is the Irish 'royal' sites, though in terms of size and complexity of structures the latter are on a much grander scale. The outer ring-work, with its more normal hillfort arrangement of external ditch, he assigned to group 2. Though the later material assemblage from Thwing seemed domestic in range and composition, the excavator believed that the earlier phase included a ritual element, and he did not exclude some continuity of purpose into the ring-work phase. The distinguishing feature of Mucking South and Thwing, however, remains the regularity in layout of circular ditches and diametrically opposed entrances, and the emphasis upon a single, centrally located building. Hillforts are very seldom so circular, the geometry of enclosure commonly being more adapted to local topographical constraints, so that we might infer that some greater significance was attached to the ring-works' plans. The orientation of their entrances falls within the bracket of midwinter sunrise and midsummer sunset that Oswald (1997) believed had cosmological significance for roundhouse entrances.

The other key later Bronze Age site that is frequently included in the ring-work classification is Springfield Lyons, overlooking the Chelmer valley in Essex (Buckley and Hedges 1987). The enclosure here is not quite circular, but more importantly the ditch is causewayed, having five gaps around its circuit (Figure 3.8D) in addition to one on its east side, which was presumably the main or only entrance in view of the corresponding elaboration of the timber passageway through the internal bank. That bank was supported by a double line of posts, around 1.5 metres apart, and set some 6 metres inside the ditch. The excavators assumed that this formed a revetment or internal range on the inside of the bank, presumed to be a simple dump, rather than containing the bank itself, which would have left a wider than usual berm in front of the wall. This leaves open the question whether secondary access was provided through any of the causeways, but assuming that this was not the case with the narrowest, then any comparison with the Scottish causewayed forts is less obvious. Centrally located within the enclosure at Springfield Lyons, with its entrance aligned on the enclosure entrance, was a roundhouse of standard post-hole construction. Two or perhaps three other roundhouses within the enclosure may have been contemporary, so that there is little to indicate it was other than a normal domestic and agricultural settlement.

A number of other sites in eastern England, predominantly from south of the Humber, have been assigned to the ring-work category, some with more irregular plans than the examples considered here. Sub-circular enclosures of more variable plan are doubtless representative of late Bronze Age and Iron Age settlement in the region, but are hardly sufficiently distinctive in plan from a range of enclosures known throughout Britain, including those from

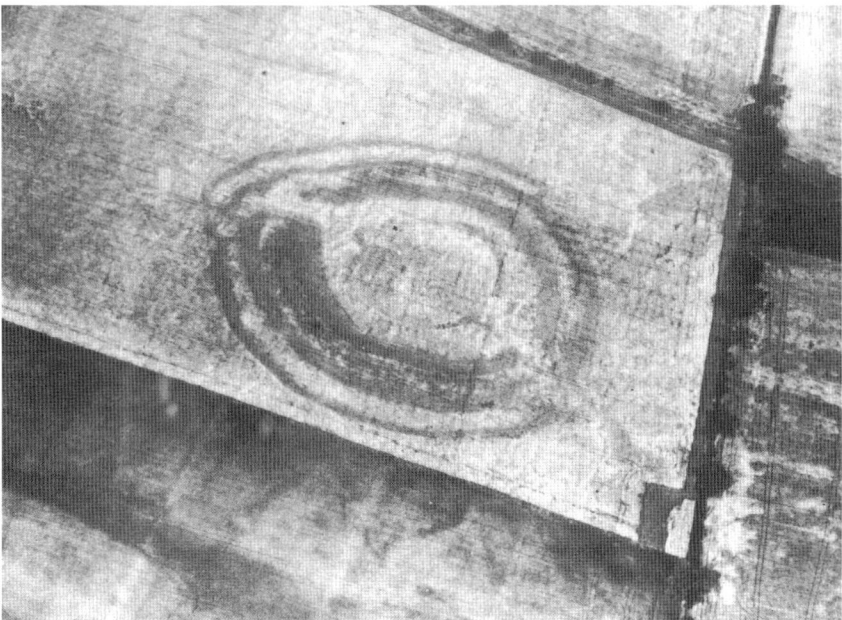

Figure 5.7. Flodden, Northumberland, multi-period ring-work. Air photograph by D. W. Harding.

the far south-west (Jones 2010) to warrant special characterization. Further north, however, one site may be a contender for the ring-work category, the multiple-ditched enclosure at Flodden, Northumberland (Figure 5.7), the innermost ring of which was tentatively identified by Anthony Harding as a henge that had been reused for defensive purposes at a later period, presumed to be in the first millennium BC (Harding 1987: 210, No. 124). The site is plainly multi-period, and if it represents the conscious reuse of an earlier monument of henge type, then the parallel with Thwing would be striking.

Landscape of eastern Yorkshire

In contrasting the Iron Age landscapes of Wessex and eastern Yorkshire, Bevan remarked that the 'most notable differences are the *presence* of square barrow burials and *absence* of hillforts in eastern Yorkshire' (Bevan 1999b: 123). This fundamental observation must have seemed so self-evident that hitherto archaeologists have not found it necessary to articulate, still less to examine whether there might be some causal relationship between the presence of one and the absence of another. In fact the absence of hillforts extends beyond the core concentration of square-ditched barrow cemeteries, into the Vale of York and south of the Humber to the Lincolnshire Wolds and the Trent valley. On the Yorkshire Wolds, Grimthorpe is an obvious exception, but with its notably circular plan and latest Bronze Age dates it might well belong to the ring-work category rather than to the conventional hillfort class. Among crop-mark sites Greenlands, Rudston, and Driffield Wold, Nafferton, and some smaller ditched enclosures, all undated, resemble small hillforts in plan, while the Duggleby Howe interrupted-ditch enclosure has on that account hitherto appeared to be more anomalous. Palisaded enclosures, as at Staple Howe and Devil's Hill, were evidently in use around the second quarter of the first millennium BC. These earlier first millennium sites were evidently contemporary with some of the earlier linear earthworks that progressively came to typify the landscape of the Wolds in the Iron Age, but they are not actually articulated into them, even though they occupy coherent entities of land at intervals within them (Stoertz 1997: Figure 33). In the case of Paddock Hill, Thwing, however, it is tempting to see the proximity of the Late Bronze Age ring-work to the convergence of three major sets of landscape boundaries as significant, whether they were aligned on it, or it in relation to them (ibid. Figure 42).

If we were applying Cunliffe's Wessex model, we might suggest that what was different in the eastern Yorkshire sequence was that none of the early enclosures acquired the status of a 'developed' hillfort, or indeed survived in use into the early and middle Iron Age. Instead a different form of settlement pattern, centred on the linear village, came to typify the region in the later Iron Age and Romano-British period.

The linear earthworks comprise boundaries, trackways and enclosures that were progressively constructed or elaborated throughout the first millennium BC, and which signify a highly ordered landscape, even if it was subject to dynamic change. Extensive linear earthworks are indicative of strict land-use management that may have been necessitated by population pressures. Trackways may have facilitated the movement of stock, affording transit through arable land to pasture, or providing access to water sources, or on a larger scale providing routes of communication between adjacent groups of settlements. Larger-scale boundary earthworks, sometimes multiple and sometimes incorporating extensive pit-alignments, appear to divide major blocks of land with limited points of access between them, and with clear implications in terms of rights to place (Giles 2007). A striking example is the series that converges at Burton Fleming on either side of the Gypsey Race watercourse. Double-ditched earthworks are explicable as drove-ways, and where these are combined with pit alignments especially, it is quite possible that the multiple effect is the product of cumulative rebuilding or redefining of boundaries over centuries. In some cases re-digging of pit alignments may have resulted in the creating of continuous ditches (Powlesland 1988), or pits may have been dug into ditches that had partially silted up (Stoertz 1997: 41). The overall pattern implies 'well-defined land-use rights and routines' (Bevan 1999b: 129) over a protracted period of time.

Plate 1. St David's promontory fort, Pembrokeshire: (a) view from south-east, (b) stone roundhouses in inner fort. Photographs by D. W. Harding.

Plate 2. Crickley Hill, Gloucestershire: (a) Period 3 rampart, (b) Period 3 entrance. Photographs courtesy of Philip Dixon.

(a)

(b)

Plate 3. Irish royal sites: (a) Tara, Co Meath, ditch and bank of the Ráith na Ríg; (b) Dún Ailinne, Co Wicklow, view from east. Photographs by D. W. Harding.

(a)

(b)

Plate 4. Continental hillforts 1: (a) Mont Lassois, Châtillon-sur-Seine, general view across upper Seine; (b) Entremont, Aix-en-Provence, wall with bastion. Photographs by D. W. Harding.

(a)

(b)

Plate 5. Shetland blockhouses: (a) Clickhimin, mainland Shetland; (b) Ness of Burgi, mainland Shetland. Photographs by D. W. Harding.

Plate 6. Northern Scottish forts: (a) Tap o' Noth, Aberdeenshire, from south; (b) Cnoc an Duin (Dun Goll), Ross-shire, inner wall. Photographs by D. W. Harding.

Plate 7. Hownam Law, Roxburghshire: (a) air view with house platforms under snow; (b) view from south-west. Photographs by D. W. Harding.

Plate 8. Pennine forts: (a) Ingleborough, Yorkshire, view from west; (b) Mam Tor, Derbyshire, view from south. Photographs by D. W. Harding.

(a)

(b)

Plate 9. Tre'r Ceiri, Caernarvonshire: (a) air view (2006 0498), © Crown Copyright: Royal Commission on the Ancient and Historical Monuments of Wales, Hawlfraint y Goron: Comisiwn Brenhinol Henebion Cymru; (b) houses within hillfort, photograph by D. W. Harding.

Plate 10. Navan fort, Co. Armagh: (a) Professor J. Mallory beside site B restored mound, (b) ditch and bank. Photographs by D. W. Harding.

Plate 11. Late Iron Age hillforts in northern Britain: (a) Mote of Mark overlooking Urr estuary, Colvend, Dumfriesshire; (b) Dundurn, Perthshire air photograph. Photographs by D. W. Harding.

Plate 12. Dunagoil, Bute: (a) general view from east, (b) vitrified wall at north end of citadel. Photographs by D. W. Harding.

Plate 13. Irish south-western stone forts: (a) Ballykinvarga, Co. Clare, fort wall with *chevaux-de-frise*; (b) Dun Dubh Cathair, Inishmore, Co. Galway, general view. Photographs by D. W. Harding.

(a)

(b)

Plate 14. Pembrokeshire hillforts from the air: (a) Carn Alw, D12011 0872; (b) Foel Trigarn, D12011 0873; © Crown Copyright: Royal Commission on the Ancient and Historical Monuments of Wales, Hawlfraint y Goron: Comisiwn Brenhinol Henebion Cymru.

(a)

(b)

Plate 15. Continental hillforts 2: (a) Plateau de Merdogne, traditional location of Gergovia; (b) Citânia de Santa Luzia, Viana do Castelo, Portugal. Photographs by D. W. Harding.

(a)

(b)

Plate 16. Hillforts and triple hills: (a) Tre'r Ceiri and Yr Eifl, Caernarvonshire, from north; (b) Eildon Hills, Roxburghshire, from south-east. Photographs by D. W. Harding.

The pattern of linear earthworks evidently encouraged successively the linear distribution of cemeteries and settlements. In some instances, like Wetwang Slack, the square-ditched barrows are closely contained within the alignment of successive linear ditches, while in other instances their linear distribution is not obviously constrained by extant earthworks but may nevertheless have respected some less substantial boundary. Wetwang is one of the few sites in which roundhouses survive in some numbers in proximity to the cemetery, with more than eighty houses spread out over a kilometre along the south-facing slope. The later pre-Roman arrangement of village settlements also follows an extended linear pattern that is often aligned along a trackway. These 'ladder settlements' doubtless incorporated a series of individual holdings with paddocks, and occasionally with visible roundhouses. They have been dated from the late second or first centuries BC, but evidently continued into the Roman period and perhaps beyond. Their rise to dominance in the landscape broadly coincides with the decline in square-ditched barrow cemeteries, though the reasons for these trends and whether they are related remain unresolved.

Attention in the past was primarily focused on the origins of the square-ditched barrow cemeteries, including the distinctive chariot- or cart-burials, and their similarities to and differences from continental burial practices of Early and Middle La Tène. The demise of these funerary monuments has never attracted the same attention archaeologically, though it equally demands explanation. A first step may be to recognize that the abandonment of barrow monuments may not mean the demise of the funerary ritual altogether, merely its final act of deposition, which is what survives in the archaeological record. If the creation of a permanent monument to the dead is an affirmation of identity and sense of place on the part of the living, then it is possible that at different times communities expressed that sense of place in different types of monument, including hillforts or domestic settlements. The linear villages of the later pre-Roman Iron Age in eastern Yorkshire are certainly a radical departure from anything known in Wessex or the south-east of England, though similar 'developed linear enclosure complexes' have been recognized from crop marks in the Trent valley (Whimster 1989) and in the Lincolnshire fens. It is not clear how the linear villages, or more particularly the open roundhouse settlements that apparently preceded them, fulfilled the functions that elsewhere were served by hillforts, but it is clear that here was a vibrant settlement tradition that survived for more than a millennium without the need for hillforts. The early ring-works of the Yorkshire Wolds, like Thwing and Grimthorpe, may have served a more limited range of functions, including those related to funerary ritual that could have been absorbed within the purview of the square-barrow cemeteries, so that hillforts never developed in this region by acquiring a wider range of roles, as they evidently did in Wessex.

Iron Age landscapes in Atlantic Scotland

The one major area of Britain where hillforts as generally defined are virtually absent is Atlantic Scotland, more especially the Outer Hebrides, Caithness and Sutherland, Orkney and Shetland. There are certainly stone forts in Argyll and the Inner Hebrides (Harding 1997), and there are promontory forts throughout Atlantic Scotland, though their extraordinarily exposed locations and precipitous topography must raise doubts regarding their viability as occupation sites.

The dominant field monument of the earlier Iron Age in Atlantic Scotland is the broch, or complex Atlantic roundhouse, with a somewhat less monumental counterpart in the 'dun houses' of Argyll (Harding 1984). Though there are regional differences in broch construction, there is little indication in architecture or layout within regional groupings for any social hierarchy within the broch class. Equally, the absence of demonstrably contemporary alternative types of settlement makes it difficult to argue that brochs were elite sites in a hierarchy of settlement. Their relative frequency in the landscape, even assuming that all were not in contemporaneous occupation, could result in the impression of 'all chiefs and no indians', unless the higher social status of individual households was reflected by factors such as the size of stock holdings that do not register in the archaeological or architectural record.

For Shetland, Fojut (1982, 2005) based his analysis of broch territories upon the assumption that the majority of sites would have been in contemporary occupation, an inference that is perhaps less justified with the new longer chronology for brochs than when they were constrained within the older short 'middle Iron Age' time span. As anticipated by both Joseph Anderson and Gordon Childe, availability of good arable land was a major factor in site location, though proximity to the sea and to pasture were also important considerations. Fojut calculated 'an average distance to nearest neighbour of 2.787 km', but a more recent study of the cluster at the southern tip of mainland Shetland (Turner and Dockrill 2005) shows sites in Dunrossness not much more than a kilometre apart. In terms of potential population, Fojut wisely estimated an average of eighty persons per broch territory, well below the theoretical carrying capacity of the land in terms of optimum cereal yields, and double what he regarded as a minimum viable number, giving a total population for Shetland around 10,000, around half the twentieth-century figure and well below early modern peaks. Excavation has shown that the principal crop of the agricultural economy of Shetland brochs was six-row barley, and Dockrill (2002) has argued persuasively that the 'power base' of the Shetland brochs was 'the centralised control and storage' of this resource. Though broch communities and broch territories were much smaller than their counterparts in the hillfort-dominated zone of central southern England, therefore, essentially they may have operated on a similar client/patron basis in which centralized control of resources provided stability against economic uncertainties and a margin of surplus to facilitate external trade and exchange.

Less clear is the relationship between brochs and what Fojut (1993: 44) called 'Shetland's non-broch forts'. These were located on 'cliffed promontories and on small islands in lochs or sheltered voes', but morphologically similar earthworks or walls also enclose some brochs in both types of location. In the case of the Burland broch (Figure 5.8a), its siting so close to the entrance passage through the earthwork walls that block the neck of the promontory might suggest different episodes of activity, while excavation (Carter *et al.* 1995: 464–6) has shown that the earthworks themselves represent more than one episode of construction. But the banks that enclose the cliff-edge broch of Houbie on Fetlar (RCAHMS 1946: No. 1212), for example, look more like a unitary design with the broch, as do the earthworks surrounding the broch at Dalsetter.

The most obvious site for establishing the relative chronology of forts and brochs, of course, should have been Clickhimin, where Hamilton (1968) proposed a sequence in which the fort or ring-work (not to be confused with the 'ring-work' platform on which the broch was constructed), together with the blockhouse, represented an early Iron Age phase of occupation that preceded the construction of the broch. Unfortunately, establishing clear stratigraphic relationships was always going to prove problematical, and the relative position of the blockhouse in particular has been a matter of contention. Fojut (1998) accepted the priority of the enclosure ring-work over the broch, though saw them as closely sequential. More recently MacKie has argued that the ring-work and the blockhouse at Clickhimin both pre-date the broch, and from a reappraisal of their ceramic associations could cover a longer span of the first millennium BC than was formerly allowed. If the ring-work itself was the earliest structure on the site, then it may have been built in the Late Bronze Age or earliest Iron Age, consistent with the few sherds of Late Bronze Age pottery found in the north-west sector of the site both within and outwith the enclosure wall.

If the later use of the site was primarily for domestic occupation, it need not follow that this was its original purpose. Hamilton argued that the carved footprints incorporated into the later causeway were more probably originally from the ring-work phase, and that they were used for inauguration rituals by the Iron Age community for which Clickhimin was presumably therefore a special place of assembly. Such a function would also make more sense of the blockhouse, which self-evidently as it stands cannot have served a defensive purpose. As an impressive symbolic barrier, from which the elect might declaim to the assembled throng, its truncated width allows controlled access round each end, and more limited access through its central passage (Plate 5a). There remains an issue, however, regarding the chronological relationship

146 *Iron Age Hillforts in Britain and Beyond*

(a)

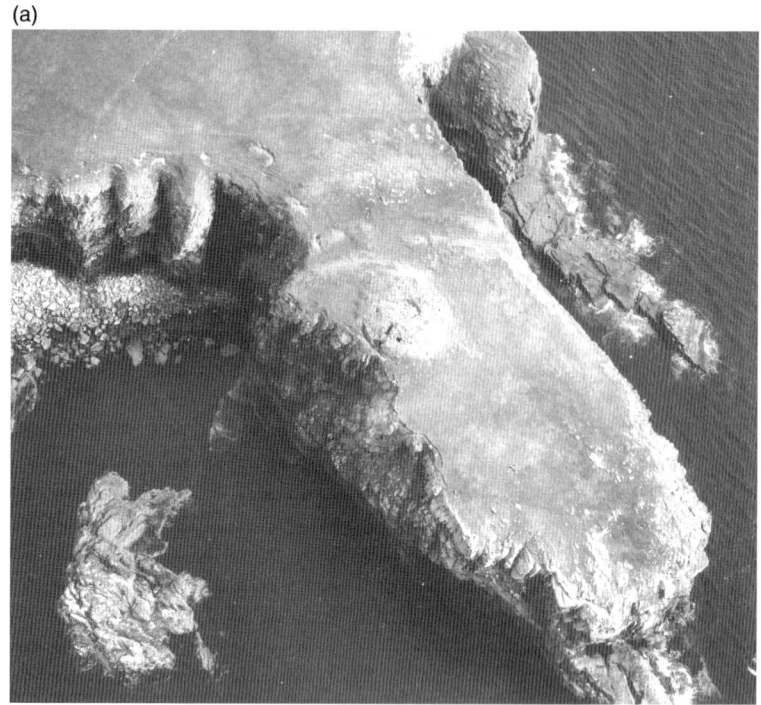

(b)

Figure 5.8. Shetland promontory forts: (a) Burland fort, and broch, (b) Hog Island eroded former promontory fort. Air photographs by D. W. Harding.

between the ring-work and the blockhouse. Though their two entrances are aligned, the simplicity of the ring-work entrance and the complex 'broch architecture' of the blockhouse stand in marked contrast, and it is possible therefore that the latter is a later elaboration.

Dating of other Shetland blockhouses, as we have noted, is equally uncertain. At Ness of Burgi (Plate 5b), there is no evidence for the date of construction and primary use of either earthworks or blockhouse, beyond some indeterminate plain-ware sherds from the latter (Mowbray 1936). Further north on the same peninsula at Scatness (Carter *et al.* 1995) there was no evidence to associate the blockhouse with the external bank and ditch, and no dating evidence, radiometric or artefactual, for either, since the only radiocarbon dates obtained, spanning the second half of the first millennium AD, were all from deposits subsequent to secondary structural modifications. At the Loch of Huxter on Whalsay, the blockhouse component, though contiguous with the ring-work wall, has butt-joints at either end, so that here the general assumption is that the ring-work was secondary.

Among other promontory forts on Shetland one of the largest and most suitable for occupation is the now completely eroded peninsula of Hog Island, Nesting, the neck of which was originally protected by multivallate earthworks (Figure 5.8b). The main rampart, which was reinforced with visible large stones, was the innermost, on the higher, insular side of the eroded system. The three outer dump banks on the landward side are less substantial, with shallow quarry-scoops, the whole producing an arrangement which Lamb (1980: 43–50) termed 'three-and-one' and likened to the Landberg on Fair Isle. Entrance gaps aligned through all four banks suggests unitary design, but there is no surface evidence for occupation and no indication of date. Like other promontory forts located around Shetland, however, it could have been built at any time during the first millennium BC or first millennium AD.

In the Hebridean west, promontory forts likewise had a potentially long chronological span. Gob Eirer on Lewis has produced radiocarbon dates in the Late Bronze Age–Iron Age transition (Ashmore 1999: 115; Church *et al.* forthcoming), while others in local tradition have a much more recent history. There are no blockhouses in the Shetland sense in the Hebrides, but there are at least two sites where stone walls with features of broch architecture cut off a headland to similar effect; on Skye at Rubh an Dunain, and Sròn an Dùin at Barra Head lighthouse on Berneray. These were both classified by MacKie as 'cross-wall semibrochs' (1965: 104), which were never intended to form complete, roofed structures and the curvatures of which describe arcs considerably greater than any known broch. The only elements in common with brochs therefore are architectural, which in themselves need not indicate contemporaneity, since they could have been emulated from surviving ruins well into the later Iron Age, or they could represent the earliest manifestation of complex architecture, as MacKie's model proposed. Rubh an Dunain had a door-check in the entrance passage, a gallery in its wall thickness, and a scarcement along its inner wall face suggesting a timber range backing the wall or perhaps supporting an upper level. At Sròn an Dùin the entrance too has a door-check, with a bar-hole, and the wall to the south has a ground-floor gallery and evidence for an upper gallery as well. The location of Sròn an Dùin is particularly spectacular, the cliffs of its headland rising 185 m (600 ft) above the Atlantic, so that, like the promontory forts of Shetland, it is possible that it was a site of special significance for the Iron Age communities from the neighbouring islands. What is curious is that the parallel headland, Rubha Sgait, shows no evidence of similar works, though it seems likely that the twin headlands would have had reciprocal significance.

The distribution of brochs in North Uist and Barra was analysed by Armit (1992), who estimated the population of broch territories rather lower than Fojut's figures for Shetland, perhaps even half the Shetland estimate. In view of the extent of environmental change, notably the spread of blanket peat, calculating carrying capacity of the Western Isles in the Iron Age would be highly speculative, so that Armit used instead comparisons with the known population figures for 1755 with appropriate qualification. Where brochs occur in close proximity to each other, even in small clusters, we may again raise the question whether they were all in contemporary use or subject to intermittent abandonment with generational social change. Most sites have not been excavated, and even if they had it is doubtful whether excavation techniques would have detected periods of generational change in any system of rotating utilization. Nevertheless, the 49 recorded brochs in North Uist still outnumber the known tackmen's houses of the early eighteenth century, which represent the lowest rank among the clan elite of that period. Wheel-houses in general still appear to belong to a later period than brochs, even though their currency may overlap, so that attempts to see these as representative of a lower social order (Barber 1985) are hardly convincing. Unless there were considerable numbers of hitherto unrecognized non-broch settlements, therefore, and in consequence a much larger Iron Age population than can currently be sustained, brochs can hardly all have been the fortified homesteads of a ruling elite, though there could still have been a hierarchy, perhaps involving a system of clientage, within broch communities. One possible model might see several adjacent broch territories as linked by kinship, so that social primacy within the group could have shifted from one broch to another, generation by generation. Armit's territorial analyses nevertheless revealed a broad similarity in the size of putative broch territories in Barra and the outlying islands, with Vatersay supporting two brochs, the lesser islands one each, and Bernerary, of course, having just the one site, the promontory fort at Sròn an Dùin. This might suggest that the promontory fort was broadly contemporary with the brochs, spanning the second half of the first millennium BC and the beginning of the first millennium AD, but serving a different function.

In sum, Atlantic Scotland is conspicuously lacking in hillforts, even in the smaller community sense of southern and eastern Scotland. The fact that brochs or Atlantic roundhouses developed in the second half of the first millennium BC as the territorial foci of dispersed Iron Age communities suggests that the social structure or economy did not require or could not sustain larger regional centres of the kind that hillforts served as elsewhere. The existence of promontory forts therefore represents a different phenomenon altogether, possibly originating from an earlier date, and probably serving a specific function in their distinctive locations. If we regard hillforts generally as having a range of purposes, this need not preclude some among them, such as promontory forts, being more limited in function, in this instance perhaps connected with ritual and inaugural ceremonies.

6

Chronology

Hillforts are conventionally regarded as a phenomenon of the Late Bronze Age and Iron Age of temperate Europe, with some sites being constructed or reoccupied in the post-Roman Iron Age or Early Medieval period. In broad chronological terms, 1000 BC to AD 1000 covers the two millennia of the 'long Iron Age' in which hillforts are a major field monument.

The concept of enclosure nevertheless has a much longer ancestry, from at least the earliest Neolithic. Some enclosed sites of the Neolithic and earlier Bronze Age in central Europe may be located on elevated ground or on promontories and may involve palisades or earthworks around their perimeter, just like Iron Age hillforts, so that the question arises whether these should not qualify as hillforts. To argue that their topographic location, or the scale or layout of enclosure, is not indicative of a primarily defensive purpose will not do, because some Iron Age hillforts seem to be compromised on these criteria. Nevertheless, by not entirely rational convention, hillforts as a regular class of field monuments are generally recognized from the Late Bronze Age, when their appearance in central and western Europe coincides with an intensification in the quantity and number of types of weaponry and defensive armour associated especially with the Urnfield culture.

NEOLITHIC CAMPS AND FORTIFIED SITES

There are a number of hillfort sites in Britain where there is underlying evidence of Neolithic occupation, including occupation that was originally defined by enclosing works of earth or stone. There is no question of claiming continuity of occupation from Neolithic to Iron Age, but since the earlier earthworks would almost certainly still have been visible—at Maiden Castle, for instance, where the earliest Iron Age hillfort follows almost exactly the extent of the Neolithic enclosure—there is every reason to suppose that the existence of earthworks that would have been recognized as ancient, even if they were not formally venerated as places of ancestors, may have encouraged choice of these sites. An alternative interpretation would be simply to assume that the same advantages of location that commended themselves to Neolithic communities coincidentally satisfied equally the requirements of their Iron Age successors. But in that event the earlier monuments, like the Hambledon Hill long barrow or the Foel Trigarn cairns (Plate 14b), would hardly have been accorded the respect by later occupants that their condition indicates they were. So it seems probable that a sense of place in all its aspects was important to Iron Age societies and that this was an important factor in the location of hillforts.

The function or multiple functions of Neolithic enclosures, however, is as debatable as is the purpose of hillforts. In the case of the inland promontory works at Crickley Hill, there seems little doubt that defence was one purpose, since the distribution of over 400 leaf-shaped arrowheads, clustered especially in the twin entrances through the outer earthworks (Figure 6.1) is hard to interpret as other than the product of an attack by archers. The concentration of arrowheads along the line of the breastwork at the rear of the bank suggests an attempt to force defenders to take cover while the gates were stormed, just as Caesar (*dBG* II, 6) described the tactics used by stoners in the initial stages of assault on hillfort gates. This is very much the kind of evidence that

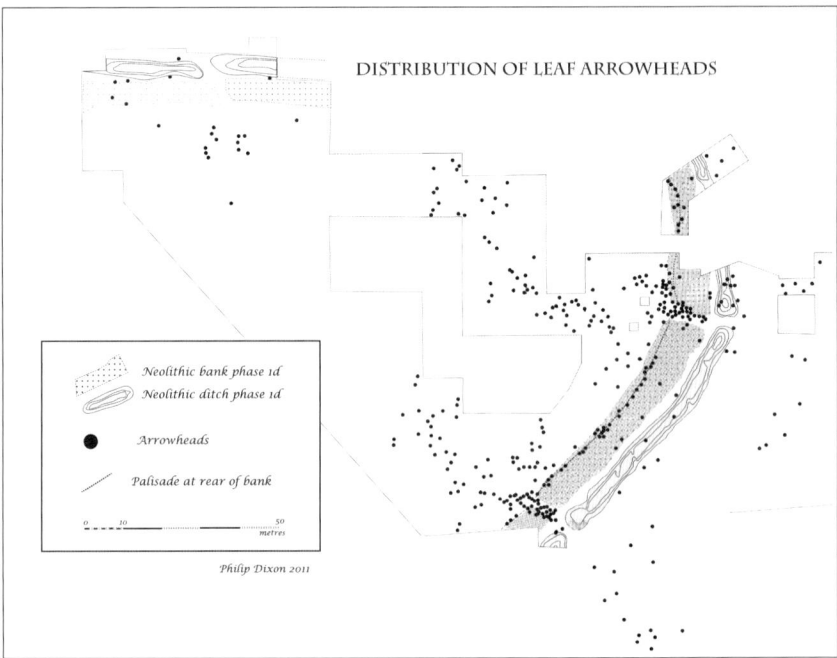

Figure 6.1. Crickley Hill, Gloucestershire, distribution of Neolithic leaf-shaped arrowheads around Neolithic defences. Drawing courtesy of Philip Dixon.

archaeologists seeking to demonstrate a defensive role for hillforts might have wished for, the nearest parallel in the British Iron Age being the scatter of sling-stones through the eastern entrance in period 6 at Danebury. For the Neolithic, one other possible instance of attack by archers is Hembury in Devon (Liddell 1930, 1931, 1932, 1935), though the evidence is more equivocal.

The phenomenon of the interrupted, as opposed to continuous, ditch is one especially associated with causewayed enclosures of the Neolithic, sites that often have more than one and sometimes multiple circuits. Following the pioneer studies of Alexander Keiller at Windmill Hill in Wiltshire (Smith 1965) and Cecil Curwen in Sussex, 'causewayed camps' were recognized as the principal class of non-funerary monuments of the southern English Neolithic, and the distribution remains emphatically south and east of a line from the Severn to the Wash, though a very few related sites have been recognized in the past thirty years in north Wales and northern Ireland. On the continent they are found from Denmark to northern France, where in some cases the evidence for permanent settlement is more convincing. The function of causewayed enclosures has been contentious from the outset. Any unnecessary break in a system of bank-and-ditch defence would compromise security, so that the causewayed technique of Neolithic camps may appear inherently non-defensive. A gap in the ditch, of course, need not imply a corresponding break in the bank (Mercer 1988: 89), and the very poor survival of many causewayed enclosures makes it hard to be certain whether bank or ditch was the primary element. The idea that each section might have been the responsibility of different groups within a dispersed society has its attractions, a token of separate identities in collective endeavour. The irregularity of some plans, however, has given rise to the suggestion that causewayed enclosures could also be the product of episodic activity rather than a single phase of construction (Oswald *et al.* 2001). Evidence for occupation has generally been equivocal, and in the case of enclosures with multiple circuits, different activities may have been segregated. Causewayed enclosures like hillforts almost certainly fulfilled a variety of different agricultural, social, and ceremonial roles, but unlike hillforts, because of their interrupted ditch systems, a defensive purpose has never been the primary presumption.

At Hambledon Hill in Dorset (Mercer and Healy 2008), the ditches of the main causewayed enclosure contained a variety of human remains, skull fragments, sections of articulated trunk, and disarticulated bones. This led Mercer to suggest that this was a place of periodic assembly where communities congregated from considerable distances, bringing with them the remains of the dead for final deposition, already partially disarticulated from exposure elsewhere. Other debris from the ditches suggested that one purpose of assembly was communal feasting, again consistent with periodic, ceremonial, or ritual use of the site. The causewayed enclosure on the Stepleton spur, on the other hand, appears to have been used for domestic occupation. Its modest bank and ditch was progressively enhanced, eventually being encompassed by a substantial timber-framed rampart that extended for 800 metres along the southern edge of the spur. This defensive work was destroyed by fire in an episode that also resulted in the discovery of the skeleton of a young man in the causewayed ditch, apparently killed by an arrow shot to the thorax, with a child smothered beneath him. Further Neolithic outworks cut off the Shroton spur east of the main causewayed enclosure, while the presence of a long barrow within the circuit of the Iron Age fort could well point to further Neolithic activity on the northern spur. Together with the Crickley evidence, Hambledon Hill has done much to reverse the 'pacification' of the Neolithic, but we should beware the danger of allowing this, and evidence for ritual activities, to outweigh evidence for the diversity of usage of causewayed enclosures in the Neolithic.

There is of course no question of causewayed camps being precursors of hillforts in any direct sense (Brown 2009: 25), not least because there is no tradition of continuity through the second millennium BC and because the percentage of sites where hillforts physically overlay causewayed enclosures is very small. Furthermore, the distribution of causewayed enclosures is hardly coincident with that of hillforts, being predominantly south and east of the Jurassic Ridge. Topographically they occur in a range of locations from upland to river valleys, with perhaps a slight preponderance towards the latter (Oswald *et al.* 2001), whereas in the Iron Age, despite notable exceptions, hillforts show a preference for upland locations. More recently the case has been made that the dating of causewayed enclosures even within the Neolithic falls within a very narrow span of less than 200 years from around 3700 BC (Whittle *et al.* 2011), making their interpretation even more contentious.

BRONZE AGE ANTECEDENTS

In central and eastern Europe, the progression from enclosed hill settlement to hillfort is one of degree, and already by the Early Bronze Age there are sites in Slovakia like Spišský Štvrtok (Harding 2006: Figure 7.13) and Nitriansky Hrádok (Točik 1981) that have substantial stone walls, or like Barca (Kabát 1955; Točik 1994) where the rampart was apparently timber-framed within a broad ditch, and enclosing a compact and ordered layout of rectangular buildings. From the Early Bronze Age too, the wetland environment of the Federsee in Baden-Württemberg was being exploited at the Forschner settlement (Torke 1990) with the addition of rampart and palisade, a forerunner of the Late Bronze Age 'Wasserburg' (Kimmig 1992). By the Lausitz culture phase in central and eastern Europe, a variety of rampart constructions in timber and stone were being used (Coblenz 1970; Hawkes 1971: Figure 1), both for hillforts like Niederneundorf in Middle Germany or in lower-lying wetlands like Biskupin in Poland. Further west, excavation of later Bronze Age hillforts had either focused on their defensive structures, as at the Wittnauer Horn in Switzerland (Bersu 1945; Berger *et al.* 1996), or on their Urnfield material assemblages as at the Fort Harrouard in northern France (Mohen and Bailloud 1987). Their rise to dominance was attributed by Anthony Harding to two factors, the formalization of Bronze Age warfare and the emergence of 'quasi-political territorial units' (Harding 2006: 108), both factors that may have catalysed the construction of hillforts in Late Bronze Age and Iron Age Britain.

In Britain, an intermediate class of Middle/Late Bronze Age enclosure was first recognized at the inner earthwork at Rams Hill on the Berkshire Downs, initially supposed by Piggott to have been a causewayed enclosure (Piggott and Piggott 1940; Bradley and Ellison 1975), where it preceded a conventional Iron Age hillfort. Three construction phases were identified, which hardly accorded with the usual Iron Age sequence, in that the earliest comprised a simple dump bank which was later enhanced by a timber framework. The final phase, in which a timber-framed wall or double palisade was built in the silted-up ditch, may reflect the problems posed by renovating a derelict timber-framed rampart. Whilst the enclosure was hardly of hillfort proportions, its wall-rampart and the timber-lined passageway of its southern entrance certainly anticipates aspects of hillfort architecture. Dating of Rams Hill has been reviewed since excavation, with a more reliable set of radiocarbon dates, based upon bone samples rather than charcoal. The results nevertheless point to a Middle Bronze Age origin (*pace* Ralston 2006: 18), indicating that the enclosure was first established by the last quarter of the second millennium, broadly in the Penard period, with major structural modifications around the eleventh or tenth centuries BC, and contemporary with the currency of Wilburton metalwork (Needham and Ambers 1994: 235).

More recently, two other enclosures of similar area and proportions have been dated to the Late Bronze Age. Again within an Iron Age hillfort at Castle Hill, Little Wittenham (Allen and Lamdin-Whymark 2005, Allen *et al.* 2011), an earlier ditched enclosure, yielding sherds of Late Bronze Age pottery, apparently had only a simple dump rampart, or conceivably one supported by turf revetment (Allen *et al.* 2009: 195). More securely dated to around the eleventh century BC was the Late Bronze Age enclosure at Taplow Court (Allen *et al.* 2009), where the complex sequence included palisade, twin post-rows, either successive stockades or part of a timber-framed wall with raised walkway, and a V-shaped ditch with simple, dump rampart, and possible *chevaux-de-frise*. Further post alignments within the excavated area were interpreted as belonging to internal compounds rather than to the perimeter enclosure. Once again, the site was refortified in the early–middle Iron Age, after a significant period of abandonment, but the fact that this later enclosure embraced the whole of the hilltop suggests that it may have been designed to fulfil a rather different purpose from its Late Bronze Age precursor.

These Middle or Later Bronze Age ditched enclosures from the Thames valley and Berkshire Downs prompt reappraisal of the ditch across the inner western entrance of Blewburton Hill (Figure 3.9A), which always seemed unlikely to be part of the phase 1 entrance, whilst the phase 2 inner post-pits had patently been dug when it was fully silted up. An abraded Neolithic axe fragment had raised the possibility of a causewayed enclosure within the Iron Age hillfort, but pottery sherds from the ditch filling appeared to be later prehistoric rather than Neolithic. Though the ditch was inadequately investigated at the time, in retrospect it affords a plausible parallel to Ram's Hill or Castle Hill, Little Wittenham.

One early candidate for a Late Bronze Age hillfort was Mam Tor in Derbyshire (Plate 8b; Coombes and Thompson 1979), where radiocarbon dates for houses within the interior appeared to indicate occupation in the later second millennium BC. The dates have since been challenged, but pottery and a fragment of bronze axe still argue for a later Bronze Age phase of activity, even if this cannot be directly associated with the defences. It was, however, excavations of 1969–76 at the Breiddin in the northern Welsh Marches (Musson 1991) that demonstrated most decisively the existence of Late Bronze Age hillforts in Britain. An unprecedented length of 60 metres of the multi-period ramparts was excavated, yielding radiocarbon dates from structural contexts that confirmed a likely Late Bronze Age construction for the earliest phase. Furthermore, the deposits along the back of the Late Bronze Age rampart had been sealed by its broader Iron Age successor. In consequence, a series of undisputed Late Bronze Age bronzes found in this sealed context could be associated with the occupation of the earliest hillfort, together with further bronzes from the stratigraphically contiguous, though not sealed, deposits behind the Iron Age rampart. In addition to these bronzes, including socketed axe and hammer, tweezers, pins, ring, and awl, numerous sherds of coarse pottery were consistent with a Late Bronze Age domestic assemblage. Dating evidence elsewhere may be more equivocal, but recent research on the promontory forts of Pembrokeshire has suggested the possibility that some may have their origins in the Late Bronze Age.

We have already reviewed the evidence for Late Bronze Age occupation at some of the larger hillforts of south-eastern Scotland like Eildon Hill and Traprain Law, for which evidence of activity in the pre-Roman Iron Age is surprisingly sparse. Taking Anthony Harding's two criteria cited above, we might certainly regard the scale of these sites as evidence for the emergence of larger social units, even if the sites themselves functioned primarily as places of periodic assembly rather than in any overtly centralizing capacity.

Some of the most persuasive evidence for Late Bronze Age construction and occupation of hillforts comes from Ireland. Raftery's (1976) excavations at Rathgall produced abundant evidence for Late Bronze Age occupation both within the interior and outwith the hillfort on the slopes to the south-east. Dating of the ramparts themselves remains unproven, as we have seen, though their association with the Late Bronze Age occupation seems the most economical explanation. Apart from some evidence of iron working pits, and an unassociated later Iron Age bronze strap-tag with openwork triskele design, there is little evidence of Iron Age occupation on the site. The Late Bronze Age activity, on the other hand, points to the site's special significance, not simply in the presence of gold-work from the ring-groove house in the centre of the interior, and hundreds of clay mould fragments from its adjacent workshop, but also from the special compound adjacent to it containing three cremation burials (Raftery 1981). Equally, Mallory's trial excavations at Haughey's Fort in Co. Armagh (Mallory 1988, 1991, 1995; Mallory *et al.* 1996) produced gold-work as well as bronzes and pottery of Late Bronze Age date, though the character of the internal occupation of the site remains unclear. We have argued earlier that this site may have had a special significance in conjunction with the adjacent sites at Navan fort, the King's Stables, and Loughnashade.

Dating is also problematic in the case of the western stone forts, but once again the most economic argument might associate the construction and use of Dun Aengus with the Late Bronze Age assemblage, including pins and mould fragments, and radiocarbon dates. The walls of one roundhouse and underlying Bronze Age levels both extend under the adjacent inner fort wall, which stratigraphically therefore must post-date the Bronze Age occupation, though the absence of Late Bronze Age deposits *outside* this wall on its west side suggests that there may have been an earlier wall on an adjacent alignment. The surviving plan of Dun Aengus certainly indicates radical reorganization, though the structural sequence is far from clear. Some later use of the site was attested by some finds from cutting 1, from the wall-chamber in wall 1, and from a burial of the second half of the first millennium AD in the entrance passage of wall 2a, but occupation of the site during the earlier Iron Age was not well represented (Cotter 1996: 14). This of course raises the perennial problem of how we recognize occupation from periods which are not characterized by diagnostic artefacts. Late Bronze Age bronzes or moulds are readily dateable, as are finds of the Early Christian period, but many everyday artefacts like hammer stones and whetstones are undiagnostic as to period. In the case of the earlier Iron Age in south-west Ireland, beyond the distribution of La Tène types, and in the absence of clearly defined stratigraphic horizons, it is hard to be confident that non-diagnostic artefacts of the earlier Iron Age have not been subsumed within earlier or later assemblages.

If Dun Aengus was indeed fortified already in the Late Bronze Age, we might expect that others among the stone-built cashels had early origins too.

At Mooghaun South, Co. Clare (Grogan 1995), there was material evidence of habitation on the site in the later Bronze Age preceding the construction of the ramparts, though a single radiocarbon date providing a *terminus post quem* for the outer rampart (Grogan 1996: 56) does not exclude the possibility that the earthworks were constructed during the course of this phase of occupation. Certainly there is evidence for Late Bronze Age activity in the Mooghaun region, in the nearby gold hoard of more than a hundred items (Eogan 1983) and in the lakeside site at Knocknalappa (Raftery 1942). It seems reasonable to conclude that some of the stone forts of the Irish south-west were built in the later Bronze Age, continuing in use through the Iron Age, despite the problems of identifying the non-La Tène material assemblage.

ROMAN PERIOD OCCUPATION OF HILLFORTS

With the Roman conquest, we might have expected that hillforts would have been forceably evacuated and their defences slighted, as a potential focus for anti-Roman sentiment and resistance. Certainly Hod Hill was suppressed by the imposition of a Claudian fort within the confines of the hillfort itself, which Richmond (1968: 121) assumed had been cleared of its native inhabitants after its assault and capture. In fact, there are problems with Richmond's interpretation of the hillfort's surrender, and the ballista barrage has alternatively been attributed to post-conquest artillery practice (Maxfield 1989). In the absence of any evidence of firing or destruction of the houses, or of a 'war cemetery', we might question whether the inhabitants of Hod Hill offered any resistance at all. The presence of Aucissa and Dolphin brooches from the annexe gully of Hut 56 and a third brooch from a similar context in the intersecting gullies of Huts 36 and 37 might indicate some continuing occupation, until the Roman fort itself was abandoned less than a decade after the initial invasion.

At Maiden Castle, Wheeler (1943: 64–8) inferred short-term continuity of occupation from the evidence of the east gate, where the roadway had been re-metalled after the episode of destruction. Finds including samian ware indicated occupation till around AD 70, when the population may have been relocated in the new town of Durnovaria (Dorchester, Dorset). Todd (1984b), however, argued that it was a small military unit that was present, rather than a native population, a view that may gain force from the discovery of rectangular timber buildings in the 1985–6 excavations (Sharples 1991a: 101–2). In fact, several hillforts in the territory of the Durotriges and in the south-west of England may have had military installations within their captured precincts. Hembury in Devon (Todd 1984a), Cadbury Castle, Somerset, and Brandon Camp in Herefordshire (Frere 1987) certainly had a military or police presence, while others like Ham Hill, Somerset, may well have had. In fact, Wheeler's original premise, that the generation after the conquest saw in this region a period of 'guarded *status quo*' (Wheeler 1943: 66), in which hillforts were not wholly abandoned, still seems a real possibility.

Further east in central southern England, however, a different situation appears to have prevailed. At Yarnbury in Wiltshire, Cunnington's investigations (1933) suggested that occupation continued through the Roman period, while Tidbury Rings, Hampshire, may have been the site of a Roman villa settlement (Payne *et al.* 2006: 141). An aisled building of later Roman date was found within the Balksbury hillfort (Wainwright and Davies 1995), and Alfred's Castle on the Berkshire Ridgeway was reoccupied from the late first to late third centuries by a substantial rectangular building (Gosden and Lock 2003). This contrasting pattern would suggest that the Roman attitude towards re-use of hillforts in the territory of the Atrebates, for example, was more sympathetic than it was further west.

In the south-east of England, continuity of occupation into the Roman period is certainly attested at the sites of the former terrain *oppida*, though not without substantial change. At Camulodunum in the Gosbecks complex, the enclosure that has been tentatively identified as that of Cunobelinus was modified in its layout and encompassed by Roman fort, temple, and theatre, the latter combination perhaps reflecting the ritualized status of the preexisting Iron Age centre (Millett 1990: 106). Just east of the Sheepen complex in the early years of the conquest a legionary fortress was established, which became the site of a *colonia* in AD 49. The imposition of a colony of veterans must have been regarded as a punitive act, involving confiscation of land and serving as a symbol of subjugation of the native authorities in their tribal centre. In the event it hardly helped promote political stability, Colchester being one of the prime targets of the Boudiccan revolt.

Beyond the lowland zone, in regions where the impact of Romanization was more marginal, it is hardly surprising to find evidence of continuing occupation, or reoccupation of hillforts. In north Wales there is abundant evidence of activity at Dinorben (Gardner and Savory 1964; Savory 1971) in the later third and fourth centuries in the form of more than 250 Roman coins widely scattered across the site, together with later Roman coarse pottery, though the reason for the site's reoccupation at this time is a matter of speculation, and the nature of the structures is controversial. Later Roman pottery from the Breiddin (Musson 1991) suggested agricultural reuse of a conveniently located enclosure, rather than the refurbishing of the hillfort's defences. The evidence from Tre'r Ceiri is perhaps the most problematic, given the density of stone-walled houses, the subdivided or cellular construction of which suggests occupation in the Romano-British period, adapting the earlier Iron Age circular plans (Hogg 1960). In terms of material remains, there is no samian from Tre'r Ceiri, though there is Romano-British coarse pottery, and no coins, so that it seems probable that the occurrence of Roman material types was highly selective, and in consequence, absence of diagnostic types cannot necessarily be equated with periods of abandonment. Contrary to any suggestion that it was a low-status agricultural settlement (Arnold and Davies 2000: 88), what is striking at Tre'r Ceiri is not just the density and substantial nature of the houses, but the discovery from early excavations of a gilt-bronze brooch of later first-century date, similar to the well-known Aesica brooch from Great Chesters, from hut 10 (Baring-Gould and Burnard 1904) and fragments of a beaded torc from hut 41 (Hughes 1907), neither properly stratified but nevertheless surely indicative of high-status occupation. Despite the absence of querns, it is hard to accept Alcock's (1965) contention that these remains result from purely seasonal occupation. Tre'r Ceiri among all British Iron Age hillforts has the appearance of a small town, even allowing for the fact that its surviving internal layout is plainly cumulative.

At first impression, a striking example in northern Britain of the Roman army imposing its presence on a native hillfort is Burnswark hill in Dumfriesshire, where Roman camps were established on its northern and southern flanks. Visible even from Hadrian's Wall, Burnswark (Figure 6.2a) must have been one of those landmark sites that proclaimed status and identity for miles around, so that it is not unreasonable to suppose that it had an important role locally and regionally. The evidence of radiocarbon dates from its rampart defences, however, suggest that these belong to the earlier first millennium BC,

(a)

Figure 6.2. Burnswark, Dumfriesshire: (a) view of hillfort from the south, (b) (opposite) air photograph showing Roman camps and siegeworks. Photographs by D. W. Harding.

whilst limited excavation of the interior (Jobey 1978) indicated occupation in the second century AD. In effect, rather like Traprain Law and some other Borders forts, evidence for occupation and use in the immediately pre-Roman Iron Age, when these sites might have been expected to have been a focus for resistance against the Roman advance, is lacking. Whether the Roman camps (Figure 6.2b) are nevertheless regarded as evidence for the storming of the native stronghold or as bases for subsequent military exercises and practice, the two principal interpretations that have been advanced by Roman archaeologists (Keppie 2009), their presence must surely have been intended primarily to signal the suppression of native authority in the region. We have seen, nevertheless, that Castle O'er at least continued to flourish during the period of the Roman occupation.

Among northern British hillforts, the role of Traprain Law in the Roman period is quite exceptional in the volume of Roman artefacts that investigations over many years have yielded. The hillfort's origins, as we have seen, lay in the later Bronze Age, and though its sequence of enclosing walls may include activity in the earlier Iron Age, its significance at this period may well have been as a centre for periodic and seasonal activities, since the evidence of occupation is scanty. During the Roman period, by contrast, though the enclosing walls were no longer maintained, occupation was relatively intense, culminating in its busiest phase in the late Roman period, when there may have been an influx from the surrounding settlements. Dating of native sites on the basis of Roman imports, as Fraser Hunter (2009) has shown, can be bedevilled by factors of supply and selectivity. Hence, for

(b)

example, there is a paucity of Flavian samian, when the coin evidence is at a peak, and a lack of coin evidence for the century between AD 160–250, when activity is attested by glass and pottery (ibid. 227). One facet of the Traprain imports is the correlation between the range of samian vessels with those from Roman military sites (Erdrich *et al.* 2000: 453), including a wide spectrum of bowls, dishes, and cups, rather than the limited selection found on normal settlement sites, which might lead to speculation that the resident community had gone further towards the adoption of Roman eating habits than was the custom elsewhere. This would also account for the higher-than-average occurrence of Roman coarse-ware vessels, the attraction of which would doubtless have been their contents rather than the vessels themselves. The range of brooch types at Traprain likewise accords closer to the types found on military sites (Hunter 1996: 121–3), in contrast to native sites generally, on which trumpet and dragonesque variants, more in tune with traditional La Tène fashion, predominate. The implication of this might be that the army was indirectly instrumental in the supply of goods to Traprain, perhaps through the local *vicus* at Inveresk, rather than goods being acquired independently from Roman *mercatores* or *negotiatores*. Nevertheless, just as the lowland brochs may have acted as intermediaries in the later first and second centuries AD in the redistribution of Roman imports to native settlements (Macinnes 1984), so it seems likely that Traprain Law had favoured status in the acquisition and redistribution of Roman goods throughout this part of south-east Scotland. The Votadini have traditionally been regarded as pro-Roman in political sympathies, and the evidence from Traprain certainly affords archaeological endorsement for that belief. By the late Roman period, the special significance of the site is attested by the famous hoard of silverware, mostly cut into fragments (*Hacksilber*), and currently dated to the mid-fifth century. By this time the perimeter had been refortified by the so-called 'Cruden wall', perhaps reflecting the political instability of the times. Beyond the fifth century there is very little evidence of the site's occupation, though equally no evidence that its abandonment was occasioned by violent destruction.

POST-ROMAN HILLFORTS IN WALES AND THE WEST

That hillforts in southern and more especially western Britain may have been built or reoccupied in the post-Roman period has been long suspected, but identifying material evidence to substantiate a Dark Age date has proved more problematic. E. T. Leeds' (1927, 1931) investigations at Chun Castle in Cornwall attributed the site primarily to the Iron Age, but Charles Thomas (1956) was able to demonstrate that the assemblage also included post-Roman pottery. Radford's (1951) proposal of a later occupation at Castle Dore was based on the presence of rectangular buildings, which could not be related to the earlier Iron Age occupation, rather than any associated material assemblage, and on the site's traditional historical associations. Dinas Emrys also had historical associations based on Nennius's *Historia Brittonum*, and on excavation (Savory 1960) proved to have been fortified and occupied in the sub-Roman period.

The most important contribution to the study of hillforts of the post-Roman period in western and northern Britain in the past fifty years has been that of Leslie Alcock, whose excavations from the 1950s at Dinas Powys in Glamorgan, Deganwy in north Wales, and more controversially, at Cadbury Castle in Somerset, were precursors to his systematic investigation of early historic sites in Scotland in the 1980s. The promontory fort at Dinas Powys (Alcock 1963) was exceptionally small in area, even by the standards of south-western Welsh hillforts—less than half an acre (0.2 ha) within the simple dump bank that enclosed the Dark Age settlement. Yet on the basis of a relatively exotic material assemblage, including class B amphorae, a range of D-ware and E-ware, and quantities of fragmentary continental glass of fifth–sixth century date, Alcock was able to propose that the site had been the residence or *llys* of a local chieftain. Metalworking on the site was relatively well attested. Iron was undoubtedly being smelted on site, and a bronzesmith and jeweller was inferred from the number of crucible fragments. Much of the bronzework was interpreted as scrap from Germanic sources imported for re-use, and at the time the same argument was applied to much of the imported glass, which was seen as cullet intended for reworking as beads or inlay. Current fashion has since swung in favour of the view that glass was imported in the early historic period as whole vessels (Campbell 2007: 96), but Alcock's original argument, based on the paucity of base to rim fragments, in this case still seems persuasive. The structural evidence for occupation was tenuous in the extreme. Two pairs of attenuated gullies enclosed sub-rectangular areas, which the excavator interpreted as drainage trenches around the site of stone buildings, the masonry of which had been robbed without trace for the revetment of the later Medieval defences, preferring this to the alternative option of timber buildings founded on sill-beams rather than earth-fast post-holes. For the present writer, the experience of excavating putative structures in such intractable surfaces as the carboniferous limestone of Dinas Powys was an early introduction to the limitations of field archaeology, but the gullies must indeed have been the residual remains of buildings and the material assemblage seems indisputable evidence for the site's status in the post-Roman centuries. The enclosing earthworks of the Dark Age fort nevertheless were hardly impressive in terms of the site's status any more than was its size of enclosure, and in view of the evidence for metal-working, we might consider the alternative possibility that the site, like the Mote of Mark on the northern Solway coast, was a specialist metal-working centre rather than the hillfort of a petty potentate.

The excavation at Cadbury Castle was unfortunately promoted and publicized as a quest for King Arthur's Camelot, as a result of which a good deal of professional criticism and controversy was generated. In retrospect, the excavator appears to have regretted the emphasis on the Arthurian dimension, which hardly features in the account presented in the final report on the early Medieval archaeology of the site (Alcock 1995), and which is expressly repudiated in its preface. What was remarkable about the early post-Roman occupation of Cadbury was that it entailed the refurbishment of the entire circuit of the inner rampart, making this one of the largest known hillforts of the period in Britain. The renovated rampart, designated the Stony Bank in earlier reports and Rampart E, of Cadbury period 11, in the final account, occupied a position stratigraphically between the ultimate pre-Roman Iron Age defences and the Late Saxon mortared rampart. Though dating evidence in direct association with this structure was limited, its date was reasonably inferred as fifth to sixth century AD on the basis of imported Mediterranean amphorae from several relevant contexts. The construction of the rampart was of particular interest, with a stone-faced, timber framework that was not earth-fast. Between outer and inner faces, some 4.5–5.0 metres apart, two rows of longitudinal timbers were jointed, rather than nailed, to transverse timbers, the positions of which were betrayed by alignments of stonework forming distinct compartments. The structure was not unlike that recovered at Green Castle, Portknockie, Banffshire (Ralston 1987), though somewhat earlier in the first millennium AD. One phase of construction at the south-west gate was also attributed to this early post-Roman occupation, but internal structures contemporary with the Cadbury 11 defences were harder to define. A concentration of amphora sherds in Area L led to the tentative recognition of a timber hall, around 19 m in length and 10 m in width. It was centred on a length of gully, slightly bowed, containing two amphora sherds, that divided the building transversely. It is acknowledged that the identification of post-holes that formed the outline of this building is not supported by statistical analysis of size or depth, and not really by any consistency in alignment or spacing. A measure of the uncertainty likewise surrounds the cruciform ditch on Site E, which Alcock (1972, 1995) consistently regarded as the foundations of a late Saxon church, the masonry walls of which were never actually built. Barrett *et al.* (2000: 176–8) alternatively suggested that this was the robbed foundations of a late Roman temple, despite the absence of supporting coin evidence (Casey 2000) or any apparent evidence of the invariable residual mortar and debris resultant from robbing of stone walls. The issue is more than incidental, since the temple was apparently central to the maintenance of the hill's role as a 'place where assumptions about the order of the world were empirically validated by routine and diverse experiences' (Barrett *et al.* 2000: 324).

Cadbury hillfort at Congresbury in Somerset (Rahtz *et al.* 1992), excavated around the same time as its better-known namesake, is around half the size of Cadbury Castle, less prominently located, though defended like the latter in its post-Roman period with a single rampart. Internally several buildings were tentatively identified and attributed to this phase of occupation, including a circular building some 10 metres in diameter, which was interpreted as a shrine, or perhaps as a building in which ritual feasting may have taken place. What the two sites had in common was the import of considerable quantities of continental pottery, which in both cases came to an end before the introduction of E-ware around the late sixth and seventh centuries. The reason for the breakdown in continental trade, which equally appears to have affected the major trading and redistribution centre at Tintagel on the north Cornish coast, may have been a reorientation of continental trading patterns away from Mediterranean control to sources in western Gaul. Equally, however, the volatile political situation consequent upon the expansion of Anglo-Saxon settlement, amply testified in the *Chronicle*, may also have been a factor, whilst Irish incursions from the west will undoubtedly have had an impact on trading activities along the western seaways.

The social and political context of these early post-Roman hillforts remains contentious. How rapidly the administrative and military order of late Roman Britain broke down after Honorius' edict of AD 410 is uncertain, but it is generally assumed that in the later fifth century, western Britain would have been ruled by a number of regional kings, as may be inferred from the writings of Gildas around the mid-sixth century. On the basis of the better-documented political structure of northern Britain in the post-Roman period Alcock (2003) argued for a hierarchy of settlements there, leading him to propose that Cadbury 11 may have had the status of a *civitas* in the late fifth or early sixth century (Alcock 1995: 151).

EARLY HISTORIC HILLFORTS IN NORTHERN BRITAIN

In view of the relatively short period of Roman occupation in southern Scotland, we might expect that traditional strongholds of the pre-Roman Iron Age could have remained in use intermittently during the early first millennium, and might well have been reoccupied on a regular basis in the post-Roman period. Despite the poverty of the material assemblage and the lack of chronologically diagnostic artefacts, a case can be made for reoccupation at Bonchester Hill, Roxburghshire, on the strength of the construction of the intermediate rampart using edge-set boulders with horizontal coursing above

(Piggott 1950: cutting X, Figure 8). A number of other sites likewise might have been reoccupied on the evidence of their multi-period plans (Harding 2004a). The citadel with outworks at Rubers Law, Roxburghshire (Figure 6.3a; RCAHMS 1956: No. 145) is clearly post-Roman, because of the incorporation into its walls of reused Roman masonry, which may have had greater significance than simply taking advantage of a convenient source of supply. The outermost circuit at Rubers Law, however, enclosing a total of just under 3 ha (7 acres), shows no evidence of Roman stonework, from which we might infer that the early historic fort had reoccupied and reinforced an earlier Iron Age hillfort.

North of the Forth the hillfort on Clatchard Craig (Close-Brooks 1986), one of several hillforts in south-east Scotland that have been casualties of quarrying, produced radiocarbon dates for its innermost and third rampart circuits, both of which had been timber-laced and burnt, that centred on the sixth and seventh centuries AD. The intermediate rampart 2, followed a slightly different alignment, but again incorporated re-used mortared Roman stonework and was evidently also part of the post-Roman sequence. Nevertheless, the exact sequence of rampart construction is not without problems, and it is still possible that there was an Earlier Iron Age phase of enclosure contemporary with the apparently earlier pottery assemblage from the site. Among the early historic material assemblage were a couple of sherds of 'E-ware' and a number of fragments of moulds for pins and penannular brooches, the latter probably dating to the eighth century, together with ornamental bronzework,

(a)

Figure 6.3. Late Iron Age hillforts in north Britain: (a) air photograph of Rubers Law, Cavers, Roxburghshire, (b) (opposite) Dunadd, mid. Argyll. Photographs by D. W. Harding.

all perhaps indicative of relatively high-status occupation. Further north important fieldwork has been undertaken in Strathdon, Aberdeenshire (Cook forthcoming), following the Alcock tradition of small-scale reconnaissance excavation, which has confirmed that half of the hillforts investigated were occupied in the early historic period.

In the south-west of Scotland, one of the more productive hillforts is the Mote of Mark overlooking the Urr estuary in Dumfriesshire (Plate 11a; Laing and Longley 2006). The hillfort was first defended with a stone-faced rampart in the sixth century AD, and was a centre for the production of high-quality bronzes until the later seventh century, when the site was burnt and its defences slighted, possibly as a result of Anglian expansion westward. The Mote of Mark was evidently a relatively high-status site, witnessed not only by its metalworking but by the presence of continental imports, notably E-ware and glass, or perhaps more accurately the perishable products such as wine, dyes, or spices that may have been contained within them. Whether these were direct imports via the western seaways, or whether they were the result of redistribution from some other major centre remains unclear. The excavators did not regard the site as royal, seeing it instead as 'the residence of a master smith rather than that of a lord who retained such a craftsman under his patronage' (ibid. 174), an interpretation that accords with the very small area enclosed by the fort (0.3 ha, ¾ acre). They nevertheless saw it as functioning within a hierarchical social system, receiving dues from lesser clients and

(b)

owing renders to a higher overlord or king. Geographically, the Mote of Mark would almost certainly have been within the territory of British Rheged, the extent of which kingdom has been much debated. It may have included parts of pre-Roman Brigantia, though by the sixth century much of the eastern Pennines will have been absorbed by Anglian expansion. How far it extended along the northern side of the Solway estuary depends in some measure upon the interpretation of the place-name Dunragit, overlooking Luce Bay towards the Rhinns of Galloway (McCarthy 2002; Laing and Longley 2006: 163–4).

The issue of correlating the evidence of archaeology and history, and more specifically archaeological sites with documentary records recurs, of course, in the context of the settlement of Argyll by Dál Riata, traditionally dated around AD 500 or earlier on the basis of brief references in the Irish Annals and in Bede's *Ecclesiastical History*. The authenticity of this episode of colonization has been called into question (Campbell 1999) on the grounds that the principal classes of settlement in Argyll do not mirror those of the assumed region of origin in Northern Ireland, where the ringfort is the dominant settlement type of the first millennium AD, if anything reflecting instead insular continuity from the earlier Iron Age. Crannogs are found in both areas, but Scottish examples have been securely dated from the earlier Iron Age, whereas their Irish counterparts on current evidence would appear to belong to the early Christian period. This line of argument, however, depends upon the expectation that archaeological distributions, whether of settlements or material types, will reflect distinct populations, in accordance with Childe's view of archaeological cultures. The reality is that it is seldom possible to make such correlations, because of the dynamic nature of cultural interaction, and in this instance, the assumed homeland of Dalriadic settlers is no more distinctive within northern Ireland in terms of its structural or material types than is early historic Argyll. It is certainly possible that the documentary entries reflect a politically motivated attempt to authenticate the sovereignty of Scottish Gaels over Irish Dál Riata (ibid. 15), and it seems probable that connections across the North Channel had a much longer ancestry than the documentary record might suggest. Comparison might be made with cross-channel connections in the later pre-Roman Iron Age in southern and southeastern England, where it seems likely that Caesar's report of Belgic settlement probably conflates and obscures a much more complex process of cross-channel acculturation over several centuries.

In Argyll and the Inner Hebrides, Alcock was insistent that the majority of excavated duns were of first millennium AD date (Alcock and Alcock 1987: 131), only Rahoy (Childe and Thorneycroft 1938a) having yielded clearly earlier Iron Age material. What he failed to acknowledge is that most of the others, such as the rectangular dun at Dun Fhinn or the sub-triangular enclosure at Kildonan, were self-evidently different from the circular or sub-circular duns of the Rahoy class that most probably represented the western counterpart to the Atlantic roundhouses of the Northern Atlantic region. Nevertheless, the fact that some duns were built and occupied in the early historic period, and that later hillforts were small in area and often little more than large 'dun enclosures' (Harding 1984) indicates a shift in the settlement pattern from the Earlier Iron Age.

'Nuclear' forts and 'citadel' forts

In essence a *nuclear fort*, first identified by R. B. K. Stevenson (1949b) at Dalmahoy on the Pentland Hills in Midlothian, comprised a summit plateau or citadel, around which a series of lower plateaux were clustered in a manner that could be adapted for a descending hierarchy of enclosures. Excavation at Dunadd (Lane and Campbell 2000), however, has shown that the permanent enclosure walls or boundaries may in fact have been cumulative over a protracted period of time, rather than a unitary construction from the outset. Even so, if the concept of hierarchy was integral from the start, then some more ephemeral form of physical boundary may have served initially, only later being reinforced by permanent walls.

Among the most prominent of the Scottish nuclear forts are those that feature in the documentary sources as regional strongholds of political importance, such as Dunadd, Argyll (Figure 6.3b; Lane and Campbell 2000), Dundurn, Perthshire (Plate 11b; Alcock *et al.* 1989: 209), and Dumbarton Rock on the Clyde (Alcock and Alcock 1990), the last two among others being included in Alcock's uniquely productive and highly economic 'reconnaissance excavation' programme. Some of these sites, including those that historically and archaeologically are among the most important, are extremely small compared to earlier Iron Age forts. At its greatest extent, Dunadd covers rather less than a hectare, and its summit citadel enclosed an area just 20 m by 13 m, which, if roofed, would have been no bigger than a large house. Furthermore, evidence for the nature of the occupation or use of nuclear forts is surprisingly sparse, and, though there was abundant occupational debris at Dundurn, for example, the small scale of the excavation trenches inevitably precluded any possibility of uncovering building plans. On the plus side is the recovery of high-status goods, notably imported pottery and glass, from a number of sites in western Scotland mainly, not just hillforts but crannogs and monastic sites too, indicating seaborne trade from the late sixth and seventh centuries along the western seaways from continental Europe (Campbell 2007). At Dundurn, this amounted to just two sherds of imported pottery, one of 'E-ware', the other possibly Rhenish, and two fragments of glass, either Rhenish or southern Gaulish. If the quantities seem pitifully small, their presence nevertheless is undeniably significant, in much the same way that Mediterranean imports are important to an evaluation of the role of Late Hallstatt and Early La Tène *Fürstensitze*.

Stevenson had thought of these sites as the product of a 'proto-feudal world in which chiefs or kings of various degrees, each with their retainers, dominate the pattern of society' (1949b: 197). Alcock *et al.* (1989: 209) anticipated 'a number of royal strongholds, among which the king would have made periodic circuits and progresses', by implication defining a rather different role for hillforts than the 'central place' model commonly envisaged for the earlier Iron Age. As Alcock recognized, a hierarchical nuclear plan could be extrapolated from other sites in Argyll, such as Dun A' Chrannag in Knapdale (RCAHMS 1988: no. 266; Alcock *et al.* 1989: 209). On a small scale, a possible contender is Little Dunagoil at the southern tip of Bute, set within the broader area of an earlier Iron Age terrain *oppidum* (Harding 2004b), where Dorothy Marshall's excavations from the late 1950s (Marshall 1964) demonstrated occupation from the sixth century, perhaps the secular counterpart to the nearby monastic settlement of St Blane's. In the east the King's Seat at Dunkeld is an obvious candidate, as could be Moredun on Moncrieffe Hill near Perth, though this may well be an adaptation of an earlier Iron Age enclosure. In the south-east is Moat Knowe at Buchtrig, Roxburghshire (RCAHMS 1956: No. 307; Harding 2004a: Figure 8.3a), the terraced layout of which, together with its used of edge-set slabs in its wall, may indicate an early historic construction. In the south-west a possible contender is Trusty's Hill, Anwoth (Thomas 1960), which again could have been an early Iron Age fort around which later outworks were added, although dating on the basis of the Class 1-derived symbols carved on rock outcropping beside the southern entrance of the vitrified citadel has been challenged by Laing (1999).

Alcock was adamant that the nuclear fort was an innovation of the early historic period, and plainly bridled at Feachem's (1966: 85) view that these forts, including Dunadd and Dundurn, were essentially Early Iron Age forts, not just reused but repaired by 'undiscriminating or desperate persons' as late as the seventh century. For the most part it is true that sites that present the 'hierarchical' terraced structure of the typical nuclear fort do not in general appear to have commended themselves to earlier Iron Age communities. But the problem of dating sites on the basis of enclosure morphology is highlighted by the case of the Dunion in Roxburghshire (Rideout 1992), now regrettably obliterated by quarrying. On the basis of surface survey, notably the absence of ditches, the use of substantial boulders in the wall construction and the incorporation of natural outcrop into the defensive circuit, this had been classified as a Dark Age fort. Yet both radiocarbon and thermoluminescent dating from the 1980s excavations indicated instead occupation in the later pre-Roman Iron Age. The plan of the Dunion did not wholly accord with the nuclear model, however, since, despite its enclosed summit plateau, it lacked a true citadel, being instead an agglomeration of linked units. It nevertheless raises the possibility that a form of nuclear hillfort, not perhaps yet fully developed into the early historic hierarchical model, had its origins in the later pre-Roman Iron Age in the Borders.

Some of these hillforts are closer in plan to a related class defined by Feachem (1955) as *citadel forts*. Like nuclear forts, the focus of these was the small, highest enclosure or citadel, but instead of a series of lesser and lower enclosures looping out from it, the citadel fort generally lies within the larger and often lower circuit of the surrounding outworks. He cited Dumyat in the Ochil Hills (ibid. Figure 5) and Chatto Craig, Hownam (RCAHMS 1956: No. 305), as possible examples. The problem with this classification was that in some instances the citadels seemed to be secondary constructions taking advantage of, but not necessarily maintaining, earlier Iron Age enclosures, so that even if the early historic date of the citadel could be sustained, there was little justification for regarding these as any different from later, smaller ringforts that were built, for example, at the summit of Garn Boduan.

Promontory forts

One of the larger and more elaborate promontory forts of north-east Scotland was at Burghead in Morayshire, largely destroyed when the harbour and town were remodelled in the early nineteenth century, but recorded in General Roy's mid-eighteenth-century plan (Figure 2.1b). On its south-eastern landward side it appears to have been defended by triple ramparts and ditches, though it is not certain whether these were cumulative or part of a unitary design, and equally unclear whether they originated in the earlier Iron Age or were part of the early historic defences (Ralston 1980: 38; 1987: 16; 2006: 175). Differences in building technique between the walls of the upper citadel and lower enclosure may well indicate a difference in date of construction. The western wall of the upper compound was exceptionally massive, being more than 8 metres thick at base and surviving to a height of 3 metres. It was constructed with an internal framework of transverse and longitudinal timbers, fronted and backed by a stone revetment (Small 1969). But there was no evidence for the use of iron spikes in the timber framework, as was reported in Young's late nineteenth-century investigation of the ramparts of the lower headland (Young 1891, 1893). Radiocarbon dating established its early historic context, though there has been some debate over the length of the rampart's use (Alcock 1984: 21). Burghead would be exceptional in its apparent use of iron spikes, which are more commonly associated with the *murus Gallicus* type of wall construction of Late La Tène fortifications in continental Europe, and it would be hard to sustain any realistic link with the earlier Iron Age tradition, which in any event is otherwise unknown in the British Iron Age. The often-cited nails from Dundurn (Alcock *et al.* 1989) are much smaller, and fit only to secure planks, whereas the Burghead spikes could have secured the main framework, especially if the timbers were half-checked. The bull carvings from Burghead (Harding 2004a: Figure 9.3), of which six survive from thirty or more claimed in the antiquarian record, again testify to the exceptional nature of the site, which may well have been a royal centre in the early historic period, even though it is not identified as such in any historical record.

Further east along the Moray coastline the much smaller promontory fort at Green Castle, Portknockie (Ralston 1980), may also have had a wall around the entire cliff-edge, though if so it had long since eroded on the seaward side. The surviving wall, dating to the second half of the first millennium AD, consisted of a ground-level framework of longitudinal and transverse timbers, with verticals half-lapped into them rather than set in post-holes (at least within the excavated area), to which the outer stone revetment had been added by way of cladding (Ralston 2004). Internally at Green Castle, the only contender as a contemporary structure was a truncated rectangular building with stone foundations and rounded corners, some 4 metres in width and a minimum of 7 metres in length, from which a number of crucible fragments were recovered (Ralston 1987: 19–21 and Figure 3). The site is too small and the material assemblage too sparse to support any claim to its being a high-status settlement, but it would be entirely consistent with the model of a hierarchical Later Iron Age society in which access to and control of sea routes was an important political and economic consideration.

IRISH RINGFORTS

The definition, dating, and function of Irish ringforts are even more contentious than those issues are in relation to duns in western Scotland, but the arguments stem from similar problems. Like the Scottish dun, 'ringfort' tends to be an umbrella term that embraces sites of very considerable morphological diversity in terms of size, layout, and construction, which may obscure an equal diversity in date, function, and social context. The term has been applied to both earthen raths with bank and ditch and stone-walled structures, generally without a ditch, otherwise referred to as *cathair* or *caiseal*, a practice that was widely adopted following the publication of Ó Ríordáin's *Antiquities of the Irish Countryside* in 1953. The assumption that stone forts were simply a counterpart of earthen ringforts in regions where the underlying geomorphology favoured building in stone has rightly been challenged (Fitzpatrick 2009: 275), not just because there may be occasional coincidence of distribution, but because stone ringforts appear to have exploited the potential for monumentality in a way that earthen ringforts seldom attempted.

Also like Scottish duns, dating of ringforts has been a vexed issue. The great majority of sites on available evidence were occupied in the Early Christian period, from around the sixth to ninth centuries AD, and opinion generally discounts earlier origins (Lynn 1983). Stout (1997) in particular marshalled the corpus of radiocarbon and dendrochronological dates to demonstrate that ringforts were occupied predominantly in this relatively narrow span. While not dissenting from this conclusion, Fitzpatrick (2009: 277) pointed to the limitations of the data, namely that, of these dated sites, 71 per cent were from Ulster and no less than 45 per cent from Co. Antrim, and that, of 156 sites excavated between 1970 and 2004 on the Department of the Environment's database, no less than 50 per cent had no dating evidence whatsoever. Given the diversity of sites and the fact that there are an estimated 45,000 ringforts throughout Ireland, the probability that their chronology will need to be reassessed as reliable dates, especially from primary contexts, become available, seems assured. Limbert (1996) pointed to several factors that militated against the demonstration of early origins for ringforts, some of which echo the problems of dating the primary construction and use of brochs and duns in Atlantic Scotland. Where the assemblage is essentially aceramic, as in the earlier Iron Age in Ireland, the task of identifying an earlier occupational horizon on the basis of material associations becomes even more difficult. Assigning occupation on the basis of negative evidence is, of course, highly problematic. It is possible that other explanations might account for the 50 per cent of ringforts that have yielded no dating evidence. Taphonomic or environmental factors may have militated against artefact survival; social or economic factors may have been different from those sites that yielded dateable assemblages. But the possibility that some of these sites belonged to an earlier period from which material finds are generally lacking should not be discounted.

Stone forts of south-west Ireland

The problems of dating a site's construction and initial occupation, where there was secondary occupation, even if intermittent, over a very protracted span of time, is nowhere better illustrated than in the stone forts of south-west Ireland. We have already seen that the sites at Dun Aengus and Mooghaun were occupied in the Late Bronze Age, as is clearly testified by material remains of that period. Whether forts themselves were built at this early date is less certain, simply because of the difficulty of establishing an unequivocal stratigraphic relationship between occupation deposits and enclosing walls, but the probability must be that the forts did have their origins in the later prehistoric period. At the same time it is evident that a site like Cahercommaun had an important Early Christian phase of occupation, equally testified by artefacts of distinctive type. What seems scarcely credible to someone who has studied the counterparts of stone forts in Atlantic Scotland, where sites were not uncommonly occupied and reoccupied over a millennium or more, is how short a span is generally attributed to the occupation at Cahercommaun, and the resistance to the possibility that the stone forts of the south-west were essentially a phenomenon of the 'long Iron Age'.

The late dating of Cahercommaun was challenged by Barry Raftery (1972), who made a number of cogent points about the artefact assemblage that hardly seem to be invalidated by his subsequent retraction. The fact that a number of types, hammer stones, simple bone points, spindle whorls, iron bill hooks, blue glass beads, and the like could as easily date from the earlier Iron Age is tacitly acknowledged in the number of references cited in the report to All Cannings Cross or the Glastonbury sites, whilst dumb-bell beads and stone strike-a-lights are known in Ireland and Britain in contexts of the first century AD or thereabouts. The seven saddle querns from Cahercommaun are unlikely to have been in contemporary usage with the rotary querns, as Hencken (1938: 60) imagined, and it is generally accepted that in domestic usage, the saddle quern was essentially a Late Bronze Age type that may have continued in use in the earlier Iron Age (Caulfield 1981; Connolly 1994). The latest reappraisal of the site (Cotter 1999) acknowledges therefore that the saddle querns represent later prehistoric activity on the site, but evidently concluded that this predated the construction of the fort, even though the prospectively earlier material was wholly confined within the limits of the inner enclosure (ibid. 61–2).

Cotter's review acknowledges that the souterrains were secondary features, as patently are several of the hearths that are shown overlying earlier features at a height of up to a metre above bedrock. The secondary walls are described as hardly ever having two faces (the walls of structure 8 and its contiguous neighbour structure 7 seem to be exceptions), or indeed being faced at all, though sometimes they were 'bordered by slabs set on edge' (Hencken 1938: 15, 18). This description matches well the techniques of construction used in later Iron Age, mid-first millennium AD cellular building in Atlantic Scotland, and indeed Ralegh Radford (1940) remarked upon the same technique at Tintagel in his review of Hencken's publication of Cahercommaun. Given the problems of stratigraphy at Cahercommaun which 'made the depths at which finds occurred in it of no significance' (Hencken 1938: 14) it is fruitless trying to attempt to define what structurally might represent the earliest occupation. For Ó Floinn (1999), as for Hencken, the deposit of the silver brooch in souterrain B is evidently the key, when the bulk of evidence suggests earlier occupation in the first millennium AD, if not before. On the analogy of Aldclune, Perthshire (Hingley *et al*. 1997), it is arguable that the ninth century brooch, especially in this instance given its association with a complete skull and other human remains, represents a deliberate deposit on a site of importance in folk memory well after its occupational *floruit*, rather than the period of occupation itself.

In sum, analogies with the archaeological problems of dating the stone-built duns of Argyll and Atlantic Scotland, or more correctly, recognizing the complexity of their occupational sequence, seems to point to the probability that evidence for the earliest occupation of the stone forts has often been obscured, being prone to obliteration by or stratigraphic confusion with, subsequent phases of activity, while distinctive artefactual types are liable to be accorded disproportionate weight in any assessment of site sequence. This is not special pleading in the absence of evidence; it is a simple recognition of the inherent limitations of archaeological evidence.

7

Function 1: Defence

For much of the past two hundred years, a basic assumption has been that hillforts had a primarily defensive function. That they served also as settlements or for community gatherings, perhaps even for ritual or ceremonial activities such as seasonal festivals or inaugurations of kings, has been variously inferred, but it was not until relatively recently that the purpose of community defence within the framework of a hierarchical society was so fundamentally challenged. The reasons, however, were often based upon individual site circumstances, from which generalization hardly seems justified. At the Chesters, Drem in East Lothian (Figure 5.2a), for example, it was argued (Bowden and McOmish 1987) that the hillfort's defensive capability was compromised by being overlooked from the south by higher ground, from which missiles might have been projected into the enclosure. Tactically this seems odd, since the fort's multiple lines of enclosure, especially at its northwest- and east-facing entrances, makes it on plan one of the more complex multivallate hillforts in Britain. Whether these had realistic defensive capability or were intended primarily for display and status remains open to debate.

Whilst it is certainly true in individual cases that hillforts were not sited topographically with tactical advantage as a paramount consideration, or that a regional class like the hill-slope forts of the south-west were apparently at a disadvantage from higher ground, or that the area enclosed by some hillforts was so great as to make their defence logistically impractical, equally we could cite hillforts where the enclosing earthworks by any standard would have been a very formidable barrier to assault. Every generation reads its archaeology in the conceptual context of its own time, and it is hardly surprising that a generation brought up with two world wars should have interpreted hillforts in terms of 'invasions'. Wheeler's (1953: 12) description of Bindon Hill, Dorset, as a 'beach-head' could hardly have been conceived by anyone other than the brigadier who had fought through North Africa and the Salerno landing in Italy. Nevertheless it is hard to avoid the conclusion that the current challenge to the defensive role of hillforts stems not so much from individually anomalous sites as from a more general objection to the concept of conflict in prehistory, and is one facet of what has been noted earlier as the 'pacification of the past' (Keeley 1996: 23). Lock (2011) is surely absolutely right in suggesting that some hillforts may have had no defensive aspect whatsoever; but equally, given that there is almost universal acceptance of the diversity of hillfort functions, it is irrational not to accept that others may well have done.

WARFARE IN PREHISTORY

Identifying evidence for prehistoric battles archaeologically is extremely problematic, and later Bronze Age discoveries from the Tollense valley in northern Germany (Jantzen *et al.* 2011) are quite exceptional. In general, pathological evidence for inter-personal conflict or warfare for the Late Bronze Age and Iron Age is not abundant (Armit 2011b), and, where it occurs, it is not always self-evident exactly what was the cause of violent injury. A number of reasons could be advanced for this, but the principal problem, as for any period of prehistory but especially so for the British Iron Age where formal cemeteries are not the norm, is that those burials that are known from the archaeological record are too few to be fully representative, and since we cannot infer the basis of selection, it is hard to evaluate their significance. Some cemeteries and individual burials have been found in the context of hillfort excavations, however, and these will be considered below.

A first step to understanding the possible role of hillforts in this context would be to consider the nature of Iron Age conflict and ancient warfare generally (Carman and Harding 1999). Conflict could be at a range of levels from individuals ('interpersonal violence' in the current jargon) or small groups to warfare on a larger scale between coordinated forces. It might occur spontaneously or as part of a planned or long-term strategy, and it might take place between community groups or within them. The causes of conflict can be infinite. They might include practical issues such as competition for land or access to water, matters of sometimes violent disagreement even among 'peaceable' farmers. But ethnographic analogies suggest that blood feuds and the prestige that accrues from productive aggression were equally potent factors in perpetuating conflict. A further issue is the degree to which Iron Age warfare was 'ritualized'; that is, the extent to which it was governed by conventions. This need not imply that it was any less destructive or bloody in its outcome, and the idea that 'primitive' or 'ritualized' warfare was less destructive than 'real' or 'non-ritualized' war surely misses the point that there are elements of ritual in most forms of warfare. James (2007: 168) is probably therefore right to argue that the 'default situation' in the Iron Age was neither peace nor war but chronic insecurity, in which the role of the hillfort as a deterrent to aggressors, among its other roles, was doubtless significant. A hillfort, nevertheless, was not an offensive installation, as siege-works plainly were, neither can it 'control' territory or routes of communication that they overlook in the same way that a hill fortified with artillery might in a later era. The assumption must be, therefore, that most engagements between hostile forces, large or small, took place outwith hillforts, and that the hillfort itself in times of conflict was a refuge of last resort. This is presumably why they were sometimes the sites of 'war cemeteries' or 'massacres'.

'WAR CEMETERIES' AND MASSACRE SITES

It might seem self-evident that the discovery of a 'war cemetery' in the immediate environs of an Iron Age hillfort reflected the site's military role in episodes of conflict. The classic case, of course, is the Maiden Castle 'war cemetery' in the eastern entrance that led to Wheeler's graphic reconstruction of the attack on the hillfort by Vespasian's Second Legion in AD 43/44. Three aspects of Wheeler's account (1943) might be open to challenge: first, that the dead were victims of a battle with the Romans; second, that the battle took place at the east gateway to the hillfort; and third, that the episode was part of the Roman advance of AD 43/44. Sharples, whose own excavation brief at Maiden Castle in 1985–6 (Sharples 1991a) did not include a re-examination of the war cemetery, nevertheless questioned Wheeler's interpretation of the cemetery and sacking of Maiden Castle (Sharples 1991c). The evidence for burning in the east gateway, which Wheeler saw as part of the storming of the gates and firing of huts, he attributed instead to debris from industrial activity. But he conceded that the slighting of the defences, represented by the collapse of stone revetment of the entrance passage, must indeed have taken place at around the time of the conquest, on the basis of material stratigraphically sealing it and sealed by it. Difficult to discount are the dozen iron bolt-heads and spear-heads found in the vicinity of the entrance, which cannot simply be dismissed as probably belonging to the late Iron Age occupation (Sharples 1991b: 125). The fact that several skeletons bore injuries that had healed certainly suggests that some individuals had been involved in episodes of inter-personal conflict or warfare prior to the Roman conquest, in contrast to the evidence from Durotrigian cemeteries generally (Redfern 2011). Multiple cuts to the head (Wheeler 1943: Pl. LIVA) endorse Wheeler's view of the savagery of the attack, and most clearly one individual with a ballista-bolt in the spine (Figure 7.1a; ibid. Pl. LVIIIA) and another with a square-shaped wound to the head (ibid. Pl. LIIID) support his contention that these fatal blows were inflicted by Roman forces. The fact that not all the skeletons show similar evidence is hardly surprising, since not all fatal wounds need have left anatomical traces. Avery (1993, vol. II, Maiden Castle paras 9, 37, 51, 78, and note 97) did not deny the identification of the cemetery as the result of conflict, but suggested that the suppression by Paulinus of the Boudiccan revolt of AD 60–61 was a more likely horizon (cp. *infra* the dating issues of the Cadbury Castle massacre), when Maiden Castle was finally abandoned for the settlement at Dorchester. Since it is clear that there was an established cemetery in the vicinity of the eastern entrance prior to the sack of the fort, it is quite probable that some graves pre-dated the 'war cemetery', and indeed some may have post-dated it. The double grave P22/P23, for example, on the fringes of the main group, included a Roman ear-scoop in P23, which could indicate that these were slightly later interments (Avery 1993, Vol. II: 227, and note 97). There need therefore be no presumption that the dead were buried where they fell, even though ballista bolts and Roman iron arrowheads indicate that the entrance came under attack. Furthermore, with regular orientation and the provision of grave-goods, Wheeler's vision of disorder, anxiety, and haste is hardly demanded by the evidence. His graphic reconstruction of events may have been characteristically flamboyant, but in broad outline it was not necessarily wrong.

Wheeler believed that native occupation of Maiden Castle continued after its sack by Vespasian's forces into the early Flavian period. This view, as we have seen, was challenged by Todd (1984b), who argued instead that a small garrison may have occupied the reduced fort, a suggestion that gained support from Sharples' discovery of rectangular timber building of the conquest or

Figure 7.1. 'War cemetery' and 'massacre' sites: (a) Maiden Castle, Dorset, burial P7A with iron spear-bolt in spine; reproduced by kind permission of the Society of Antiquaries of London from Wheeler, 1943, © reserved; (b) (opposite) Sutton Walls, Herefordshire, skeletons in ditch by west entrance. Photograph courtesy of the Royal Archaeological Institute.

Function 1: defence

immediately post-conquest period (1991a: 101–2). Cadbury Castle certainly appears to have been occupied by a Roman military contingent in the post-conquest period, though its size and composition is not clear from the very truncated remains so far revealed within the hillfort interior (Barrett *et al.* 2000: 173ff.). Here, however, the evidence for massacre comes in the form of mass burial, the circumstances and implications of which are by no means straightforward. That the hillfort gateway and ramparts were subject to burning and destruction is not in doubt, and the presence of both Roman and native weaponry with the dead in the south-west gate might warrant the assumption that this had been the principal focus of attack. The problem relates to dating, since Alcock (1972: 170–2) believed that the material remains indicated a date around AD 70 for the massacre, for which there was no obvious historical context. It may seem improbable that a hillfort of Cadbury Castle's importance was 'by-passed in the mid-40s' (ibid. 170), and re-examination of the evidence for final publication concluded that there had been more than one episode of destruction at Cadbury in the first century AD. According to this version, the massacre related to the first of these episodes. After a period of abandonment, the bones were sealed with rubble and the gateway was rebuilt. The second episode of destruction, which saw the reduction of the stone-lined passageway, related to the later occupation that

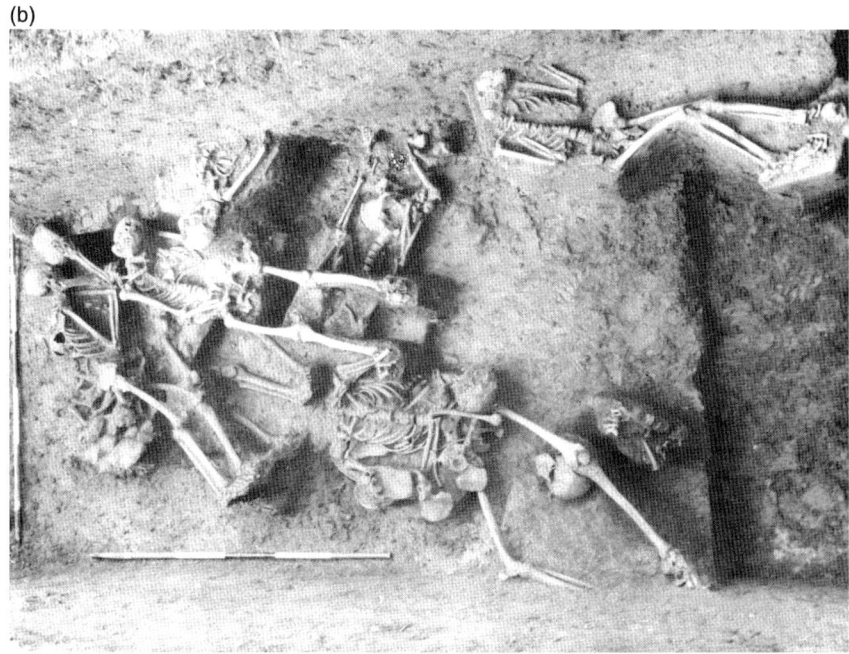

(b)

may have extended into the early second century AD. It seems unlikely that the remains of the dead were simply left where they fell, and the probability that the entrance was selected as the site for their pyre for symbolic reasons seems consistent with evidence elsewhere for deposits made in or near the gateway to hillforts. The presence of Roman equipment, including a set of spears and shield from the west guard chamber, could indicate the presence of Roman casualties (Woodward and Hill 2000) or perhaps of trophies among the weapons and dress ornaments of the native victims. The date of the massacre remains unresolved, the options being the period of the conquest, immediate post-conquest unrest recorded by Tacitus (*Annals* 12, 31), the period of the Boudiccan uprising of AD 60/61, or some other episode not documented in the historical record. Not surprisingly, however, this is not regarded as 'central to any full understanding of the human processes that were taking place. The questions to be answered are how and why, not when' (Barrett *et al.* 2000: 116). Others might not see these as mutually exclusive alternatives, even for a proper understanding of 'human processes'.

Location within the gateway of the fort and mutilation of the human remains are two aspects of the Cadbury 'massacre' that link it with discoveries made in the 1930s at Bredon Hill on the border between Gloucestershire and Worcestershire (Hencken 1938). There is no question of this constituting a formal cemetery, since the remains were severely mutilated with torsos dismembered and limbs scattered around the entrance passage. The numbers involved were hard to estimate; on the basis of cranial material a minimum number of 27 was represented, on the basis of mandibles 46 and from non-cranial remains a minimum of 64. It is thus clear that significant parts of the skeletons were missing, deliberately or by accident. In the circumstances, sex was hard to determine, but virtually all the remains were adult between 25–35 years of age. It is difficult to distinguish possible depredation by scavengers from what also plainly must have been an orgy of extreme savagery, possibly carried out in ritualistic frenzy. Though the excavator not unreasonably assumed that the dead had fallen defending the gates to their fort, it is not inconceivable that the remains had been brought here for deposit from elsewhere, and that the weaponry found with them was part of the ritual deposition. The problem is compounded by the suggestion that a line of broken skulls across the inner gateway may have been from trophies suspended on the gates, which had been fired. It is not clear whether these were part of the massacre ritual, or whether the trophies were from previous events, perhaps even the occasion of reprisal. Mrs Hencken noted that the gates and flanking walls of the passage had collapsed or been thrown down on to the mutilated remains, and concluded that the hillfort had been totally abandoned thereafter. She was also adamant that there was no evidence that the hillfort had been subject to attack by Roman forces, and in fact attributed the massacre to a conflict with hostile 'Iron Age C Belgic' settlers expanding from south-eastern England. No explicitly post-conquest material was recovered from the excavation, and both pottery and metalwork would be consistent with a date in the early decades of the first century AD. Avery (1993 Vol. II: 40, 43 note 50) nevertheless argued that the Roman conquest was the most likely context for the Bredon massacre, on the basis of pottery sherds found in the massacre levels which he believed should be post-conquest, and a fragment of possible Roman helmet flap from among the massacre deposits. Furthermore Manning (1985) maintained that the spearheads were Roman, so that current opinion has swung in favour of Bredon having been stormed in the early years of the conquest.

The evidence for a massacre by advancing Roman forces at Sutton Walls in Herefordshire (Kenyon 1953) differs from Cadbury Castle and Bredon Hill in one significant respect, the victims having been bundled unceremoniously into the ditch immediately adjacent to the entrance (Figure 7.1b). Twenty-four bodies were uncovered in a limited excavation, and the excavator was sure there were more to the north. Several had been decapitated, and others bore evidence of severe wounds to the head or limbs. Though there were no associated artefacts and no stratified dating evidence, the ditch in which the skeletons lay had accumulated minimal silt since the defences had been refurbished in the early decades AD, and the ramparts and entrance revetment had in the excavator's estimation been slighted in accordance with Roman practice. A striking feature of Sutton Walls, nevertheless, is that occupation of the hillfort continued through the second century AD, so that the presence of the massacred remains in the flanking ditch did not seemingly deter access through the gateway, as the gruesome relics in the inner gateway at Bredon Hill evidently had done.

The evidence for what has been regarded as a massacre site or war cemetery at Spetisbury Rings in Dorset (Gresham 1939) was uncovered in the mid-nineteenth century in the course of construction of the central Dorset railway, which infringed on the north-east sector of the defences. Between eighty and ninety skeletons were said to have been uncovered in 1857, 'laid irregularly' in a pit in what was probably the partially silted ditch. There is no suggestion of mutilation or dismemberment; in fact, Henry Durden, the local antiquary and collector, remarked on the good state of preservation of the skeletal remains. A variety of artefacts were reputedly recovered at the same time by Durden and J. Y. Akerman, secretary of the Society of Antiquaries of London. These included an iron sword and several currency bars, and a fragment of bronze scabbard binding, as well as bronze brooches and rings and bone pins and needles. These, together with a complete bronze cauldron and an iron torc (Hawkes 1940), are indicative of the high status and special character of the deposits, which is hardly consistent with the image of a Roman 'tidying-up operation' (Cunliffe 2005: 187, 222). The inclusion of Roman spearheads as well as examples of native type certainly suggests that the hillfort was one of

Suetonius' twenty *oppida*, but there are problems in regarding the Spetisbury collection as a uniform assemblage. The two brooches of La Tène 2 type, apart from being comparative rarities in Britain, must date from more than a century before the conquest, while a complete bronze chape is again of a form that must have been current in the later third or second centuries BC. Durden's record of a further forty or more skeletons having been discovered in January 1858, in circumstances that are obscure raises the possibility that there was a second group of burials further along the track, perhaps including a cemetery already established before the conquest. This might then replicate the sequence at Maiden Castle, where casualties of the conquest were buried in proximity to an established burial ground. In the case of Spetisbury, it is significant that it must have been located in or just beyond the enclosure ditch, just beyond the boundary of the hillfort.

One example of mass burial comes from well beyond the Wessex–Welsh Marches axis of previous discoveries, from Maiden Bower in Bedfordshire, first the site of a Neolithic causewayed camp, thereafter an Iron Age hillfort. In the south-east entrance in 1913 the landowner and farmer uncovered a burial pit in which were the remains of more than fifty individuals in a jumbled mass of skeletal remains, including animal remains (Hawkes 1976b: ix). The date of this deposit remains uncertain, and there is no evidence to confirm that it was contemporary with the hillfort (though this seems likely), still less that it was the result of Roman attack. Nevertheless, the importance of the entrance and the flanking ditches seems once again to go beyond the simple belief that this was where the dead had fallen.

The most recently-excavated example of what appears to have been a massacre comes from Fin Cop in Derbyshire (Waddington 2011, and forthcoming). Here a minimum of nine skeletons was found in two quite widely separated sections across the hillfort ditch, unlike most of the above examples, where the burials were concentrated, notably near the entrance. The excavator therefore inferred that there could have been a hundred or more if they had been distributed around the perimeter defences, a pattern which has not been noted elsewhere, and which would certainly have ritualistic or symbolic overtones. A significant factor in the Fin Cop find is that all the skeletons so far identified were of women or children, which might suggest not so much a battle as a punitive massacre. Finally, a key element was that the Fin Cop massacre pre-dates the other Roman-period massacres by several centuries, being dated to a span around 440–390 BC. Whatever its explanation, therefore, it cannot be dismissed as an anomaly of the Roman political horizon, and it certainly reflects an episode involving earlier Iron Age native communities, and one that had a lasting impact, since the site was apparently never again reoccupied thereafter.

Whilst these and other possible sites where there is evidence for the burial of victims of battle undoubtedly reflect the violent side of Iron Age life, it is still arguable whether this necessarily means that defence was a primary function of hillforts. Hillforts may well have been a target for attack, and therefore a locus for defensive engagements, because they were identified with the community under attack, and the capture and sack of the hillfort would therefore be symbolic as well as tactical. It is hard to be certain that burial of the dead in the ditches flanking the entrance or within the entrance passage itself was therefore the result of a failed attempt to defend the hillfort, rather than because burial in proximity to the gates of the hillfort of those who had fallen in an engagement outside the hillfort was regarded as special. The 'massacre' sites plainly are not examples of respectful deposition, even in haste. They must therefore have been carried out by hostile forces, or by forced labour under coercion by hostile forces. Where quantities of dismembered remains are included, however, we may question whether these were not the product of acts of calculated profanity, such as the dispersal of remains that had been exposed to excarnation within a sacred precinct in or near the hillfort, rather than the macabre mutilation of the defeated dead. Cunliffe's 'tidying up operations' might well have been necessary where the Roman army chose to occupy the hillfort even temporarily, a practice that may have been adopted more frequently in Britain that had previously been imagined. Hod Hill may appear exceptional, but we have seen that there is evidence for a Roman contingent at Cadbury Castle, and equally positive evidence has been uncovered for Roman occupation of the hillfort at Hembury in Devon. But in addition to these, a Roman presence might be inferred, as we have seen, at Maiden Castle, at Brandon Camp, Herefordshire (Frere 1987), and possibly, on the basis of several finds of Roman military equipment (Webster 1958: 80–3), at Ham Hill in Somerset too (Todd 1984a: 265). In these circumstances it is certainly possible that the unceremonious deposit of massacre victims and excarnated remains into the hillfort ditches might well result from clearance by forced labour squads after defeat.

EVIDENCE OF DESTRUCTION

The most obvious evidence of destruction is afforded by those hillforts where there is evidence of burning of the structural defences. Unlike the New England Indians (Malone 1993), where firing as a military tactic was universally eschewed because of an abhorrence of its consequences, fire was recognized by Caesar as an effective tactic against both ramparts and gates, and its use in the early historic period in northern Britain is certainly recorded in documentary sources. Finding traces of burning archaeologically, of course, need not mean that this was the result of aggressive destruction rather than by accident, or by design as part of some esoteric act of symbolic closure, so that we can only weigh the balance of probabilities in individual cases. Avery may have been right in arguing that the shift in later pre-Roman Iron Age hillforts from timber revetment to stone in entrance passageways was in part a response to the vulnerability of timber passages to attack by firing (Avery 1993, II: 75–6), though the main objective of attack would presumably have been to breach the gates, which would still have been susceptible to firing.

Among hillforts where firing is attested archaeologically, the burning of the entrance at Rainsborough, Northamptonshire, was so intense and sustained that the filling of the major post-pits in the passage comprised material burnt bright red and purple with quantities of charcoal up to a metre in depth (Avery et al. 1967: Figures 10a, 10b, and 232). The guardrooms had also been destroyed by fire, the roof of the north guardroom apparently collapsing on to one of the defenders (Avery 1993, II: 282). The intensity of burning indicated by the Rainsborough post-pits raises the possibility that the fire could have been deliberately fuelled by the defenders once they had failed to prevent it from taking hold. As a defensive tactic, this may have been an effective last resort, since an attacking force would be unlikely to relish the prospect of mounting a charge across 20 metres of deep, smouldering embers. Another instance of an entrance apparently being destroyed by fire is period 6c of the main east entrance at Danebury. This gateway had once previously been burnt, in period 2, when in plan it most closely resembled the gateway at St Catharine's Hill, Winchester, which was also destroyed by fire. But the period 6c destruction at Danebury evidently signalled a major shift in its fortunes and functions, the gate itself never being rebuilt, though the entrance passage remained open to traffic. Evidence for this destruction is nevertheless confined to the postholes of the inner entrance, in which the charred stumps of posts survived, packed with flints 'shattered by intense heat from the burning post' (Cunliffe 1984a: Fiche 1, C5, postholes 16, 23, 30, 61). There is no reference to the fire having scorched the flint revetment lining the long passageway, so that in this instance the evidence may indeed point to the specific targeting of the gate, rather than to systematic sack after capture. At St Catharine's Hill, by contrast, not only were the gates and timbers of the entrance passage burnt and strewn across the roadway, the rampart itself suffered, reducing its core material to a 'light brick-red powder' (Hawkes et al. 1930: 64–6).

There are numerous examples of hillforts where evidence has been claimed for the burning or partial dismantling of ramparts, which is often treated under the same heading as the firing of gateways, both being regarded as evidence of military assault. The specific case of vitrified forts in northern Britain will be considered below, but from Wessex to the Welsh Marches there are instances of ramparts having been fired deliberately, and more probably after capture than in the process of attack. A good demonstration of this was the burning of the period 2 rampart at Crickley Hill, where the burning of the rampart's timber framework generated enough heat to turn the core material into quicklime. Dixon reasoned that the survival of the front wall face indicated that the process of destruction had begun from within, with the dismantling of the rear wall to expose the timber framework: 'it seems inconceivable that this would have occurred by accident, particularly when the same fire seems to have involved the buildings within the fort, and one must consider that the destruction of the first hillfort was a deliberate slighting of the defences, after abandonment or capture' (Dixon 1994: 186). The destruction of the period 3b defences was equally systematic and decisive, but this time the evidence points to damage inflicted by the assault, the walls of the bastions flanking the entrance being fire-reddened by the burning of the gates and bridge. Within the fort, the roundhouse and four-posters of the contemporary settlement likewise showed evidence of burning (ibid. 194), which could have happened in the course of the attack or as part of the subsequent destruction. This time, apart from much later, partial occupation, the hillfort was never rebuilt. Broadly contemporary with the later defences at Crickley Hill was the single-period rampart at nearby Leckhampton, where the rampart south of the entrance had been severely burnt, the slaked lime core overlying a framework of charred timbers (Champion 1971, 1976). Here it was unclear whether the gates had been fired at the same time, since excavation had not reached the lowest levels in the entrance passage, but seemingly the rampart to the north was unaffected.

In the Welsh Marches, the south-west entrance at Croft Ambrey was possibly targeted with fire at the end of period Vb (Stanford 1974). A layer of charcoal extended right through the entrance, including substantial timbers that lay across the passageway from the gateway superstructure. The southern entrance at Ffridd Faldwyn in period 3 seems to have suffered a similar fate. Not only was the stone revetment at the entrance reddened by burning, the ramparts themselves had been subjected to such intensive heat that the excavator regarded the effect as tantamount to vitrification, with quantities of 'clinker' being found in the ditch fill (O'Neil 1942: 36–7). We might perhaps infer that the more extensive and systematic the destruction, the more likely it is to have been the product of punitive razing after capture, whereas more limited evidence of burning, especially where concentrated around the gates, may be indicative of tactical use of fire in an attack on the hillfort itself.

The fact that all of the examples so far considered are from southern Britain may reflect the reality that hillfort excavation in the north and west has generally been on a smaller scale, and therefore insufficient to demonstrate extensive evidence of destruction. One exception was the Broxmouth, East Lothian, salvage excavation, where the hillfort's defences and entrances underwent a succession of structural phases, several of which included elaborate timber-revetted passageways between the ramparts and ditches. For the most part these displayed no evidence of destruction, deliberate or accidental, but the period VI structures at the south-west entrance clearly had suffered intense firing, incinerating the revetment posts on the east side of the entrance especially, but also reducing the rampart material itself to what the excavator described as 'vitrified gravel', which was also found in the adjacent ditch filling (Hill 1982a: 164). The timber-laced fort of period 2 at Craigmarloch, Renfrewshire, was also comprehensively burnt to the point of vitrification, but in this case there was also some evidence that the earlier double palisade had been destroyed by fire (Nisbet 1996; Alexander 1996b: 17–18).

Though entrances, ramparts, and internal buildings may all have been fired in the course of attack and capture, therefore, slighting and firing of ramparts and burning of buildings within the fort more probably would have resulted from punitive reprisals after a hillfort's capture, intended both to discourage its future reuse and to signal widely its fate. Dismantling stonework of the walls would have been necessary in order to expose the internal timber-work sufficiently to facilitate firing. Prior to both, the main confrontation may have taken place somewhere outside and beyond the hillfort. Where only the gates have been burnt, however, with no evidence of wider destruction, we should not discount the possibility that an attack was successfully repelled.

'VITRIFIED FORTS' AND BURNT RAMPARTS

Vitrified forts are not a special class of hillfort that belong to any specific cultural or chronological horizon. They are simply forts the stone and timber ramparts of which have been subject to intense burning to temperatures over 1000 degrees Celsius, resulting in vitrification. The belief that vitrification was an ingenious device on the part of hillfort builders for creating a stronger defensive wall still has its exponents more than a century after the issue was first addressed in the archaeological literature, and long after the myth of creative vitrification should have been laid to rest. Christison (1898) on balance believed that those examples in which the defensive circuit was more or less completely vitrified represented a construction process, though he was uncertain as to its purpose. He did, however, recognize that many so-called vitrified forts had only very limited vitrification, or showed evidence of burning without actual fusing of the rock. The essential weakness of the constructional vitrification theory, therefore, is that it was generally only partially or selectively achieved. It is equally unclear what benefit could have accrued from vitrification, since its effect appears to be distortion rather than consolidation of the wall. These factors had already been recognized by Joseph Anderson, who rightly concluded (1883: 279) that 'vitrified forts do not differ in any essential point of their character from forts that are not vitrified. . . . The results of former investigations have not produced evidence sufficient to carry the conclusion that the vitrification was accomplished at the time of their construction, or that it was a method of construction.'

In the 1930s, Childe (1935a, 1935b) had initially assumed that vitrified forts were a culturally distinctive group, but following his own excavations and exercises in experimental archaeology (Childe and Thorneycroft 1938a, 1938b), he too concluded that 'a vitrified rampart is just a Gallic wall that has been burned' (Childe 1946: 14), effectively concurring with Anderson's conclusion more than sixty years later. MacKie's (1976) excavations at several key sites demonstrated clearly that the burnt debris had collapsed into the interior to rest upon the accumulated deposits of occupation, so that firing was plainly secondary and not part of the construction process. Setting fire to the ramparts in the prevailing weather of eastern Scotland, especially under onslaught from defenders, would surely have been wholly impractical. Experimental firing (Ralston 1986) has shown just how difficult it is under favourable circumstances to get a timber-framed rampart to burn to the point of vitrification, requiring repeated attention and addition of combustible material. The clear implication of empirical experiment, therefore, must be that firing of the ramparts was undertaken subsequent to capture, as a deliberate and punitive act of repression. The fact that the rampart core shows an intensity of vitrification, as at Dunagoil on Bute (Plates 12a,b), may again reflect the fact that the facing walls were torn down to expose the timber of the interior. Once alight, the ramparts could have burnt or smouldered for days and nights, sending a dire signal for miles around and violating the communal sense of place that the hillfort embodied. Burning a hillfort after capture would have symbolized the destruction of a community's ancestral homeland with the finality that was evidently intended by the Helvetii when they destroyed their own strongholds before migration (Caesar *dBG* I, 5).

An alternative explanation for vitrification has been advanced for Moel y Gaer, Llanbedr, in the Vale of Clywd (Karl and Butler 2009), where it was argued that vitrified material from elsewhere was deliberately introduced to the site as part of a foundation ritual, intended to affirm the builders' rights of place and to ward off malevolent forces. Such an interpretation seems scarcely applicable to the scale of vitrification witnessed elsewhere, and it is plainly inadmissible in the case of Dunagoil, where the process of vitrification had affected *in situ* outcrop (Harding 2004b). Dunagoil, with its outer works, was plainly a complex site, though among the secondary scatter of vitrified material its subtleties are not easy to detect (Geddes and Hale 2010).

As to distribution, MacKie (1976) showed that the distribution of vitrified forts was essentially coincident in Scotland with timber-framed ramparts, though there appeared to be some regional clusters around the Moray Firth, in central Scotland from the Tay to the Clyde, and in the south-west. Vitrified or calcined ramparts are also found quite widely over continental Europe from southern Scandinavia to the Hispanic peninsula. In southern Britain there are instances of limestone ramparts like Leckhampton (Champion 1971, 1976), where firing at high temperature has resulted in calcination of the rampart core. Notwithstanding the case that has been made for constructive vitrification for the early historic site at Broborg in Uppland (Kresten *et al.* 1993), the evidence in Britain overwhelmingly confirms the conclusion that this was the result of destruction rather than any intended purpose on the part of the builders.

CHEVAUX-DE-FRISE

Chevaux-de-frise in military technology are massive frames of criss-cross spiked timbers designed to impede a cavalry attack, the name being derived ironically from the Frisians' reputed lack of cavalry. Archaeologically the term refers to any barrier of close-set stones or stakes that would cause horses to rear or stumble, and through which even infantry would have to thread their way with care. At their most effective, in the swathes of razor-sharp stones surrounding Dun Aengus, for example (Figure 3.6b), they present a daunting obstacle that even the visitor today should attempt to cross with caution. In north-west Europe the Irish examples are certainly the most impressive, and the best designed in terms of a serious obstruction to assault, in that the broad bands of stones that surround the fort at Ballykinvarga, Co. Clare (Plate 13a), or the promontory fort at Dun Dubh Cathair on Inishmore (Plate 13b; Westropp 1910b), for example, at least cover extensive swathes of the approaches to the fort.

The Scottish examples, by contrast, are both smaller in size and so selective in their surviving placement in relation to the fort's circuit that they could surely have been circumvented by any attacking force. At Dreva in Peeblesshire (RCAHMS 1967: No. 275), the *chevaux-de-frise* outside the south-western outer wall of the hillfort occupies the central part of the plateau that gives access to the fort but well back from the walls, and would have had the effect of forcing any attackers into narrower approaches on either side. They might therefore have impeded a direct onslaught by diverting its direction, though the slopes adjoining the plateau are hardly so steep as to present much of a natural obstacle. Settings of individual stones would of course have been vulnerable to later stone-robbing, as may have been the case at Dreva, where the secondary settlement on the north-east side of the fort could have reused stones from an earlier *chevaux de frise*. At Cademuir West, Peeblesshire (RCAHMS 1967: No. 264), a linear spread extends along the eastern flank of the hillfort where they would have been concealed from view of any attacking force approaching from the north-east until it was upon them. The excavated examples at Kaimes Hill, Midlothian (Simpson 1969) were so diminutive and so limited in extent that it is hard to believe they were more than token in purpose, being adjacent to the south-east entrance, but hardly obstructing access to it. Small size need not preclude effectiveness in bringing down a horse at the gallop, but it seems unlikely that they could serve much purpose so close to the walls. Ralston (2006: 88), following Moret (1991: 11) and Lorrio (1997: 93), was surely right in envisaging their purpose, if defensive, as directed against infantry as much as cavalry, a conclusion that had actually been reached by Christison (1898: 227) rather earlier.

One of the more impressive examples of *chevaux-de-frise* in Wales, at Pen-y-Gaer, Llanbedr-y-Cennin, Caernarvonshire (RCAHMWM 1956: no. 315), was evidently radically modified when the construction of an the outer rampart on the south side of the fort intruded across the earlier extent of the southern setting. Detailed survey of the small hilltop enclosure at Carn Alw, Dyfed (Plate 14a; Mytum and Webster 1989) showed that the *chevaux-de-frise* formed a protective swathe across the only easy approach to the site, with access strictly controlled through a trackway lined with boulders leading to the main entrance. The purpose of the *chevaux-de-frise* may indeed have been to impede frontal attack, but it is equally clear that control of access and impressing visitors was also part of the effect.

Beyond Scotland, Wales, and Ireland *chevaux-de-frise* are best represented in the north-west of the Hispanic peninsula, as Harbison (1968, 1971) showed, with a lesser concentration in the territory of the Celtiberians (Lorrio 1997). An issue that inevitably arises from the difficulty of dating *chevaux de frise* is whether they were an integral part of the rampart and ditch system, or whether they belong to an independent, possibly earlier occupation, which might thus account for the rather sparse, residual remains associated with some British hillforts. In the case of the Celtiberian sites, however, their location in front of the ditch, or on occasion between wall and ditch, certainly suggests a planned unity. Their dating, however, remains problematic. Among the earliest, the fort at Els Vilars, Arbeca, where the *chevaux-de-frise* abuts a wall of *murus duplex* type and projecting bastions, is dated to the seventh century BC, though elsewhere they are undoubtedly later in the pre-Roman Iron Age. Ralston (2006: 88) is probably right in favouring an origin for *chevaux-de-frise* in the Hispanic peninsula, where the distribution seems densest, and their presence in northern and western Britain and Ireland argues for maritime contacts along the western seaways. Harbison suggested that the stone variant that survives in Atlantic Europe may have been derived from a more widely distributed use of timber *chevaux-de-frise*, dating at least from the earlier Iron Age and from which the Roman technique of using wooden *lilia* may have derived, but the evidence for this has been inconclusive. A possible contender as a wooden *chevaux-de-frise* is the post alignment 1104 fronting the later Bronze Age defences at Taplow Court (Allen *et al.* 2009: 195–6, and Figure 4.4c), where a greater original breadth may have been curtailed by the subsequent construction of the U-profiled ditch. A question of definition thus arises as to when multiple lines of posts are not palisades but *chevaux-de-frise*: apart from not being part of a contiguous barrier, presumably the latter would entail sharpened, if shorter, stakes, but neither distinction need be obvious in the archaeological record.

If *chevaux-de-frise* were indeed in origin designed to impede a cavalry attack, then we might infer that cavalry was deployed from at least the later Bronze Age or earlier Iron Age. This, of course, was Cowen's (1967) inference from the introduction of the long Hallstatt sword, and especially the Mindelheim type, which he regarded as a high-status weapon. He was persuaded that, in addition to wagons with paired draught, testified by the vehicles and horse-gear in aristocratic graves, the evidence of horse-bits and scabbard-chapes also pointed to mounted warriors. The evidence from horse-burials such as those from Blewburton Hill or the various deposits from Danebury, nevertheless, suggest that Iron Age horses were no larger than medium-sized ponies by modern standards, standing around 11–13 hands. This evidently was true of most of western and north-western Europe in the Iron Age (Johnstone 2004), and appears still to have been the case in the later pre-Roman Iron Age, if the proportions between horse and rider depicted on Iron Age coins are indicative. The same relative proportions likewise seem incongruous to the modern eye on 'Pictish' sculptures. There is little evidence for selective breeding in the Iron Age (Grant 1984), though the Danebury evidence did suggest that horses were regarded as special by Iron Age communities.

WEAPONRY AND SLING-STONE HOARDS

The principal weapons of the Iron Age in Britain as in continental Europe were the sword and spear or lance. These are widely attested in the Urnfield Late Bronze Age and through the Hallstatt and La Tène Iron Ages, notably as grave-goods in La Tène inhumations that perhaps controversially have been labelled as 'warrior burials'. The fact that weapons occur in graves and in hoards, both with ritual associations, prompts the question whether their automatic interpretation as evidence for warfare or interpersonal violence is justified. Kristiansen (1984, 1999) argued on the basis of an analysis of Danish and Hungarian later Bronze Age swords that there was clear evidence of resharpening and repair as a result of actual use. In Britain swords and scabbards of the La Tène period have been found in graves, notably in cemeteries of the Arras series in eastern Yorkshire of the middle Iron Age (Stead 1965, 1979, 1991), and occasionally elsewhere, like Mill Hill, Deal (Parfitt 1995) or in northern Britain, as at Mortonhall, Edinburgh (Stead

2006: no. 206), or Alloa, Clackmannanshire (Mills 2004). Equally notably, they have been recovered from watery contexts, like the Witham sword from Lincolnshire (Harding 2007: Figure 7.2) and the remarkable series from the River Bann in Co. Antrim (Raftery 1984). Some of these weapons were contained within highly ornamented scabbards, sometimes with motifs like the so-called dragon-pairs that may have had supernatural significance beyond simple decoration. As with some of the parade armour of the middle and later pre-Roman Iron Age, like the Witham and Battersea shields, it is hard to imagine that such prestige pieces of equipment were not designed more for ritual and ceremonial usage than for practical service in conflict. Spearheads, or more specifically lance-heads, on the other hand, with the notable exception of the example from the Thames at Datchet, were not generally ornamented, any more than were the iron swords themselves. Kristiansen (1999) regarded the lance as the basic weapon of combat of the later Bronze Age and Iron Age from Greece to Northern Europe, numerically outnumbering swords in the order of ten to one. In the European Iron Age, spear- or lance-heads occur in graves with swords and sometimes shields as part of the martial panoply, so presumably were still prestigious items of equipment. They also occur not infrequently on hillfort sites in pre-Roman contexts as at Danebury (Cunliffe 1984b; Cunliffe and Poole 1991b).

One weapon for which there is little evidence archaeologically in the British Iron Age is the bow. The bow had certainly been in widespread use in the European Neolithic and Copper Age (Mercer 1999), and in the continental Iron Age, the well-known quiver of arrows from grave VI at the Hohmichele in Baden-Württemberg (Riek 1962) indicates its survival into the earlier Iron Age, if mainly perhaps as a sporting or hunting weapon. Caesar encountered archers in his Gallic campaigns, and he makes a point of stressing the great number of archers that Vercingetorix was able to summon up for the defence of Alesia (Caesar *dBG*, VII, 31, 36, and 80). So it is surprising that evidence of archery is virtually absent from the archaeological record in late La Tène Gaul. Caesar makes no mention of the use of archers by the native forces in Britain, and he is surprisingly unspecific regarding the nature of weapons and missiles deployed by the Britons. Since the weaponry of the native forces can hardly have been a matter of indifference to him, the most likely reason for his failure to elaborate is that they were essentially the same as those used by his own troops, which included both slingers and archers. Archers, of course, can be used tactically in two quite different ways; to put down a barrage of arrows or to target the enemy individually. This latter was what the Gaulish archers did as rear-guard snipers at Alesia, evidently so effectively that it prompted Caesar to comment on that tactic. It may therefore be that the use of stoning rather than archery barrage as an assault tactic accounts for the rarity of arrowheads among finds from hillforts, though a couple of iron arrowheads were found in the Pimperne, Dorset, roundhouse (Harding *et al.* 1993: Figures 26, 12, 13).

Alternatively, we may wonder whether bone tips or simply fire-hardened hardwood tips were used, for which surviving archaeological evidence would be minimal. This raises the question whether there were different classes of weaponry, among which high-status weapons are more conspicuous in the archaeological record, whereas basic weapons for hunting and personal defence among lesser ranks may have been more common but less readily distinguished. Archery does not feature in the early Irish epic tales, from which we might conclude either that the bow was unknown, or that it was not considered to be a suitably heroic weapon.

Sling warfare and sling-stones as a significant component of the Iron Age armoury came to prominence with the excavation of Maiden Castle, Dorset, and the discovery there of several huge hoards of stones, apparently assembled for the defence of the hillfort. Wheeler (1943) argued that sling warfare became dominant with the introduction of multivallate defences, though it was never entirely clear how the concept of 'defence in depth', linked to the critical range of around one hundred yards for effective sling fire, worked in practice. Wheeler's explanation of the introduction of multivallation has been largely discredited, but his recognition of the increased use of stoning, whether with the aid of a sling or as a hand-thrown barrage, in the later pre-Roman Iron Age seems to have been vindicated (Avery 1986). Sharples (1991c) pointed to the possible use of the sling for other purposes, such as the protection of flocks by shepherds, and doubtless slings could equally have been used for wildfowling and other activities. But the hoard of 22,260 stones in a pit just behind the sentry box in the east gateway at Maiden Castle, or the two further caches, one of 16,044, the other 15,000, behind the inner hornwork, surely were located in anticipation of a major attack on the hillfort, and not just for the convenience of shepherds.

These conclusions are endorsed by the more recent evidence from Danebury. Sling-stones were found from all phases of the site's occupation, but the number increased substantially in ceramic phase 7 (Brown 1984: 425). In particular, a hoard of 11,000 was found in a pit just inside the east gate, while other pits in the vicinity contained lesser numbers. Furthermore, the excavator's interpretation of the east gateway and its outworks in period 6 (Cunliffe 1983: 76–7) is predicated upon the use of the sling as the principal weapon of defence, the entire hornwork area being within range of the 'command post' located at the outer end of the north inner hornwork (Figure 3.12). Quantities of sling-stones were recovered from the entrance, particularly flanking the north inner hornwork (Cunliffe 1984a: 425, Figures 3, 25), so that the combination of hoards with spent stones in numbers is surely conclusive.

Not all hillforts have produced sling-stones in the quantities recovered at Maiden Castle and Danebury. At Cadbury Castle relatively few were found, though an increase in numbers towards the end of the pre-Roman Iron Age was certainly noted (Poole 2000: 247), a trend also noted in the 1980s excavations at Maiden Castle (Sharples 1991a: 261). Not all presumed sling bullets, however, are of stone. A baked clay variant, commonly ovoid in its longer axis, is known from non-hillfort settlements, notably from Glastonbury (Gray 1917). Being lighter in weight than stone, these are sometimes regarded as weapons for use in hunting small game, while the heavier stone slingshot would be more appropriate in combat (Poole 1984: 398). Meare, on the other hand, had few of the baked clay variety, and many more of stone (Gray and Cotton 1966: 377–8), so that availability may have been a key factor for non-military activities.

Outside Wessex, there are no comparable numbers of sling-stones in hoards, perhaps because of the lack of large-scale investigation. The nearest comparable discovery was the collection of over eleven hundred stones from Conway Mountain (Griffiths and Hogg 1956), where 612 came from the hut just inside the southern gateway, while a further 33 stones were found within the entrance passage. These numbers hardly compare with Maiden Castle and Danebury, but they stand in marked contrast to the paucity of such finds from Tre'r Ceiri or Garn Boduan.

The archaeological evidence, then, is consistent with the use of sling-stones or hand-thrown stones in the defence of hillforts in Wessex at least, so that it is perhaps surprising that Caesar made no specific reference to coming under attack from Gaulish or British slingers. He described the Gaulish method of attack on fortified positions by putting down a hail of stones to clear the ramparts of defenders (Caesar *dBG* II, 6), though he does not specifically attribute this to slingers as opposed to a hand-thrown barrage. Roman forces used slingers throughout the Gallic campaign, including the raids on Britain, when they are invariably accompanied by archers. In the classical sources, Balearic slingers were singled out as especially skilful, having different slings for long-range, medium-range, and short-range usage according to Strabo (*Geography* 3, 5, 1), and serving with Hannibal at the fateful battle of Cannae in 216 BC according to Livy (*Histories* 21, 21).

The phrase that Caesar uses repeatedly of attacks by the Britons is 'tela conicere', 'to hurl missiles' of an otherwise unspecified type (*dBG*, IV, 24, 26, 32, 33). This suggests that the native forces were not segregated like his own into slingers or archers, but simply launched whatever missiles they could muster in a general barrage. Where their tactics caught him by surprise, as with chariots in Britain or the use of archers as rear-guard snipers at Alesia, he remarked upon them, but otherwise he appears to have regarded them as a motley rabble, even when they were momentarily effective. Whilst some would doubtless have been better equipped with swords and spears, it seems probable that the arms and equipment of the rank and file were much more basic, thereby accounting for Caesar's very generalized description of their onslaught.

RITUALIZED WARFARE

It is widely recognized that all forms of warfare are ritualized to some degree, so that to draw a distinction between ritualized warfare and other forms of warfare, particularly if the implication is that the former resulted in fewer or less grievous casualties, may be misleading. Ethnographic examples like the Dani of New Guinea may be cited to promote the view that some forms of ritualized warfare were highly stylized, approximating to ritual dance, and resulting in minimal casualties. But even this kind of formulaic confrontation could on occasion escalate to more lethal outcomes (Heider 1979). In the context of conflict in the Andes, Arkush and Stanish (2005) proposed an amended distinction between festive combat and destructive warfare, recognizing that ritual aspects were common to both.

The appearance through the second millennium BC in Europe of progressively more advanced weaponry and defensive armour, by the Late Bronze Age resulting in a range of technically very complex designs of swords, has generally be taken as evidence for an increased concern with warfare or martial aspirations. Kristiansen (1999) equated these developments with the rise of a warrior aristocracy, whose aggression was directed at the control of resources of production and trade, and with the creation through alliances of larger networks of regional polities. By contrast, Neustupný (1998b, 2006) argued that warfare was not a significant factor in prehistoric European societies, the 'weapons' in question being ritual and symbolic in purpose rather than functional. Kristiansen (1999: 188) did not deny the importance of their symbolic role, but argued nevertheless that 'there can be no rituals or symbols without the reality of what they signify'.

In the context of the British and European Iron Age, destructive conflict could have been ritualized to a significant degree, while festive combat may have been a regular feature of communal gatherings on a seasonal cycle. In both cases, hillforts could well have been designed in part to provide a suitable location. Some indications of the ritualized nature of Iron Age warfare is given in the classical sources. Athenaeus (IV, 40) quoting Posidonius, who was writing about the north Alpine $K\epsilon\lambda\tau o\iota$ of the early second century BC, describes the custom of feasting in which the participants engage in simulated combat, perhaps a version of festive combat or the playing-out of time-honoured legends. This is linked by Athenaeus, and by Diodorus Siculus (V, 28), drawing on the same source, to competition for the champion's portion and the practice of single combat, which may indeed have been formulaic themes in Iron Age folklore and bardic traditions, as they were in later Irish epic literature. But how this related to actual Iron Age practice, even among the elite, is more debatable. The challenge of single combat as a precursor to battle is itself a highly formulaic ritual, according to Diodorus' source (V, 29), in which the champions recite their own credentials whilst denigrating those of their opponents. Caesar's record of the Gallic campaign or its extension into Britain, however, has no evidence of any Gaulish or British champions challenging Romans to single combat, so that this practice appears to have fallen into abeyance by the later pre-Roman Iron Age, either because it had receded into the realms of myth or because its exponents had recognized that it had no impact on the outcome.

Archaeologically the ritualization of warfare is hard to demonstrate, although there are a number of depictions from continental Europe that appear to portray individuals either in combat or in some kind of ceremonial combat-dance. La Tène art is essentially non-figural, so that ornamented metalwork in Britain or neighbouring regions of the continent, notwithstanding its potential for abstract symbolism, does not depict warriors or battle scenes. Further afield the mounted lancers and foot soldiers in procession on the La Tène A scabbard from grave 994 at Hallstatt (Jacobsthal 1944: No. 96) are plainly related to the processional friezes of situla art of the sixth to fourth centuries around the head of the Adriatic, though engraved rather than executed in *repoussé*. The charioteers, riders and foot soldiers of situla art, however, are invariably in procession rather than depicted in conflict. Individuals, often naked, are shown engaged in some kind of face-to-face contest clutching dumb-bells, but it is not clear that they are fighting as opposed to acting out a ritual dance. Indeed, the emphasis of situla art is on feasting and music, together with processions of men and mythical beasts, integrating what may have reflected reality with what is plainly supernatural (Kastelic 1965). The Gundestrup cauldron (Klindt-Jensen 1961), too, on one celebrated panel depicts processions of foot soldiers and cavalry, with weaponry, helmets, and war-trumpets or *carnyxes* that would be entirely in keeping with the aristocratic warrior's equipment of the La Tène Iron Age, and the iconography of squatting heroes or deities wearing torcs is equally La Tène. But stylistically, the silver-gilt plates are Thracian not La Tène, and they were deposited in a bog in Germanic Jutland, not in La Tène Europe, which renders their dating to the first century BC or thereabouts somewhat speculative. Nevertheless, the panels plainly have a symbolic, if not a narrative, significance, reinforcing the belief that martial parading was an important element in ceremonial and ritual practice in Iron Age Europe. Finally among earlier Iron Age figural representations, from the far south-west, the painted ceramics of the first century BC from the Celtiberian town of Numantia include a pair of warrior figures armed with sword and spear confronting each other, which could be a scene of single combat. But other representations in the same series depict individuals with human bodies and animal or bird heads, or perhaps humans wearing exotic zoomorphic head-gear, suggesting that these are supernatural figures, or perhaps humans participating in festive or ritual ceremonies (Lorrio 1997: Figures 79, 109).

From the later Iron Age in northern Britain, figural representations are characteristic of Class 2 'Pictish' stones, commonly depicting hunting scenes or Biblical figures. The eighth century Aberlemno churchyard slab is unusual in depicting panels of warriors apparently engaged in battle, a scene that has been equated speculatively with the battle of Nechtansmere of AD 685 (Ritchie 1989). Both cavalry and infantry are represented, the former with swords and spears, the latter having sword, spear, lance and bow, the bow having reasserted itself in the Later Iron Age. Some riders, putatively Anglians in the historical interpretation, wear helmets and carry round shields. The Aberlemno battle scene is unique in 'Pictish' stone art (Henderson and Henderson 2004: 134–5), so it is not impossible that it could be commemorative of an actual engagement, rather than of a mythical battle or one drawn from literary epic tradition. In any event, we may suppose that the sculptor would have depicted figures equipped and performing roles that were broadly familiar, even if in an artistically stylized form.

CONCLUSIONS

It has long been recognized that many hillforts have limitations as defensive strongholds, perhaps as a result of compromising tactical considerations in favour of other criteria that were considered as important. Walls and entrance structures, ostensibly designed for defence, may equally have been aggrandized as symbols of status and power. The fact that there is little unequivocal archaeological evidence for hillforts coming under attack in the pre-Roman Iron Age need occasion no surprise, since the purpose of deterrence is to avoid its being put to the test. Where there is evidence of burning and slighting of defences, as in the vitrified forts, the evidence suggests that this is the result of punitive destruction after defeat in battle, the main event of which may have taken place elsewhere. Part of that punitive process may have been the symbolic destruction of a community's hillfort with ritual dismemberment and deposition of the kind witnessed at Cadbury Castle and elsewhere.

In more than two millennia of potential use of hillforts, it is evident that, even assuming a significant defensive role, this could have changed quite radically over time, not least in response to changes in military tactics. Though in southern Britain, there appears to be a greater number of wall ramparts with vertical external face of timber or stone in the later Bronze Age and earlier Iron Age, and of dump ramparts in the later pre-Roman Iron Age, this is by no means an invariable formula, and it may be that resource availability and logistics of construction were factors in changing military tactics. There is certainly evidence to support the contention that stoning or the use of slings increased in the later pre-Roman Iron Age in southern Britain, but any link between this tactic and multivallation is best regarded as unproven. One tactical development that appears to be broadly coincident with the widespread construction of hillforts is the use of horses for riding as well as for draught, though any causal relationship between the two is undemonstrated. Nevertheless, we should not underestimate the importance of horse-riding as an innovation of the first millennium BC. More rapid communication and access must have had social and economic consequences, not least the capability of mounting an attack with minimal warning.

In reviewing the evidence for weaponry, it seems fairly clear that what is normally accepted archaeologically as representative of the weaponry or defensive equipment of a given age, based almost invariably on objects preserved in graves, need not be representative of the equipment used in actual combat, at least by any combatants other than an elite corps. Equally, river finds of high-status artefacts, most probably votive deposits, were surely designed for ceremonial rather than for practical use. So the common image of the panoply of the 'Celtic' warrior, sword, spear or lance, helmet and shield, might fit the heroic ideal perpetuated in high-status burials and doubtless also in oral epic, but it may not match the full reality of Iron Age conflict. The archaeological record of weaponry, together with artefacts associated with feasting and drinking, may therefore all be a reflection upon the 'ritualization' of warfare and interpersonal rivalry in the Late Bronze Age and Iron Age.

8

Function 2: Social, Economic, Ritual

PERMANENT, PERIODIC, OR SEASONAL OCCUPATION?

In southern England, in terms of prevailing environmental conditions most hillforts could have been occupied or used on a permanent rather than seasonal basis. With the exception of Exmoor and Dartmoor in the far south-west, none are located above the 300 m contour and therefore could potentially have sustained a mixed agricultural regime. In northern England, Wales, and Scotland, on the other hand, there are hillforts at altitudes that make seasonal use more likely, although even with some of the larger hillforts in southern Scotland and Northumberland, like Eildon Hill, Hownam Law, and Yeavering Bell, higher altitude may not have precluded occupation on a significant scale.

We have already seen that some hillforts in southern Scotland and the Cheviots show ample evidence of occupation in the form of house stances, so that a residential function as a primary purpose is hardly in doubt. Sites like Hayhope Knowe or Camp Tops may be categorized as protected villages, and though some might seem scarcely to qualify as hillforts at all (Frodsham *et al.* 2007), others like Sundhope Kipp boast defensive earthworks, which seem almost disproportionate in scale to the area of the internal settlement. Sometimes the houses are so densely arranged within the interior as to exclude the possibility of division into different activity zones, unless some of these seemingly identical roundhouses actually served as workshops or stores rather than just for domestic occupation. Despite their relatively high altitude and exposed locations, there is every reason to believe that some sites were permanently occupied, since evidence of cord-rig agriculture often lies in immediate proximity to the enclosure. Even so, these cultivation plots must have been on the margins of viability in the Iron Age, and it is possible that these Borders upland sites by the later first millennium BC were used only seasonally. Indeed, progressive environmental deterioration may be a reason why the earthwork phase of enclosure at Hayhope Knowe was never completed.

Archaeologically it is hard to point to evidence that might distinguish seasonal from permanent occupation. The number of buildings may be indicative of the intensity of use, but might stake-wall construction with numerous episodes of rebuilding indicate seasonal construction, as opposed to more permanent post-built houses? On the other hand, stone foundations could have been renovated seasonally in a manner than might be hard to distinguish archaeologically from permanent use. Proximity to trackways that could have been used for transhumance might provide a clue to a hillfort's possible use. Upland hillforts may have had a relatively small resident group that was supplemented seasonally when herds from the lowlands were driven into upland pasture. This is a pattern that has been proposed for some Northumbrian hillforts (Oswald *et al.* 2006: 88), based on traditional practice from historic times for the driving of herds into the uplands at Ellenmass (3 May), and retrieving them on All Hallows' Day (1 November), corresponding to the Celtic festivals of Beltane and Samhain. It does not follow that the entire community group moved to upland summer pastures; more probably only the younger and fitter members would have undertaken this task. The inference may be that extended families that occupied homestead settlements in the lowlands may have used hillforts maintained by their larger kin groups in the uplands for communal security during the period of summer pasture, the hillforts perhaps additionally serving for seasonal or festive gatherings during that period. Abundant traces of cord-rig agriculture in the Borders in regular association with palisaded enclosures and ring-ditch houses should date from at least the mid-first millennium BC, and although the dating of hillforts is not easy to establish, research in the Northumberland National Park (Frodsham 2004) and its environs suggests that their origins may be earlier than has been conventionally assumed.

In Wales and the Marches, Alcock (1965) noted that only a minority of hillforts were located above the 250 m (800 ft) contour, and highlighted their probable role in both arable and pastoral economy. The hillforts overlooking the east side of the Vale of Clwyd, for example, seem sited tactically at the interface between arable land and upland pasture, where the larger forts, Moel Hirraddug (10 ha), Penycloddiau (19 ha), and Moel Fenlli (9.5 ha), would have been especially suitable for protecting herds and flocks from threat of seasonal raiding. Brown (2009: 209) pointed out that the Clwydian range has among the highest concentration in Wales of Bronze Age burial cairns, perhaps demarcating territorial boundaries that the later hillforts likewise respected.

CENTRAL PLACES, STORAGE, REDISTRIBUTION, AND STATUS

Much of the thinking that dominated hillfort studies from the 1970s was predicated on the assumption that 'developed' hillforts at least served as central places within the defined territory of a coherent community group. Whether that community was dependent upon the central place or serviced by it depends upon our perception of whether it was hierarchical or egalitarian, and in recent years the pendulum of archaeological fashion in Britain has tended towards the latter. The basic assumption is that the community will have developed economically or otherwise to the point where certain functions were better fulfilled centrally than in multiple dispersed settlements, with the implication that the central place would accrue a degree of authority in the exercise of these functions. That authority in turn would enable it to articulate with neighbouring polities and even with more distant contacts that might control, for example, required mineral resources or desirable exotic imports.

There are issues enough with this model when there are exotic goods in evidence and artefacts of unquestioned value in significant quantity, as was conventionally argued for the *Fürstensitze* or princely strongholds of late Hallstatt and early La Tène north Alpine Europe (Kimmig 1969; Frankenstein and Rowlands 1978; Härke 1979; Eggert 1989). For hillforts of the British Iron Age, by contrast, there is very little in the material assemblage that could not be paralleled on non-hillfort settlements. Even where the assemblage is substantial, as at Danebury, the case is not easily made. Cunliffe nevertheless argued in the context of Danebury that 'a central place may function as a focus in a redistribution network embedded in a system of reciprocity' (1995: 93), and proceeded to enumerate raw materials from beyond the local region that had been found on site. These included currency bars and billets from Northamptonshire or the Forest of Dean, shale from Kimmeridge on the Dorset coast, copper alloy from the south-west of England or Wales, and stone artefacts of non-local origin. Some south-western-style pottery vessels may have been containers for unspecified goods and briquetage would have contained salt from the south coast. Though none of these items, except briquetage, was exclusive to the hillfort, as opposed to neighbouring settlements, the relative quantities at Danebury suggested that these goods may have been brought to the hillfort and redistributed from the central place. The general lack of briquetage on non-hillfort settlements certainly supports this view. Salt was a dietary essential which in many societies also acquired a symbolic aspect, but for practical purposes it was one of the main methods of preserving meat and fish. It may well have been redistributed from hillforts as a matter of practical convenience, or because some additional levy was attached to it in the process, but it is equally probable that meat surpluses were salted *en masse* at the hillfort for future redistribution or export. Other exchange goods for these imports could most obviously have included corn and wool, retained for the purpose in the hillfort's ample storage facilities. Wine was not among the imports to Danebury, though its introduction in the period around 100 BC to southern and south-eastern England may have been coincident with a complex series of changes that brought about the hillfort's eventual decline and abandonment, and that of other hillforts in southern and south-eastern England.

Comparing hillforts with non-hillfort settlements in Wessex it is apparent that some hillforts had a substantially greater storage capacity, absolutely and proportionately, than non-hillfort settlements. Quite clearly not all hillforts fulfilled this function, and in other regions like the Upper Thames, dense concentrations of pits at Gravelly Guy, for example (Lambrick and Allen 2004) suggest that communal storage may have been provided within the context of a non-hillfort, essentially open-settlement regime. But pits and four-post structures are known in some hillforts in such concentrations that their storage capacity must have been substantially in excess of the requirements of any resident community. The hillforts of the Welsh Marches are conspicuous, as we have seen, in their apparent concentration of four-posters, and the regularity with which their post-holes were recut, implying both density of numbers restricting space for lateral expansion and longevity of use. In most cases excavation has been selective, but there is no question of the density of building in the areas sampled. On the continent the obvious parallel is the Altburg von Bundenbach in the Hunsrück (Schindler 1977). Among innumerable post-holes that could not be attributed to meaningful plans, a substantial number of four- and six-poster buildings were considered by the excavator on balance to have been for storage. A separate compound on the west side of the interior, itself divided into two halves, could have housed a resident group.

One other group of continental sites is worth considering in this context; the walled enclosures of the northern Netherlands (Waterbolk 1977). The key sites at Zeijen, Vries and Rhee date from around the fourth or third centuries BC to the first century AD. Internal structures included four-posters, but more especially long, rectangular, post-built structures, in some instances, as in Phase 3 at Zeijen 1, up to 25 m in length and 6 m in width, arranged around the inner perimeter of the enclosure (Figure 8.1B). Because these buildings lacked the normal internal subdivisions of domestic houses, Waterbolk interpreted them as communal barns within fortified enclosures that were occupied seasonally for stock-gathering and were otherwise used primarily for storage of agricultural produce. The location of the enclosures in areas where there were extensive field systems certainly would be consistent with their agricultural function, but Waterbolk also argued that the walled enclosures may have had a ritual dimension. The combination of communal assembly, agricultural

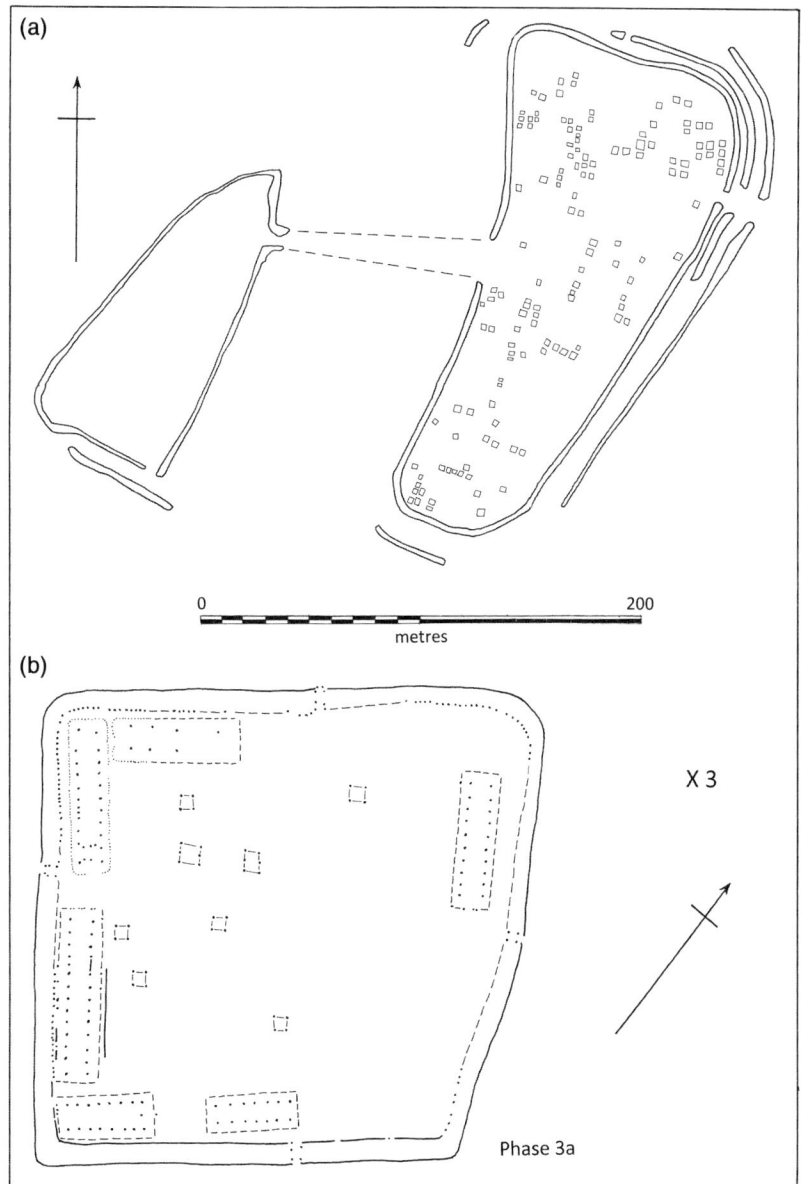

Figure 8.1. Special function enclosures: (A) Sutton Common, South Yorkshire; (B) Zeijen 1, northern Netherlands. Drawings by D. W. Harding adapted from van de Noort *et al.* 2007 and Waterbolk 1977.

storage for security and seasonal ritual is one that could easily fit the role of some hillforts in Britain, and perhaps sites like the 'marsh-fort' at Sutton Common in South Yorkshire (Figure 8.1, A; van de Noort *et al.* 2007).

Unless we imagine a large resident hillfort community, actively engaged in farming an extensive area around the hillfort and bringing home the consequent harvest for processing and storage, which hardly seems justified at Danebury by the number of surviving houses, we must alternatively presume that storage was of produce from surrounding, dependent settlements. This alternative seems to be supported by the evidence from Danebury for prior processing of the cereals and cereal residues (Cunliffe 1995: 90). Whether this surplus was extracted by way of levy, or voluntarily brought to the hillfort for storage and safe keeping, depends upon what model of social reconstruction we choose to apply. Cunliffe ultimately favoured the hierarchical model, in which an elite controlled agricultural surpluses, using them to acquire exchange goods from outwith the local territory, redistributing some of the benefits and thereby reinforcing its own authority and status.

Evidence of status in terms of material artefacts in comparison to non-hillfort settlements was lacking at Danebury (Stopford 1987; Cunliffe 1995: 90). Apart from formal burials or votive deposits, however, prestige goods would not normally be expected among domestic assemblages, unless the site was overwhelmed by disaster or abandoned in circumstances that did not permit the recovery of anything of value that could be reused or recycled. In any event, it is more likely that wealth and status would have been measured in terms of livestock and agricultural surpluses than through extravagant metalwork, like parade weaponry and armour, which may not anyway have been individual possessions in a capitalist sense. Ethnographic studies suggest that custody of valuable items would undoubtedly have conferred prestige upon their keepers, and they may well have been important symbols displayed on ceremonial or ritual occasions, which might have taken place within hillforts. But they are unlikely to have been a measure of an individual's disposable wealth as in modern consumer society.

If it is unrealistic and simplistic to expect status to be reflected in the surviving material assemblage, the most obvious measure of the status of a hillfort must surely be the scale and grandeur of its monumental architecture. A widely rehearsed example is the stone-founded mud-brick wall with bastions of the period IVb defences at the Heuneburg in Baden-Württemberg (Gersbach 1995), a Mediterranean innovation that must have been inspired by prestige rather than practicality. The British counterpart was less exotic but equally impressive, walls faced with timber and stone surmounted by parapet, long entrance passages flanked by bastions and guardrooms and bridged by gatehouses on which gruesome trophies might be displayed, and multiple circuits of ramparts and ditches that proclaimed colossal expenditure of resources. The idea that bivallation or multivallation was indicative of an ascending hierarchy

Function 2: social, economic, ritual

in hillforts has lost favour, but the basic principle that the extravagant expenditure of resource was an index of status must surely hold good.

For the larger hillforts of southern Britain, the evidence for internal occupation is, as we have seen, extremely variable, sufficient to indicate that not all were intended as permanent settlements. Wheeler nevertheless evidently regarded Maiden Castle as functioning as a town, doubtless encouraged by Suetonius' use of the term *oppida*, or walled towns, to describe the strongholds captured by Vespasian, and by the fact that their counterparts in Gaul were likewise described by Caesar as *oppida*, or even as an *urbs* in the case of Avaricum (Bourges). Without being distracted into a debate about incipient urbanization or state formation in Gaul, it is clear that there were fundamental changes taking place in Iron Age society in Gaul and in Britain in the century before the Roman conquest, from which it would be unwise to make retrospective inferences regarding the role of British Iron Age hillforts of the preceding centuries. Furthermore, any definition of urbanization that is based upon a Mediterranean or Middle Eastern model, in which criteria such as administrative functions, public buildings, and commercial specialization are paramount, may not be appropriate in the context of complex Iron Age societies in non-Mediterranean Europe. In West Africa among the Yoruba, for example, towns developed even among non-industrial farming communities, which we would not expect to judge by the criteria of classical urbanization.

One criterion of a town might be size, both the physical area enclosed and the density of occupation within. In terms of absolute area even the largest of the British hillforts, Ham Hill in Somerset (80 ha; 200 acres), pales into insignificance beside the largest of the continental enclosures, like the massive Heidengraben bei Grabenstetten in Baden-Württemberg (Fischer 1982), which overall embraces some 1500 ha. Not even the terrain *oppida* of the later pre-Roman Iron Age in Britain like the Colchester dykes or Stanwick are in this league. But as excavations at Manching in Bavaria (Sievers 2003) have shown, a vast enclosure does not necessarily contain evidence of uniformly dense occupation within, so that a large area need not be synonymous with a very large resident population. Some of the larger hillforts of Wessex and the Marches might equate in area enclosed with the smaller walled towns of Roman Britain, but the latter would be distinguished by their planned layout and public buildings. Hillforts might certainly compare on more equal terms of size and population density with early Medieval towns, as Alcock's (1965) comparison of Tre'Ceiri and Medieval Conway graphically demonstrated.

A measure of interior planning has generally been regarded as an index of incipient urbanization in which hillforts 'took on the character of small towns' (Cunliffe 1974: 256–60). The concept of 'town planning' was quite widely canvassed in the 1970s with the emerging evidence from Danebury of different structural concentrations segregated by a pattern of streets, and as a result of excavations at Moel y Gaer, Rhosesmor (Guilbert 1976), where the layout underwent major episodes of reorganization. As Guilbert (1975b: 203) pointed out, the important inference from the phase 2 plan at Moel y Gaer was that the layout was predetermined and not simply the result of organic growth over time. This indicated intentional zoning into separate activity areas, which might be regarded as one measure of urbanization. Guilbert nevertheless concluded that British Iron Age hillforts fell short of fully urban status, since their economy was still essentially agricultural, rather than being based upon a wider range of specialized commercial or industrial activities. Cunliffe's criteria for 'developed' hillforts, which he regarded as exhibiting 'characteristics appropriate to a proto-urban organization' (1976b: 141), included the manufacturing of goods surplus to need, but still presumed a basic dependence on agriculture and stock-raising. Twenty years later (Cunliffe 1995) much the same criteria were advanced to characterize Danebury's role as a focus within the regional economic and social system, but the terms 'town' and 'urbanization' were no longer part of the current vocabulary. The reason perhaps is that in recent years the urban or proto-urban status of continental *oppida* and the concept of state formation in Late La Tène Gaul have come under rigorous scrutiny, so that the even more tenuous claims of British *oppida* and hillforts have in consequence been sidelined.

BURIAL AND FUNERARY RITUALS

At Broxmouth in East Lothian in 1978, a small cemetery of nine, mainly slab-built cist graves was uncovered just outside the outermost hillfort ditch on its northern side (Figure 8.2A). The construction of the graves was not identical, though the inhumations were all flexed and aligned north-east to south-west or vice versa, and radiocarbon dates suggested that they were broadly contemporary in the pre-Roman Iron Age. The choice of location, just beyond the hillfort boundary, is surely significant; the cemetery was also on the seaward side of the hillfort, but not in close proximity to either its eastern or southern entrance. Apart from the cemetery, three more burials were located within the defences in simple pit-graves, with one slab-lined pit-burial in the south gateway. The sample is obviously too small to represent the resident population's normal means of disposing of the dead. Unlike the pit burials within this and other hillforts, however, described in the interim report (Hill 1982a) as 'stray burials', the external graves had a sufficient consistency in proximity, form, and orientation to be regarded as a cemetery. If cemeteries were regularly located immediately outside hillfort enclosures, then the fact that excavations have invariably concentrated on ramparts, entrances, and interiors might in part account for the apparent paucity of cemeteries in the insular Iron Age.

The clearest example of a cemetery in juxtaposition to a hillfort, of course, is Maiden Castle, Dorset (Figure 8.2B). Setting aside issues regarding the 'war

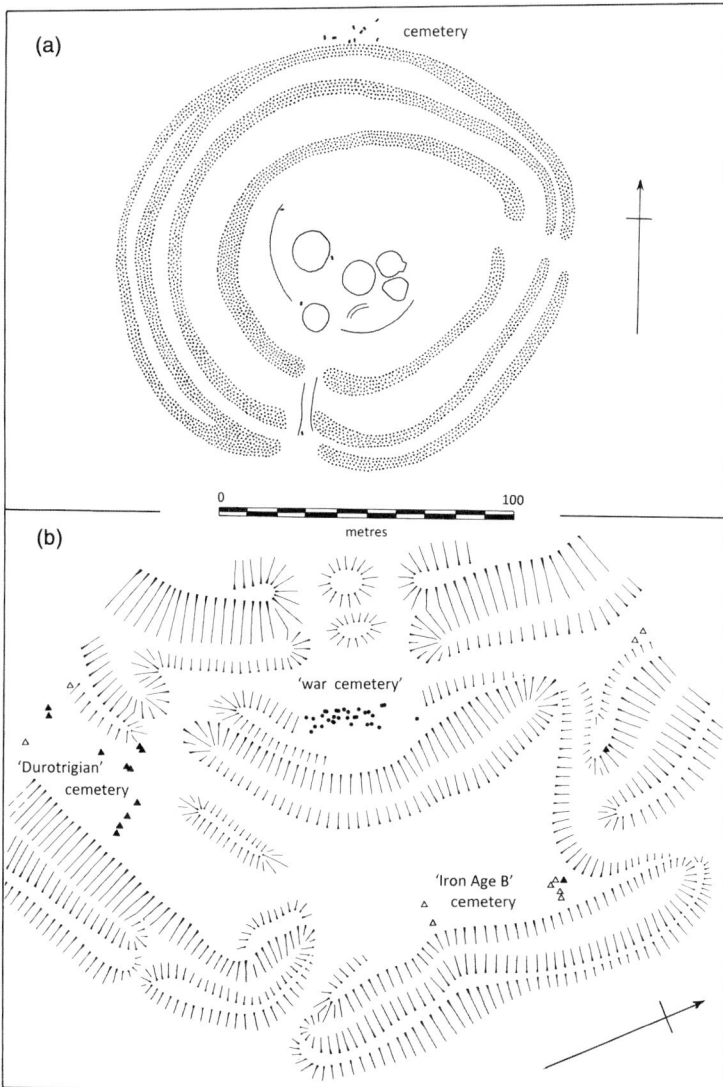

Figure 8.2. Hillfort cemeteries: (A) Broxmouth, East Lothian; (B) Maiden Castle, Dorset, eastern entrance. Note that the Broxmouth hillfort in its entirety occupies a similar area to the final entrance at Maiden Castle. Drawings by D. W. Harding adapted from Hill 1982a, and Wheeler 1943.

cemetery', there is no dispute that there was a pre-existing tradition of burial in proximity to the east gate at Maiden Castle. The 'earth-graves' at Maiden Castle are not significantly different from those of other 'Durotrigian' cemeteries in southern Dorset (Whimster 1981), among which cist-graves are a comparatively rare alternative found mainly in Purbeck and the coastal area around Weymouth and Portland. The 'non-war grave' burials were either in pits, ditches, or shallow earth graves, as might be found at other hillforts, with the important difference that at Maiden Castle they were apparently grouped together, rather than being more randomly disposed between other, presumably non-funerary, pits. The Maiden Castle burials were seemingly oriented deliberately, but so are some apparently 'casual' pit burials. On the other hand, the Maiden Castle 'war cemetery' graves contained grave goods, 'the proper and traditional perquisites of the dead' in Wheeler's (1943: 62) graphic reconstruction, which 'casual' pit burials seldom do, though what constitutes grave goods or 'structured deposition' is open to debate. Wheeler's plan (ibid. Plate XCIX) showed clearly that these two dozen burials were simply those that his narrow trenches had uncovered; the reality was surely a much more extensive cemetery dating from the middle Iron Age and possibly from a time when it was established *outside* the hillfort defences.

In discussing the considerable volume of evidence for the burial of human remains from Danebury, Cunliffe (1995: 72–9) was emphatic that pit-burials did not represent a 'normative rite'. Pit burials, in and around hillforts and lesser, enclosed settlements, have been recognized for many years (Whimster 1981; Wilson 1981), whilst the occurrence of partial deposits of human remains have likewise been seen as 'structured deposits' (Hill 1995a) rather than the result of casual discard. So why, in the absence of any other recurrent form of burial, are pit burials denied recognition as a 'normative rite'? One reason might be that not all the pits within a pit cluster contain burials, though sometimes, as at Castle Hill, Little Wittenham (Allen and Lamdin-Whymark 2005; Allen *et al.* 2011), a significant majority of the fourteen Iron Age pits excavated contained burials or fragments of human bones. At Danebury, certainly, the number of burials as a percentage of the total number of pits is minimal, and as Cunliffe argued, represents only a very small number when spread over the span of occupation, though increasing in later phases in proportion to the intensification of activity. A second reason why these burials are regarded as abnormal is the absence of unequivocal grave-goods. These factors certainly mark pit burials as different from 'regular' cemeteries of the kind that characterize the La Tène series in eastern Yorkshire or even the 'Durotrigian' cemeteries of south Dorset, or indeed of funerary practice represented by the barrow cemeteries of the Bronze Age or Neolithic. In any event, as Cunliffe subsequently acknowledged (1995: 79), it has long been recognized that supposedly 'regular' forms of burial cannot account for more than a small minority of the total population, so that other methods of disposal, which archaeologically have escaped detection for the most part, must have been the 'norm' for the majority of the community. For the British Iron Age, the problem is highlighted by the absence of regular and recurrent cemeteries outside the so-called Arras and Aylesford–Welwyn groups, each geographically and chronologically restricted. In fact, the number of known Iron Age cemeteries has steadily increased over the past thirty years, though still insufficient to fill the deficiency. A small Iron Age cemetery at Yarnton in Oxfordshire (Hey et al. 1999) lacked grave-goods, and in the context of a multi-period palimpsest of occupation might well have been attributed to other periods, had not radiocarbon dating surprised the excavators by showing that the burials belonged to the middle pre-Roman Iron Age. The limited number of burials and their relatively short time span led to speculation that only two or three families over a couple of generations might be represented. Though there were other burials within the settlement area, the two groups in the main cemetery appeared to lie outside the settlement, the boundaries of which had not obviously survived.

The burial of detached whole skulls at Danebury was regarded as something special, and, with the possibility prompted by documentary sources of head-hunting among Iron Age communities, these were regarded as 'trophies' introduced from the 'external world' (Cunliffe 1995: 78). The further possibility of ritual sacrifices may be implied by the mutilated pelvic girdle from Pit 1020 (Hooper 1984: 471-2). The Danebury funerary assemblage was also notable for the number of neonatal or infant burials. Infant burials had also been recorded at Maiden Castle from all phases of the Iron Age occupation. At Danebury, Cunliffe observed that neonatal inhumations were either accorded a small pit of their own, or deposited in the middle or upper fillings of larger pits, in contrast to juvenile or adult inhumations, which were placed at or near the bottom of the pit. He concluded therefore that treatment of infants was different from that of adults, but was unable to offer the reason for this. Nevertheless, it is clear that neonatal burials formed a meaningful part of the hillfort's role in funerary practices.

In addition to cemeteries and pit burials, individual burials are regularly found on hillfort excavations under ramparts or in ditches. Both in contemporary jargon would be regarded as liminal locations, marking the division between outside and inside, included and excluded, them and us. Burials under ramparts, provided they can be shown not simply to antedate the phase of enclosure, might be regarded as foundation deposits. Such was the explanation offered by Wheeler (1943: 38-9) for the pit-burial found at Maiden Castle beneath the rampart of the early Iron Age univallate enclosure at the point of its junction with the extended hillfort. On the basis of observed stratigraphy, the excavator was characteristically unequivocal in regarding the burial and rampart as contemporary, invoking biblical precedent for foundation burials. Richmond too invoked biblical authority for his interpretation of the burial under the counterscarp bank at the Stepleton gate at Hod Hill as a foundation burial (Richmond 1968: 16). At Sutton Walls (Kenyon 1953: 12), the foundation burial was exposed by commercial quarrying of the southern rampart, but the excavator was in no doubt that it had been deposited at the same time as the construction of the rampart. A similar role was claimed for a burial inserted in a pit into the back of the rampart at Cadbury Castle

(Alcock 1972: 102–3), although the complexity of stratigraphy compounded by mechanical excavation of the rampart section made it impossible to assign the burial reliably to the appropriate phase of construction (Barrett *et al.* 2000: 67–9). Plainly there must be an element of doubt as to the relationship of these burials to the overlying rampart, especially where, as in the case of the Stepleton burial at Hod Hill, the grave lay outside the hillfort ditch adjacent to the entrance, where an external cemetery might have been located. But the judgement of excavators of the calibre of Wheeler and Kenyon should be respected. They were aware that, even assuming contemporaneity, the explanation of the burials as ritualistic in purpose was inevitably speculative.

Burials in ditches have been more difficult to explain, since their deposit implies that any purpose that the ditch might have served as a functioning barrier had fallen into abeyance. Plainly the ditch's initial function as a quarry for material to construct the rampart becomes redundant after the episode of construction, though there are ample examples of ditches being periodically cleaned out and the material being re-deposited to heighten a dump rampart or counterscarp. This process implies a role for the earthworks in which the maintenance of an effective barrier is crucial. The deposition of burials in the ditch, on the contrary, suggests that maintaining a practical barrier was not the issue, though it is possible that the spirits of the dead could have afforded a more potent disincentive to potential intruders. Individual burials have been recorded in hillfort ditches widely across southern England, ranging in date from earlier to later pre-Roman Iron Age, at Maiden Bower, Bedfordshire (Matthews 1976), at Wilbury Hill, Hertfordshire (Applebaum 1949), at Ham Hill, Somerset (Gray 1925, 1926, 1927) and at Cassington Mill, Oxfordshire (Case and Kirk 1951: 79). One notable example is Yarnbury, Wiltshire, where Mrs Cunnington (1933) found no less than nine infant burials in four separate sections across the ditches. This suggests a highly unusual distribution pattern, though infant burials in ditches of settlements are known from Rotherley, Wiltshire (Pitt-Rivers 1888), and Gussage All Saints, Dorset (Wainwright 1979). From older hillfort excavations it was unlikely that more than occasional discoveries would be made, given that cuttings were invariably extremely narrow and designed simply to establish the profile of the defences, which may therefore belie the scale of the practice.

The most remarkable burial from a hillfort ditch in southern England, however, is without doubt the horse, rider, and dog from Blewburton Hill, the rider having one leg over and the other under the horse's hind quarters, as if 'the man had been cast into the ditch riding the horse, with his feet tied together under its belly' (Collins 1953: 31). Despite this improbable scenario, man, horse, and dog were evidently an assemblage, deposited at the point in the vertical sequence where the original ditch was widened for the construction of the dump rampart around the fourth or third centuries BC. Associated with the deposit were an iron adze, an iron pin, and fragments of a black, burnished pot, though whether these were intended as grave goods is unclear. Horse burials are not common in Iron Age Britain or Europe, though they are more common in the early medieval period (Müller-Wille and Vierck 1971), and alluded to in documentary sources of this period. The draught teams are notably not included in the vehicle burials of central and western Europe, either four-wheeled wagons of the Hallstatt phase or the two-wheeled carts/chariots of the La Tène Iron Age, though further east they are well attested in Scythian burials. In the Arras group, the only unequivocal example of horse burial is the pair from the King's Barrow, though other possible examples were discussed by Stead (1965: 18–19). More recently a lone horse was found in the south-west cemetery at Mill Hill, Deal (Parfitt 1995), where it was considered to be contemporary with the adjacent inhumations. So the recent excavation in the Auvergne outside the *oppidum* of Gondole of eight horses and their presumed riders buried side by side (but not mounted) is a truly unique discovery (Deberge *et al.* 2009). The excavators nevertheless recalled Caesar's observation of lavish Gaulish funerals, in which 'everything that they regard as having been dear to the dead in life, even animals, they cast into the pyre' (Caesar *dBG* VI, 19). Ironically, the human skeletons are tucked in at the side of the tomb, in which the horses are dominant, so that the appearance is more of horses buried with grooms, rather than riders buried with their mounts. The reference to Caesar's report could therefore be a complete red herring. The Blewburton burial is modest by comparison, but the decision to inter the dead man in the ditch with his pony and dog is surely a significant choice of a 'liminal' location.

Somewhat later in the site's occupation in the main entrance to the hillfort two pairs of horses (presumably implying teams) were found buried in the inner passageway (Collins 1953; Harding 1976b). These are not the only horse burials found in the entrance: the 1967 excavations recorded another disarticulated horse within a pit at the inner end of the entrance. Furthermore, Collins (1953: 39) found fragmentary remains of horse, cow, and deer, as well as disarticulated infant bones scattered across the entrance passage beneath the collapsed stonework of the flanking walls. He interpreted this as evidence for a violent sack of the hillfort, which, acknowledging the absence of dating evidence pointing to a Roman horizon, he assigned to the first century BC. In fact, the evidence for destruction through force of arms is slight, and although the revetment walls may have been thrown down, there is nothing to compare with the intense burning witnessed, for example, at Rainsborough Camp. It would be tempting therefore to see the evidence of the Blewburton entrance as a 'closure episode' involving ritual deposition and symbolic destruction, but not necessarily inflicted by a vengeful enemy. The later choice of the area adjacent to the entrance for the location of an Anglo-Saxon cemetery may reflect a continuing tradition of the site's sanctity.

The deposit of both human and animal burials, complete, disarticulated, or fragmentary, in boundary locations of hillforts, in their ramparts, ditches, or entrances, with some evidence for formal burials immediately beyond these liminal points, raises important questions regarding rituals of deposition of human remains, in which burial intact in a grave within a cemetery was evidently only one, perhaps minority, option. Apart from burials within the hillfort at Castle Hill, Little Wittenham, sampling of the extensive external occupation on its western and south-western flanks produced some evidence for pit-burial (Allen and Lamdin-Whymark 2005: trench 15) but not such as to occasion special note. At Battlesbury, Mrs Cunnington (1924: 373) had recorded inhumation burials, according to local information found just outside the north-west entrance from time to time in the course of quarrying chalk. The reports were hardly specific, but reference to burials in a crouched position up to two feet below the turf might suggest a formal cemetery. More recently, the relatively narrow strip excavated along the northern ridge from Battlesbury Bowl (Ellis and Powell 2008) yielded a variety of burial remains, including intact pit burials as well as disarticulated human and animal remains from the adjacent ditches. Two pit burials containing double inhumations were plainly formal interments, but much of the remaining material suggests the curation and disposal of skeletal remains, perhaps with indications of selectivity, subsequent to excarnation. The role of the hillfort in this process remains unclear, given the inadequate evidence from the hillfort itself, and in view of the fact that the external settlement could have been significantly larger in extent than the area so far uncovered. But together with its near neighbour at Scratchbury, it is possible that Battlesbury was an important regional focus of ceremonial and ritual significance.

Whilst hillforts may have fulfilled particular functions in Iron Age funerary rites, evidence for burial and the disposal of human remains is equally forthcoming from settlements that would not normally qualify as hillforts. The main enclosure at Pimperne in Dorset (Harding *et al.* 1993) was 4.5 ha (11.5 acres) in area, and might have qualified as an early hillfort had its earthworks been more substantial, and had it not been located just off the summit of the ridge. That the ditch was not maintained as a defensive barrier was indicated by its infilling shortly after construction for thirty feet adjacent to the east entrance with a capping of packed natural flints, neatly filling the ditch like a negative cairn. Below this capping at one end was a half human skull, split vertically, and at the other a human femur, presumably ritual deposits, though the basis for selecting these elements, and the fate of the remainder of the skeleton is completely unknown. The special character of the entrance is further demonstrated by the deposit of fragments of human skull, notably centred on the temporal bones, in post-holes within the entrance passage and in the opposite ditch terminal. These deliberate deposits of human remains contrasted with the evidence of the southern gateway, where a ditch terminal had been backfilled with the fragmentary remains of a horse and skull of an ox. The fact that two small chalk lamps had been placed together with the animal remains suggests a deliberate deposit, perhaps reflecting the function of the southern gateway in relation to the lesser enclosure, possibly used for corralling stock, to which it was linked. Whatever the purpose, however, the Pimperne evidence underlines the special significance of entrances and ditches in Iron Age settlements beyond any putative defensive or protective role, whether homesteads, villages or hillforts.

EXCARNATION AND 'NORMATIVE' BURIAL

The evidence for burials in relation to hillforts underlines the fact that Iron Age burial practices for large parts of Britain are not readily characterized by a predominant and recurrent rite like the cremation cemeteries of the late La Tène in south-eastern England or by structural layout like the square-ditched barrows of eastern Yorkshire. Instead, funerary practice evidently entailed an immensely complex set of conventions that might result in a great diversity of evidence in the archaeological record. In all probability so too did the funerary conventions of the Arras culture group and of the later pre-Roman Iron Age communities in south-eastern England, but the identification archaeologically of a distinctive and recurrent type of burial has relieved us of the responsibility for examining the evidence more critically. In consequence, it is misleading to say of pit-burials, for instance, that they or any other of the various practices considered above cannot have constituted a 'normative rite', since cumulatively or selectively they all constituted the accepted convention for the disposal of the dead.

The solution generally favoured by prehistorians to the apparent absence of formal burial is some form of disposal that leaves minimal trace, such as cremation and scattering, but an alternative that has attracted widespread support in recent years is excarnation and summary disposal of the remnants. The fact that there are so many instances, associated both with hillforts and with non-fortified settlements, of burials of incomplete human skeletal remains is most satisfactorily explained by regarding these as evidence for secondary burial, that is, deposition after a period in which the body has been subject to excarnation (Carr and Knüsel 1997). If the process involved exposure on an unprotected mortuary platform, the probability is that smaller and some larger bones may have been carried off by carrion birds or animal scavengers. The likely impact on the archaeological record will obviously depend upon the method of excarnation and the period of time involved, which may well have varied between communities or according to whatever rite was being observed. Nevertheless, the evidence from Iron Age sites in

Wessex points convincingly to the practice of excarnation and selective secondary burial as a widespread convention, and one that would certainly account for the apparent absence of a standardized burial rite. The obvious candidates for excarnation platforms are four-post settings, the interpretation of some of which as such certainly need not exclude other explanations, including the widely accepted view that they were the foundations for raised granaries. A relevant analogy is afforded by Bradley's (2005) argument that Late Bronze Age 'house urns', used to contain cremated human ashes, were in fact modelled on storehouses, including some on raised pediments, and as such they illustrated the fundamental link between the rite of passage of death and storage for the regeneration of crops.

The idea that some four-poster structures might have been excarnation platforms was first suggested by Ellison and Drewett (1971) on the basis of ethnographic practice among North American Indians, who disposed of the accumulated remnants in periodic ceremonies, sometimes after the lapse of some years. This, however, commonly involved disinterring human remains before transferring them to their permanent resting place, a practice necessitated particularly in regions where settlements regularly shifted after a generation (*vide infra* Chapter 10). Forty years ago, when socio-political and economic explanations for hillforts were more fashionable than ritual or symbolic, the suggestion was not widely adopted. But in a climate in which excarnation is generally accepted as an important element in the funerary rites of passage, it seems reasonable to reconsider this as one possible interpretation of some of the four-post structures within hillforts. In fact, the evidence from chambered long barrows has long indicated secondary burial, and the possibility that excarnation was practised at least from the Neolithic.

For Danebury, Cunliffe accepted that the human skeletal remains found within pits in the hillfort interior were the outcome of excarnation, 'brought from elsewhere to be placed in the pits . . . from the place where dead bodies were excarnated' or special 'excarnation grounds' elsewhere (1995: 76, 88). Whilst it is possible that there were special places, archaeologically undetected, where excarnation took place, surely the more logical assumption would be that excarnation took place within the hillfort itself, where the dead might be protected from unwanted intrusion. There is no reason to suppose that this function would have been incompatible with the hillfort's having served as a storage depot for communal cereals and other produce, since both would have been regarded as vital to the community's well-being.

On the other hand, we may note the caveat raised by Ellison and Drewett (1971: 192) regarding the likely inhibition on settlement in close proximity to an area dedicated to excarnation. This, of course, raises the question whether hillforts like Danebury were ever used as regular settlements. Danebury is not obviously dominated by residential buildings, in the way that Hod Hill, Hambledon, or Chalbury are. The interior at Danebury is largely given over to pits north of the main road and four-posters to the south, with roundhouses arranged for the most part peripherally to these. Whilst it is true that the ephemeral traces of stake-wall roundhouses may not have survived stripping of the topsoil in excavation, other than where they had been protected in the lee of the rampart, the basic form of the stake-wall construction is not the norm in Wessex Iron Age settlements, and it is arguable whether the resident population of Danebury was more than a custodial group. The most probable solution therefore is to think of some of the four-poster structures, perhaps those in the centre of the hillfort near the supposed shrines, as excarnation platforms. One of the key functions of this enclosed, special site would thus have been the performance of propitiation rituals, following the appropriate period of exposure of the dead where they could be protected from unwanted intrusions. Some of the remains thereafter may have been removed for disposal elsewhere, some may have been given dedicated burial within the hillfort, and other smaller parts may have ended up, as a result of the excarnation process, in one of the 211 separate contexts in which they were found. To explain a number of the four-post structures this way need not preclude the great majority having served as raised granaries or for other storage purposes. The structural remains are so basic that there is no reason to discount multiple purposes, any more than roundhouses need have been exclusively for domestic occupation. To suppose that there were external excarnation sites hitherto unrecognized and unrecorded archaeologically seems unnecessary, when the basic requirements of security from intrusion or violation by the impious could be best met within a hillfort, which additionally would have afforded a location redolent with a sense of place as a focus for community activities.

OTHER RITUAL OR CEREMONIAL ROLES

Accepting that a ritual dimension was endemic in all hillforts, whatever other functions they served, there are nevertheless some sites that seem improbably located as settlements, permanent or seasonal, or even as defensive refuges, and for which a ritual role may therefore have been dominant. At 650 m (2174 ft) OD, Carrock Fell in Cumbria (Figure 8.3a), which Collingwood (1938) took to be an Iron Age tribal centre, but which could have had much earlier origins (Pearson and Topping 2002) seems exceptionally high, even for the later second millennium BC, and there is no surviving evidence of occupation in the form of houses within the enclosure. The only internal features are two cairns of uncertain date, while other cairns lie in proximity to the site (Barker 1934). Nevertheless, it is situated on the north-east fringe of the Cumbrian Fells, and commands an extensive outlook to north and east over

(a)

Figure 8.3. 'Special sites' in remote locations: (a) Carrock Fell, Cumbria; (b) (opposite) Burgi Geos, Shetland. Air photographs by D. W. Harding.

a much lower-lying landscape. There are a number of breaks in the wall that are evidently not original entrances, which Hogg (1975) thought was the result of deliberate slighting by the Romans, an outcome that could be consistent with the site having a special significance to the native population. A similar case for the special character of the hillfort could be made for England's highest at 720 m (2350 ft) OD at Ingleborough in north-west Yorkshire (Plate 8a; King 1987; Bowden et al. 1989). Unlike Carrock Fell, there is evidence of internal activity at Ingleborough, in the form of twenty 'hut-circles', generally interpreted as houses rather than as cairns (Luke 2011), of which those that have visible entrances have a predominantly easterly orientation. Nevertheless, it is hard to imagine that Ingleborough was ever occupied on more than a seasonal or occasional basis, and the site's outstanding prominence in the landscape alone suggests that it may have had a special purpose. Brown (2009: 215) drew attention to the fact that this part of Yorkshire is cave and pothole country, so that any ritual associations may equally have been with depths as well as height.

If exceptional height prompts the question whether a hillfort was ever intended for normal occupation, then the remote and precipitous location of some of the northern promontory forts must equally raise doubts. Most bizarre of all is Burgi Geos on the northern edge of Yell, Shetland (Figure 8.3b). Here the cliffs fall sheer on either side for 60 m, while on the

(b)

landward side access is today across accumulated peat in places 10 m deep, which can hardly have accumulated wholly since the Iron Age (Lamb 1980). The outer 'defences' consist principally of an alignment of boulders and a swathe of *chevaux de frise*, but instead of being arranged transversely across the access route, they are aligned alongside the path as if intended to channel access between them. The path then crosses a lower saddle, barely 4 metres wide in places before climbing to the end of the promontory. Here there is what may have been a blockhouse, not centred across the main access but to one side. The entire configuration is hardly designed as an effective defence, and in any event the location is so awesomely inhospitable that it is difficult to see why it should have been chosen unless location was determined by ritual, custom, and belief rather than for community occupation.

That too was the conclusion reached by Rynne (1991; 1992) for the cliff-edge fort of Dun Aengus on Inishmore. With its sheer 100 m drop into the Atlantic, the inner fort at Dun Aengus seems very exposed, even for a fortified settlement, and the natural platform at the very edge of the cliff would have made for an imposing inauguration setting (Figures 8.4a, b). The ramparts could as easily have provided a viewing platform as defensive wall, and the *chevaux-de-frise* likewise could have been to provide symbolic protection as much as physical. An obvious complication, however, is the site's self-evident multiphase construction and alteration, which might have coincided with changes in its role. Fieldwork as part of the Discovery Programme

220   *Iron Age Hillforts in Britain and Beyond*

(a)

(b)

Figure 8.4. Dun Aengus, Inishmore, Co. Galway: (a) Professor E. Rynne on platform at cliff-edge, (b) view from cliff-edge. Photographs by D. W. Harding.

(Cotter 1993; 1995; 1996) has shown a significant presence on the site from the late Bronze Age to the Early Christian era, and a site of this prominence could have undergone significant changes in function as well as structural layout. In any event, architectural similarities shared by the stone forts of south-western Ireland need not preclude a range of different functions for different sites, or perhaps a different emphasis within the range of functions shared by them, with the same basic structure over the best part of two millennia. Not all promontory forts, it should be stressed, need have had a special ritual or ceremonial function. In Pembrokeshire, Flimston Bay, with its precipitous cliffs and treacherous blow-hole, might well fall into the exceptional category, but other promontory forts evidently were focal points within a productive and settled coastal landscape (Barker and Driver 2011), as was Trevelgue Head on the north Cornish coast (Nowakowski and Quinnell 2011).

One of the difficulties in the British Iron Age in demonstrating a ritual or ceremonial role is the absence of any distinctive architectural form of temple or shrine, at least until the Romano-British period. This does not mean that there were not buildings dedicated to ritual activity, or that buildings primarily used for domestic or agricultural purposes did not also have an implicit ritual dimension. It simply means that identification of ritual activity is dependent upon other, often more tenuous, criteria, such as 'votive' deposits or even more rarely iconic representations in metalwork or sculpture. The one structure for which a ritual role has been generally accepted, the 'temple' within Caesar's Camp, Heathrow (Grimes and Close-Brooks 1993), had neither. Its identification by the original excavator was based upon the resemblance of its 'concentric rectangular' plan to later Romano-Celtic temples or perhaps more accurately to Greek temples, and by Close-Brooks on the basis of comparison with rectangular structures subsequently excavated at Danebury and Cadbury Castle. The Heathrow plan certainly appears to define a structure with inner *cella* and outer *porticus*, but as a prototype Romano-Celtic temple it is not only precocious, but should also have been square rather than rectangular. Cunliffe (1984a: 87) quite rightly observed that, if the plan published in the interim report (Grimes 1961: Figure 7 inset) was accurate, then the inner and outer rectangles represent successive structures rather than a single building, though the final report glossed over this point. The *temenos* enclosure was levelled long before Grimes' wartime rescue excavations, which could only confirm that its ditch was of hillfort proportions, though Stukeley's drawing shows it as an extant earthwork with single entrance. In terms of Venclovà's (1993) criteria for the identification of 'non-profane activity', therefore, we have only the building's distinctive plan to support its special role.

The identification of the rectangular structures at Danebury as shrines is even more tenuous. They occupy a false summit in the centre of the fort facing, and clearly visible from, the entrance. If RS2 had been centred within RS1 there might have been a resemblance to the Heathrow building (Cunliffe 1983:

117), but otherwise there was no associated evidence in the form of special deposits to support their interpretation as shrines. In fact, dating evidence was limited, and they probably represent a sequence of building. Their post-trench construction suggests walled structures, in which respect they differ from those four-posters that are normally interpreted as raised granaries (Bradley 2005: 189), with the smaller ones at least most probably roofed. They more closely resemble the small, trench-built 'shrines' associated with the late pre-Roman Iron Age cremation cemetery at Westhampnett, Sussex (Fitzpatrick 1997), where they may have housed the dead in a period of 'laying out' prior to cremation. With domestic buildings of the Iron Age in Britain predominantly circular in plan (Harding 2009), in contrast to the widespread tradition of rectangular building in central and west-central Europe, self-fulfilling circular argument allows any rectangular plan here to be regarded as special.

Equally problematic was the late pre-Roman Iron Age rectangular 'megaron' from Cadbury Castle, the ritual function of which seemed initially to be endorsed by a number of pits with animal burials disposed in front of its veranda (Alcock 1972: 81–4). Subsequent study of the Cadbury evidence has suggested a rather more complex sequence of activity, in which the animal burials probably pre-date the shrine by a century or more (Downes 1997). Hamilton-Dyer and Maltby, however, confirmed the special nature of the deposits represented by 34 neonatal calves, but argued that the rest of the assemblage was 'better explained as an accumulation of butchery and domestic waste' (Hamilton-Dyer and Maltby 2000: 291). The 'shrine' itself was late, possibly post-conquest, and constructed at a time when the hillfort was not in regular occupation. Nevertheless, there appears to have been a long tradition of activity that reflected the special significance of place, which does not require the identification of any specific structure as a 'shrine' or focus of ritual.

That hillforts embodied a veneration of place almost certainly accounts for their being chosen as sites for the construction of temples in the later Roman period. The best known example, of course, is Maiden Castle, Dorset, where immediately south of the Romano-Celtic temple was an additional fourth-century oval building, from which a collection of 171 Roman coins, together with fragments of a bronze and a marble statuette, would be consistent with its interpretation as part of the temple complex (Wheeler 1943: Plates XX, XXII). This building was located directly over a circular structure of late pre-Roman Iron Age date, the entrance to which fronted a roadway leading directly to the eastern gateway of the hillfort. Although there were no special deposits to suggest the sanctity or special character of this earlier building, the exact superimposition of the oval building may not have been coincidental, and the fact that the hillfort should have been chosen after a lapse of three centuries for the late Roman ritual complex is in itself a measure of the site's enduring significance to the local community. As Woodward and Leach reminded us (1993: 305), the proximity of this complex to one of the longest Neolithic long barrows in Britain, extending down the spine of the enlarged hillfort, is surely not fortuitous.

Although often cited, the known examples of Romano-British temples within hillforts are comparatively rare by comparison with sequential use of non-fortified sites like Woodeaton and Frilford in Oxfordshire (Harding 1987), or Cold Kitchen Hill in Wiltshire. At Chanctonbury in Sussex (Bedwin 1980; Rudling 2001), the enclosure dates from the later Bronze Age and there was little evidence of occupation from the middle pre-Roman Iron Age. It is small by hillfort standards, and may instead have been a sacred enclosure that was eventually replaced by the Romano-British *temenos* wall. No positive evidence of a pre-Roman focus was found, but the most obvious location would have been directly below its Romano-British successor, and the excavation policy precluded investigation of the primary levels. The siting of the square-within-a-square temple centrally within the compound certainly prompts the idea that there may have been an earlier shrine on the site. Of the two Romano-British temples, the polygonal shrine was of particular interest in a number of deposits of pigs' heads, reminiscent of the significance of boar imagery in Iron Age culture and art. At Lydney in Gloucestershire (Wheeler and Wheeler 1932), where a major religious centre dedicated to Nodens was built in the later third century, the local community was engaged in an iron-working industry, and the promontory fort within which the temple was located may also have served a specialist function in the Iron Age, prompting its later prosperity and ritual dedication (Yeates 2008). The presence of a temple or shrine of the Romano-British period could be regarded as evidence of continuity of sanctity from earlier periods, but equally the significance of sites may change over a millennium, and what began as an agricultural and domestic settlement or a defensive enclosure to protect communal property may have acquired venerated status through longevity and tradition.

CURRENCY BAR HOARDS AND METALWORKING

Hoards from the Late Bronze Age and Iron Age in Britain are found in a wide variety of locations, but one class of artefact that appears to be especially associated with hillforts is iron 'currency bars' (Allen 1967; Hingley 1990). The term derives from a reference by Caesar to the Britons' alternative to the use of gold and bronze coinage:

> taleis ferries ad certum pondus examinatis pro nummo
> bars of iron checked for standard weight in place of money

(Caesar *dBG* V, 12; for resumé of the textual issues, see Allen 1967: 319 and footnote 1)

As Hingley (ibid. 105) pointed out, however, the distribution of currency bars in Britain shows an almost total absence of recorded finds in those regions of south-eastern England with which Caesar was familiar, and it seems more likely that they were valuable as ingots, perhaps used in trade and exchange, rather than as currency in the normal sense. Find-spots include both non-fortified settlements and hillforts, including Meon Hill, Warwickshire (394), Salmondsbury, Gloucestershire (147), Ham Hill, Somerset (70–80), as well as lesser deposits, such as Madmarston, Oxfordshire (12), Hod Hill (17), and Danebury (20). The other significant choice of location is in rivers, like the Orton Meadows, Northamptonshire deposit (9) and several from the Thames. Other natural contexts include Wyche Rocks, Malvern, Worcestershire, where two separate hoards of some 150 bars or fragments, which might well be regarded as votive deposits, were found within a few yards of each other in 1856–7. Hingley detected a significant preference for hoards from hillforts and settlements to be deposited in liminal locations, such as ramparts and ditches, and the discovery of a hoard of 48 in a pit-alignment at Gretton, Northamptonshire (Jackson 1974) certainly endorses this idea. That they were deliberate, 'non-profane' deposits seems a reasonable inference, since burial would hardly be conducive to preservation of iron if recovery was intended. Hingley also regarded the shape of currency bars, particularly the sword-shaped and ploughshare-shaped variants, as bearing symbolic significance, and their deposits therefore as intended to invoke protection for the community and productive yields of their crops. The spit-shaped bars, which Hingley did not stress, might equally be regarded as symbolic of hearth and home. The distribution of hillfort and settlement related finds of currency bars is centred on the distribution area of Durotrigian and Dobunnic coins, though the date of production and use of the bars in the last three centuries BC initially precedes the introduction of coinage in these territories. On the basis of metal analyses (Hedges and Salter 1979), it appears that production was essentially local, but as Hingley argued (1990: 108), if currency bars were produced to a broadly standardized form and weight, the implication is that control was being exercised over production and circulation, which might have implications for our understanding of the role of hillforts. Crew (1994), however, has argued that similarity in shape and weight arises only from the production process, not from any more systematic control of weights and measures.

At Danebury, the hoard of twenty currency bars found in circular structure 22 was interpreted as a propitiatory deposit in view of a number of such offerings on the site (Cunliffe 1995: 86). In addition, however, there was evidence for currency bars being cut up in preparation for manufacture into tools and weapons (Crew 1995: 279); the sword-shaped bars, for example, lending themselves to use for knives and cutting tools. It seems possible that the distinctive shapes of the bars were a means of identifying to the user the source of production, which in this case was potentially either Northamptonshire, the Weald or the Forest of Dean (Cunliffe 1995: 93). Despite the size of the assemblage (some 489 iron artefacts), it seems that the scale of iron production at Danebury was domestic rather than industrial. From the last ten years of the Danebury excavation, only 14 kg of slag was recovered (ibid. 69) compared, for instance, with 700 kg from Gussage All Saints (Crew 1995: 281), suggesting that the latter was a more important production centre. On the other hand, some small walled sites in Wales like Bryn y Castell, Merioneth (Crew 1984, 1986; Mighall and Chambers 1997) evidently were industrial sites, though at one of the most prolific sites in terms of ironworking debris (600 kg) and multiple bowl furnaces, Crawcwellt West, Merioneth (Crew 1989), the wall was not so much a protecting enclosure as an attached annexe.

On current evidence there would seem to be no case for regarding hillforts in Britain as having any special association with iron production or distribution, beyond the local needs of whatever communities they sustained. There is certainly some evidence for an increase in iron products and iron working in the late pre-Roman Iron Age at sites like Danebury, but not remotely on the scale of some of the Late La Tène *oppida* of central Europe like Manching or Kelheim in Bavaria (Wells 1993). The scale of production in evidence at these sites was prodigious, and the range of tools and equipment for blacksmithing, agriculture, and joinery was at a level that Wells reckoned 'changed very little between the late Iron Age and the Industrial Revolution' (1984: 145). Even so, iron was smelted and forged on smaller sites as well, though it seems probable that there was a measure of hierarchy in iron production, with more specialized work being concentrated in the *oppida*. Apart from the social and economic functions of the central European *oppida*, sites like Manching that adopted the *murus Gallicus* type of defensive circuit required a massive consumption of iron for the spikes used to fix the timber framework of its internal construction.

CONCLUSIONS

It is hardly necessary to summarize the range of functions, social, economic, and ritual, that hillforts may have served, except to stress that Iron Age communities would almost certainly not have viewed the role of hillforts in this way. Just conceivably, some individual hillforts may have had a primary dominant role, as stock-enclosures or for secure storage of produce, for example, but in general it seems more likely that they were viewed by their users as communal sites, in which different activities may have been seasonally dominant, but in which otherwise social, economic, and ceremonial or ritual roles were mutually embedded. Of these, hillforts' role in burial ritual has almost certainly been underrated, because archaeologists have conventionally expected burial practices to be witnessed by a regular and recurrent rite.

9

Documentary Sources

Prehistorians like to think of prehistoric archaeology as the 'purest' branch of the discipline, in that interpretation and reconstruction of prehistoric societies is solely dependent upon the principles and techniques of archaeology, untainted by the predisposition of history. The unfortunate polarization of attitudes was only too evident at a recent International Congress of Celtic Studies, at which some younger archaeologists were utterly dismissive of any argument that was based upon classical sources, an intolerance that was only comprehensible in the face of the equally irrational faith placed in these sources, irrespective of context or chronology, by some of their senior colleagues. This kind of uncritical use of texts doubtless underlies Hill's (1989) exhortation that Iron Age archaeological studies should become more like the Neolithic. For others, the present writer included, the challenge of the Iron Age derives largely from the fact that it *does* span the threshold of history, and that Britain and Europe are therefore populated by named individuals and known communities, not just by inanimate pots and stone artefacts. The age of hillforts is substantially *protohistoric*, though Christopher Hawkes' (1954) term *parahistoric* is probably more accurate for much of the British Iron Age, for which the relevant texts derive from literate neighbours rather than from even a minority literate group among the native community. Archaeologists since Hawkes have sometimes talked about such periods as *text-aided*, as opposed to prehistoric periods that were *text-free*. It may be arguable whether the presence of textual sources is an aid or a complication, but the phrase *text-free* implies a measure of relief that for these periods at least the archaeologist is free to interpret the evidence uninhibited by possible contradiction from historical records.

The problem with text-aided archaeology, of course, was that it tended to be *text-led*; that is, that archaeology was seen as a means of 'proving' or at least illuminating history. The subordination of archaeology to history that was implicit in this approach is well illustrated by the way that Sir Leonard Woolley's excavations at Ur were popularly heralded as proving the flood of Genesis, or Kathleen Kenyon's excavations at Jericho were presented as discovering the walls destroyed by Joshua, notwithstanding the fact that the

Neolithic town with which she was primarily concerned pre-dated Iron Age Joshua by several millennia. More directly relevant to hillforts is Wheeler's interpretation of evidence from excavations at Stanwick, focused expressly on Tacitus' account of the rivalry between Venutius and his pro-Roman queen Cartimandua, which in retrospect and in the light of renewed excavation can be seen to be open to quite contrary reading. Even in the late 1960s, the excavation at Cadbury Castle was widely promoted as a search for King Arthur's Camelot. Despite the retrospective distancing of the director from the Camelot bandwagon (Alcock 1995: ix), it is clear from contemporary accounts (e.g. Thomas 1969; *Irish Times*, April 4, 1968; March 13, 1969; June 19, 1969) that the Camelot Research Committee under Sir Mortimer Wheeler was vigorously exploiting the Arthurian connection in its fund-raising pitch. For R. G. Collingwood, archaeology may have been the handmaid of history, but archaeology as a discipline has moved on a long way since then.

Textual sources too needed to be scrutinized carefully. Editors over the years have commonly proposed emendations for textual cruces, notably where manuscripts are ungrammatical or inconsistent, but sometimes without obvious good reason. It has sometimes also been suggested that whole paragraphs are later interpolations, though it is not always clear by whom, when, or to what purpose. So texts are not infallible, and it is as likely that archaeology can cast light on the documentary sources as it is that those sources can inform archaeology.

CAESAR, TACITUS, AND CLASSICAL SOURCES

In dealing with any of the Greek or Roman sources relating to the barbarian west, a fundamental question is whether we are dealing with a report based upon personal knowledge or experience, or one based upon earlier records, or simply on unsubstantiated traditions. In the past it was accepted that accounts of Gaulish society, its structure, conventions and beliefs, based upon reports by Caesar, Strabo, Diodorus Siculus, and others, reflected a pan-European Celtic way of life that was equally relevant to Iron Age Britain. With an increasing awareness of the highly regionalized character of European Iron Age communities has come a recognition that, for all their apparent similarities, these accounts may obscure quite marked local differences in custom and practice. Furthermore, changes over time may have accelerated in the immediately pre-Roman period so that some of the attributes of Gaulish societies of the first century BC may not be a true reflection of custom and practice in the preceding centuries, even if they ever reflected reality as opposed to the world of heroic fiction. To this extent, at least, Caesar's personal reports, as opposed to his interpolations of general ethnography, may be taken as reflecting, reliably or otherwise, actual events in actual places.

There are two fundamental qualifications that must inform our evaluation of any statement or opinion, the first attributable to ignorance of or disinterest in factual accuracy, the second to unconscious or wilful bias in the presentation of the evidence. In the first category we might include much of the generalized ethnography of the non-Greek or non-Roman world, based upon traditional accounts of earlier writers like Posidonius, some of which can be seen to be borrowed second-hand from the fact that they are repeated almost verbatim by different sources. At best these lack the authority of first-hand reports, at worst they are in the league of fantastic travellers' tales. In the second category are statements that are deliberately contrived, either to present native communities as savage barbarians, and therefore deserving of whatever might be inflicted on them in the name of civilization, or as propaganda to satisfy the Senate and popular opinion in Rome. In this league we might rank Caesar's insistence, contrary to the testimony of other sources such as Strabo, that the Rhine formed a significant ethnic boundary between Gauls and Germans. Strabo (*Geography* 7.1.2) argued that there was little difference between the peoples east and west of the Rhine, explaining that this was why the Germani were so named, to indicate that they were blood brothers with their neighbours. Caesar by contrast wished to justify not extending his campaign further, and an ethnographic boundary would have been regarded as an appropriate point at which to draw the line. There are also occasions in which Caesar's accounts, though not perhaps factually inaccurate, put a decidedly one-sided gloss on the outcome of encounters with native forces. In the debacle at Gergovia, for example, now once again believed to have been located on the Plateau de Merdogne (Plate 15a) south of Clermont-Ferrand, he admitted to the loss of forty-six centurions, but tried to mitigate the disaster by stressing the valour, if foolhardiness, of his men to cover his tactical withdrawal.

In practice, however, it is often difficult to distinguish ignorance from opportunistic misrepresentation. Caesar was not studying the Gauls as an anthropologist, so that his account of the class structure (*dBG* VI, 13) is doubtless a gross over-simplification, and his assessment of the common people as oppressed by the nobility to the point of being effectively slaves surely obscures a subtle hierarchy of debts and obligations. Equally, in describing the practice of sacrificing criminals to appease the gods (*dBG* VI, 16), his additional suggestion that, when no criminals are available, the innocent would be executed instead, seems calculated to induce revulsion in a Roman audience. His report that in Britain the people of the interior know little about agriculture and crop cultivation but instead are pastoralists living off meat and milk (*dBG* V, 14) might, on the face of it, seem like an objective statement of observed fact. It was accepted by Piggott (1958a) in support of his concept of a 'Stanwick economy' based on pastoralism for northern Britain, in contrast to the mixed agricultural regime of his southern British 'Woodbury economy'. As an estimate of the insular Iron Age economy, however, Caesar's statement presents several problems. First it is not clear that by 'interior' he meant northern Britain (with which he had no acquaintance whatsoever) as opposed to Britain north of the Thames (with which he was familiar). Second, he uses an almost identical formula in discussing the Germans beyond the Rhine (*dBG* IV, 1), whom he was trying to dissociate from communities west of the Rhine for reasons of political expediency. The formulaic nature of the statement is based upon the Roman equation of cultivation with civilization, so that in both instances Caesar was attempting to cast both northern Britons and Germans as uncivilized pastoralists, whom he could therefore conveniently discount. As statements on agricultural economy, therefore, his opinion is probably wilfully misleading. On the other hand, some of Caesar's observations at least are based on first-hand experience, and what he says about military tactics and defensive structures carries greater authority because they must have mattered to him.

With both the principal Roman sources relating to Britain, Caesar and Tacitus, even if we can be reasonably confident that any observation regarding social structure or military tactics is authentic, there remains the issue of whether events of the first centuries BC and AD have any bearing on the situation over the preceding millennium. Quite obviously, circumstances during the Gallic wars or in the conquest of Britain, where native forces were in conflict with a highly specialized army whose discipline and field equipment will have been quite alien to traditional combat practices between indigenous foes, have limited relevance to conventional inter- or intra-tribal Iron Age warfare. But it has been argued that the changes in Iron Age society itself, in southern Britain at any rate, in the first century BC were much more fundamental in terms of the reordering of methods of production and exchange (Gosden 1989), and consequentially in the structure of society itself. Plainly the capture and destruction of *oppida* in Gaul and hillforts in Britain was central to the Roman policy of subjugating the local population, but it is unlikely that Iron Age antagonists would have targeted hillforts quite so systematically. The impact of a Roman presence in southern Gaul from the end of the second century, and Caesar's protracted campaigns in Gaul evidently gave the native forces time to adapt to novel circumstances, as Caesar himself remarked at the siege of Avaricum in 52 BC:

> Singulari militum nostrorum virtuti consilia cuiusque modi Gallorum occurrebant ut est summae genus sollertiae atque ad omnia imitanda et efficienda quae ab quoque traduntur aptissimum
>
> The outstanding valour of our troops was countered with all kinds of tactics by the Gauls, for they are a nation of the greatest resourcefulness and most apt to copy and put into effect anything that they are introduced to.
>
> (Caesar *dBG* VII, 22)

Among the tactics deployed by the Gauls in imitation of the Romans was the use of towers on the rampart walls, which they heightened to counter the Roman assault towers. Five years earlier at Noviodunum of the Suessiones Caesar claimed that the Gauls had sued for peace, overwhelmed by the scale of the siege-works, with which they were totally unfamiliar. In fact, however, his initial assault had been repelled by a small defending force

> propter latitudinem fossae murique altitudinem
> on account of the width of the ditch and height of the wall
> (Caesar *dBG* II, 12)

which sounds very like a massive dump rampart with broad ditch of the kind that would have been much better adapted to match assault machinery than a lesser dump rampart or older conventional wall-rampart with narrow ditch. The Suessiones, with the intercession of their Remic allies, may well have decided on this occasion that discretion was the better part of valour, but it seems unlikely that they were so unfamiliar with Roman tactics that must have been well known to their southern neighbours for several generations. Another Roman tactic adopted by the Gauls was the use of circumvallation, which would have been totally alien to any likely military deployment in the earlier Iron Age, and which again Caesar attributes directly to experience of Roman tactics:

> Nervii vallo pedum ix et fossa pedum xv hiberna cingunt. Haec et superiorum annorum consuetudine ab nobis cognoverant et quos clam de exercitu habebant captivos ab eis docebantur.
>
> The Nervii surrounded the Roman winter quarters with a rampart nine feet high and fifteen feet wide. These tactics they had learned from us through encounters in previous years, and they had been instructed by prisoners whom they had secretly captured from the army.
> (Caesar *dBG* 5, 42)

The most comprehensive instance of circumvallation, however, was Caesar's investment of Alesia in 52 BC (Figure 1.9b), designed both to contain the besieged forces and to impede any attempt to penetrate the blockade by relieving troops.

Less certain is whether the Gauls had previously used the 'tortoise' tactic, the practice of interlocking shields over the heads of an assault group in an attack on the gates or ramparts of a hillfort. Caesar actually attributes this to the Gauls in his account of the campaign against the Belgae:

> Gallorum eadem atque Belgarum oppugnatio est haec. Ubi circumiecta multitudine hominem totis moenibus undique in murum lapides iaci coepti sunt murusque defensoribus nudatus est, testudine facta portas succendunt murumque subruunt.

> The method of attack of the Gauls and the Belgae is the same. When a host of men have surrounded the entire ramparts, and a hail of stones has been launched from all sides, stripping the walls of defenders, having formed a 'tortoise', they fire the gates and undermine the walls. (Caesar *dBG* II, 6)

Despite numerous attempts by editors to emend *succendunt* to *succedunt*, Rivet (1971) mounted a vigorous defence of the manuscript originals, on the very reasonable grounds that firing of hillfort gates was amply demonstrated in the archaeological record, and there was therefore no reason to exclude it when archaeological and documentary records appeared to be in complete accord. The nature of the 'tortoise', however, might be questioned. This was certainly a Roman tactic, efficiently deployed with shields of standard, matching size. Whether, when used by native forces, it amounted to more than raising shields above the head for obvious protection against a defensive barrage is doubtful. When Caesar reported that Vercingetorix's troops formed a tortoise (*testudine facta*) at Alesia (*dBG* VII, 85), he may simply have been using a familiar Roman term to describe a practice that approximated less formally to a known tactic. Stoning, whether projected by hand or by sling, was undoubtedly a basic tactic of the later pre-Roman Iron Age. Unlike Roman artillery, which presumably would very rapidly have adjusted to the correct range, Gaulish (and British) stone fire would probably have been less accurate, and part of the purpose of the Gaulish 'tortoise' may have been to protect the attackers from misplaced 'friendly fire'. The reference to undermining of the walls is significant, since archaeologically it has seldom been considered from the evidence of excavation, where damage such as the collapse of the flanking walls of entrance passages at Blewburton Hill (Collins 1953) or at Bredon Hill (Hencken 1938) has generally been attributed to post-capture demolition.

One celebrated passage in Caesar's record that accords closely with archaeological evidence is his description of the 'Gallic wall' at Avaricum, which appears to be based upon personal experience of attacking and subsequently slighting the defences. The *murus Gallicus* variant of wall rampart (Cotton 1957) was distinguished by the combination of transverse and longitudinal beams internally with minimal exposure in the external stone wall faces. The advantage of this form of construction over earlier types of timber-with-stone ramparts is summarized with the authority of an expert in defensive and offensive tactics:

> et ab incendio lapis et ab ariete materia defendit, quae perpetuis trabibus pedes quadragenos plerumque introrsus revincta neque perrumpi neque distrahi potest.
>
> the stonework protects it from fire and the timber from the battering-ram, which, with continuous beams commonly forty feet in length, held firmly in place internally, can neither be breached nor pulled apart. (Caesar *dBG* VII, 23)

A point of contention is the internal fixing of the intersecting timbers. On a number of late La Tène *oppida* in Gaul, such as the Mont Beuvray or Le Camp d'Artus, Huelgoat, and Le Petit Celland (Wheeler and Richardson 1957), massive iron spikes have been recovered in some numbers that evidently served this purpose. It is generally maintained, however (Harding 1974: 64), that Caesar's terms *revinciuntur, revincta,* and *coagmentatis* do not necessitate nails or spikes, though it might be argued that the *vinc-* element implies a metal bond. In practice, however, this was plainly a major component in many Gaulish *oppida*, with very significant ramifications in terms of the industrial production of iron.

In 56 BC Caesar extended the campaign to the Veneti of the Breton peninsula. Here he encountered a different kind of fortification and different defensive tactics. The Veneti were renowned for their seamanship and the robust build of their vessels, so that it is hardly surprising that their strongholds were coastal, and evidently with easy access to the sea. As Caesar explained, they were located

> in extremis lingulis promontoriisque neque pedibus aditum haberent cum ex alto se aestus incitavisset
>
> on the ends of spits of land and promontories so that there could be no access on foot once the tide itself had rushed in from the sea   (Caesar *dBG* III, 12)

Yet whenever the Romans constructed barriers to the incoming tide or otherwise threatened to breach the stronghold, the Veneti took to their ships and made off to another location. This description was widely regarded, following Wheeler's pre-war campaign of excavations in northern France (Wheeler and Richardson 1957), to refer to the coastal cliff-castles of southern Brittany, which share with sites in south-western Britain their precipitous promontory locations. Unfortunately, as Hogg pointed out (1972: 22), this equation hardly matches the description of sites that were daily cut off by the tide and from which the defenders could readily launch their ships. In fact, the cliff castles of Brittany, like their counterparts in Cornwall, can now be shown to date somewhat earlier than the period of the Gallic campaign, and any search for the sites referred to by Caesar should be directed to the lower-lying coastal reaches of Brittany.

Caesar only twice encountered a fortified site in Britain in 54 BC. The first he described simply using a formulaic phrase,

> et natura et opera munitum
>
> fortified both by nature and by defensive works   (Caesar *dBG* V, 9)

Despite the older conventional identification of this site with Bigbury in Kent, not far from the Stour and about the right distance from Caesar's assumed landing place between Deal and Sandwich, the description does not really match a conventional hillfort. In fact Bigbury stands very much in isolation in eastern Kent, which is otherwise devoid of hillforts east of Tunbridge Wells, despite the seeming suitability of the North Downs. The site described by Caesar was located in the woods rather than around the contours of a low hill, from which periodically the local forces emerged to engage the Romans. Certainly the *locus* (not an *oppidum* and still less anything grander) had a rampart, against which the Seventh Legion built a ramp, but the fact that multiple entries had been blocked, not with makeshift gates but a great number of felled trees, sounds more like an extensive area of low-lying woodland earthworks sharing some of the features of a terrain *oppidum*. Reckless pursuit of guerrilla attacks into the woods and uplands resulted in casualties, suggesting that these sites were designed to serve as killing grounds, whatever may have been their other community uses in more peaceful times.

Having negotiated the underwater obstacles placed in the Thames to impede his crossing, Caesar advanced on the stronghold of Cassivellaunus, which is described in similar terms:

> silvis paludibusque munitum...
> fortified by woods and marshes
>
> Oppidum autem Britanni vocant, cum silvas impeditas vallo atque fossa munierunt...
> Now the Britons call it an *oppidum* when they have fortified dense woodland with rampart and ditch
>
> egregie natura atque opera munitum
> excellently fortified by nature and defensive works (again)   (Caesar *dBG* V, 21)

The fact that a great number of cattle were found here need not imply that this had anything to do with the normal, as opposed to emergency function of the *oppidum*, since we are told that along the route of the Roman advance, communities had driven their herds into the woods for protection. What is clear is that the native forces did not attempt to hold their position, but made good their escape.

The other major source of interest in terms of Iron Age warfare is Caesar's account of the British use of chariots (*dBG* IV, 33). Already obsolete on the continent, the last recorded use being at the battle of Telamon (Polybius *Histories* II, 28), he admits to the consternation that this novel form of engagement caused to the legions, though it is hard to believe that his advance intelligence had failed to get any intimation of this tactic. By the time of Agricola the practice was not universal among the British tribes (Tacitus *Agricola* 12), and it may already have been in limited use by the first century BC. Caesar's account of chariot warfare among the Britons needs no rehearsing, except perhaps to ask how many fighting men were carried in each chariot. There are, of course, Egyptian and Mediterranean representations of single charioteers, and on rock art of the Bronze Age in Scandinavia

(Kristiansen 1999: Figure 5), and that is the image depicted on a bronze coin of Eppillus from Kent (Nash 1987: Plates 3, 13). The standard image of the Celtic war chariot in action is of a single warrior, the social superior, with one driver, his subordinate, which is doubtless in significant part inspired by images of the Celtic superhero of Irish legend or classical accounts of its ceremonial or sporting usage. But these images all relate to ceremonial or legendary events, and may not reflect the actuality of real combat. If this was really the normal fighting practice, how can chariots possibly have provided

> mobilitatem equitum stabilitatem peditum in proelis
>
> in battle the mobility of cavalry and the stability of infantry   (Caesar *dBG* IV, 33)

unless groups could be deployed as infantry in concert? Furthermore, we are told that

> si illi a multitudine hostium premantur, expeditum ad suos receptum habeant
>
> if the warriors are overwhelmed by the numbers of the enemy, they have a ready means of withdrawal to their own side   (ibid. 33)

which would hardly be undertaken one at a time. The chariot more probably served as an armed personnel carrier, designed to deploy groups rapidly to wherever they were required. This was evidently what happened in 54 BC, when the native forces

> numquam conferti sed rari magnisque intervallis proeliarentur stationesque dispositas haberent, atque alios alii deinceps exciperent integrique et recentes defetigatis succederent
>
> never fought in close rank but in small numbers widely separated, and had their detachments disposed so that one group could relieve another in succession, and fresh troops could take over from the battle-weary   (Caesar *dBG* V, 16)

This certainly makes more sense if there was more than one fighting man per chariot, a conclusion which is further supported by Tacitus' observation that the warrior of senior rank was the driver while his plural dependants fought in his defence (*Agricola* 12). That there was sufficient room is corroborated by the report (Tacitus, *Annals* XIV, 34) that Boudicca paraded before her army with her daughters in her chariot. In this instance, however, the chariot appears to have been a symbol of rank or perhaps intended to invoke memories of past successes, since otherwise her forces apparently comprised only large numbers of infantry and cavalry.

Essential to this tactic was the coordination of cavalry with chariots. Prior to this engagement, Caesar three times mentions the deployment of chariots (*dBG* IV, 24; IV, 32; V, 9); on every occasion cavalry and chariots are referred to as an entity. A major role of the cavalry was evidently to draw off the Roman cavalry, thus enabling the chariot infantry to control the field. After Cassivellaunus had abandoned hope of a decisive engagement and disbanded the greater part of his forces, he used the remaining chariot warriors to harry the Roman cavalry, but avoided direct engagement with the Roman infantry. This residual force Caesar estimated at around four thousand charioteers (*dBG* V, 19), the operative word being *essedarii* not *essedi*. Four thousand chariots requiring eight thousand horses always seemed an extravagant estimate, and even propaganda has to be credible. But four thousand mobile infantry using chariots does not sound nearly so much of an exaggeration.

That Caesar's account can illuminate aspects of Iron Age strongholds and the tactics deployed in their defence is hardly in doubt. Equally interesting are the political rifts that emerge from the account that may reflect significant differences in the local communities in southern Britain on the eve of the conquest. Too easily dismissed as evidence of native fickleness, it seems more likely that they reflect inter-tribal hostilities and intra-tribal rivalries between dominant kin groups. The first hint of discord among the native population comes before the first raid of 55 BC:

> a compluribus insulae civitatibus ad eum legati veniunt qui polliceantur obsides dare atque imperio Romani obtemperare
>
> from several of the island states envoys came to Caesar who promised to give hostages and submit to Roman rule   (Caesar *dBG* IV, 21)

Sending Commius back with them suggests that these envoys were from tribes of the Atrebatic confederation, rather than, for instance, those from the eastern coastal regions flanking and north of the Thames estuary. Caesar subsequently admits, however, that he had made previous contact with high-ranking representatives of the eastern 'maritime' tribes in Mandubracius, who had come to the Continent after his father had been killed by Cassivellaunus:

> Mandubracius adulescens Caesaris fidem secutus ad eum in continentem Galliam venerat
>
> young Mandubracius had come to Caesar in mainland Gaul to seek his allegiance
> (Caesar *dBG* V, 20)

The fact that Commius had then been seized and imprisoned, only to be returned with the promise of hostages after the initial defeat of the native resistance to Caesar's landing, suggests a power struggle between rival elites within the native communities, in effect between appeasers and those who wished to defend their territory. With Caesar's fleet suffering storm damage, the resistance party once more seized the initiative, and the seventh legion had to be rescued from ambush. After consolidating his beach-head camp and deploying Commius' cavalry, Caesar doubled the number of hostages required and rapidly departed for the continent.

In his second campaign in 54 BC, Caesar landed further east, which would have been the preferred landing the previous year, and where initially he met no resistance. After a preliminary foray inland, he once again experienced storm damage to the fleet, and delayed for ten days securing his base before setting out again. In the meantime we are told that the native forces had united under Cassivellaunus,

> cuius fines a maritimis civitatibus flumen dividit, quod appellatur Tamesis
>
> whose territory is divided from the maritime states by the river called the Thames
> (Caesar *dBG* V, 11)

so that we may infer that the anti-Roman faction was once again in the ascendant. From the following geographical division we may infer that Cassivellaunus is allied to the 'interior pars', inhabited by pastoral barbarians, unlike the people of the 'maritima pars', who had come over from Belgic Gaul ('ex Belgio transierunt', *dBG* V, 12) or who, in the case of the maritime inhabitants of Kent, differed little from their civilized Gallic neighbours (*dBG* V, 14), and who by implication included pro-Roman sympathizers. It was at this point, as Caesar pressed forward north of the Thames, that the Trinovantes renewed their request for protection from Cassivellaunus, and four other tribes, among whom only the Cenimagni had a name that might be equated with otherwise known groups, likewise came to terms. Cassivellaunus evidently commanded sufficient authority among the maritime states to incite four separate 'regiones' to attack Caesar's naval base behind his advance. After the apparent failure of this, and chiefly concerned by potential defection among his allies ('permotus defectione civitatum', *dBG* V, 22), however, he too came to terms with Caesar, who, having charged Cassivellaunus somewhat optimistically not to terrorise the Trinovantes, again rapidly departed.

From this account it would appear that there were at least three main confederations of whom Caesar had direct experience. The people of the 'maritime states' included Kent, but the description may also have applied to the Trinovantes of coastal Essex. These evidently included a significant pro-Roman faction, if only in the case of the Trinovantes because of pre-existing enmity with Cassivellaunus. Cassivellaunus is not historically identified with the Catuvellauni, but his territory north of the Thames and inland from maritime Essex would not be inconsistent with that identification. He plainly was a major protagonist of anti-Roman resistance. Finally, it seems likely that Caesar was familiar through Commius with the Atrebates to the west in Hampshire, Surrey, Sussex, and Berkshire. Within the 'maritime' groups at least, there appear to have been at least four sub-groups or 'regiones', which presumably exacerbated the potential divisions between pro-Roman and anti-Roman factions. The overall picture, therefore, is one of inter-tribal rivalry or outright enmity, but perhaps with diplomatic liaisons between powerful communities or their leaders that could have been based upon long-standing social or economic alliances. Society may have become more hierarchical, but underlying social bonds and tensions between groups are likely to have been longer-standing.

Tacitus' record of events in Britain in the first century AD makes a few references to native fortifications, though insufficient to identify the sites in question. The crude defences attacked by Ostorius' forces in putting down the Icenian revolt of around AD 48 were tentatively identified by Frere (1967/1998: 60) as Stonea Camp in Cambridgeshire, a possibility that has been broadly endorsed by the site's subsequent excavators (Malim 1992; Jackson and Potter 1996). After securing his back, Ostorius in AD 51 advanced into the territory of the Ordovices to face Caractacus, who had selected a hilltop position overlooking a river to make his stand. Where the hill was accessible, its circuit was barred by stone ramparts, but it would appear that Caractacus had squads initially in front of the stronghold as well as defending the hillfort itself. The Romans breached the defences using the customary *testudo*, forcing the defenders to retreat to higher ground with severe losses. Thereafter the destruction of Druidic sacred sites in Anglesey by Paulinus and the subsequent defeat of Boudicca in AD 61 make no reference to the use of hillforts.

Though Tacitus is generally regarded as a reliable historian, his accounts of political and military discord of the mid-first century among the Brigantian ruling hierarchy, assumed by Wheeler to be successive episodes in a continuing quarrel, present a possible conflict of dating if they refer to the same events (Ross 2011: 37–40). In one account (*Annals* 12, 40), dated to AD 51, Cartimandua's surrender of Caractacus to the Romans triggered widespread dissent among the anti-Roman faction, including her husband Venutius, who had previously been sympathetic to the Romans, to the point that she required Roman military support. This bitter quarrel, described in similar terms, but compounded by the fact that Cartimandua had consorted with Venutius' armour-bearer, is introduced in a second account in the context of events of AD 69 (*Histories* III, 45). This episode, as we have seen, was crucial to Wheeler's dating of Phase III of the Stanwick fortifications, which he assumed was held by the anti-Roman Venutius. He favoured an older archaeological tradition that Castle Hill, Almondbury, identified as the *Camulodunum* of Ptolemy's geography (Richmond 1925: 83–4), was Cartimandua's southern Brigantian capital, an identification that has long been rendered improbable by the evidence of excavation for that hillfort's much earlier construction and occupation (Varley 1976). With the evidence of more recent excavations at Stanwick for flourishing trading relations with the Romanized south-east (Haselgrove *et al.* 1990), its role in the documented discord between pro-Roman and anti-Roman factions among the Brigantes is no longer self-evident. To the archaeologist, of course, this hardly affects the crucial issues in evaluating the role and significance of Stanwick, but it affords a salutary reminder of the pitfalls in reconciling archaeological evidence with documentary history.

Finally in Tacitus' record the Caledonians were routed at Mons Graupius. Despite detailed description of the defending forces drawn up on a higher place with troops seemingly ranked above each other, and reinforcements, who had occupied the hilltops, subsequently descending to engage the Roman forces, there is no reference to fortifications, and the defeated natives fled to the forests rather than to a hillfort. What does emerge from Tacitus' account, however, is that the native forces, notwithstanding their capacity to adapt to a different type of warfare, were still hopelessly ill-equipped with their massive swords and small shields (*Agricola* 36, 1) for close combat with Batavian and Tungrian auxiliaries. Archaeologically the evidence for Iron Age shields of this period in northern Britain is minimal, not least because regular shields, unlike parade armour, would have been made largely of wood or leather. Ritchie (1969) nevertheless inferred a relatively small, rectangular type with circular boss from sculpted representations of contemporary native warriors in submission or defeat, analogous to the leather shield from a bog at Clonoura, Co. Tipperary (Raftery 1984: Figure 70). The massive swords alluded to could well have been of the same general class as the Stanwick sword (Wheeler 1954; Stead 2006: no. 245), the blade of which (i.e. excluding hilt) is 697 mm long. The small shield was presumably light enough to be raised to parry a swinging blow from such a sword in one-to-one combat, but would have been inadequate and cumbersome in a close-order group engagement of the kind described at Mons Graupius.

Chariots were deployed at Mons Graupius, though not as effectively as they had been against Caesar. According to Dio Cassius (*History* 77, 12), the Caledonii including the Maeatae used chariots for warfare in the early third century, indicating a degree of tactical conservatism in northern Britain.

With due allowance for the fact that events of the Romano-British wars may not have reflected pre-Roman practice, it seems probable that hillforts seldom featured as the sites of battles. Perhaps their impressive ramparts and elaborately guarded entrances served as sufficient deterrent. Pre-Roman Iron Age conflict more likely took the form of small-scale ambushes and raids, and even when larger scale engagements took place it is probable that these were on open ground below hillforts where cavalry and chariots could operate effectively. Hillforts undoubtedly were burnt and their defences slighted, but this was more probably in post-battle circumstances, where the hillfort had functioned as a refuge of last resort, mainly for non-combatants, their livestock, and entourage.

IRISH LITERARY SOURCES

Over the past twenty years, the pendulum of opinion has swung away from the older view that the epic tales of early Medieval Ireland might incorporate traditions regarding social structure and conventions that derived through long oral tradition from the pre-Roman Iron Age. The principal limitations in the use of Irish sources were that 'one thousand years of changes—including the impact of the Roman Empire, Christianity, literacy, the transition to feudalism etc.' (Hill 1995b: 47) invalidated their use as a 'window on the Iron Age' (Jackson 1964). Hill's objection to the uncritical use of medieval Irish law tracts is certainly justified; as Wailes (1988) observed, they are prescriptive rather than descriptive, and may incorporate archaisms no longer relevant in a changing social order. Similar qualifications should be applied to medieval Welsh sources for the same reasons (Alcock 1965: 189).

Central to Jackson's argument was the fact that the impact of Roman contact in Ireland had been minimal and that the tales from their content indicated their pre-Christian origin. The fact that Ulster was ruled from a royal centre at Emain Macha indicated that the setting of the tales pre-dated the fifth-century reorganization of the kingdom, after which the ascendency of the Ui Néill dramatically changed the political geography of northern Ireland. The central thrust of Jackson's case, however, was the similarities in the social order of the epic tales—kings, warriors, druids, clients, and so forth—and the accounts of Gaulish, and to a lesser degree British, Iron Age society given by Caesar, Strabo, and Diodorus Siculus. The existence of druids and the practice of fosterage were equally testified in both contexts. The boastful behaviour of claimants of the champion's portion at the feast had echoes in the classical sources, and combat between champions was another common theme. Weaponry and warfare were comparable, including the use of the chariot, which was surely telling, since not a single chariot or convincing chariot parts (as opposed to evidence of paired draught of a non-combatant variety) have ever been recovered archaeologically in Ireland. Jackson's conclusion, therefore, was that the tales were based on a pre-Christian oral tradition that had its origin in the La Tène cultural world of north-western Europe. His problem was to explain how that tradition could have been introduced into Ireland, and more especially whether oral transmission could account for its survival for perhaps as long as five hundred years.

In the past twenty years or so, opinion among Irish scholars has shifted away from a belief in a long oral tradition as the source of the heroic tales of the Ulster Cycle. Aitchison (1987) contended that Jackson's approach was concerned with content and transmission rather than structure and social context, and that an examination of the *Tain* and other epics suggested that, if tales were recited orally by the *filidh*, they were composed in written form rather than from an oral tradition. He pointed to an absence of prosodic systems, apart from repetition, which he did not believe could be the result of transcription and omission from oral sources. He conceded nevertheless that there were some verse elements, notably to heighten the mood in relation to love, anger, or death, and in direct speech as opposed to narrative in the epic tales. The language and syntax of these *roscada* was often archaic, and, he conceded, 'that some of the *roscada* within the Ulster Cycle originated from an orally-transmitted tradition maintained by the *filidh* is perfectly plausible' (ibid. 98). But he argued that these had been deliberately introduced for historical authenticity.

Aitchison argued that the *Tain* was composed in the late eighth century, perhaps in the monastic *scriptorium* at Armagh, with the intention of appropriating the authority of the traditional centre of Emain Macha to the Christian centre. Bruford followed a similar line, suggesting that 'Armagh was the real centre of power, while Emain was an occasionally visited inaugural site' (Bruford 1994: 25). Navan fort itself apparently ceased to be a major centre after the first century BC, and though it may still have been a focus for periodic activities of a ceremonial kind, it was certainly not in the second half of the first millennium AD a fortified settlement of the kind depicted in the epic tales. Archaeologically there can be no doubt that the Navan complex was an important regional centre in the early Iron Age, but not so much as a fortified settlement as for its ceremonial and ritual structures. As a symbol of pagan cults, any folk memory of Navan would surely have been anathema to the Christian hierarchy in Armagh. Reviving a 'traditional' image of Emain Macha as a secular royal centre might therefore have been preferable to its pagan reality.

The absence of any explicit Christian material in the tales surely remains puzzling, if they were composed in the later eighth century in a Christian *scriptorium*. And the similarities cited by Jackson with classical sources cannot all convincingly be dismissed as so generalized that they would be 'difficult not to parallel among many "barbarian" societies of Iron Age and early historic north-western Europe' (Aitchison 1987: 91). Druids, for example, are referred to in the early Irish sources and are otherwise only known in Iron Age Gaul and Britain, though this need not imply similarity or continuity of role. Aitchison (ibid. 95) dismissed Jackson's reference to the Gaulish druids' oral learning (*dBG* VI, 14) in support of an oral tradition on the grounds of their 'spatial, temporal and cultural remoteness' from the Irish *filidh*. The druids, of course, were not a bardic order (Caesar's use of *versuum* need not imply poetic lines), and their use of oral learning is expressly attributed to their desire to maintain exclusivity, though any such constraint need not have applied to the *bardi* of Iron Age Gaul or Britain.

Nevertheless, the consensus among Celtic linguists appears to be that 'it now be regarded as axiomatic that, assumed oral origins for some of its constituents notwithstanding, the proper frame of reference for early Irish literature is early Christian Ireland rather than the preceding pagan period' (McCone 1990/2000: 3). Yet if early Medieval Ireland no longer affords a 'window on the Iron Age', it still remains a source for social analogy no less valid that ethnographic analogies drawn from regions and periods far more remote from the British Iron Age. On this basis, Karl (2008) made a reasoned case for reinstating the view of social organization of the British Iron Age as Celtic.

Part of the problem is the apparent lack of archaeological continuity in Ireland. The Irish La Tène, which, as Raftery (1994: 226) acknowledged, could have resulted from a relatively small but highly influential group, is especially well represented in the vicinity of Navan fort, though its continental (or less probably British) origins and affinities are not easy to identify. Furthermore, though some artefacts like Monasterevin-type discs can be assigned to the first or second centuries AD, it is difficult to span the centuries between the apparent demise of La Tène metalwork and the early historic period. Though there is a La Tène component in early Christian art (Harding 2007), notably the hair-spring spiral and the trumpet motif picked out by Jackson, it is far from dominant and the case for continuity strains the limited surviving evidence. Equally, the evidence of field monuments hardly supports the case for continuity. The principal class of field monument of the early Christian period is the ringfort, and although evidence can be adduced for a few sites of this general class dating from the early first millennium, such as Raffin, Co. Meath (Newman 1993a, 1993b), the great majority of dated sites, as we have seen, were of the early historic period. Information regarding defences in the tales is not elaborated beyond reference to ramparts or gates, which could apply to virtually any class of enclosure. As regards the buildings within, despite attempts to correlate the texts with archaeological evidence for Iron Age structures (e.g. Hamilton 1968), the descriptions are generally insufficient to sustain any convincing comparison. For Navan itself the descriptions in the tales were measured against the archaeological evidence by Mallory (1997), who reluctantly concluded that any equation between the two was 'on the periphery of archaeological inference'.

EARLY HISTORIC NORTHERN BRITAIN

Widely regarded as authoritative by contemporary standards, the principal documentary source for historical events in northern Britain is Bede's *Historia Ecclesiastica Gentis Anglorum*, written in AD 731. Since two-thirds of the time span covered was before his birth in 672/3, Bede's evidence was necessarily second-hand for much of the record. Furthermore, as its name implies, the

Historia Ecclesiastica is intended to celebrate the English, and makes no secret of the author's contempt for the Britons. Other contemporary sources too were written from an Anglian perspective regarding political, religious or military conflict with their Pictish or British neighbours, so that problems of bias inevitably arise. Equally, reliance on annals, notionally compiled annually in monastic *scriptoria*, is fraught with problems arising from possible corruption through transcription errors, deliberate alterations, and interpolations between the date of the event recorded and the much later date of the earliest extant manuscripts. Alcock (1988: 6) illustrated the problem by citing a reference in an eleventh-century northern version of the *Anglo-Saxon Chronicle*, which claimed that in 547, Ida had first enclosed the royal stronghold at Bamburgh with a palisade and later with a wall, a sequence which was not impossible, but which was so like the pattern of Late Saxon *burhs* that we might suspect that the record was reflecting tenth-century practice rather than sixth.

Much of the archaeological literature of the early historic period hinges on the identification of the location of sites named in the records. One that is beyond dispute is the prominent site of Castle Rock, Dumbarton on the Clyde, described by Bede as

> civitas Brettonum munitissima usque hodie quae vocatur Alcluith
>
> a stronghold of the Britons very strongly defended to the present day, which is called Alt Clut   (*Historia Ecclesiastica* 1, 1)

which he subsequently amplifies:

> urbem Alcluith, quod lingua eorum significat Petram Cluit, est enim iuxta fluvium nominis illius
>
> the stronghold Alt Clut, which in their language means Clyde Rock, as it is by the river of that name   (*Historia Ecclesiastica* 1, 12)

The use of *civitas* and *urbs* implies that the site was of some status, but it is evident throughout the sources that these terms do not carry the same meanings as they did, for instance, for Caesar in the first century BC in Gaul. They do not appear to be applied with any great consistency, but there is reason to suppose that they are indicative of a hierarchy of settlement. Alcock (1988: 11) proposed a threefold hierarchy, based upon the terms used by Bede and Stephen, with *civitas* indicating the highest level, *urbs* and *castellum* an intermediate order, and *villa* or *vicus* the lowest of the three, though even a *villa* could be designated as royal by *regia*. He cited Stephen's description in the *Life of Wilfred* of Ecgfrith and his queen in a royal progress as evidence of such a hierarchy:

> rex cum regina sua per civitates et castellos vicosque cotidie gaudentes et epulantes in pompa saeculari circumeuntes

the king with his queen going around through cities and forts and townships in worldly pomp, rejoicing and feasting daily   (Stephen, *Vita Sancti Wilfrithi* 39)

This certainly suggests that in Anglian society in the late seventh century, the royal progress, effectively a means of extracting dues in kind whilst at the same time reinforcing the king's authority over his territory, was a recognized practice. The concept of food-renders, including livestock and agricultural produce of all kinds, is exemplified in the thirteenth century Welsh Laws of Hywel Dda, which might include material as early as the tenth century. The correlation of *urbs* and *castellum* may seem contradictory, but presumably implies both a civil and military function for such sites, thus mirroring the two contrasting roles that have polarized opinion regarding earlier Iron Age hillforts.

Alcock (2003: 180) listed instances in which hillforts or allied sites were documented as having been sacked or subject to siege, mostly on the basis of records in the *Annals of Ulster*. Major centres were evidently targeted. Dunadd was besieged in 683, together with Dundurn, though the aggressors are not named. Dunadd was successfully attacked in 736 by Oengas, son of Fergus, king of the Picts, who captured two of the sons of Selbaich and laid waste to the territory of Dál Riata. In 870, two Norse kings from Dublin laid siege to Alt Clut, ultimately destroying it and returning with great quantities of booty and many slaves, including Angles, Picts, and Britons, as a result of their rampaging. There can be little doubt therefore that these forts were subject to military attack, though the *Annals* seldom elaborate beyond the bare statement of fact. Bede (*Historia Ecclesiastica* 3, 16) offers marginally more detail of the attack on Bamburgh at some date before 651 by Penda, king of Mercia. Being apparently unable to take the fort by assault or by siege, he is said to have piled up combustible material scavenged from timber buildings in the vicinity to a great height on the landward side of the fortifications and set fire to it. Seemingly the wind veered so that the flames blew back over the assailants, frustrating the attack and saving the city, through divine intervention in response to the prayers of Bishop Aidan, according to Bede (though experienced archaeological air photographers might recognize a not uncommon meteorological phenomenon of the north-east coast).

All of these strongholds were attacked, presumably, because they were centres of wealth and power, but also because they offered prospects of booty. But like earlier Iron Age forts, they could be by-passed by marauding forces intent on rustling and destruction, so that defending forces must have been prepared to engage in the open. Such was the case when the Dál Riatan king Áedán met the army of Aethelfrith around 603 at Degsastan, reckoned to be a site in the western Cheviots (Bede, *Historia Ecclesiastica* 1, 34). Áedán's army was annihilated, and Aethelfrith's also suffered severe losses, but otherwise we are told little of the engagement or how it was conducted. The other important account of a battle is Ecgfrith's defeat by the Picts under Brude mac Bile in 685 at Nechtansmere, because it marks the point at which the Anglian expansion in Scotland was arrested and reversed. The identification of the location of the battle site continues to elude conclusive demonstration. Bede (*Historia Ecclesiastica* 4, 26) merely informs us that the Picts used the tactic of feigning flight to draw Ecgfrith's forces into an ambush in narrow passes amid inaccessible mountains. The event is recorded in the *Annals of Ulster* as '*bellum duin Nechtan*', which must surely be correlated with the name Dunnichen, but there is no suggestion in Bede's or any other account that there was an attack on the hillfort itself. Alcock (2003: 133–6 and Figure 42) favoured the valley between Dunnichen Hill and Turin Hill, notable for its lakes and swamps, dismissing Bede's account of the topography as the exaggerated reports of a defeated army. More recently, Fraser (2002) has reviewed the evidence, including the report in Nennius' *Historia Brittonum* (57) that the battle was known as *Gueith Lin Garan*, the battle of the Crane Lake, perhaps equating with the *Nechtansmere* or lake of Nechtan. He concluded that the battle was fought on the lower slopes of Dunnichen hill, an interpretation that certainly seems to satisfy the limited evidence available. That there is no evidence of the hillfort itself being attacked or sacked is immaterial; there doubtless would have been if the outcome had gone the other way.

Ten kilometres north of Dunnichen, the Aberlemno churchyard cross-slab on its reverse side depicts a battle scene between two opposed forces that has been widely identified as a representation of Ecgfrith's defeat at Nechtansmere (Ritchie 1989: 24–5; Cruickshank 1991; Ralston and Armit 1997: Plate 12.4; Mack 1997: 61). Stylistically the Aberlemno cross-slab dates from up to a century after the battle of Dunnichen, so that, if it does indeed commemorate the decisive battle, it did so very much in retrospect. Seductive though it may be to historical archaeologists to wring out of the sources tantalizing clues to the site of the battle, or to read historical events into sculptural representations, to others it might seem like a rather old-fashioned exercise in text-led archaeology, the result of which is wholly immaterial to any understanding of the social, political, economic, or cultural significance of hillforts or warfare in early historic societies.

A final textual reference illustrates the inherent dangers of sources that have an implicit religious agenda. Adomnán's *Vita Sancti Columbae* (ii, 35) includes an episode that purportedly occurred when the holy man visited the fortress of king Bridei, presumed to be somewhere in the vicinity of Inverness. Finding the gates (*regiae munitionis portae*) barred to him, he made the sign of the cross on them, whereupon the gates sprung open and the king, suitably impressed, duly accorded him a civil reception. The fact that the entrance to the royal fort was stoutly barred hardly occasions surprise, but the subsequent claim that Columba performed a similar miraculous feat in Ireland (*VC* ii, 36) tends to undermine historical credibility.

CONCLUSIONS

It is generally acknowledged that any of the documentary sources reviewed here, whether classical or early historic, must be evaluated in the light of standard criteria, whether they are first-hand accounts by contemporary witnesses or reports written long after the event on the basis of sources of unverifiable reliability, whether they include traditional ethnology of dubious validity or reports based on personal experience, however understood or misinterpreted, and whether the source had an inbuilt bias, political or religious. The issues regarding the Irish sources, on the other hand, are of a different order altogether. The tales of the Ulster Cycle in particular are special in that they are in the category of epic fiction in which individuals and events are of heroic proportions, in which any reflection of everyday reality would inevitably be distorted or exaggerated. The question whether they draw upon an oral tradition, and if so, over what span of time that oral tradition could have been sustained, does not alter the fact that there are striking similarities between the customs and beliefs reflected in the tales and those alluded to in classical sources in relation to Gaulish society of the first century BC. The real problem for archaeologists is whether the latter bear any more relationship to actual custom and practice in Gaul and Britain in the Iron Age than the former did to life in early historic Ireland. The world of the tales is heroic fiction and if it provides any 'window on the Iron Age', it would be a window on the traditional heroic tales told by Iron Age bards at the feast rather than a reflection on the reality of everyday life. Whether it ever had a basis in reality at some stage in the remote past seems doubtful, though not impossible.

Though Caesar's account of the Gauls may evoke the ideals of an heroic society, these are hardly evident in the actual engagements described. Even the 'tradition' of single combat, which might have had some practical utility as well as ritualized significance in resolving conflict among Iron Age antagonists, is nowhere recorded in Caesar's account, and is only attested in other classical sources in very few, exceptional circumstances. Ritual deposits like the weapons piled into the ditch at Gournay-sur-Aronde (Brunaux *et al.* 1985; Brunaux and Rapin 1994; Lejars 1994) certainly suggest that in elite circles at any rate, a mystique still attached to warfare and weaponry, but Brunaux (1988: 125) notes that the inventory did not include arrows or sling bullets as these were 'weapons of auxiliaries rather than warriors'. This reinforces the idea that there may have been a considerable gulf between the aristocratic cult of the warrior, as celebrated in tales and song, and the more mundane reality of the supporting cast in major conflicts, and no doubt the reality also of local skirmishes between minor neighbouring factions.

The role of hillforts specifically remains ambivalent from the documentary record. There can be no doubt from both Roman and early historic accounts that hillforts were subject to siege and sacking, but the fact that they were political targets or targets for plunder need not mean that military defence was their primary function. Only from Caesar's campaign in Gaul do we get any detailed indication of how they might have been attacked, and how in consequence their installations may have been designed to counter attack, and even this need not be applicable to inter- or intra-tribal warfare of an earlier period. What is significant from the Roman sources, however, is the frequency of engagements away from hillforts, reinforcing the belief that the hillfort itself was a refuge of last resort.

10

Ethnographic Models

Evaluating the contribution that a study of ethnographic models can make to an understanding of the role of hillforts in Iron Age society is as fraught with difficulties as is a critical assessment of documentary sources. Divorced in space and time from the Iron Age in Britain and north-western Europe, there can plainly be no direct cultural association or expectation that the social, political, economic, or belief systems that governed behaviour were necessarily comparable. Nevertheless, the basic requirements of providing food, shelter from the environment, and protection from hostile threat are universal, and communities widely separated in time and space may respond independently to similar situations in ways that may potentially illuminate the archaeological issues under review. As with experimental archaeology, we cannot say as a result of studying ethnographic analogies, that Iron Age communities in Britain built hillforts for such-and-such purposes or in the process believed this or that; only that these possibilities might be examined as potentially satisfying the available evidence. When it comes to social reconstruction, it may be possible to identify broad categories of social structures in which patterns of behaviour are recurrent, and more tentatively the same might be inferred for cognitive systems. The fact that we may never know what Iron Age communities believed is no reason for failing to address the question, which is not the same as simply asserting what they believed without presenting evidence or due qualification.

Modern or early modern ethnographic models suffer from the inevitable disadvantage that they derive from contact between the native communities and European colonists. In consequence there is the probability that, as with Roman records of contacts with Gaulish or British Iron Age communities, native behaviour will in some measure have adapted to the alien cultural presence. This would apply even if the nature of contact were peaceable exploration, commercial, or evangelical, since the introduction of new technology and novel goods and practices would inevitably impact on local conventions. In the context of any defensive sites or protected settlements, the introduction of firearms plainly will have transformed any established convention of warfare that pertained in the pre-colonial era. Establishing the native tradition from earlier periods is not an easy or wholly reliable exercise, especially given that practices may have changed significantly if slowly over generations.

An examination of settlement enclosures dating from the early modern era in North America, Central and South America, Africa, and New Zealand and Polynesia, however, raises many of the issues of functional interpretation that apply with equal force to British and European Iron Age hillforts. Three geographically widely divergent regions illustrate the issues involved.

PĀ SITES OF NEW ZEALAND

Despite their self-evident detachment geographically, chronologically, and culturally from Iron Age hillforts in Britain and north-western Europe, the New Zealand *pā* have frequently been cited as ethnographically analogous since Aileen Fox's (1976) comparative study, not least because they present problems not unfamiliar to students, including Lady Fox, of British Iron Age hillforts (Armit 2007). Immediately apparent is the imbalance in distribution of *pā* in New Zealand, with estimates between 6,000 and 7,000 in North Island, but only a hundred or so in South Island, and most of those concentrated in the north around Tasman Bay. One of the principal functions of *pā* appears to have been the storage of sweet potatoes (*kumara*), which were introduced by the earliest Polynesian settlers of New Zealand, but which could not successfully be cultivated in the cooler climate of the south. In the north, however, they became a dietary staple, and it has been argued therefore that increased competition for good horticultural land may have been a major factor in the rise of fortified *pā* (Groube 1970). The limited extent of investigation of *pā* in South Island has almost entirely concentrated on sites along the east coast (Schmidt 1996: Figure 3).

Although *pā* had obviously attracted attention since the time of James Cook and Joseph Banks, it was not until the 1950s that serious archaeological fieldwork was undertaken to investigate them. Not surprisingly, initial research addressed the classification of *pā* based either upon topographical, morphological, or inferred functional criteria. The first distinguished between sites on headlands, ridges or swamps in much the same way that British Iron Age forts have been classified by contour, ridge, promontory, or valley locations. Groube (1970) used defensive works as the basis for classification, whether the site had simply reinforced terraces, transverse banks, and ditches across the easiest routes of access, or were enclosed by a continuous or near-continuous 'ring-ditch' (a term that in New Zealand archaeology implies a larger enclosure than in British usage, where 'ring-work' might be the nearest equivalent). He had earlier (1964) also proposed a functional division between fortified villages, citadels, retreats in times of unrest and fortresses for garrisons. These schemes might be equally appropriate in the context of later prehistoric or early historic sites in Britain, but their limitations would be equally apparent; namely, that there can be no presumption that similar topographic location, defensive morphology, or inferred function implies chronological, socio-political, or cultural affinity. As in the case of Mrs Piggott's (1948) 'Hownam sequence' in Britain, comparable schemes of classification were devised with the expectation that fortifications would follow a pattern of increasing complexity, with the most complex, multivallate defences being the latest. Whilst in some instances, longevity of usage does indeed result in cumulatively more complex enclosure, individual sites may depart radically from any progressive model. The Pouerua *pā* (Sutton *et al.* 2003) is just one example of episodes in which the defences fell into decline alternating with periods in which they were built or renewed.

One of the early achievements of archaeological research on New Zealand *pā* was the clarification of a basic chronology prior to the period of colonial contact, though there was inevitably, as in Britain and elsewhere, too great a reliance on a limited number of radiocarbon dates from earlier excavations. As with British hillforts, the date of first occupation is not necessarily coincident with the date of construction of perimeter defences, and correlating the two is always problematic. It is clear, however, that a number of sites, including the volcanic cone sites of Mount Wellington, Mount Roskill, and Pouerua, were all occupied well before bank and ditch defences were erected. Unlike British hillforts, however, where it had been suggested (Bradley 1971) that the earliest hillforts developed out of pastoral enclosures, there can be no such explanation of the Maori *pā*, which originated in a society that had no tradition of animal husbandry. Kauri Point (Green 1978) and Te Awanga (Fox 1978; Davidson 1987: 251) are probably among the earliest *pā* to have earthwork defences, around the fifteenth century AD, and here too there was earlier occupation. The earliest constructional activity at Pouerua consisted of the building of terraces, involving earthmoving and significant remodelling of the contours of the hill. This activity may nevertheless have enhanced the defensibility of the hill, since in several instances where *pā* have formal palisades, it is the terrace above that initially provides the fighting platform (Fox 1976: Figure 24). With the addition of bank and ditch, the defences effectively employ the same tactical principle as a European timber-faced wall rampart. A distinctive feature of the defences of the final phase at Otakanini, South Kaipara Harbour (Bellwood 1971, 1972), and Te Awanga were fighting towers raised above the level of the bank and palisade, to provide defending forces with an additional advantage of height. This is a feature not widely recorded in British Iron Age hillforts, although Ellison and Drewett (1971) drew attention to the pairs of four-post structures set back from either side of the entrance at Grimthorpe, Yorkshire (Stead 1968) immediately behind the rampart, but not otherwise in proximity to groups of four-post storage buildings. The four-posters flanking the Period 2 entrance at Crickley Hill (Dixon 1994: Ills. 175, 180) might have served a similar purpose. Larger than average post-holes in the defensive circuit of other *pā* may likewise have supported higher fighting platforms. Fox and Bellwood both drew attention to the descriptions of 1769 by Cook and Banks at Mercury Bay and the sketch made by the du Fresne expedition in 1772 of Paeroa *pā*, Bay of Islands, as a satisfactory demonstration of the correlation of archaeological and documentary evidence. Although the equation may appear to be valid in this instance, we should nevertheless beware of assuming that observations or impressions from the colonial era will necessarily reflect older indigenous traditions, and the introduction of the musket certainly brought an end to traditional fighting tactics and the role of the *pā*.

Actual evidence for fighting in and around the fortified *pā* is as scarce and equivocal as it is in British Iron Age hillforts. Bellwood (1971: 80–1) suggested that the disproportionate concentration of artefacts, mostly fragments of weaponry, in the narrow entrance at Mangakaware 2 *pā* was the result of a battle. The presence of fragments of human bone, smashed, burnt, and covered in red ochre, however, suggests ritual activity that need not be an immediate consequence of battle. Davidson (1987: 192) cited the extensive burning and quantity of artefacts from Peketa *Pā*, Kaikoura, as possible evidence of violent destruction, while there are instances of burials where the cranial trauma indicates a violent death. But the consensus appears to favour small-scale conflicts between disaffected groups rather than warfare on a larger scale. Competition for good horticultural land, perhaps resulting from population pressure, may have increased the risk of conflict, but fighting may just as easily have been triggered as a reprisal for trespass or insult. It seems likely, however, that aggression was also motivated by the prospect of enhanced status and prestige. Warfare sparked by competition and revenge was endemic in Polynesian societies, and elsewhere did not necessitate the construction of monumental fortifications. Without discounting the obvious defensive dimensions of *pā*, therefore, which will necessarily have appeared dominant at the time of European colonization, we may consider other reasons for the construction of these impressive sites.

A significant sub-group within the *pā* class is the marsh or swamp *pā*, which Fox (1976: 23–5) compared to the crannogs or 'lake-villages' (or, as we might now prefer, 'lakeside villages') of western Europe. They were commonly located at the margins of lakes where the ground was only seriously flooded in winter; sometimes, like some Scottish crannogs, where a natural island afforded a focus for artificial extension. Trees and shrubbery from the lakeside were cleared and used to create a platform for the settlement, one or more lines of palisading enclosed the site especially from the landward side, and sand and silt was used to build up foundations for individual houses.

The location was evidently designed to provide natural protection, at the same time exploiting the resources of the lake and wetland margins and being within easy access of fertile horticultural land. Communication and transport by water is attested, for example, by the discovery of three dugout canoes in Lake Mangakaware in the Waikato basin, where one of three swamp *pā* has been extensively excavated (Bellwood 1971). Mangakaware 2 enclosed around 2 ha, but probably never exceeded a community of around thirty individuals, occupying the limited number of houses in evidence. In contrast to the three Mangakaware *pā*, where Bellwood estimated a maximum population of around a hundred, even assuming all three were occupied simultaneously, the settlement at Ngaroto, at over 5 ha in area traditionally one of the major centres in the region, may have sustained a much larger and more concentrated population, although the excavator's estimate of up to 100 houses does not demand that all were in occupation at any one time (Shawcross 1968).

Analysis of environmental and organic material persuaded the excavator that Mangakaware 2 had been occupied throughout the year, but there remained the possibility that the number of occupants on site could have varied seasonally, with some migrating temporarily to cultivation areas away from the base camp, as had been suggested on ethnographic grounds (Best 1952: 255). One major advantage to the archaeologist of a wetland environment, as in the Scottish crannogs, is the preservation of organic artefacts. For a culture that did not have metal technology or ceramics, the artefactual inventory of sites like Mangakaware 2 is enhanced comprehensively by the preservation of wooden artefacts, including spears and knife-handles, digging implements, beaters and clubs, bowls and domestic tools, as well as structural timbers from buildings. Unfortunately this also meant that swamp *pā* like Ngaroto were more vulnerable to depredation by earlier twentieth-century collectors of Maori artefacts (Schmidt 1996: 9), much as were European lakeside sites like La Tène in the nineteenth.

As regards function, it is highly probable that over a period of half a millennium the role of *pā* will have changed, just as the role of hillforts in Britain and the near continent will have changed over the half millennium before the Roman conquest. Sutton *et al.* (2003: 2) in particular criticized New Zealand archaeologists for their 'static view of pre-contact Maori socio-political organisation', which they believed to be too dependent upon eighteenth- and nineteenth-century European sources. The parallel with Britain and Gaul in the first century BC is striking, and serves as a salutary warning that, however accurate classical sources may (or may not) be regarding social structure, customs, and beliefs of Iron Age societies, these accounts may reflect a period of fundamental change catalysed by external contact.

A principal issue relates to the nature of occupation of *pā*. Fox noted particularly the journals of the early nineteenth-century missionaries Samuel Marsden and J. L. Nicholas, whose first-hand accounts suggest that *pā* were occupied on a permanent basis, describing them as towns with estimates of their population in hundreds. On the other hand, other travellers like Augustus Earle clearly viewed *pā* as refuges for communities that abandoned their undefended villages in time of threat. Maori communities are generally assumed to have moved seasonally within recognized territories, so that the *pā* was essentially a 'home base for a seasonally mobile population' (Bellwood 1971: 91). This of course need not mean that the same groups did not return to the *pā* at different seasons: in fact, Bellwood distinguished between 'houses' and 'shelters' at Mangakawara 2 on the basis that the latter were for summer occupation. Early nineteenth-century drawings show buildings within the *pā*, notably storage buildings but also dwelling houses, but this does not mean that they were permanently occupied fortified settlements. Some drawings and descriptions suggest that houses were grouped around an open, central space, but this pattern was evidently not universal. Houses have been recognized archaeologically within *pā*, rectangular in plan and within low-pitched roofs. Internal hearths were for heating, and their principal use was for sleeping, since the preparation of food was undertaken outside or confined to attached cooking sheds. Houses might be of standard size around 3 metres in width and 5 metres in length, or larger, up to 6 metres in width and 9 in length, though it is unclear whether this reflects size of household or status of occupants. At Te Awanga, Fox (1978) suggested that a large house, 11.6 metres in length by 3.9 metres wide, was the chieftain's residence, used also as a place for assembly and for receiving guests.

Whatever the status of *pā* in terms of residential occupation, it is clear that storage of food produce was an important, if not the major role. Some storage may have been on raised platforms, some supported by a single massive upright, but the principal method of storage was in rectangular pits up to 1.5 metres in depth, that evidently served as semi-subterranean cellars. Some have been shown archaeologically to have had a line of posts down the long axis, or in some cases double rows creating the equivalent of an aisled *Grubenhaus*. An alternative variant was a circular, bell-shaped pit with domed roof, in basic design not unlike storage pits in Iron Age Britain. The key difference, of course, was that the British storage pits were principally for grain, for which an air-tight seal was essential to preservation. Within the Maori pits produce was stored in bins or baskets, and drains were provided to combat the risk of damp and mould. Eventually the storage pit would become sour, when it would be filled with domestic rubbish and abandoned for a new one, much as was formerly suggested for Iron Age pit storage in Britain. The importance of storage is evident from the fact that these pits may be predominant within the interior of the *pā*, as at Taniwha (Figure 10.1) near Te Kauwhata, which appears to have been designed primarily as a fortified storage depot (Law and Green 1972). Here, nearly four dozen storage pits occupy an alignment along the crest of the hill, with half as many potential houses at a

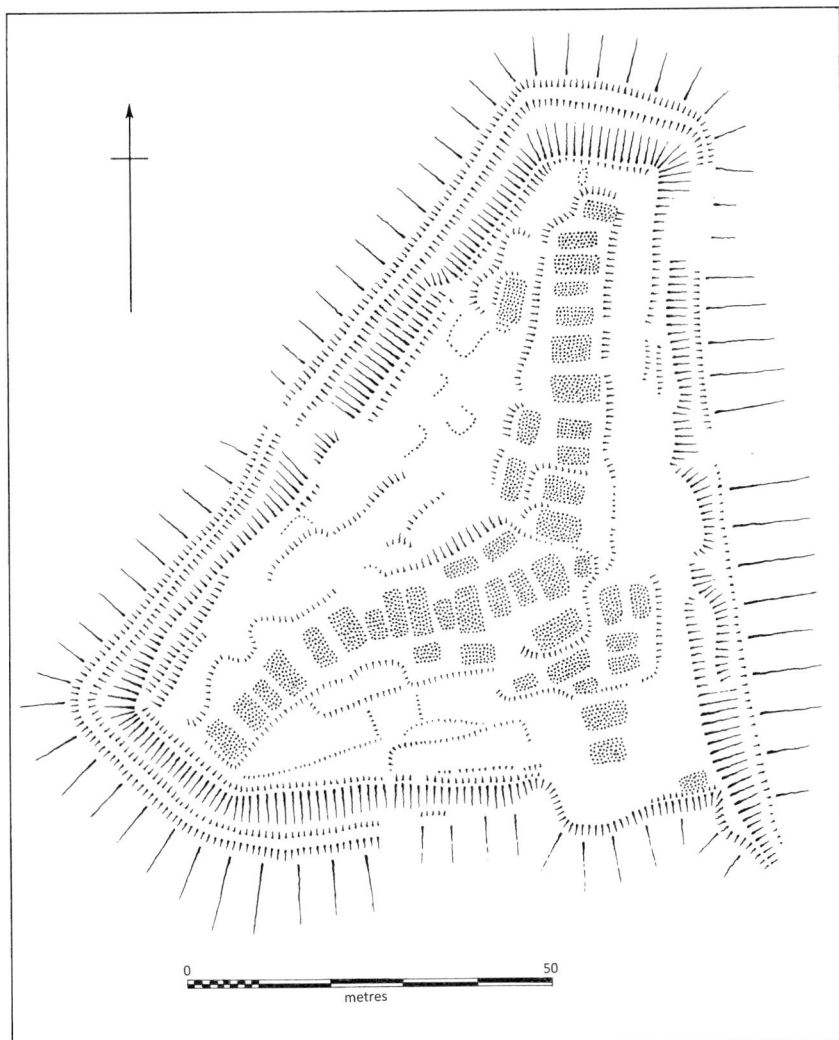

Figure 10.1. Taniwha *pā*, Lower Waikato, New Zealand, plan. Drawing by D. W. Harding, adapted from Law and Green 1972.

lower level on either side, suggestive of an element of town planning in the site's design. The implication is that storage of food produce was a communal responsibility, stored and protected collectively. The excavators' conclusion (ibid. 263–4) that the site was occupied perhaps as late as the nineteenth century was based upon its state of preservation rather than any diagnostic artefacts, which in comparison with other sites might argue a pre-contact date.

Unlike other East Polynesian communities, the Maori of New Zealand apparently did not construct designated ritual enclosures or shrines, and evidence that *pā* were used for explicitly ritual activities in the form of special structures or deposits is almost totally lacking archaeologically. Occasionally there is evidence for some special episode, such as the deposit of artefacts in the entrance of Mangakaware 2 (Bellwood 1971: 80–1), which might have had a ritual significance, or the burial at Waioneke of two individuals with severe head wounds that apparently coincided with the abandonment of the *pā* (McKinlay 1971; Davidson 1987: 175 and 192). The deposit of ornamental wooden combs and obsidian flakes in the swamp adjacent the Kauri Point *pā* in the Bay of Plenty (Shawcross 1976) has been interpreted as the ritual disposal of objects that had become *tapu* (forbidden). Apart from such clues, information regarding ritual practices is largely derived or inferred from ethnographic sources.

Although an expressly ritual function for *pā* seems to be precluded by the lack of definitive evidence, it seems likely that the constructional effort invested in some of the more monumental sites implies a conscious element of display, in much the same way that this has been inferred for the more developed hillforts of the British Iron Age. Though some *pā* have houses within their circuits, most domestic settlement appears to have been in small hamlets or open sites. Within *pā* themselves there certainly is evidence of an ordered layout, but not obviously in household groups of structures as can be seen in open settlements. Settlement patterns can be distorted within an enclosure, of course, not least by the palimpsest of successive occupation. At a site like Pouerua there was clearly a good deal of activity, but the excavators were not persuaded that it ever constituted a normal domestic settlement. Their summary of its significance might equally have been written about one of the major Wessex hillforts:

> The alteration of the large, physically dominating cone was a clear statement about 'place'... covering those terraced spaces with structures filled with stored wealth amplified that statement. (Sutton *et al.* 2003: 233)

In sum, the New Zealand *pā* sites display considerable diversity in terms of location, constructional morphology, social, political, economic, and perhaps ritual function. They span half a millennium or more during which time individual sites may have undergone significant changes in their roles. Communal storage may have been a dominant function for some, though permanent or seasonal occupation, supplemented in times of conflict, should not be discounted. The problems that they pose archaeologically are not unlike those of Iron Age hillforts in Britain, and, remote as they are in time and space, the issues raised in addressing those problems may well be mutually informative. Nevertheless, superficial comparisons between topographical location and perimeter defences that have attracted attention from Fox (1976) onwards should not obscure obvious differences, not least in size and scale of earthworks. For most *pā*, as the name implies, the palisade is the key element, and the earthworks do not display anything like the structural complexity of British and European hillforts. Furthermore, as Armit remarked (2007: 34), *pā* entrances are small and simple, not just because Maori did not raise stock or have wheeled vehicles, but because, unlike hillfort entrances, most were meant to be inconspicuous. Where the defensive lines were multiple, the narrow entrance gaps were not in alignment but offset, to leave intruders open to flank attack (Challis 1978: 19). Yet it is hard to believe that the terraced *pā*, especially the volcanic cones of the Auckland region, were not intended to be monumental statements in the landscape, their tiered effect perhaps reflecting an ascending hierarchy, social or ritual. The absence of any surviving evidence of ritual activity, other than might be implicit in the remains of cooking or feasting, for example, need not mean that a ritual and ceremonial aspect was not important in the major *pā*. Finally, if conventional interpretations of Iron Age hillforts in Britain and beyond have been criticized for being *text-led*, too ready to match the archaeological evidence to classical sources, then the perception of *pā* might equally in the past have been *ethnographically-led* and too ready to accept accounts of early explorers as valid for *pā* in prehistory.

NORTH AMERICAN PALISADED SETTLEMENTS

Among the North American Indians one group that regularly occupied enclosed villages or towns were the Iroquoian tribes of the southern Great Lakes region and Saint Lawrence River, with their Huron neighbours who shared many of their cultural traditions (Engelbrecht 2003/5). These indigenous groups came into contact with Europeans from the first half of the sixteenth century, as a result of which some traditional practices would inevitably have been radically changed. Nevertheless, the basic structure of society and its belief systems, insofar as they can be determined, remained substantially unimpaired, and may serve to inform archaeological interpretation for periods before European contact.

In terms of subsistence economy, the Iroquois practised slash-and-burn cultivation, in consequence of which the land eventually became exhausted, requiring the relocation of the entire settlement to a new or regenerated locality. Technology was basic, with farming tools being essentially hoes made of wood or bone. Without livestock, there was neither draft for ploughs or wheeled transport nor a natural source of fertilizer. Smaller settlements of the earlier pre-contact period might have survived for several decades before needing to move, and then perhaps only a kilometre or so. After a few years, the original site would have regenerated, and once again would have been available for resettlement and cultivation (Snow 1994). By late pre-contact times, however, when fortified villages had grown to sizeable communities, and when the demands of a secure location may have taken priority over proximity to the most fertile land, settlements may have needed to shift after as little as ten or a dozen years. Basic crops were maize, kidney beans, and squash, the beans being inter-planted among the corn with squash cultivated in separate plots. Among the Huron optimum yields for maize were around 20–30 bushels per acre, dropping to around 10 bushels per acre by the time the decision was made to shift settlement. Cultivating and tending the crops was essentially a female occupation, with women and children occupying much of the summer months in the fields. Accordingly, the cleared fields up to the forest edge were the women's domain, with the men controlling activities further afield. Hunting was apparently more important to the Iroquois, for whom it was a prestigious activity, than to the Huron, though the latter did hunt deer, and, given that horticulture and hunting were seasonal activities, it is difficult to assess their relative importance (Fenton 1978). Fishing was common to all the tribes.

The traditional view of the three staple crops as fundamental to Iroquoian horticulture has undergone some revision in recent years (Hart and Brumbach 2003), with maize now known to have been cultivated in southern Ontario from the mid-first millennium AD (Warrick 2000, 2008), and in New York State possibly earlier still (Thompson *et al.* 2004). Squash may not have been grown as early in northern Iroquoia as previously thought, though in western New York its cultivation may originate in the later first millennium. Beans, on the other hand, were a relatively late introduction across the north-east of North America, perhaps not much earlier than the fourteenth century. So the maize-bean-squash equation as typically Iroquoian is now shown to be a late development.

Iroquoian settlements at the time of contact combined the requirements of defence with the pragmatic demands of a resident population engaged in agriculture or horticulture (Jones 2006). The sites chosen generally had to meet four essential preconditions: they should be on elevated ground, well-drained, and potentially defensible, but in reasonable proximity to good, cultivable land, a source of timber for construction and firewood, and an accessible source of drinking water. The settlement enclosures were constructed of timber, of which massive quantities were required, and seldom involved earthworks. The primary defensive barrier was a palisade, commonly in double or triple circuits. Among the Huron these could be in excess of 5 metres in height, with upper galleries in which stone missiles were stored together with water for extinguishing fires, while watchtowers could be located at strategic points. The enclosure was entered by means of one or two gates, which, unlike British Iron Age hillforts, were designed expressly not to be conspicuous to potential enemies, and were narrow enough to be readily blocked. The settlements were evidently not intended to fulfil a role involving regular traffic on a commercial scale.

Within the enclosure, which could cover two to three hectares and accommodate 1,000 or more people, the principal buildings were domestic longhouses, some 7 to 8 metres wide and averaging 25 metres long, depending on the number of families they housed. Among the Mohawk houses might attain 60 metres in length, with vaulted, rather than pitched roofs. The basic unit occupying these houses was the nuclear family, each with apartments sharing a central fire, of which there could be 3 to 5 arranged along the length of a Mohawk house. Domestic space included living areas and sleeping platforms, together with space for storage. In earlier houses produce might be stored in cylindrical or bell-shaped pits, which, after they had become sour, might be used as rubbish pits or for burial (Snow 1994: 30), once again prompting comparison with British Iron Age sites. Champlain, writing in 1616, referred to storage of maize in large casks made of tree-bark within the houses. The houses were spaced out, sometimes regular groups with no obvious distinction between them, except for the houses of civil and war chieftains, which were larger on account of their use as meeting houses in addition to their normal domestic functions.

The quantities of timber that would have been required for these defended villages were prodigious. Heidenreich (1978) calculated that even a single-palisaded Huron village of thirty-six longhouses accommodating a population of 1,000 would have required 20,000 poles and 15,000 m^2 (18,000 sq yds) of elm-bark roofing, estimates that seem conservative, considering that most enclosures had double or triple palisades and allowing for the size that longhouses could attain. Given that settlements needed to be relocated perhaps twice in a generation on account of the practice of shifting agriculture, this would seem to be a profligate use of resources unless a good deal of timber could be salvaged in the process of planned removal. In terms of detail, the early French accounts are not in fact very informative, and near-contemporary illustrations may not be at all reliable. Trigger and Pendergast (1978: Figure 2) cited an Italian engraving of c.1556 of the village of Hochelaga, the principal village of the Iroquoians of Montreal Island, that has been long recognized as the artist's imaginative reconstruction of the textual account, in which the ordered layout of the interior especially represents an imposition of Renaissance ideals. Jacques Cartier's account of 1535/1545 nevertheless referred to its threefold palisaded enclosure and described the internal layout of its fifty houses, 'each about fifty paces long'. It also remarked that the land about the settlement was 'ploughed and very fertile'.

If we were to make an initial comparison between Iroquoian and Huron enclosed settlements and British Iron Age hillforts, some key differences would be immediately apparent. The fact that the former were constructed almost exclusively of timbers rather than involving earthworks need not in itself be particularly significant, but may well be accounted for by the fact that the Iroquois settlements were not expected to be occupied for any extended period of time on account of the shifting agriculture regime. Furthermore, from the layout of structures internally there can equally be little doubt that the primary purpose of these sites was residential occupation by farming communities who cultivated the land in immediate proximity. A similar inference might be drawn for some of the small enclosed village hillforts of the Scottish Borders, and perhaps even for some larger hillforts like Hod Hill or Hambledon Hill, where house stances have survived in considerable numbers, but in general the role of hillforts in Britain appears to have been more complex than the simple fortified settlements of farming communities. There is no evidence, ethnographical nor archaeological, for example, of Iroquoian or Huron settlements having served as centres of specialized production or as markets for wider regional trading or exchange.

Nevertheless, there has been little doubt among North American archaeologists that a primary purpose of the late pre-contact palisaded enclosures was defensive, and not just from the period of European contact: 'the new settlement pattern was clearly adopted for defensive reasons. The villages were larger and more heavily fortified than before, either by ravines or by artificial earthworks and multiple palisades' (Snow 1994: 52). More recently that view has been qualified by Birch (2010), who has pointed out that among the northern Iroquois and Huron, warfare was undertaken in response to blood feuds and to enhance personal status by taking captives, heads or scalps, and not as a political expedient for acquiring territory or capturing entire villages. The construction of multiple palisades therefore may have had a social and symbolic significance as great as its function as a practical defence. Nevertheless, in a climate of increased inter-community aggression, safeguarding family and food supply may have acquired socially enhanced importance.

Iroquoian settlements were largely self-sufficient, and appear not to have engaged in extensive long-distance exchange. The Huron, on the other hand, traded corn, tobacco, and fishing nets with hunter groups from the north, from whom they acquired hides, dried fish, and meat (Trigger 1978b). Insofar as it was practised, gift-exchange and the forging of alliances was a means of gaining prestige and status, and might involve the enlisting of the treaty-partner's aid in some military enterprise. Hence, for example, the Huron in the early seventeenth century sought Champlain's military support in their conflict with the Iroquois as a precondition of their engaging with the French in fur trading. Trade routes nevertheless were strictly controlled by the lineages that operated them, and any poaching of these monopolies could easily lead to conflict. In fact, violation of territorial integrity of any sort without consent or without paying the required transit dues could result in inter-group warfare.

The formation of alliances was plainly crucial to controlling the escalation of blood-feuds, which were endemic and inherently debilitating in Iroquoian society. The need to contain internecine warfare has been advanced as one reason for the coalescence of smaller villages into larger units, a trend which is archaeologically detectable in western New York State and Ontario from around AD 1000 onwards (Tuck 1978), but more especially in the Middle Iroquoian period of the fourteenth century. With the introduction of horticulture it is possible that there was an expansion of population resulting in increased competition for resources. Small farming or fishing settlements, initially no larger than a single family unit, on poorly defended sites or riverside situations were relocated to larger, palisaded hilltop villages and towns in a process of progressive amalgamation of clan groups. Some villages grew to five hectares in area with populations up to 2,000, with planned village layouts, an increasing concern for collective defence and doubtless with correspondingly more complex social structures. Climatic factors may have played a part in this process (Snow 1994); with the ending of the Medieval optimum and the onset of the Little Ice Age it is possible that a shortening growing season and increase in crop failures may have contributed to competition for better land and limited resources. The process of coalescence invites comparison with the shift in the southern British Iron Age from a distribution pattern of numerous small, early hillforts to one in which there were fewer 'developed' hillforts by the middle Iron Age, a change which has been generally acknowledged but seldom adequately explained. By the fourteenth century the pattern that met the European explorers of hilltop settlements of the Iroquois with palisaded perimeter defences and ordered ranks of longhouses occupying most of the interior was already established. The creation of larger alliances culminated in the Iroquoian confederacy of five tribes, probably as late as the sixteenth century. These large communities may nevertheless have created their own, internal tensions, as clan groups vied for position in the internal social hierarchy (Birch 2010). Among the Huron, creating external alliances might involve the exchange of 'hostages', whose role could be ambivalent, being as much spies in the opposing camp as hostages (Heidenreich 1978: 383). This ambivalence perhaps casts a different light on Caesar's practice of taking hostages during his Gallic campaign, which may at times have been as much a liability as a safeguard against perfidy.

Authority among the Iroquois resided in the chiefs and their councils. The ruling hierarchy was exclusively male, though they derived their credentials for office through the female line, and within the household the senior woman was matriarch. The chiefs seemingly exercised no coercive authority, so that young men might instigate a war party on their own initiative, but in general majority opinion was a compelling factor in maintaining a stable order. Nevertheless, making war, often in pursuit of a vendetta, was a means of achieving status, especially if it resulted in bringing back of scalps or of prisoners. Head-hunting or scalp-hunting was endemic to warfare, and among the Huron, heads might be displayed, as in the British Iron Age, on the outside of the palisaded enclosure. Evidence for interpersonal conflict is increasingly common in the late pre-contact period in the form of 'modified human bone' that is, artefacts like rattles made from human skulls that may have been used in war ceremonies (Birch 2010: 41).

Relatively less is known of Iroquoian burial customs in the pre-contact period than from the time of European contact, when clan cemeteries were located away from the settlement. Among the Huron and their neighbours, however, burials were interred temporarily, until at intervals of around ten years villages collectively organized a Great Feast of the Dead, at which point the dead from individual villages would be disinterred and brought to a specially designated place for collective permanent burial. The funerary ritual nevertheless involved feasting and bringing of gifts, not just to accompany the dead but for the bereaved as well, and it is clear from accounts that extravagance in funerary gift-giving was highly esteemed. The Iroquois evidently had a highly complex cosmology, belief systems, and seasonal and diurnal rituals (Fenton 1978), though none appears to have been focused especially upon the settlement enclosure as such, which appears to have been of transient significance.

WEST AFRICAN FORTIFIED VILLAGES AND TOWNS

West African settlements have a particular bearing upon the study of British Iron Age hillforts in terms of their role as incipient towns. From the accounts of European traders and explorers from the fifteenth to nineteenth centuries, it is clear that the communities that occupied the major centres in the hinterland of the Guinea Coast, like Benin or Ife, had developed relatively advanced urban civilizations with a form of state organization that controlled resources and production and could summon military service from sizeable populations. How early these city-states had developed prior to their nineteenth-century heyday, or how far the enclosed settlements of northern Nigeria or the middle Niger delta had progressed towards urban status, is more debatable, and depends significantly upon our definition of urbanization and state society.

The criteria for measuring urbanization and state formation in Iron Age Britain and Europe commonly emphasize the importance of controlling trade and exchange, sometimes over considerable distances, and of craft specialization as a mirror of a community's capacity for producing a surplus. Both of these are important factors in the assessment of West African societies, though archaeological evidence is not yet as conclusive in some regions as in others. Size of settlement or of area enclosed alone would not normally be regarded as adequate evidence of urbanization, although in the case of some sites the scale of territorial enclosure is so immense that it does not seem unreasonable (*contra* for example Sharples 2010: 241) to infer a coercive organizing agency with a hierarchical social structure.

The fortifications around the city of Benin were on a prodigious scale. The inner wall consisted of an earthen bank and ditch presenting a combined obstacle up to 17 m in vertical height and with a circuit more than 11 kilometres in length (Connah 1975). Oral tradition and historical records, with the support of radiocarbon dating, suggest that this walled city was in existence by the time of European contact in the later fifteenth century, while occupation of the interior has been shown to date from at least the thirteenth century. Still more remarkable, however, is the network of enclosures surrounding the city, and extending on both sides of the Ikpoba river, covering many square kilometres, and the much more extensive pattern of earthworks beyond these (Darling 1984). Even assuming that these earthworks were cumulative over a period of five hundred years or more, they are surely indicative of a substantial population and an agricultural capacity to match. The extent of the earthworks may reflect not just competition for agricultural land, but the fact that the lengthy fallowing required to regenerate soil fertility meant that much more extensive tracts needed to be cleared to provide for adequate rotation.

North-west of Benin were the Yoruba towns of Ife and Oyo-Ile (Old Oyo), the former in the zone between forest and grassland and the latter in the southern savannah itself. Ife was evidently an important ritual and ceremonial centre, a role attested by its wide range of stone sculptures, terracottas, and bronze alloy castings. Craft specialization from the first half of the second millennium AD is also indicated at Ife by archaeological evidence for glass-working. The town's origins can be traced to the late first millennium AD, though its art reached a zenith in the fourteenth and fifteenth centuries (Willett 1967). Archaeological evidence for subsistence economy in the rainforest zone is limited, but it appears that by the early second millennium, in the northern forest regions at any rate, slash-and-burn agriculture based on a long fallow-to-cultivation cycle had been developed, and it is likely that the yam was an important element in food production. Animal husbandry was more tenuous, with limited evidence for cattle and goats. Iron and copper technology, nevertheless, had been developed to a sophisticated level by the earlier second millennium, as metalwork from Benin and Ife testifies. These artefacts cast further light on the social order as adjuncts to the institution of divine kinship indicated by ethno-historical and oral sources, and the hierarchical social structure that must have supported it. They further testify to an advanced level of craft specialization that can only have flourished on a solid basis of agricultural surplus.

In the north, Yoruba towns might be located on hilltops, but in the southern forest zone, a belt of dense forest was often left uncleared to deter access other

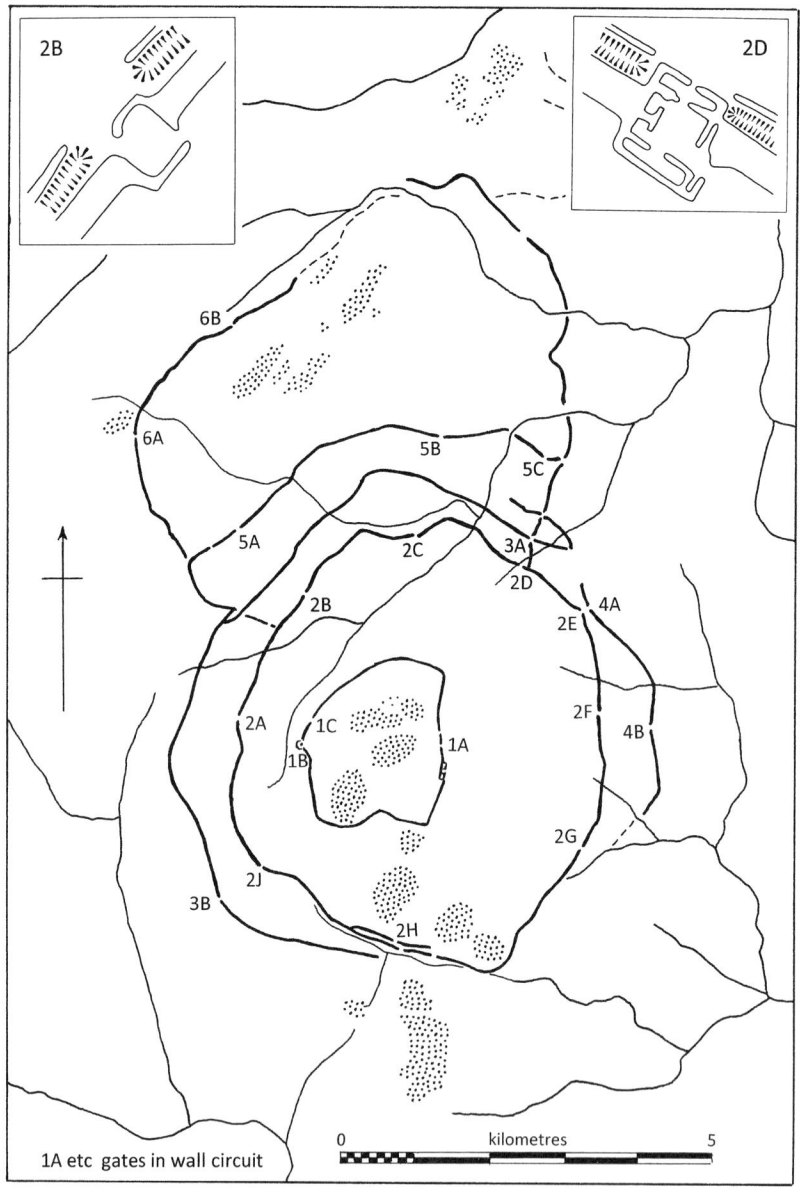

Figure 10.2. Oyo Ile, Nigeria, town walls and entrances. Drawing by D. W. Harding, adapted from Soper and Darling 1980.

than through authorized paths, where unwelcome intruders could readily be ambushed. Towns were commonly surrounded by multiple walls, widely spaced at intervals from 100 m up to a kilometre, and enclosing cultivated fields and water sources and even natural supplies of timber. This is generally supposed to have been in anticipation of lengthy sieges by hostile armies, though it is unclear how infiltration could be prevented over such large areas. The walls of Oyo-Ile itself thus covered an area some 6 by 10 kilometres in extent over a variety of terrain (Soper and Darling 1980). Its principal circuit (Figure 10.2), 18 kilometres in length and enclosing more than 2000 ha, had nine or ten entrances, which, like British Iron Age hillforts, often diverted access through the gateway to one side and could include flanking guardrooms. West African town walls could be relatively low barriers in the order of 2 metres in height, or substantially larger, up to 6 or 7 metres or more, as at Surame, the capital of the Hausa kingdom of Kebbi in north-western Nigeria. Where stone was available, it was sometimes used for wall construction, but in general, town walls among the Yoruba were earthen dumps, or faced with sundried bricks, though the latter would have been vulnerable in a rainforest environment. Timber palisades may have surmounted the mud-built walls. In the towns of the Kagoro of central Nigeria, hedges of cactus up to fifteen feet in height apparently served as an effective barrier in place of earthworks. Ditches were generally dug along the front of walled defences, for which they also served as the quarry for building material. Occasionally they were also dug along the inside, not just as additional quarry pits, as in the British Iron Age, but as part of the defensive system, suggesting perhaps a need on occasion to contain as well as to exclude. The ditches regularly filled with water in the rainy season, but when dry, thorn bushes could be introduced to provide an additional barrier (Ajayi and Smith 1964/1971). They were deep relative to their width, and were bridged at entrances by planks that could be removed in time of emergency. The gates sometimes had adjacent guardrooms for sentries and customs posts for exacting tolls, while watchtowers and fighting platforms added to the defensive capability (Smith 1989).

In northern Nigeria, the walled cities of the Hausa states probably originated in the early second millennium. Settlements of a tell-like character are known in the region south of Lake Chad dating probably from the early first millennium BC, but the addition of enclosure walls was a later development. Among early travellers Captain Hugh Clapperton in the 1820s was impressed by the extent and scale of the walled city of Kano, its mud-brick and earthen dump defences with inner as well as outer ditches, and its multiple entrances. A generation later Heinrich Barth visited the region during his expedition of 1849–1855, planning Kano and providing a description of its defences in his journal. He explicitly claimed that the walls extended well beyond the normally occupied quarters of the town to provide for the contingency of siege by including cultivated fields and room for displaced refugees from surrounding open and undefended villages (Kirk-Greene 1962: 113). Moody's survey (1970) showed that the area enclosed had expanded in successive stages, originating in the eleventh to the twelfth centuries and progressing through the fifteenth to the seventeenth.

The nature of the enclosure works leaves little doubt that they were designed to provide protection against attack, but at the same time the location of the towns themselves was not apparently primarily chosen for tactical defensibility, as opposed to proximity to resources and access to established trading routes. The purpose of these earthworks, therefore, was in significant part to demarcate boundaries and to control access and movement through the territory of the resident authority. The labour involved in the construction and maintenance of these extensive earthworks must have been substantial, involving communal effort on a regular basis. In the journal of his second expedition, Clapperton recorded observing the maintenance of the walls of Boussa, former capital of Borgou in north-eastern Nigeria:

> The walls appeared very extensive, and are at present under repair. Bands of male and female slaves, accompanied by drums and flutes, and singing in chorus, were passing to and from the river with water, to mix the clay they were building with. Each great man has his part of the wall to build, like the Jews when they built the walls of Jerusalem, every one opposite his own house.
> (Clapperton 1829, entry for Thursday, 30 March 1826)

The use of slave labour, which evidently made up a substantial proportion of the population of these towns, could be relevant to the British Iron Age, as could be the reference to responsibility of householders of rank for sections of the wall. The exact nature of the military threat to the town, and therefore the likely tactical response, is altogether less clear. Long-term siege is widely reported, involving the construction of semi-permanent camps by the investing forces that may even have engaged in cultivation to supply their own needs on campaign. But sieges were not necessarily successful, and how the stand-off was managed by both sides over such large areas remains uncertain.

According to Connah (2000), walled cities like Kano represent the culmination of a process in the West African savannah that had its origins in the later first or early second millennium AD. He argued that urbanization and state formation was not triggered by the stimulus of trans-Saharan trade and the ensuing influence of Islamic culture (ibid. 115), but was an indigenous process over a longer period of time. He cited especially the example of Jenné-jeno in the Inland Niger Delta in Mali (McIntosh and McIntosh 1980), a 12 ha settlement by the first century AD that had expanded to cover 33 ha by the ninth century. The population living in the round and rectangular houses enclosed within the mud-brick wall of this later town has been variously calculated, but would certainly have totalled several thousands. Allowing for the fact that there were at least two dozen satellite sites of possibly contemporaneous occupation within a kilometre of Jenné-jeno the population density of this region in the late first and early second millennium was relatively high. Settlements in this region evidently thrived on a mixed agricultural economy of cereal cultivation and animal husbandry, supplemented at Jenné-jeno by African rice, cultivated in the floodwaters of the Niger in what Connah (2001: 131) termed the practice of recessional cultivation. This combination evidently formed a stable subsistence base for a millennium and a half at Jenné-jeno, providing the essential foundation for incipient urbanism.

Nevertheless, the implications in terms of social complexity are more contentious. As Connah (ibid. 117–19) conceded, 'although the evidence from Jenné-jeno has established a convincing case for the indigenous development of urbanism in the Inland Niger Delta, it has not demonstrated the existence there of a highly stratified social hierarchy or of a centralized authority' (McIntosh and McIntosh 1993). He subscribed to the approach that attempted to distinguish regional hierarchies of settlement rather than simply identifying the sites of historically recorded towns and cities, as had been the archaeological convention. In the northern Cameroon, for example, Holl (1996) had recognized three levels of settlement from unenclosed, tell-type mounds to walled villages that he equated with district chiefs and large centralized settlements of up to 20 ha in extent that were probably the antecedents of the walled cities of the later second millennium AD.

One of the problems in evaluating the West African evidence, of course, is not simply the perennial issue of the impact upon indigenous practice of contact with European explorers and traders, and in particular the effect on warfare and defences of the introduction of firearms from the later sixteenth and seventeenth centuries, first by the Portuguese to Benin, then across the Sahara, but also the possibility that fundamental changes took place within the indigenous communities. Many commentators assume that the rise of towns among the Yoruba, for example, was a largely nineteenth-century development, in part stimulated by the civil wars of that period. Indeed, Smith (1989) argued that warfare and the diplomatic liaisons that commonly accompanied it were major factors in the concentration of political power leading to statehood. But the city of Oyo Ile itself and a number of the towns surrounding it were abandoned as a result of the Fulani wars of the 1820s, so clearly the origins of urban settlement are much earlier. Plainly there is an issue with the definition of urbanization, since some of the earliest 'towns' in West Africa seem to be little more than large concentrations of population for mutual protection and subsistence, without clear evidence of any marked degree of social complexity or state-level organization. By the seventeenth and eighteenth centuries, however, more sophisticated social organization is certainly in evidence in the major cities like Benin, Oyo Ile, and Kano, and the material evidence of archaeology surely reflects this.

CONCLUSIONS

A survey of the ethnographic evidence for palisaded or walled enclosures, though from contexts that are geographically, chronologically, and cultural remote from the British Iron Age, nevertheless shows that there are common issues in their study and interpretation. Archaeological approaches to hillforts and the ethnographic comparanda have often followed familiar lines, giving priority to identifying sites that are highlighted in the historical record, or classifying earthworks on the basis of topography or earthwork morphology. In almost every instance, military defence has been assumed, though equally frequently the actual archaeological evidence for conflict is minimal. Almost invariably, tactical defence is compromised by the need for sites to be located in reasonable proximity to agricultural land, or in relation to natural and long-established routes of communication and trade. The enclosing walls were commonly of a scale that seems to make a statement beyond simple practicality of protection, though entrances may be narrow and concealed rather than conspicuous and dependent upon elaborate passageways or outworks. In some instances the use of resources, such as timber for palisades, may be on an extravagant scale that could have been intended as a demonstration of status. A key issue is the extent to which enclosures were primarily habitation sites: other functions like storage of produce were clearly important. Where the purpose of enclosure was primarily to afford protection for a resident community it seems reasonable to expect clusters of houses to register as a major component archaeologically; without this, population estimates based upon area enclosed beg a range of issues regarding other reasons for enclosure and therefore lack credibility. In the progress towards urbanization and social complexity, controlling long-distance trade and exchange is plainly an important factor, together with the political or diplomatic alliances that this might entail. Status and prestige appears to have accrued from such liaisons, as it may also have done from success in military enterprises. In considering the scale of resources and labour required for the construction of monumental earthworks, we should not overlook the role of slaves, especially since this is one of the activities among British Iron Age communities that was apparently conducted on a scale sufficient to attract the attention of classical sources.

11

Conclusion: A Sense of Place

stondeð nu on laste leofre duguþe
weal wundrum heah wyrmlicum fah

all that now remains of the beloved warrior company
is a rampart dauntingly high, warning off like a serpent
(*Wanderer*, 97–8)

It has often been supposed that the Anglo-Saxon poet lamenting the passing of an heroic society was referring to the ruins of Roman walls, for some reason decorated with serpentiform designs. But it seems more likely that the walls in question were those of an older order altogether, the grass-covered ramparts of a long-abandoned hillfort, winding serpent-like around the contours of a conspicuous local landmark like the Lambton Worm of Wearside folklore. However derelict, such sites must have retained a sense of place that heightened in collective memory the importance of people and events that were associated with them.

ARTEFACTS AS SYMBOLS

Archaeology by convention characterizes ancient societies on the basis of the artefacts that they leave behind, whether structural and monumental, or portable and ephemeral. What survives will depend in significant measure upon the durability of material or construction, and upon a variety of taphonomic and environmental factors relating to the deposit or residual context. It will also self-evidently depend upon what communities chose to create and to leave behind, since artefacts are essentially proxy expressions of what they regarded as important, reflecting not just a basic utility but something of the identity and social values of the makers. As hillforts are the most substantial, monumental constructions of Late Bronze Age and Iron Age communities in north Alpine Europe, exceeding in scale even funerary monuments of those local groups that created lasting memorials to the dead, we may infer that they were the most potent expression of what mattered to the communities that built them.

One of the recurrent frustrations of archaeology is that for periods or regions in which settlement remains are well represented, burial sites can prove elusive, and vice versa. What appears to be an exasperating demonstration of Murphy's Law nevertheless must have a significant explanation. In effect, some communities leave a mark predominantly in terms of settlement remains and others predominantly in funerary monuments. Diepeveen-Jansen (2007: 385) observed that in the Iron Age of the Marne-Moselle region, 'the use of hillforts *alternates* with the employment of increasingly ostentatious burial practices' (my emphasis), with the implication that this must reflect a meaningful shift in social expression. On this basis, the relative absence of hillforts in eastern England, including eastern Yorkshire, where the square-ditched barrow cemeteries came to prominence in the second half of the first millennium BC, could imply a different set of values from those of hillfort-dominated zones. Even within the broad hillfort zone there could be enclaves, like the Upper Thames valley, where there was a pattern of intensive settlement without apparent dependence on or direct relationship to hillforts, though here there is no distinctive mode of burial.

Equally enigmatic in respect to portable artefacts is the fact that large parts of England north of the Trent with southern and eastern Scotland are virtually aceramic in the Iron Age (Ross 2011), a characteristic shared with Ireland, and one that is virtually unique in the Old World as late as the Iron Age. By contrast, the hillfort-dominated zone of southern England on the one hand and the hillfort-devoid, broch-dominated regions of Atlantic Scotland on the other, both have distinctive ceramic assemblages. At a time when northern Britain was seen as having a predominantly pastoral economy (Piggott 1958a), this might have been explained as a consequence of a mobile lifestyle, but the 'Stanwick economy' model always was unduly simplistic and is no longer supported by the archaeological evidence. The absence of pottery in north-west England especially, however, might well reflect different traditions of food preparation and consumption from regions like the Tees valley, where Roman imports and fashions were more readily absorbed.

Some years ago, Armit (1990b: 206) detected in the Western Isles in the early first millennium AD a shift away from monumental architecture and an elaboration of small, personal ornaments like pins and brooches, with the implication that there was a change in social expression of status from the symbolism of place to personal and portable symbols. Such variations in contemporary expressions of social identity could explain in part regional variations in hillfort construction, as well as differences in the archaeological record in terms of funerary evidence.

Despite the acknowledged diversity of hillforts, therefore, an important element in common may be their role as symbols of community identity and values, of which the scale or elaboration of enclosure may have been an important physical expression. But if all forms of structural and material artefacts fulfilled symbolic as well as 'practical' functions, then the absence of hillforts from certain regions may equally have been because certain aspects of their functions were not required or were fulfilled by other, possibly quite disparate types.

HILLFORTS AND DEFENCE

The symbolic aspect of hillforts also has a bearing on the issue of their defensive role, and the polarization of opinion between those for whom the enclosing walls or earthworks of hillforts were implicitly for defence against hostile attack, and those for whom the Iron Age was essentially a period of peaceful co-existence between egalitarian neighbours engaged in ritually structured activities within hillforts that proclaimed nothing more aggressive than identity and status. The function of the enclosing walls is not necessarily indicative of the role of the site itself, as enacted in the space within, but they were surely defensive in the sense that they provided a formidable barrier to access, other than that which was strictly controlled through formal entrances and even externally regulated approaches. In some cases, they effectively screened activities that took place within from the outside world, although in others, as we have seen, they conspicuously did not. These barriers may be aggrandized to underline or enhance status and prestige, but their existence must be predicated on an assumption of protection of the community within and its property or privacy, symbolically, or physically in terms of military defence. But of themselves the enclosing works do not inform us about the nature of the community that occupied the site or the activities in which they were engaged. Most obviously they do not indicate a military garrison, as the outline of a Roman fort plainly signals, since standing armies and garrison forts were not part of the Iron Age order. The purpose of the site itself included a great range of activities, all of which would have been preferably pursued in peaceable circumstances. In some cases, the defences may never have been put to the test in practice; the most successful deterrent, of course, is the one that is never used.

Whether hillforts could ever have provided effective military defence, of course, depends upon the scale and form of attack. To claim that a site the size of Ham Hill could never have been defended presupposes a threat that required manning the entire circuit simultaneously, which in an Iron Age context is plainly as unrealistic as it would have been to mount a coordinated assault from all sides simultaneously. We have seen that Yoruba walled towns exceeded the scale of any British Iron Age hillforts, yet presumably were designed to control access, and their walls would certainly have inhibited any attempt by infiltrators to drive off stock. The defensibility of a site therefore must be measured in the light of likely threat and prevailing practice in raiding and armed conflict.

For all the concern with technicalities of rampart construction, it is surprising that some of the most obvious implications have attracted less attention. The sheer quantities of resource required to create a timber-framed rampart on the scale of Wessex hillforts raises the possibility that in consequence, this degree of elaboration might not have been applied uniformly around the perimeter enclosure. If its purpose was primarily defensive, of course, then it would be necessary to have an effective level of protection around the entire circuit, assuming fighting tactics were dictated by logic rather than by convention. But if prestigious display was paramount, then the ramparts flanking the entrance might be accorded greater priority in order to create a monumental façade, comparable, for example, to the gatehouse or blockhouse façades of Shetland forts. It has sometimes been suggested that ramparts may have been higher adjacent to the entrance, and it seems entirely plausible that greater elaboration may have been expended on the ramparts flanking the entrance in order to enhance their impressiveness (Collis 1996: 88).

In some instances, perhaps the burning of the Rainsborough entrance or the skeletons in the ditch at Fin Cop, there may be plausible evidence that hillforts were attacked, and there are certainly instances in which defences seemingly have been deliberately slighted. Where ramparts have been partially vitrified, a convincing case can be made for regarding this as the product of punitive destruction rather than damage inflicted in the course of assault. Documentary sources suggest that post-Roman hillforts in north Britain were the target of attack, but for the earlier Iron Age it is not obvious that they were a primary target. Whilst any raiding force might be content to ravage field and farm, or drive off cattle, it seems likely that the hillfort nevertheless would also contain potential booty. Furthermore, its capture might have been a target for reprisal in cases of blood feuding, which ethnographic analogy suggests was a common motivation for aggression between groups.

Past perceptions of Iron Age warfare probably reflect the world of epic tradition and heroic tales rather than the reality of everyday life, and if conflict did arise, it was probably more mundane in its causes and more squalid in its conduct than single combat over the champion's portion. Blood-feuds within and between communities, disputes over land or water sources and periodic stock-raiding probably were endemic in the Iron Age. But these would seldom have threatened hillforts, an attack on which must have been a comparative rarity, when larger issues and forces were involved. Even then, engagements almost certainly took place away from the hillfort, though as a last refuge and symbol of group identity, hillforts were doubtless vulnerable to pillage and destruction after defeat. 'That any single hillfort could not be for military defence at all' (Lock 2011: 360) is clearly a logical possibility within the spectrum of multiple inter-dependent roles of hillforts, though it is hard to see why that possibility among so many probable combinations should be stressed, other than to mollify the new 'pacified' orthodoxy.

LANDMARKS AND THE LEGACY OF THE PAST

Not all hillforts share the same prominence in the landscape, but some are so conspicuous that we are obliged to consider this as a major factor in their siting. Promontory forts, as we have seen, can occupy awesome locations that must have militated against their functioning as regular settlements. Among upland hillforts Ingleborough (Plate 8a) is positively track-stopping in its impact, dominating the skyline for miles around. Tap o' Noth (Plate 6a) likewise commands attention from a distance in a way that would be consistent with its use as a place of periodic assembly for widely dispersed communities. The three peaks of Yr Eifl on the Llŷn peninsula (Plate 16a) are similarly impressive from the north, raising intriguing questions regarding the occupation of one summit by the Tre'r Ceiri hillfort whilst its neighbours remained apparently neglected for settlement, though they too have cairns marking their summits. The parallel with the Eildon hills (Plate 16b) is striking, including the presence of earlier cairns. It hardly seems possible that Iron Age communities would have ignored the unoccupied summits, so that it is tempting to imagine that the latter held some special significance in relation to gods or ancestors that set them aside from occupation. Whether they were reserved for ritual or funerary ceremonies can only be speculated, but to focus exclusively upon one summit simply because of the extant evidence of settlement may be to misread the significance of the landscape setting. In Northern Ireland, the triple summits of Navan fort, Creeveroe, and Haughey's fort prompt similar questions, and the apparent absence of occupational evidence from the middle hill may belie its true significance.

The occurrence of barrows, cairns, or enclosures of much earlier date on sites subsequently used for hillforts could simply reflect coincidental re-use of prominent landmarks, or it could signify a genuine veneration of the past or wish to identify with monuments to the ancestors. In the case of Tre'r Ceiri, the cairn occupies the highest point of the hill at the northernmost end of the hillfort enclosure, and its survival among so many substantially-built stone houses must have been intended. The three huge cairns that give their name to Foel Trigarn (Plate 14b) in Pembrokeshire are likewise so dominant that it is impossible to believe that the hillfort was not located as it was expressly to enclose them. Yet the dense clustering of house platforms all around, and in the annexes and beyond, surely indicates that the primary purpose of the site was occupational rather than exclusively ritual or burial. The Neolithic 'long mound' at Maiden Castle and the long barrow at Hambledon Hill are more problematic. Although the Hambledon long barrow lies centrally along the spine of the hill in a manner that looks integral to the final layout of the hillfort, it would have been external to the earliest Iron Age enclosure, while at Maiden Castle, the earliest hillfort actually transected the Neolithic long mound, though it mirrored the outline of the causewayed enclosure. Given the fact that the Neolithic activity at Hambledon extended along adjacent spurs, it might appear in these cases that it was the overall sense of place rather than specific location of earlier activity that attracted the Iron Age builders.

The physical juxtaposition of hillforts and earlier monuments, especially funerary monuments, is probably not just a coincidental preference for prominent places, nor even a mark of respect for unspecified ancestors. Though we are admittedly at the limits of archaeological inference, the regularity of associations suggests that it was fundamental to the way that Iron Age communities perceived the past. The example of the monuments in the vicinity of Uffington Castle and the Berkshire Ridgeway (Figure 11.1) illustrates the

Figure 11.1. Uffington Castle and White Horse, Oxfordshire. Air photograph by Major G. W. G. Allen. Reproduced by kind permission of the Ashmolean Museum, University of Oxford.

point, where the hillfort stands adjacent not only to the White Horse, now shown to date from the later Bronze Age (Miles *et al.* 2003), but also a putative Neolithic long mound and barrows of the early and middle Bronze Age. The role of Dragon Hill and the extent to which it has been artificially reshaped to create a flattened platform remain uncertain, but it is clear that an understanding of the hillfort cannot be detached from an appreciation of its landscape context. Gosden and Lock (1998) stressed the importance in non-literate societies of genealogy as history continuing into the present, in the recollection of which features in the landscape may have served as a mnemonic. In the case of White Horse Hill, however, the emphasis may have been on mythical history, extending through into the Christian mythology surrounding Dragon Hill.

WESSEX DIVIDED

In addressing the development of hillforts, Cunliffe noted the concentration in distribution of major hillforts in a broad swathe from Wessex and Sussex through the English–Welsh borders to north Wales, which he defined as his *central southern* hillfort zone (Cunliffe 2005: Figure 21.2). Within the southern half of this zone, he treated *Wessex and adjacent areas* effectively as an entity, so that Maiden Castle and Cadbury Castle, for example, are treated alongside the Hampshire, Sussex, and Wiltshire hillforts, among which, of course, Danebury has pride of place (ibid. 378ff.). In a subsequent summary of research on Wessex hillforts (Cunliffe 2006: 162) the point is made that unlike the Durotrigian hillforts, the hillforts of the Atrebates in general did not continue in regular use after the beginning of the first century BC. The differences between the hillforts east and west of the Hampshire Avon are worth examining more closely, suggesting that Wessex in terms of hillforts is not the coherent entity that is sometimes assumed.

First, some major Dorset hillforts were plainly still flourishing at the time of the Roman conquest, even if most 'developed' hillforts in Hampshire and Sussex, including Danebury, had been abandoned as major centres, at best showing marginal evidence of activity in this period. This is presumably why hillforts in the region east of the Hampshire Avon were not suppressed by the Romans with the same rigour as befell their Durotrigian neighbours, and were even allowed to be reoccupied as domestic and agricultural settlements. In effect, hillforts in the territory of the Atrebates had largely been abandoned in favour of other forms of settlement and community centres, so that if the Atrebates and Durotriges were the two 'formidable' tribes that Vespasian faced on his westward advance, then the *oppida* that he reputedly subjugated may have included quite radically different sites, and the level of resistance that he met may have been quite different. The Atrebates may have been more directly influenced by continental fashions before Caesar's raids, and by the last decade of the first century BC, at Silchester a new form of planned settlement was emerging in a process of changing settlement patterns that would finally render hillforts obsolete.

Second, the Durotrigian hillforts were evidently occupied intensively as habitation sites, as the concentrations of house stances at Hod and Hambledon indicate. Some of these buildings could have been used for storage and other purposes and the apparent paucity of pits and four-posters suggests that individual dwellings or groups of buildings provided all that was necessary for their respective social units. Such intensive levels of habitation are seldom witnessed in the 'developed' hillforts of east-central southern England, even at Danebury, where much of the interior is given over to other purposes, including storage on a communal scale. In some other hillforts in Berkshire, the interiors show little trace of intense occupation, so that other roles have been suggested (Payne *et al.* 2006). The contrast between Liddington Castle and Barbary Castle, or between Uffington and Segsbury, suggests that hillforts in proximity to each other within the same community may have served quite different purposes.

In fact, the distribution of larger hillforts (Figure 1.3) is emphatically *not* concentrated only in Wessex, but is oriented instead between west Hampshire and east Dorset through Wiltshire and Gloucestershire to the Severn and the Welsh Marches, an axis that seems to cut across most anticipated geographical divisions since Fox's (1932). Cunliffe (2005: Figure 21.6) recognized this by accommodating it between his eastern village and open settlement zone and a western zone of defended homesteads and 'petty lords', represented here by hillforts under 3 acres (Figure 1.1). But it is hard to see his extended central southern zone as any kind of cultural or political entity, and in terms of hillforts alone, the Welsh Marches hillforts are distinguished especially by their use of guard chambers, for which there is little evidence in Wessex. In Wessex, the problem lies in whether the less dense 'Atrebatic' hillfort distribution east of the Hampshire Test belongs with the Durotrigian-Dobunnic hillfort zone, and the archaeological evidence points to the divergence of these two regions well before the closing centuries BC.

'DEVELOPED' HILLFORTS

The single and most important contribution of *Iron Age Communities* to hillfort studies was the identification of *developed hillforts* of the fourth and third centuries BC in central southern England (Cunliffe 2005: 388–96), resulting from a 'coalescence of power' (ibid. 590), previously distributed between a larger number of smaller hillforts of the early Iron Age, into fewer, more strongly defended central places like Danebury. The causes of the process of coalescence, which resulted in the enhanced status of 'developed' hillforts, has never really been adequately explained, though in an earlier paper, Cunliffe (1971: 59–64) had suggested that it may have been triggered by population growth associated with improved agricultural production and increased stock-raising, resulting in the emergence of a political and economic elite. In the central southern zone, these major hillforts were seen as 'centres of communal power dominating and serving territories' (Cunliffe 2005: 591), the progressive emergence of which could be loosely correlated with the distribution of ceramic styles that by the first centuries BC/AD in Dorset and Hampshire are described as Durotrigian or Atrebatic (ibid. Figure 21.4). We have seen in the context of Iroquoian defended settlements that the coalescence of numerous small settlements into fewer, larger centres could be brought about as a result of alliances between neighbouring communities, designed to create greater political and social stability by reducing the level of aggression triggered by ongoing blood feuds. In the Wessex Iron Age, it is seen as a consequence of the emerging dominance of individuals or elite groups over their neighbours and the politically ambitious forging of larger territorial domains, though equally it could have resulted from negotiated alliances in which the subordinate parties might also have benefited from being part of a larger confederation.

A key example of the reduction in the number of early hillforts and either the enhancement of one existing hillfort or the building of a new 'developed' hillfort was the distribution of sites along the South Downs (Cunliffe 2005: Figure 15.28). From some two dozen hillforts between St Catharine's Hill, Winchester, and Seaford Head, only eight are regarded as being occupied in the second century BC, and these are distributed at intervals suggesting territories some 15–20 kilometres apart, broadly comparable to the size of territory proposed for Danebury (Cunliffe 2000: 181). This impression is reinforced by the division of the chalk downs into sectors by the rivers Arun, Ouse, and Cuckmere, and presumably the Adur dividing Cissbury from Devil's Dyke. An initial problem is that few of these hillforts have been properly investigated, so that in many cases, dating is dependent upon chance finds. Hamilton and Manley (2001, especially Tables 1–3) listed the South Downs hillforts by evidence of apparent period of use, which showed that a number of the Sussex sites could have had later Bronze Age origins, and that, from the beginning of the Late Bronze Age to the latest pre-Roman Iron Age, the numbers of sites in occupation in any given period hardly varied. Among the hillforts in occupation in the middle Iron Age, notably Torberry (Cunliffe 1976a), Cissbury, the Trundle, and the Caburn, there is a considerable range of areas enclosed and little evidence of common function. The Trundle has surface evidence of more than a dozen circular house stances, and at the

Caburn, more than 140 pits suggest communal storage was important, but otherwise there is no consistent pattern to suggest a common role as 'developed' hillforts. Among the sites with evidence of Late Bronze Age activity, Harting Beacon appears to be related to a more extensive landscape system of dykes, which have been claimed as defining pasture (Bedwin 1979), and it seems possible that some of these earliest hillforts may have served as secure pastoral enclosures (Hamilton and Manley 2001: 25).

Much the same constraints apply to the plotting of hillforts in northern Hampshire and Berkshire (Cunliffe 2005: Figure 15.29), most of which have never been systematically investigated. Of those that have, Uffington (Miles *et al.* 2003) shows little evidence for internal structures of the kind that would be expected of a 'developed' hillfort, and the excavators suggested that it may have fulfilled a ritual role in conjunction with the nearby White Horse. So whilst the 'developed' hillfort model may be valid for the Test–Bourne region of Hampshire (Cunliffe 2005: Figure 15.27) in which Danebury became dominant in the middle Iron Age, its applicability elsewhere seems less certain in the absence of reliable excavated data. Rather than focusing on the role of 'developed' hillforts as centres of power, perhaps we should accept the probability that hillforts served communities in different capacities, some of which, like pastoral enclosures, might leave rather less evidence of activity than those that were used, for example, for secure storage of agricultural produce.

SOCIAL AND ECONOMIC ROLES

Hill (1995b) suggested that the important thing about hillforts, viewed admittedly from a limited Wessex perspective, was that they were 'not farmsteads'. That seemingly banal observation provides a starting point for evaluating what they were, though a better one might have been that they were 'not open farming settlements'. Danebury was certainly not a farmstead, but it is not so clear that more densely occupied sites like Chalbury or Beacon Hill did not develop as a 'coalescence' of farmsteads, as were some of the larger settlements from ethnographic contexts. Certainly they may have structural components in common with farmsteads, pits, four-posters, and roundhouses, and, as has been frequently remarked, their material assemblages are often not so different in kind from those of farmsteads. But if they resulted from a coalescence of farmsteads, in the process they also probably acquired additional community functions as well as more substantial perimeter works.

In northern Britain the seemingly dense Late Bronze Age settlement on Eildon Hill North could well represent the coalescence of smaller farming communities, perhaps induced by political instability resulting from climatic deterioration and consequent pressures on agricultural land. Alternatively, the site may have been occupied by a relatively small resident population 'augmented intermittently by larger numbers of the local or regional populace' (Owen 1992: 67). Either way, it seems that Eildon had already by the later Bronze Age acquired a role as an important regional or territorial focus that, in spite of the apparent lack of later pre-Roman Iron Age settlement, may ultimately have been a factor in the establishment of the Roman fort of Trimontium at its foot. The hillfort once again saw relatively dense occupation in the Roman period, though we need not assume the same status as in its earlier heyday. That depends in some measure on the date of the enclosure walls, which have yet to be shown to be contemporary with the Late Bronze Age occupation. In the absence of any convincing evidence of Iron Age activity, however, this seems probable, in which case the 16 ha (39 acre) enclosure with its concentration of 'house' foundations could well qualify as an early example of a town resulting from the coalescence of smaller agricultural communities.

Among the great diversity of sites that have been classified under the umbrella heading of 'hillforts', some of the smaller hillforts in the Borders and elsewhere display a density of roundhouses within the enclosed circuit that leaves little doubt that domestic and agricultural habitation was their primary purpose, so that in effect they were protected villages. In more dispersed upland regions this may be a standard form of independent settlement, but in the Borders individual small hillfort-villages may have shared a dependent relationship with the fewer, larger hillforts, like Eildon Hill, Hownam Law, or Yeavering Bell, which are conspicuous landmarks that could have served as places of periodic assembly for quite widely dispersed communities. Even assuming a process of fragmentation from Late Bronze Age nucleated settlements to smaller Iron Age protected villages (Halliday 1985: 238), it is still possible that the larger centres continued to serve in a different capacity for periodic assembly, without leaving evidence of substantial settlement. In any event, the sequence is certainly different from the Wessex model of progression towards fewer 'developed' hillforts.

Whether any Iron Age hillforts can be regarded as 'towns' in any meaningful sense has been sidelined by the debate over *oppida* and urbanization in south-eastern England, against the background of the wider issues of urbanization and state formation in continental Europe. As we have seen, Wheeler evidently thought of Maiden Castle and the Durotrigian hillforts as towns, and the evidence of 'houses' in greater numbers at Hod Hill and Hambledon Hill might certainly support that contention. Some of the larger *castros* of the peninsular north-west, like the Citânia de Briteiros near Guimarães or the Citânia de Santa Luzia at Viana do Castelo (Plate 15b), with a dense internal occupation represented uniquely outside Britain by roundhouses, would likewise surely qualify as towns. Adapting Hull's (1976) criteria for recognizing African towns before the European conquest, we might propose four key functions as diagnostic of towns in Iron Age temperate Europe:

- residential centres for a population engaged in agricultural activities in the immediate hinterland, but potentially also supporting craft specialization through its capacity for agricultural surplus,
- centres of governance by political and legal authorities, administered with the aid of periodic assemblies,
- centres of economic activities, such as storage of agricultural produce, local redistribution, and longer-distance trade or exchange,
- centres of religious or ritual activities, including burial rites.

In terms of their physical characteristics, as may be recognized archaeologically, the most obvious criterion would be the size of the settlement, with the expectation that a site fulfilling these 'urban' functions would be larger than dependent 'rural' settlements. In addition, centres of community activity are likely to have been defined by a walled enclosure that could also serve in times of crisis as a refuge for dependent communities in its catchment territory. But the fact that Manching had already acquired some urban characteristics before the construction of its enclosing wall indicates that this was not a *sine qua non* of urbanization. Finally, in consequence of the limitation on available space imposed by enclosure, it is probable that the interior would be subdivided into separate activity areas or allocated to groups within the community for segregated usage, as a result of which some element of 'town planning' might be detectable archaeologically in terms of structural zoning. The issue of defence may be secondary, though not negligible, perhaps influencing local siting but not determining location, but control of access may have been more important, being expressed in enclosing walls with regulated entrances.

These functions could have been applicable to some British Iron Age hillforts, though plainly not to more than a small proportion of the total that conventionally fall under that umbrella. Some hillforts may have been centres of regional governance, controlled by Cunliffe's 'coercive power', but it is still debatable whether that governing power was necessarily resident in the hillfort, or whether the latter simply served as a place of assembly and symbol of that authority. Plainly, however, this definition of a town diverges from any that Childe might have devised for Middle Eastern or Mediterranean urban civilizations, for which literacy and bureaucracy would have been essential, together with monumental architecture. Furthermore, in those urban civilizations there is a greater emphasis upon town planning, and the presence of public buildings that mark them out as the focus of the governing hierarchy and its administrative, judicial, and religious organization. Craft specialization to a more sophisticated level may also be anticipated in a state-level society.

If *residential occupation* was a function of many hillforts, *storage* was evidently an equally important, and sometimes even the dominant role. The example of the New Zealand *pā* illustrates the importance of secure storage of communal produce, and it seems probable that some hillforts of the British and European Iron Age were primarily dedicated to this purpose. The role of central storage of produce need not necessarily entail concomitant ideas of centralized control, the payment of dues to a central authority, or redistribution as part of the reciprocal obligations between social ranks, though these may have been implicit in Iron Age society. A key consideration is whether the produce stored within the hillfort was the greater proportion of the community's yield, or whether it was primarily surplus intended to support a wider network of exchange. Cereals may have been the staple of Iron Age agriculture in Britain, with quantities by the later pre-Roman period in parts of southern or eastern Britain being produced for export, as Strabo (*Geography* 4.5.2) claimed. But inter-community exchange with near neighbours was presumably more common than long-distance exchange, and we might imagine that the hillforts of the Welsh Marches, for example, with their ranks of four-posters standing testimony to a storage capacity on a substantial scale, may well reflect exchange between grain-producing communities and stock-raising neighbours. Agricultural produce was clearly vital to a community's survival, whether for local consumption or as surplus for external exchange, and as such warranted special protection against theft or damage. It therefore does not seem unreasonable to assume that hillforts were as much for the protection of these resources as of the communities that were dependent on them. It is worth reflecting, however, that our current understanding of the economy of the British Iron Age is still fundamentally based on the Bersu's (1940) interpretation of both pits and four-posters as twin methods of storing grain, a premise that is not unreasonable but not invariably demonstrable. It should also be remembered that pits in southern Britain are a feature of the middle pre-Roman Iron Age especially, and are not prolific in the earliest or late periods.

Stock-raising was clearly also an important element in the agricultural economy and cattle are also in Strabo's list of exports. Accordingly, we might presume that such an important asset would be carefully husbanded, especially since cattle would have been vulnerable to rustling. Caesar's terse summary of the Britons (*dBG* V, 12) included the observation that they kept great herds of cattle, and had assembled large numbers in the stronghold of Cassivellaunus (*dBG* V, 21). Apart from protection from cattle-raiding (Lucas 1989), there would presumably have been occasions when hillforts may have been used for seasonal round-ups, and this could have been one purpose served by those sites in which there is minimal evidence for permanent buildings. Given the status accorded to cattle, and in the Irish epic tradition, to prize bulls and cattle raiding, *stock protection* therefore seems a legitimate reason for constructing a fortified compound.

In the case of the Berkshire Downs hillforts, we might speculate whether the obviously cult symbolism of the White Horse might not have reflected a more secular interest in horses, perhaps in their training as well as breeding, for which the landscape is plainly better suited, for example, than it is for cattle-raising, though sheep are generally dominant on the chalk downs (Ingrem 2003). Evidence for horse breeding in the Iron Age in southern Britain is minimal (Grant 1984: 521–2), and the scarcity of neo-natal or young animal remains, with notable exceptions like Gravelly Guy, Oxfordshire (Lambrick and Allen 2004) and Rooksdown, Andover (Powell and Clark 1996), hitherto led to the suggestion that wild herds were periodically rounded up for training in preference to breeding (Harcourt 1979: 158). The one hillfort with conspicuous evidence for horses is Blewburton Hill, where limited excavation in the interior yielded little trace of dense structural occupation. The Blewburton horse burials do not prove that horses were bred or trained there, but they do suggest that horses were regarded as special. The paired burials at Blewburton suggest two-horse teams, and if teams on the scale of Cassivellaunus' chariot force were required by Iron Age leaders, then their breeding and training would have been a prestigious specialist occupation. In the diversity of functions that hillforts may have fulfilled, it may be that the hillforts of the Berkshire Downs had a particular interest in the breeding of horses.

Hillforts as places of *assembly* is a probable function, for seasonal festivals and other events that demanded the gathering of representatives from every section of the related or dependent community. The choice of a conspicuous landmark may be indicative, but archaeologically it is unclear what evidence we might expect from such communal events, since assembly could cover a multitude of activities, not all of which may have been communally inclusive. Assembly might thus be divided into *social assembly*—seasonal festivals, family celebrations, inaugurations and the like; *economic assembly*—involving markets, exchange, or redistribution; *diplomatic or political assembly*—in which treaties and alliances between neighbours were negotiated and sealed; and *ritual assembly*, including funerary ceremonies. It is likely that these categories were mutually embedded, so that social events would doubtless have included a ritual dimension, and in the case of exogamous marriages, for example, perhaps a diplomatic dimension as well. In the apparent absence of a regular rite for the disposal of the dead, it seems likely that the role of hillforts in *funerary ritual* has hitherto been seriously underestimated.

CEREMONIAL, RITUAL, AND BURIAL

Several studies of the orientation of roundhouse entrances have shown that a substantial proportion displays a marked preponderance towards the east and south-east. Hill extended this to include hillforts, where the outcome was more subtle. Of seventy-five hillforts in southern England in his sample survey, there was an overwhelming preference for either an eastern or western entrance orientation, the former slightly outnumbering the latter (Hill 1996: Figure 8.10). It is certainly true that a check of fifty hillforts from Hampshire, Wiltshire, Berkshire, Surrey, and Sussex endorsed that conclusion, but the two dozen hillforts listed in the Dorset *Inventory* by contrast show only a very marginal preference for any specific orientation, perhaps again revealing a measure of difference within Wessex. Among the Dorset hillforts, the special significance of the east–west orientation at Maiden Castle is emphasized by the use of 'twin portals', suggesting the possibility of ceremonial, processional use.

In south-east Scotland, a similar preponderance of opposites is accentuated by hillforts located on steep-sided ridges with entrances at either accessible ends. Though the preference in orientation is not nearly so narrowly focused as in Hill's sample, the great majority of hillfort entrances in Roxburghshire and Peeblesshire, combining sites with single entrances and those with more than one, are concentrated between north-east and south-east, or between north-west and south-west, with the proportions being much closer to equal in Peeblesshire. Whereas it is not unreasonable to argue that the orientation of a roundhouse entrance towards the south-east might be to maximize morning sunlight and avoid a prevailing westerly wind, the orientation of a hillfort entrance could well have been influenced by cosmological considerations.

Perhaps the most underrated aspect of hillforts' potential function, notwithstanding the repeated discovery of human remains in and around hillforts, has been their role in funerary practice. Setting aside the vexed question of 'massacre' sites, most excavated hillforts have yielded from pits or ditches human skeletal material that has never been considered as part of the normal ritual for disposal of the dead, simply because pits are not readily equated with graves, and the remains often do not comprise complete skeletons. If, as is widely accepted, excarnation was part of the funerary ritual, then the fragmentation of the skeletal remains becomes a real possibility, the more so if it was customary to deposit the remains in more than one place of significance to the dead or their kin. Only with an excavation as extensive as Danebury can we see the scale of the practice of pit-burial, with more than 150 pits containing human remains. Equally enigmatic is the fact that more than twice that number contain animal remains, and as many again what are regarded as propitiatory 'special burials' (Cunliffe 1995: Table 18). Any suggestion that there was a marked increase in these deposits after the fourth century BC, however, should be qualified by the relative time spans represented by the site's 'ceramic phases' (ibid. 17–18). In those regions of Britain where there is a regular and recurrent burial rite, such as eastern Yorkshire or the south-east of England in the late pre-Roman Iron Age, there are relatively fewer hillforts. Where hillforts are more numerous there are no such formal cemeteries, and it seems likely that the hillforts themselves fulfilled a major role in the rituals that accompanied the disposal of the dead. At Danebury, the 'shrines' could well have served as excarnation enclosures, though we should not discount the possibility that some four-posters likewise were excarnation platforms. What has consistently confused archaeologists is the absence of a single, uniform rite for the ultimate disposal of the remains, a constraint that may also have applied in areas where there *were* formal cemeteries, but which need not account for the totality or even the majority of the population.

In the case of the Irish 'royal' sites, no-one doubts that a ritual dimension is present and even paramount. We tend to discount these on the grounds that they are not 'true hillforts', especially those, like Dún Ailinne or the Ráith na Ríg at Tara in which the earthworks are reversed. But if we argue that British hillforts were not designed primarily to be defensive, why should we disqualify Irish sites that deviate from the defensive paradigm? Irish sites are simply at one end of a spectrum of enclosures involving a range of activities, including burial, ritual, and ceremonial activities that were at the centre of community life and identity. Had the Romans invaded Ireland, Navan, and Dún Ailinne would surely have been prime targets for annihilation, and doubtless would have preserved archaeological evidence for massacres like those of some southern British hillforts. The reason for the rigour of destruction in evidence at Cadbury Castle and elsewhere is surely testimony to the fact that some hillforts at least were much more than defended settlements.

In continental Europe too, the ritual role of hillforts has come to increasing prominence in recent years. The interior of the Mont Lassois, traditionally interpreted as a western example of the north Alpine *Fürstensitzen* of the Late Hallstatt period, and assumed by Joffroy (1960) to have been denuded of significant structural remains in its interior, has been subject to further investigation by geophysical survey with some excavation. The outcome not only suggests a regular and intensive arrangement of buildings, perhaps influenced by models from the south, but also at least one major aisled building with apsidal end that could indicate a 'royal' or 'ritual' centre within the citadel. On the northern fringe of the distribution of the Late Hallstatt–Early La Tène *Fürstensitzen*, the site of the Glauberg with its remarkable burial complex (Hermann and Frey 1996; Frey and Hermann 1997; Frey 1998; Weber 2002) is now widely regarded primarily as a ritual and ceremonial centre. Even the *oppidum* at Manching, long regarded as the prime example in central Europe of a proto-urban centre of the Late La Tène, is now known to have had a central sanctuary comprising a sub-square enclosure with circular central structure spanning the occupation of the site from La Tène B to La Tène D. It had long been clear from the adjacent La Tène B/La Tène C1 cemeteries at Steinbichel and Hunsrucken that the site was already an important focus before the *oppidum* had fully developed, but it now seems probable

HILLFORTS AND SOCIAL HIERARCHIES

that its location and development were in part at least stimulated by the site's special sense of place over many generations.

For southern Britain, it is now widely argued that change to a more hierarchically structured society may have been a relatively late development of the pre-Roman Iron Age, in a process that was accelerated in the century between Caesar and Claudius by increasing contacts with Romanized Gaul. In contrast to the middle Iron Age in Wessex, the emergence of a social and political hierarchy in south-eastern England is equated with a new order that was heralded by the adoption of coinage, the appearance of *oppida* (different from conventional hillforts, whatever their role might have been), a 'visible cremation mortuary rite', prestige goods and evidence for long-distance exchange, the latter notably evident in the exotic grave-goods from high-status burials (Hill 1995b: 47). We might add to the list of changes a class of domestic buildings that was rather less visible archaeologically, perhaps because rectilinear in plan rather than circular and built to a different technical specification. Undoubtedly there were significant changes in the archaeological record of the late pre-Roman Iron Age in south-eastern England, so that for sceptics of hierarchy, even classical sources from this period can be deemed suspect as indices of earlier Iron Age society. But the question remains whether radical change triggered the rapid rise of a hierarchical social structure, or conversely whether the established existence of a hierarchy facilitated the rapid adoption of innovation.

The question therefore arises: what other evidence is there for the existence of a social elite in the earlier Iron Age, apart from the monumentality of hillforts themselves? Rather than simply glossing the issue in terms of 'elites', it is worth recalling Caesar's description of Gaulish society, as he encountered it in the mid-first century BC. Caesar certainly referred to tribal leaders as kings or chiefs, below whom he singled out two grades as being of consequence, the *druids* and the *equites*, in that order (*dBG* VI, 15). Some of the attributes of the druids may have been confused together with those of the bards and seers, who would hardly have exercised the same authority, as Caesar must have known perfectly well. The druids could be of high social standing: Caesar's Aeduan ally Diviciacus, described as a druid by Cicero (*de Divinatione* I, 49), was brother of the Aeduan king Dumnorix. Among the warrior class, the best-endowed by birth and wealth commanded the greatest number of dependants (*ambacti*) and clients, which certainly implies a complex social hierarchy. From this we might infer that Gaulish society by the first century BC at least had a complex system involving aristocratic chiefs, a warrior hierarchy, and religious leaders.

Archaeology conventionally recognizes social rank most obviously in burials, in which, perhaps questionably, grave-goods are assumed to reflect the status of the dead. On this basis burials of the Late Hallstatt period in west-central Europe, containing lavish grave-goods, often associated with feasting and drinking like Hochdorf or Vix, are generally regarded as indicative of a social elite, whilst graves of the Early La Tène period in the Champagne that include two-wheeled vehicles, weaponry, or helmets are interpreted as those of warrior aristocrats. Whether these interpretations are simplistic, whether, for example, the grave-goods are symbolic of office rather than reflecting the personal achievements of the individual in life, or whether they are offerings to the otherworld from the mourners, displaying their status through conspicuous disposal of wealth rather than that of the deceased, is largely beside the point in the present context. The fact that some graves are lavishly furnished while others are not is indicative of a significant degree of discrimination in the treatment of the dead or in the rituals that accompanied their interment, and is therefore consistent with a hierarchical structure, whatever its basis. This certainly was the case in the late pre-Roman Iron Age in south-eastern England, where burials like Lexden, Welwyn, or Stanway stand out from the simpler cremation burials of the majority of cemeteries, with a notable emphasis again on feasting and drinking, hearth and home. The mid-first century AD burials at Stanway (Crummy et al. 2007) included both 'warrior' and 'doctor's', the latter including 'divination rods' that suggested, if not a druid specifically, someone whose healing powers were as much spiritual as physical.

Prior to the late pre-Roman Iron Age, the only regular and recurrent funerary rite is the Arras series of burials from eastern Yorkshire, where from the fourth to second centuries BC, inhumation cemeteries include a range of associated furnishings that might well be regarded as evidence for a hierarchy of ranking, from minimal grave-goods to those with weapons and the dismantled remains of two-wheeled carts or chariots. The scabbard from grave K3 at Kirkburn is as elaborately ornamented and complex in its construction as any in the European Iron Age, and together with the mail tunic from K5 attests to the importance of the warrior ethos. The fact that otherwise there is limited archaeological evidence of social hierarchy in the British Iron Age prior to the first century BC is thus demonstrably because of the absence of a regular burial rite elsewhere, with the result that one major source of status goods is simply not available (Fitzpatrick 1984: 182). Where exceptional burials are known, such as the third century 'warrior' grave from Mill Hill, Deal (Parfitt 1995), the presence of sword and shield together with ornamented bronze 'crown' suggests aristocratic as well as 'warrior' status, while the pair of bronze spoons from nearby grave X2 might imply the presence of a religious elite as well. The evidence as it stands, however, does suggest that in the earlier Iron Age status was primarily expressed through the trappings of the warrior, whereas by the late pre-Roman Iron Age in southern England, feasting and drinking once again asserted itself as a major expression of status and wealth. These examples admittedly relate only to selected regions and periods, because the archaeological record of formal cemeteries is so limited.

Aside from burials, high-status artefacts are generally only otherwise found in contexts like ritual deposits in water or in hoards, though material of La Tène type is not as prolific as Late Bronze Age or Hallstatt-derived types. Not all water deposits are of high-status artefacts, but some of the parade weaponry and armour, such as the Standlake or Witham scabbards, the scabbards from the river Bann in Co. Antrim, or the Witham or Battersea shields, were unquestionably prestigious pieces, in the case of the shields almost certainly intended for ceremonial use. Luxurious personal ornaments are relatively scarce before the first century BC in Britain, though the four gold torcs recently discovered near Stirling, for one of which an origin in south-western Gaul has been suggested, appear to be stylistically earlier. Like the buffer-terminal torc of continental La Tène B2 type from Knock (Clonmacnoise) in Ireland, these prestige pieces were surely the prized possessions of Iron Age aristocrats whose international connections gave them access to wider European sources of supply. Outside burials and hoards, artefacts of this quality are seldom found on hillforts or settlement sites, presumably for the obvious reason that valuables would normally be safeguarded or salvaged wherever possible.

Despite the current preference for the late development of a hierarchical social structure in Iron Age Britain, therefore, the limited archaeological evidence does seem to be consistent with its emergence from the later Bronze Age in Britain as in Europe, while it seems improbable that a system as complex as that implied by Caesar's account of Gaul in the first century BC should not have developed over a considerable period of time. How far hillforts reflect any such social hierarchy is another matter. In western and northern Britain, the small size of some forts with historical associations certainly suggests that they were fortified royal residences, rather than community sites, perhaps only occupied by their patrons periodically. The nuclear forts may likewise have been centres for periodic assembly, but their layout does appear to embody a hierarchical sub-division of space. In contrast, the hillforts of southern Britain in the pre-Roman period show no evidence of subdivision of space on the basis of social hierarchy, though there may be some evidence for functional subdivision, as at Danebury. In fact, the size of some of the larger Wessex hillforts argues for their being community centres with a range of communal functions, rather than elite citadels, even if they were controlled by an authority representing a social, martial, or spiritual elite, or a combination of these various forces.

CHANGE THROUGH TIME

The diversity in form and function of hillforts is hardly surprising in view of the time span over which they were constructed, which begins conservatively in the later Bronze Age and continues in some parts of Britain into the later, post-Roman Iron Age. A surprising fact is that, without excavation, it would be hard on the basis of enclosure morphology, topography, or any other form of archaeological classification to assign any individual site to period with confidence within that two thousand year span. An exception might be the terraced or tiered nuclear forts of the later Iron Age in northern Britain (and even they may have had earlier Iron Age antecedents), but for the most part hillfort earthworks are not in themselves diagnostic to period. It is true that complexity of enclosure may result from cumulative construction over time, but it certainly does not follow that simple earthworks are necessarily early and complex ones are late, and some of the smaller, multivallate sites of western and northern Britain could in fact be the product of unitary construction.

The technique of rampart construction, on the other hand, though hardly diagnostic, may be indicative of date. In southern Britain timber-framed or timber-and-stone wall ramparts mostly date from the Late Bronze Age and earlier Iron Age, giving way to dump ramparts that characterize the majority of later pre-Roman Iron Age hillforts. This pattern is so widespread and recurrent that it must have tactical or economic implications. As we have seen, Avery suggested that it was the result of a change in fighting tactics; it could equally have been necessitated by the depletion of timber resources brought about by intensive use. The two need not be incompatible. In continental Europe, on the other hand, wall ramparts with at least a vertical front face continued in use up to the time of the Roman conquest east and west of the Rhine in two principal variants, the *murus Gallicus* mainly in the west, and the Kelheim type further east, with both used successively at Manching. The quantities of materials consumed in the construction of these massive *oppida*, not least in the use of iron spikes to secure the timbers of *muri Gallici*, as at the Mont Beuvray, plainly testifies to resource management on a highly organized scale. Dump ramparts were also in evidence in the Gallic campaign, as we have seen, perhaps as a result of changing defensive tactics. In northern Britain, wall ramparts continued to be constructed in the later Iron Age, perhaps reflecting a greater conservatism in fighting tactics, or alternatively because the generally smaller scale of construction was not so demanding of resources.

It is widely acknowledged that the appearance of hillforts in increasing numbers in the Late Bronze Age may have been a consequence of increasing political instability, accompanied by an intensification of interest in martial activity or ritual associated with it that is reflected in the range of high-status weaponry and defensive armour in the archaeological assemblage of the

Urnfield and Atlantic Late Bronze Age. It is certainly possible that weapons and armour were for ritualized activity that may not have mirrored actual practice in combat, not least because, for example, sheet-bronze shields would have been extremely vulnerable in real combat unless backed by leather or wood (Coles 1962). The proliferation of weaponry nevertheless is matched by the scale and elaboration of hillfort defences, in which the element of display and conspicuous use of resources appears to have been as important as defensive utility. An equally important product of the Late Bronze Age industrial revolution was sheet-bronze for vessels associated with feasting and drinking, and it seems likely that displays of martial prowess, and songs and tales that lauded mythical heroes or ancestors for feats of arms, would have featured prominently in ritual feasts and festivals that may well have been centred on hillforts. The image of the boastful, drunken, and aggressive Gaulish warrior, challenging rivals to single combat for the champion's portion, is more probably a tradition derived from a semi-mythical heroic Bronze Age society than a true reflection of fighting practice in the late pre-Roman Iron Age.

A key to understanding the role of hillforts in later British and European prehistory must lie in progressive change in political and social organization, and in marked regional differences in when such change came about. If hillforts in southern Britain had their origins in the industrial, environmental, social, and political upheaval of the Late Bronze Age, by the earlier Iron Age, they were doubtless already acquiring a range of different roles in which defence or martial display may no longer have been paramount. In north Alpine Europe, hillfort domains from the early Iron Age were often (though not invariably) larger than those of southern Britain, thereby commanding resources over a wider area with greater opportunities for external exchange. In southern Britain, early Iron Age society may have had petty hierarchies focused on local hillforts, some of which subsequently were abandoned, while others acquired enhanced community roles, though even these 'developed' hillforts may have developed in markedly different ways. But it was probably not until the middle or later pre-Roman Iron Age that the coalescence of smaller domains resulted in territories attaining a size approaching that of the *civitates* of Roman Britain, by which time only territories 'peripheral' to the south-eastern 'core' were still focused on hillforts. By the early first century BC, many hillforts east of the Hampshire Avon were abandoned as other kinds of community *foci* like Silchester or Camulodunum came to prominence. In the north and west communities remained essentially dispersed and small-scale, doubtless with alliances between local groups that nevertheless amounted to less than confederation. Here, hillforts remained in use, and indeed some may have been a focus of resistance to the Roman invasion. There was no uniform progression, however, culminating in proto-urban status, as was once believed of northern British hillforts like Eildon Hill and Traprain Law, and some of these appear to have been occupied more intensively in the Roman period than in the preceding Iron Age.

It remains a regrettable fact that the study of post-Roman hillforts in Britain is virtually a separate discipline from later prehistoric hillfort studies. It is perhaps inevitable that the research agenda for later Iron Age hillforts should be historical and text-led, but it is unfortunate that prehistorians and archaeologists of historic periods so seldom communicate in terms of theoretical or practical approaches to hillfort interpretation. Several conclusions can be drawn from a study of later Iron Age hillforts in northern and western Britain. First, from the documentary sources it is clear that they were attacked and sacked, so that they evidently did serve a defensive role. Whilst this need not mean that hillforts over the preceding fifteen hundred years necessarily served a similar function, there is little evidence, rational or anecdotal, to believe that earlier Iron Age communities were any more pacific or egalitarian. Second, later Iron Age hillforts are not alone in having 'exotic' imports in the form of continental or Mediterranean pottery and glass. Monastic sites and crannogs too have yielded such imports, for which there is no demonstrable evidence that they were the product of redistribution from higher status centres, though this possibility should not be excluded. Again this need not invalidate the model of earlier Iron Age hillforts as centres of redistribution, though that model has certainly been challenged on independent grounds. Finally, in the case of early historic hillforts size is clearly not a reliable index of status, since some of the most important sites, based on both historical and archaeological evidence, like Dunadd, are relatively small in area. In Strathdon too, it is the smaller sites that have produced exotic imports (Cook forthcoming). Large enclosures presumably served large communities, whether hierarchically ordered or not. In the later Iron Age, elite citadels were exclusive but relatively small, and doubtless more readily defended on that account. In southern Britain as in the north there is some evidence for reoccupation and refurbishment of earlier Iron Age hillforts, notably at Cadbury Castle, where excavation has shown that the entire circuit of rampart was renovated, rather than simply a citadel around the summit. Whoever was the controlling authority in the early sixth century, this was doubtless an attempt to reinforce its legitimacy in politically unstable times through the traditional associations of the hillfort.

EPILOGUE

For a class of monument as all-embracing and diverse as hillforts, spanning two millennia, there can be no single explanation, and any expectation that this review might adduce a novel code that would unlock the meaning of hillforts is bound to be disappointed. Hillforts fulfilled a multiplicity of roles, though some may have been more important than others. Diversity of hillforts does not mean that within regional groups, hillforts may not have fulfilled similar purposes, like the defended villages of the Roxburghshire Cheviots, or the hillforts of the southern Welsh Marches with their capacity for secure storage of agricultural produce. Some hillforts in Wessex may even have served as central places for community storage and other activities. In the past, a defensive role was uncritically taken for granted; nowadays identity and symbolism may easily be overrated in a reaction against older conventions. Both surely remain valid interpretations. The so-called 'grand narrative' of Iron Age warfare was surely overstated, but fantasizing about an egalitarian and pacified Iron Age, based more on wishful thinking than sound archaeological evidence, is equally unworthy of serious scholarship.

If there is one role that has been consistently underestimated, it is the role of hillforts in burial. The varied but extensive evidence for burials in and around hillforts falls tantalizingly short of a recurrent burial rite that might satisfy the vexed question of the very disparate representation of formal cemeteries in the British Iron Age. The fact that the distribution of hillforts and that of recurrent cemetery rites are in significant measure exclusive might prompt the idea, not that hillforts fulfilled the role of cemeteries, but that communities in some regions expressed their social identity in non-hillfort settlements and cemeteries, and in others did so in more monumental enclosures, which may also have had an important role in the disposal of the dead. More specifically, the expectation of a recurrent burial rite, because for some regions and periods such are known, is misplaced; there is no reason why prehistoric communities should not have disposed of the dead in what archaeologically may appear to be a variety of different ways. Even in the Arras or Aylesford–Welwyn series of cemeteries, it is improbable that more than a select section of society was buried in the distinctive square-ditch barrow or cremation cemeteries that archaeologically are regarded as typical. These represent only the final stage in the funerary rite that happens to determine its archaeological visibility. The 'invisible rites' by definition must have been more widespread than the surviving record suggests.

As to future hillfort research, it seems unlikely in the prevailing climate that research excavation will be high on the agenda, although without it there is a real prospect that purely desk-based studies and cognitive speculation based on 'empathy' will sidetrack serious scholarship. Some priority needs have not changed in thirty-odd years. There is still an urgent need to examine the immediate exteriors of hillforts, a task to which the use of non-intrusive geophysical survey in the first instance is ideally suited, to determine whether some hillforts had contemporary occupation outside their walls in a citadel–suburbs relationship. Though it might have appeared that the potential for investigation of ramparts has been exhausted, most excavations in the past have patently failed to recover their complexities, and have seldom adequately investigated the role of ditches. Furthermore, the assumption of uniform construction certainly needs to be tested. On a regional basis, there are innumerable questions that need to be clarified regarding major sites or individual groups of hillforts, but which are unlikely to be resolved as an incidental adjunct to site management and public display. Leaving proactive field research to future generations on the grounds that improved techniques of recovery and analysis will become available is an abdication of responsibility, since *mañana* never comes.

Bibliography

Aitchison, N. (1987), 'The Ulster Cycle: Heroic image and historical reality', *JMH*, 13: 87–116.
Aitken, M. and Tite, M. (1962), 'Proton magnetometer survey on some British hillforts', *Archaeometry*, 5: 126–34.
Ajayi, J. F. Ade and Smith, R. (1964), *Yoruba Warfare in the Nineteenth Century*, Cambridge, Cambridge University Press/Institute of African Studies, Ibadan, 2nd edition 1971.
Alcock, L. (1963), *Dinas Powys, an Iron Age, Dark Age and Early Medieval Settlement in Glamorgan*, Cardiff, University of Wales Press.
——(1965), 'Hillforts in Wales and the Marches', *Antiquity*, 39: 184–95.
——(1972), *By South Cadbury is that Camelot. Excavations at Cadbury Castle 1966–70*, London, Thames and Hudson.
——(1984), 'A survey of Pictish settlement archaeology', in Friell, J. and Watson, W. (eds), 1984: 7–41.
——(1988), *Bede, Eddius and the forts of the north Britons*, Jarrow lecture 1988, Newcastle Upon Tyne.
——(1995), *Cadbury Castle, Somerset. The Early Medieval Archaeology*, Cardiff, University of Wales Press.
——(2003), *Kings and Warriors, Craftsmen and Priests in North Britain AD 550–850*, Edinburgh, Society of Antiquaries of Scotland.
——and Alcock, E. (1987), 'Reconnaissance excavations on Early Historic fortifications and other royal sites in Scotland, 1974–84: 2, Excavations at Dunollie Castle, Oban, Argyll, 1978', *PSAS*, 117: 119–47.
—— ——(1990), 'Reconnaissance excavations on Early Historic fortifications and other royal sites in Scotland, 1974–84: 4, Excavations at Alt Clut, Clyde Rock, Strathclyde, 1974–75', *PSAS*, 120: 95–149.
—— ——and Driscoll, S. (1989), 'Reconnaissance excavations on Early Historic fortifications and other royal sites in Scotland, 1974–84: 3, Excavations at Dundurn, Strathearn, Perthshire, 1976–77', *PSAS*, 119: 189–226.
Alexander, D. (ed.) (1996a), *Prehistoric Renfrewshire, Papers in Honour of Frank Newall*, Edinburgh, Renfrewshire Local History Forum.
——(1996b), 'Sites and artefacts: the prehistory of Renfrewshire', in Alexander, D. (ed.) 1996a: 5–22.
——(2002), 'An oblong fort at Finavon, Angus: an example of the over-reliance on the appliance of science', in Smith, B. B. and Banks, I. (eds), 2002: 45–54.
Allcroft, H. (1908), *Earthwork of England, Prehistoric, Roman, Saxon, Danish, Norman, and Mediaeval*, London, Macmillan.
Allen, D. (1967), 'Iron Age currency bars in Britain', *PPS*, 33: 307–35.
Allen, T., Cramp, K., Lamdin-Whymark, H. and Webley, L. (2011), *Castle Hill and its landscape. Archaeological investigations at the Wittenhams, Oxfordshire*, Oxford, Oxford Archaeology Monographs 9.

Allen, T., Hayden, C. and Lamdin-Whymark, H. (2009), *From Bronze Age enclosure to Anglo-Saxon settlement: archaeological excavations at Taplow hillfort, Buckinghamshire, 1999–2005*, Oxford, Oxford Archaeology Thames Valley Landscapes Monograph No 30.

——and Lamdin-Whymark, H. (2005), 'Little Wittenham: excavations at and around Castle Hill', *South Midlands Archaeology*, 35: 69–82.

Anderson, J. (1883), *Scotland in Pagan Times. The Iron Age*, Edinburgh, David Douglas.

——(1893), 'Notice of Dun Sron Duin, Bernera, Barra Head', *PSAS*, 27, 1892–3: 341–6.

Applebaum, S. (1949), 'Excavations at Wilbury Hill, an Iron Age hillfort near Letchworth, Hertfordshire, 1933', *Arch. J.*, 106: 12–45.

Arkush, E. and Stanish, C. (2005), 'Interpreting Conflict in the Ancient Andes: Implications for the Archaeology of Warfare', *C. Anth.*, 46, No. 1: 3–28.

Armit, I. (ed.), (1990a), *Beyond the Brochs, Changing Perspectives on the Atlantic Scottish Iron Age*, Edinburgh, Edinburgh University Press.

——(1990b), 'Epilogue: the Atlantic Scottish Iron Age', in Armit, I. (ed.) 1990a: 194–210.

——(1992), *The Later Prehistory of the Western Isles of Scotland*, Oxford, BAR British Series 221.

——(1997), *Celtic Scotland*, London, Batsford/Historic Scotland.

——(1999), 'Life after Hownam: the Iron Age in south-east Scotland', in Bevan, B. (ed.) 1999a: 65–80.

——(2007), 'Hillforts at War: From Maiden Castle to Taniwaha Pā', *PPS*, 73: 25–38.

——(2011a), Presentation to 14th ICCS, Maynooth, August, 2011.

——(2011b), 'Violence and society in the deep human past', *British Journal of Criminology*, 51 (3): 499–517.

Armit, I., Dunwell, A. and Hunter, F. (1999), *Traprain Law Summit Project, East Lothian: Data Structure Report, 1999*, Edinburgh, privately circulated professional report.

—— —— ——(2000), *Traprain Law Summit Project, East Lothian: Data Structure Report, 2000*, Edinburgh, privately circulated professional report.

——and McKenzie, J. (forthcoming), *An Inherited Place: Broxmouth and the southern Scottish Iron Age*, Edinburgh, Society of Antiquaries of Scotland.

Arnold, B. and Blair Gibson, D. (eds) (1995), *Celtic chiefdom, Celtic state. The evolution of complex social systems in prehistoric Europe*, Cambridge, Cambridge University Press.

Arnold, C. and Davies, L. (2000), *Roman and Early Medieval Wales*, Stroud, Sutton.

Ashmore, P. (1999), 'A List of Archaeological Radiocarbon Dates', *DES*, 1999: 110–15.

Atkinson, R., Piggott, S. and Sandars, N. (1951), *Excavations at Dorchester, Oxon*, Oxford, Ashmolean Museum.

Avery, M. (1986), 'Stoning and fire at hillfort entrances in southern Britain', *WA*, 18, 2: 216–30.

——(1993), *Hillfort Defences of Southern Britain*, 3 vols. Oxford, BAR British Series 231.

——Sutton, J. and Banks, J. (1967), 'Rainsborough, Northants, England: excavations 1961–65', *PPS*, 33: 207–306.
Barber, J. (1985), *Insegall, The Western Isles*, Edinburgh, John Donald.
Baring-Gould, S. and Burnard, R. (1904), 'An Exploration of some of the Cytiau in Tre'r Ceiri', *Arch. Camb.*, 4, 1: 1–16.
Barker, L. and Driver, T. (2011), 'Close to the Edge: New Perspectives on the Architecture, Function and Regional Geographies of the Coastal Promontory Forts of the Castlemartin Peninsula, South Pembrokeshire, Wales', *PPS*, 77: 65–87.
Barker, M. (1934), 'Tumuli near Carrock Fell', *TCWAS*, 34: 107–12.
Barrett, J. and Bradley, R. (eds) (1980), *Settlement and Society in Later Bronze Age Britain*, Oxford, BAR British Series 83.
——Fitzpatrick, A. and Macinnes, I. (eds) (1989), *Barbarians and Romans in Northwest Europe: from the later Republic to late Antiquity*, Oxford, BAR International Series 471.
Barrett, J. C., Freeman, P. W. M. and Woodward, A. (2000), *Cadbury Castle Somerset. The later prehistoric and early historic archaeology*, London, English Heritage.
Bedwin, O. (1979), 'Excavations at Harting Beacon, West Sussex; second season 1977', *SxAC*, 116: 225–40.
——(1980), 'Excavations at Chanctonbury Ring, Wiston, West Sussex, 1977', *Britannia*, 11: 173–222.
Bell, E. W. (1893), 'Notes on the British fort on Castle Law, at Forgandenny, Perthshire, partially excavated during the summer of 1892–3', *PSAS*, new series 3: 14–22.
Bellwood, P. (1971), 'Fortifications and Economy in Prehistoric New Zealand', *PPS*, 37: 56–95.
——(1972), 'Excavations at Otakanini Pa, South Kaipara Harbour', *JRSNZ*, 2, 3: 259–91.
Berger, L., Brianza, M., Gutzwiller, P., Joos, M. and Rentzel, P. (1996), *Sondierungen auf dem Wittnauer Horn, 1980–1982*, Basler Beiträge zur Ur- und Frühgeschichte, Bd 14, Basel, Habegger.
Bernelle, A. (ed.) (1992), *Decantations: A Tribute to Maurice Craig*, Dublin, Lilliput Press.
Bersu, G. (1940), 'Excavations at Little Woodbury, Wiltshire, part 1', *PPS*, 6: 30–111.
——(1945), *Das Wittnauer Horn im Kanton Aargau*, Monographien zur Ur- und Frühgeschichte der Schweiz, Bd IV, Basel, Birkhäuser.
——(1977), *Three Iron Age Round Houses in the Isle of Man*, (ed.) Radford, C. A. R., Douglas, Manx Museum and National Trust.
Best, E. (1952), *The Maori as he was, a brief account of Maori life as it was in pre-European days*, Wellington, 3rd impression, R. Owen, Government Printer.
Bevan, B. (ed.) (1999a), *Northern Exposure: interpretative devolution and the Iron Ages in Britain*, Leicester, Leicester University Monograph 4.
——(1999b), 'Land–Life–Death–Regeneration: interpreting a middle Iron Age landscape in eastern Yorkshire', in Bevan, B. (ed.) 1999a: 123–48.
Birch, J. (2010), 'Coalescence and Conflict in Iroquoian Ontario', *ARC*, 25: 13–28.
Blagg, T. F. C., Jones, R. and Keay, S., (eds) (1984), *Papers in Iberian Archaeology*, Oxford, BAR, International Series, 193 (1).

Bond, D. (1988), *Excavation at the North Ring, Mucking, Essex: A Late Bronze Age Enclosure*, Chelmsford, East Anglian Archaeology Reports 43.
Bowden, M. (1991), *Pitt Rivers, the life and archaeological work of Lieutenant-General Augustus Henry Lane Fox Pitt Rivers*, Cambridge, Cambridge University Press.
Bowden, M., Mackay, D. and Blood, N. K. (1989), 'A new survey of Ingleborough hillfort, North Yorkshire', *PPS*, 55: 267–72.
—— and McOmish, D. (1987), 'The required barrier', *SAR*, 4, 2: 76–84.
—— —— (1989), 'Little boxes. More about hillforts', *SAR*, 6, 1: 12–15.
Bradley, R. (1971), 'Economic Change in the Growth of Early Hill-forts', in Hill, D. and Jesson, M. (eds), 1971: 71–84.
——(2005), *Ritual and Domestic Life in Prehistoric Europe*, London, Routledge.
—— and Ellison, A. (1975), *Rams Hill: a Bronze Age Defended Enclosure and its Landscape*, Oxford, BAR British Series 19.
Brassil, K., Guilbert, G., Livens, R., Stead, W. and Bevan-Evans, M. (1982), 'Rescue Excavations at Moel Hiraddug between 1960 and 1980', *JFHS*, 30, 1981–82: 13–88.
Brewster, T. C. M. (1963), *The Excavation of Staple Howe*, Malton, East Riding Archaeological Research Committee.
Brown, I. (2009), *Beacons in the Landscape: The Hillforts of England and Wales*, Oxford, Windgather Press.
Brown, J. (1995), *Traditional Metalworking in Kenya*, Oxford, Oxbow Monograph 44.
Brown, L. (1984), 'Objects of stone', in Cunliffe, B., 1984b: 407–25.
Bruford, A. (1994), 'Why an Ulster Cycle?' in Mallory, J. P. and Stockman, G. (eds), 1994: 23–30.
Brunaux, J.-L. (1988), *The Celtic Gauls: Gods, Rites and Sanctuaries*, London, Seaby.
—— Meniel, P. and Poplin, F. (1985), *Gournay I, les fouilles sur le sanctuaire et l'oppidum (1975–1984)*, Amiens, Revue archéologique de Picardie supplement.
—— and Rapin, A. 1994. *Gournay II: Boucliers et lances, depots et trophées*, Paris, Éditions Errance.
Bryant, S. (2007), 'Central places or special places? The origins and development of "*oppida*" in Hertfordshire', in Haselgrove, C. and Moore, T. (eds), 2007a: 62–80.
—— and Niblett, R. (1997), 'The late Iron Age in Hertfordshire and the north Chilterns', in Gwilt, A. and Haselgrove, C. (eds), 1997: 270–81.
Buckley, D. and Hedges, J. (1987), *The Bronze Age and Saxon Settlements at Springfield Lyons, Essex: an Interim Report*, Chelmsford, Essex County Council Occasional Paper 5.
Bulleid, A. and Gray, H. St G. (1917), *The Glastonbury Lake Village, a full description of the excavations and the relics discovered 1892–1907, Vol. II*, Glastonbury, Glastonbury Antiquarian Society.
Burgess, C. (Christopher), Topping, P. and Lynch, F. (eds) (2007), *Beyond Stonehenge: Essays on the Bronze Age in Honour of Colin Burgess*, Oxford, Oxbow Books.
Burgess, C. (Colin), Topping, P., Mordant, C. and Maddison, M. (eds) (1988), *Enclosures and Defences in the Neolithic of Western Europe*, Oxford, BAR International Series, 403.
Burstow, G. P. and Holleyman, G. A. (1964), 'Excavations at Ranscombe Camp, 1959–60', *SxAC*, 102: 55–67.

Campbell, E. (1999), *Saints and Sea-kings, the First Kingdom of the Scots*, Edinburgh, Canongate/Historic Scotland.
——(2007), *Continental and Mediterranean Imports to Atlantic Britain and Ireland, AD 400–800*, London, CBA.
Carman, J. and Harding, A. (eds) (1999), *Ancient Warfare: Archaeological Perspectives*, Stroud, Sutton.
Carr, G. and Knüsel, C. (1997), 'The ritual framework of excarnation by exposure as the mortuary practice of the early and middle Iron Ages of central southern Britain', in Gwilt, A. and Haselgrove, C. (eds), 1997: 167–73.
Carter, S. P., McCullagh, R. and MacSween, A. (1995), 'The Iron Age in Shetland: excavations at five sites threatened by coastal erosion', *PSAS*, 125: 429–83.
Case, H. J. and Kirk, J. (1951), 'Archaeological Notes 1951', *Oxoniensia*, 16: 79–90.
Casey, J. (2000), 'The Roman coins', in Barrett, J. *et al.* (eds), 2000: 252–3.
Caulfield, S. (1981), 'Some Celtic problems in the Irish Iron Age', in Ó Corráin, D. (ed.), 1981: 205–15.
Chadwick, S. E. and Thompson, M. W. (1956), 'Notes on an Iron Age habitation site near Battlesbury Camp, Warminster', *WAM*, 56: 262–4.
Challis, A. (1978), *Motueka, An Archaeological Survey*, New Zealand Archaeological Association Monograph 7, Auckland, Longman Paul.
——and Harding, D. W. (1975), *Later Prehistory from the Trent to the Tyne*, 2 vols, Oxford, BAR British Series 20.
Chalmers, G. (1807), *Caledonia, An Account, Historical and Topographical, of North Britain from the most ancient to the present times*, London, Cadell and Davies, Edinburgh, Constable.
Champion, S. (1971), 'Excavations at Leckhampton Hill, 1969–70 Interim Report', *TBGAS*, 90: 5–21.
——(1976), 'Leckhampton Hill, Gloucestershire, 1925 and 1970', in Harding, D. W. (ed.), 1976a: 177–91.
Champion, T. C. and Collis, J. R. (eds) (1996), *The Iron Age in Britain and Ireland: Recent Trends*, Sheffield, J. R. Collis Publications/University of Sheffield.
Childe, V. G. (1935a), *The Prehistory of Scotland*, London, Kegan Paul.
——(1935b), 'Excavation of the vitrified fort at Finavon, Angus', *PSAS*, 69, 1934–5: 49–80.
——(1936), 'Supplementary excavations at the vitrified fort of Finavon, Angus', *PSAS*, 70, 1935–6: 347–52.
——(1946), *Scotland before the Scots*, London, Methuen.
——and Thorneycroft, W. (1938a), 'The vitrified fort of Rahoy, Morvern, Argyll', *PSAS*, 72, 1937–8: 23–43.
—— ——(1938b), 'The experimental production of the phenomenon distinctive of vitrified forts', *PSAS*, 72, 1937–8: 44–55.
Christison, D. (1898), *Early Fortifications in Scotland: Motes, Camps and Forts*, Edinburgh and London, Blackwood.
——(1900), 'The Forts, "Camps" and other Field-works of Perth, Forfar and Kincardine', *PSAS*, 34, 1899–1900: 43–120.
——and Anderson, J. (1899), 'On the Recently Excavated Fort on Castle Law, Abernethy, Perthshire', *PSAS*, 33, 1898–99: 13–33.

Church, M. et al. (forthcoming), 'Sea, stone and security: survey and excavation of a Late Bronze Age/Early Iron Age promontory enclosure at Gob Eirer, Lewis, Western Isles of Scotland', *PSAS* forthcoming.

Clapperton, H. (1829), *Journal of a Second Expedition into the Interior of Africa from the Bight of Benin to Soccatoo*, London, J. Murray.

Clarke, D. (ed.) (1968), *Analytical Archaeology*, London, Methuen.

——(ed.) (1972a), *Models in Archaeology*, London, Methuen.

——(1972b), 'A provisional model of an Iron Age Society and its Settlement System', in Clarke, D. (ed.) (1972a): 801–70.

Close-Brooks, J. (1986), 'Excavations at Clatchard Craig, Fife', *PSAS*, 116: 117–84.

Coblenz, W. (1970), 'Zur Frage der befestigten Siedlungen der Lausitzer Kultur', in Filip, J. (ed.), 1970: 715–19.

Coles, J. (1962), 'European Bronze Age Shields,' *PPS*, 28: 156–90.

——and Minnitt, S. (1995), *'Industrious and fairly civilized', the Glastonbury Lake Village*, Taunton, Somerset County Museum Service.

Collingwood, R. G. (1938), 'The hill-fort on Carrock Fell', *TCWAS*, 38: 32–41.

Collins, A. E. P. (1947), 'Excavations on Blewburton Hill, 1947', *BAJ*, 50: 4–29.

——(1953), 'Excavations on Blewburton Hill, 1948 and 1949', *BAJ*, 53: 21–64.

——and Collins, F. J. (1959), 'Excavations on Blewburton Hill, 1953', *BAJ*, 57: 52–73.

Collis, J. (1977a), *The Iron Age in Britain, a review*, Sheffield, University of Sheffield Department of Prehistory and Archaeology.

——(1977b), 'An Approach to the Iron Age', in Collis, J. (ed.), 1977a: 1–7.

——(1981), 'A theoretical study of hill-forts', in Guilbert, G. (ed.), 1981a: 66–77.

——(1996), 'Hill-forts, enclosures and boundaries', in Champion, T. C. and Collis, J. R. (eds), 1996: 87–94.

——(2003), *The Celts, Origins, Myths, Inventions*, Stroud, Tempus.

Connah, G. (1975), *The Archaeology of Benin*, Oxford, Oxford University Press.

——(2000), 'Contained communities in tropical Africa', in Tracy, J. (ed.), 2000: 19–45.

——(2001), *African Civilizations: an archaeological perspective*, 2nd edition, Cambridge, Cambridge University Press.

Connolly, A. (1994), 'Saddle quern stones', *UJA*, 57: 26–36.

Cook, M. (2010), 'New light on oblong forts: excavations at Dunnideer, Aberdeenshire', *PSAS*, 140: 79–92.

——(forthcoming), 'The Hillforts of Strathdon', *PSAS*, forthcoming.

Coombes, D. G. and Thompson, F. H. (1979), 'Excavation of the Hill Fort of Mam Tor, Derbyshire, 1965–69', *Derbyshire Archaeological Journal*, 99: 7–51.

Cooney, G., Becker, K., Coles, J., Ryan, M. and Sievers, S. (eds) (2009), *Relics of Old Decency: archaeological studies in later prehistory, Festschrift for Barry Raftery*, Dublin, Wordwell.

Copeland, T. (1988), 'The north Oxfordshire Grim's Ditch; a fieldwork survey', *Oxoniensia*, 53: 277–92.

Cotter, C. (1993), 'Western Stone Fort Project, Interim Report', *Discovery Programme Reports: 1, Project Results 1992*, Dublin, Royal Irish Academy: 1–19.

——(1995), 'Western Stone Fort Project, Interim Report', *Discovery Programme Reports: 2, Project Results 1993*, Dublin, Royal Irish Academy: 1–11.

——(1996), 'Western Stone Fort Project, Interim Report', *Discovery Programme Reports, 4: Project Results and Reports 1994*, Dublin, Royal Irish Academy: 1–14.
——(1999), 'Western Stone Forts Project', *Discovery Programme Reports: 5* (Cahercommaun), Dublin, Royal Irish Academy: 41–96.
Cotton, M. A. (1954), 'British camps with timber-laced ramparts', *Arch. J.*, 111: 26–105.
——(1957), '*Muri Gallici*', in Wheeler, R. E. M. and Richardson, K. M., 1957: 159–216.
——and Frere, S. S. (1968), 'Ivinghoe Beacon Excavations, 1963-5', *Records of Buckinghamshire*, 18: 187–260.
Cowen, J. D. (1967), 'The Hallstatt Sword of Bronze: on the Continent and in Britain', *PPS*, 33: 377–454.
Crawford, O. G. S. (1930), 'Grim's Ditch in Wychwood, Oxon', *Antiquity*, 4: 303–15.
——and Keiller, A. (1928), *Wessex from the Air*, Oxford, Oxford University Press.
Crew, P. (1984), 'Bryn y Castell', *Archaeology in Wales*, 24: 37–43.
——(1986), 'Excavations at Bryn y Castell hillfort, Gwynedd, North Wales: a late prehistoric iron-working settlement', in Scott, B. and Cleere, H. (eds), 1986: 91–100.
——(1989), 'Excavations at Crawcwellt West, Merioneth, 1986–1989. A late prehistoric upland iron-working settlement', *Archaeology in Wales*, 29: 11–16.
——(1994), 'Les lingots der fer en Grande Bretagne: typologie et fonction', in Mangin, M. (ed.), 1994: 345–50.
——(1995), 'Aspects of the iron supply', in Cunliffe, B., 1995: 276–84.
Crone, A. (2000), *The History of a Scottish Lowland Crannog: Excavations at Buiston, Ayrshire 1989–90*, Edinburgh, STAR Monograph, 4.
Cruickshank, G. (1991), *The battle of Dunnichen: an account of the Pictish victory at the Battle of Dunnichen, also known as Nechtansmere, fought on the 20th May 685*, Balgavies, Pinkfoot Press.
Crummy, P. (2007), 'Did Julius Caesar storm Camulodunon?', *CA*, 208: 8–16.
——Benfield, S., Crummy, N., Rigby, V. and Shimmin, D. (2007), *Stanway, an elite burial site at Camulodunum*, London, Society for the Promotion of Roman Studies.
Cunliffe, B. (1971), 'Some aspects of hill-forts and their cultural environment', in Hill, D. and Jesson, M. (eds), 1971: 53–69.
——(1974), *Iron Age Communities in Britain*, 1st edition, London, Routledge and Kegan Paul.
——(1976a), *Iron Age Sites in Central Southern England*, London, CBA Research Report 16.
——(1976b), 'The Origins of Urbanisation in Britain', in Cunliffe, B. and Rowley, T. (eds), 1976: 135–62.
——(1983), *Danebury: Anatomy of an Iron Age Hillfort*, London, Batsford.
——(1984a), *Danebury: An Iron Age Hillfort in Hampshire. Vol. 1: The Excavations, 1969–78: the Site*, London, CBA Research Report 52.
——(1984b), *Danebury: An Iron Age Hillfort in Hampshire. Vol. 2: The Excavations, 1969–78: the Finds*, London, CBA Research Report 52.
——(1995), *Danebury, an Iron Age hillfort in Hampshire, Volume 6, A hillfort community in perspective*, London, CBA Research Report 102.

Cunliffe, B. W. (2000), *The Danebury Environs Programme, The Prehistory of a Wessex Landscape, Vol. 1, Introduction*, Oxford, English Heritage and Oxford University Committee for Archaeology.

—— (2005), *Iron Age Communities in Britain*, 4th edn., Abingdon, Routledge.

—— (2006), 'Understanding hillforts: have we progressed?' in Payne, A. *et al.*, 2006: 151–62.

—— and Miles, D. (eds) (1984), *Aspects of the Iron Age in Central Southern Britain*, Oxford, Oxford Committee for Archaeology.

—— and Poole, C. (1991a), *Danebury: An Iron Age Hillfort in Hampshire. Vol. 4: The Excavations, 1979–88: the site*, London, CBA Research Report 73.

—— —— (1991b), *Danebury: An Iron Age Hillfort in Hampshire. Vol. 5: The Excavations, 1979–88: the finds*, London, CBA Research Report 73.

—— and Rowley, T. (eds) (1976), *Oppida in Barbarian Europe*, Oxford, BAR Supplementary Series, 11.

Cunnington, M. E. (1924), 'Pits in Battlesbury Camp', *WAM*, 42: 368–73.

—— (1933), 'Excavations at Yarnbury Castle', *WAM*, 46: 198–221.

Curwen, E. C. (1932), 'Excavations at Hollingbury Camp, Sussex', *Ant. J.*, 12: 1–16.

Darling, P. (1984), *Archaeology and History of Southern Nigeria: the ancient earthworks of Benin and Ishan*, Oxford, BAR International Series 215.

Davidson, J. (1987), *The Prehistory of New Zealand*, 2nd edition, Auckland, Longman Paul.

Davis, O., Sharples, N. and Waddington, K. (2008), *Changing Perspectives on the First Millennium BC: Proceedings of the Iron Age research Student Seminar 2006*, Oxford, Oxbow Books.

Deberge, Y., Cabezuelo, U., Cabanio, M., Fouercas, S., Garcia, M., Gruel, K., Loughton, M., Blondel, F. and Caillat, P., (2009), 'L'opppidum arverne de Gondole (Le Cendre, Puy-de-Dôme). Topographie de l'occupation protohistorique (La Tène D2) et fouille du quartier artisanal: un premier bilan', *RAC*, 48: 1–251.

Diepeveen-Jansen, M. (2007), 'Early La Tène burial practices and social (re)construction in the Marne-Moselle region', in Haselgrove, C. and Pope, R. (eds), 2007: 374–89.

Dixon, P. (1976), 'Crickley Hill 1969–72', in Harding, D. W. (ed.), 1976a: 162–76.

—— (1988), 'The Neolithic Settlements on Crickley Hill', in Burgess, C. *et al.* (eds), 1988: 75–87.

—— (1994), *Crickley Hill volume 1. The Hillfort Defences*, Nottingham, Crickley Hill Trust and Department of Archaeology, University of Nottingham.

—— and Borne, P. (1977), *Crickley Hill and Gloucestershire Prehistory*, Gloucester, Crickley Hill Trust.

Dockrill, S. (2002), 'Brochs, economy and power', in Smith, B. B. and Banks, I. (eds), 2002: 153–62.

Dowling, G. (2006), 'The liminal boundary: an analysis of the sacred potency of the ditch at Ráith na Ríg, Tara, Co. Meath', *JIA*, 15: 15–37.

Downes, J. (1997), The shrine at South Cadbury Castle: belief enshrined?', in Gwilt, A. and Haselgrove, C. (eds), 1997: 145–52.

Driver, T. (2007), 'Hillforts and human movement: unlocking the Iron Age landscapes of mid Wales', in Fleming, A. and Hingley, R. (eds), 2007: 83–100.

Dunwell, A. (2007), *Cist burials and a palisaded settlement at Dryburn Bridge, Innerwick, East Lothian*, Edinburgh, SAIR 24.

Dunwell, A. and Strachan, R. (2007), *Excavations at Brown Caterthun and White Caterthun hillforts, Angus, 1995–1997*, Tayside and Fife Archaeological Committee Monographs 5.

Dymond, C. W. (1902), *Worlebury, an ancient stronghold in the county of Somerset*, Bristol, Crofton Hemmons.

Eagles, B. N. (1991), 'A new survey of the hillfort on Beacon Hill, Burghclere, Hampshire', *Arch. J.*, 148: 98–103.

Edwards, K. and Ralston, I. (eds) (1997), *Scotland: Environment and Archaeology, 8000BC–AD1000*, Chichester, John Wiley.

Eggert, M. (1989), 'Die "Fürstensitze" der Späthallstattzeit: Bemerkungen zu einem archäologischen Konstrukt', *Hammaburg*, NF 9: 53–66.

Ellis, C. and Powell, A. B. (2008), *An Iron Age Settlement outside Battlesbury Hillfort, Warminster, and Sites along the Southern Range Road*, Salisbury, Wessex Archaeology Report 22.

——and Rawlings, M. (2001), 'Excavations at Balksbury Camp, Andover, 1995–97', *HFC*, 56: 21–94.

Ellison, A. and Drewett, P. (1971), 'Pits and post-holes in the British early Iron Age: some alternative explanations', *PPS*, 37: 183–94.

Engelbrecht, W. (2003/2005), *Iroquoia: the Development of a Native World*, New York, Syracuse University Press.

Eogan, G. (1983), *The Hoards of the Irish Later Bronze Age*, Dublin, University College.

Erdrich, M., Giannotta, K. and Hanson, W. (2000), 'Traprain Law: native and Roman on the northern frontier', *PSAS*, 130: 441–56.

Fairhurst, H. (1939), 'The galleried dun at Kildonan Bay, Kintyre', *PSAS*, 73, 1938–9: 185–228.

Feachem, R. W. (1955), 'Fortifications', in Wainwright, F. T. (ed.), 1955: 66–86.

——(1956), 'The Fortifications on Traprain Law', *PSAS*, 89: 284–9.

——(1960), 'The Palisaded Settlements at Harehope, Peeblesshire. Excavations, 1960', *PSAS*, 93, 1959–60: 174–91.

——(1966), 'The Hill-Forts of Northern Britain', in Rivet, A. L. F. (ed.), 1966: 59–88.

——(1971), 'Unfinished hill-forts', in Hill, D. and Jesson, M. (eds), 1971: 19–39.

Fenton, W. (1978), 'Northern Iroquoian Culture Patterns', in Trigger, B. (ed.), 1978a: 296–321.

Fichtl, S. (2000), *La Ville Celtique, Les oppida de 150 av. J.-C. à 15 ap. J.-C.*, Paris, Éditions Errance.

Filip, J. (ed.), (1970), *Actes du VIIe Congrés International des Sciences Préhistoriques et Protohistoriques, Prague 21–27 Août 1966*, Prague, Académie Tchécoslovaque des Sciences.

Finney, J. B. (2006), *Middle Iron Age Warfare in the Hillfort dominated Zone, c. 400 BC–c. 150 BC*, Oxford, BAR British Series 423.

Fischer, F. (1982), *Der Heidengraben bei Grabenstetten, ein keltisches Oppidum auf der Schwäbischen Alb bei Urach*, Stuttgart, Konrad Theiss.

Fisher, A. R. (1985), 'Winklebury Hillfort: a study of artefact distribution from subsoil features', *PPS*, 51: 167–80.

Fitts, R. L., Haselgrove, C. C., Lowther, P.C. and Willis, S. H. (1999), 'Melsonby revisited: survey and excavation 1992–1995 at the site of the "Stanwick", North Yorkshire hoard of 1843', *Durham Archaeological Journal*, 14–15: 1–52.

Fitzpatrick, A. (1984), 'The Deposition of La Tène Iron Age Metalwork in Watery Contexts in Southern England', in Cunliffe, B. and Miles, (eds), 1984: 178–90.

——(1997), *Archaeological Excavations on the Route of the A27 Westhampnett Bypass, West Sussex, 1992. Vol. 2: The Late Iron Age, Romano-British and Anglo-Saxon Cemeteries*, Salisbury, Wessex Archaeology Report 12.

Fitzpatrick, E. (2009), 'Native Enclosed Settlement and the Problem of the Irish "Ringfort"', *MA*, 53: 271–306.

Fleming, A. and Hingley, R. (eds) (2007), *Prehistoric and Roman Landscapes, Landscape History after Hoskins*, Vol. 1, Oxford, Windgather Press.

Fojut, N. (1982), 'Towards a Geography of Shetland Brochs', *GAJ*, 9: 38–59.

——(1993), *A Guide to Prehistoric and Viking Shetland*, Lerwick, Shetland Times.

——(1998), 'How did we get here? Shetland studies to 1995', in Nicholson, S. and Dockrill, S. (eds), 1998: 1–41.

——(2005), 'Any closer towards a geography of Shetland brochs?' in Turner, V. *et al.* (eds), 2005: 166–71.

Forde-Johnston, J. (1976), *Hillforts of the Iron Age in England and Wales, a survey of the surface evidence*, Liverpool, Liverpool University Press.

Foster, S. and Smout, T. C. (1994), *The History of Soils and Field Systems*, Aberdeen, Scottish Cultural Press.

Fowler, P. (1960), 'Excavations at Madmarston Camp, Swalcliffe, 1957–58', *Oxoniensia*, 25: 3–48.

Fox, A. (1952), 'Hill-slope forts and related earthworks in South-West England and South Wales', *Arch. J.*, 109: 1–22.

——(1961), 'South-Western Hill-Forts', in Frere, S. S. (ed.), 1961: 35–60.

——(1976), *Prehistoric Maori Fortifications in the North Island of New Zealand*, Auckland, Longman Paul.

——(1978), *Tiromoana Pa, Te Awanga, Hawkes Bay. Excavations 1974–75*, Otago, Otago University Studies in Prehistoric Anthropology 11/New Zealand Archaeological Association Monograph 8.

Fox, C. (1932/38), *The Personality of Britain*, Cardiff, National Museum of Wales.

Frankenstein, S. and Rowlands, M. (1978), 'The Internal Structure and Regional Context of Early Iron Age Society in Southwest Germany', *BLUIA*, 15: 73–112.

Fraser, J. (2002), *The Battle of Dunnichen 685*, Stroud, Tempus.

Frere, S. S. (ed.) (1961), *Problems of the Iron Age in Southern Britain*, University of London Institute of Archaeology Occasional Paper No. 11, London.

——(1967), *Britannia, a History of Roman Britain*, London, Routledge and Kegan Paul, Pimlico edition 1998.

——(1987), 'Brandon Camp, Herefordshire', *Britannia*, 18: 49–92.

Frey, O.-H. (1998), 'The Stone Knight, the Sphinx and the Hare: New Aspects of Early Figural Art', *PPS*, 64: 1–14.

——and Hermann, F.-R. (1997), 'Ein Frühkeltischer Fürstengrabhügel am Glauberg im Wetteraukreis, Hessen. Bericht über die Forschungen 1994–1996', *Germania*, 75: 459–550.

Friell, J. and Watson, W. (eds) (1984), *Pictish Studies: Settlement, Burial and Art in Dark Age North Britain*, Oxford, BAR, British Series 125.

Frodsham, P. (2004), *Archaeology in Northumberland National Park*, York, CBA Research Report 136.

——Hedley, I. and Young, R. (2007), 'Putting the neighbours in their place? Displays of position and possession in northern Cheviot "hillfort" design', in Haselgrove, C. and Moore, T. (eds), 2007a: 250–65.

——and O'Brien, C. (eds) (2005), *Yeavering: People, Power and Place*, Stroud, Tempus.

——Topping, P. and Cowley, D. (eds) (1999), *We were always chasing time. Papers presented to Keith Blood. Northern Archaeology*, 17/18, Newcastle upon Tyne, Northern Archaeology Group.

Fulford, M. (1987), '*Calleva Atrebatum*: An Interim Report on the Excavation of the Oppidum, 1980–86', *PPS*, 53: 271–8.

——and Clarke, A. (2011), 'Silchester; how it all began', *CA*, 250: 12–19.

——and Timby, J. (2000), *Late Iron Age and Roman Silchester: Excavations on the Site of the Forum-Basilica 1977, 1980–6*, London, Society for the Promotion of Roman Studies, Britannia Monograph 15.

Gannon, A. R. (1999), 'Challenging the past: the resurvey of Braidwood hillfort', in Frodsham, P. *et al.* (eds), 1999: 105–12.

Gardner, W. and Savory, H. N. (1964), *Dinorben, A Hill-fort occupied in Early Iron Age and Roman times*, Cardiff, National Museum of Wales.

Geddes, G. and Hale, A. (2010), *The Archaeological Landscape of Bute*, Edinburgh, RCAHMS.

Gersbach, E. (1995), *Baubefunde der Perioden IVc–IVa der Heuneburg*, Heuneburg-studien IX, RGF Band 53, Mainz, von Zabern.

Ghey, E., Edwards, N., Johnston, R. and Pope, R. (2007), *Characterising the Welsh Roundhouse: Chronology, Inhabitation and Landscape*, York, Internet Archaeology 23.

Gibson, D. B. and Geselowitz, M. (eds) (1988), *Tribe and Polity in Late Prehistoric Europe*, New York, Plenum Press.

Giles, M. (2007), 'Reconfiguring rights in the Early Iron Age landscapes of East Yorkshire', in Haselgrove, C. and Pope, R. (eds), 2007: 103–18.

Gillies, W. and Harding, D. W. (eds) (2005), *Celtic Connections. Papers from the Tenth International Congress of Celtic Studies, Edinburgh, 1995, Volume Two, Archaeology, Numismatics, Historical Linguistics*, Edinburgh, University of Edinburgh Archaeology Mon. Ser. 2.

Gilmour, S. M. G. (2000), *Later Prehistoric and Early Historic Settlement Archaeology of the Atlantic Seaways*, Edinburgh, University of Edinburgh Ph.D. Thesis.

Gordon, A. (1940), 'The excavation at Gurnard's Head, an Iron Age cliff castle in western Cornwall', *Arch. J.*, 97: 96–111.

Gosden, C. (1989), 'Debt, production and prehistory', *JAA*, 8: 355–87.

——(1998), 'Prehistoric Histories', *WA*, 30 (1): 1–12.

——and Lock, G. (2003), 'Becoming Roman on the Berkshire Downs: the evidence from Alfred's Castle', *Britannia*, 34: 65–80.

Grant, A. (1984), 'Animal Husbandry', in Cunliffe, B., 1984b: 496–548.

——(1991), 'Animal husbandry', in Cunliffe, B. and Poole, C., 1991b: 447–87.

Gray, H. St G. (1917), 'Objects of baked clay', in Bulleid, A. and Gray, H. St G., 1917: 558–81.
——(1925), 'Excavations at Ham Hill, south Somerset (part 1)', *PSANHS*, 70: 104–16.
——(1926), 'Excavations at Ham Hill, south Somerset (part 2)', *PSANHS*, 71: 57–76.
——(1927), 'Excavations at Ham Hill, south Somerset (part 3)', *PSANHS*, 72: 55–68.
——and Cotton, M. A. (1966), *The Meare Lake Village, a full description of the excavations and relics from the eastern half of the west village, 1910–1933*, Vol. III, Taunton Castle, printed privately.
Green, R. (1978), 'Dating the Kauri Point sequence', *HR*, 26, 1: 32–45.
——and Kelly, M. (eds) (1970), *Studies in Oceanic Culture History*, 1, Pacific Anthropological Records 11, Honolulu, Bishop Museum.
Gresham, C. (1939), 'Spettisbury Rings, Dorset', *Arch. J.*, 96, 1: 114–30.
Griffiths, W. E. and Hogg, A. H. A. (1956), 'The Hill-Fort on Conway mountain, Caernarvonshire', *Arch. Camb.*, 105, 1–2: 49–80.
Grimes, W. (1944), 'Excavations at Stanton Harcourt, Oxon, 1940', *Oxoniensia*, 8–9, 1943–4: 19–63.
——(1961), 'Some Smaller Settlements: A Symposium', in Frere, S. S. (ed.), 1961: 17–34.
——and Close-Brooks, J. (1993), 'The excavation at Caesar's Camp, Heathrow, Harmondsworth, Middlesex, 1944', *PPS*, 59:303–60.
Grogan, E. (1995), 'Excavations at Mooghaun South, 1993', *Discovery Programme Reports: 2 Project Results 1993*, Dublin, Royal Irish Academy, 57–61.
——(1996), 'Excavations at Mooghaun South, 1994', *Discovery Programme Reports: 4 Project Results and Reports 1994*, Dubin, Royal Irish Academy, 47–57.
——(2005a), *The North Munster Project, Vol. 1. The later prehistoric landscape of south-east Clare*, Discovery Programme Monograph No. 5, Bray, Wordwell.
——(2005b), *The North Munster Project, Vol. 2. The prehistoric landscape of North Munster*, Discovery Programme Monograph No. 6, Bray, Wordwell.
——(2008), *The Rath of the Synods, Tara, Co. Meath: excavations by Seán P. Ó Ríordáin*, UCD School of Archaeology, Dublin, Wordwell.
Groube, L. (1964), *Settlement Patterns in Prehistoric New Zealand*, MA thesis, Departmemt of Anthropology, University of Auckland, Auckland, New Zealand.
——(1970), 'The origins and development of earthwork fortifications in the Pacific', in Green, R. and Kelly, M. (eds), 1970: 133–64.
Guichard, V., Sievers, S. and Urban, O.-H. (eds) (2000), *Les processus d'urbanisation à l'âge du Fer*, Gluxe-en-Glenne, Collection Bibracte 4.
Guilbert, G. (1975a), 'Moel y Gaer, 1973: an area excavation on the defences', *Antiquity*, 49: 109–17.
——(1975b), 'Planned Hillfort Interiors', *PPS*, 41, 203–21.
——(1976), 'Moel y Gaer (Rhosesmor) 1972–1973: An Area Excavation of the Interior', in Harding, D. W. (ed.) 1976a: 303–18.
——(1979a), 'Dinorben 1977–8', *CA*, No. 65: 182–8.
——(1979b), 'The Guard-chamber Gateways at Dinorben and Moel Hiraddug Hillforts, and the Problem of Dating the Type in North Wales', *BBCS*, 28, Pt. 3: 516–20.
——(1980), 'Dinorben C14 dates', *CA*, No. 70: 336–8.
——ed. (1981a), *Hill-Fort Studies, Essays for A. H. A. Hogg*, Leicester, Leicester University Press.

——(1981b), 'Hill-fort functions and populations: a sceptical viewpoint', in Guilbert, G. (ed.), 1981a: 104–21.
Gwilt, A. and Haselgrove, C. (eds) (1997), *Reconstructing Iron Age Societies*, Oxford, Oxbow Monograph 71.
Halliday, S. P. (1982), 'Later prehistoric farming in south-east Scotland', in Harding, D. W. (ed.), 1982: 57–91.
——(1985), 'Unenclosed upland settlement in the east and south-east of Scotland', in Spratt, D. and Burgess, C. B. (eds), 1985: 231–51.
——(1993), 'Marginal agriculture in Scotland', in Smout, T. C. (ed.) 1993: 64–78.
Hamilton, J. R. C. (1968), *Excavations at Clickhimin, Shetland*, Edinburgh, HMSO.
Hamilton, S. and Manley, J. (2001), 'Hillforts, monumentality and place: a chronological and topographical review of first millennium BC hillforts in southeast England', *EJA*, 4: 7–42.
Hamilton-Dyer, S. and Maltby, M. (2000), 'The animal bones from a sample of Iron Age contexts', in Barrett, J. *et al.*, 2000: 278–91.
Hanson, W. (ed.) (2009), *The Army and Frontiers of Rome, Papers offered to David J. Breeze*, JRA Supp. Ser. 74, Portsmouth, R.I.
Harbison, P. (1968), 'Castros with *Chevaux-de-frise* in Spain and Portugal', *Madrider Mitteilungen*, 9: 116–47.
——(1971), 'Wooden and stone *Chevaux-de-frise* in Central and Western Europe', *PPS*, 37: 195–225.
Harcourt, R. (1979), 'The Animal Bones', in Wainwright, G., 1979: 150–60.
Harding, A. (1987), *Henge Monuments and Related Sites of Great Britain: airphotographic evidence and catalogue*, Oxford, BAR British Series 175.
——(2006), 'Enclosing and excluding in Bronze Age Europe', in Harding, A. *et al.* (eds), 2006: 97–115.
Harding, A. F., Sievers, S. and Venclová, N. (eds) (2006), *Enclosing the Past: inside and outside in prehistory*, Sheffield, J. R. Collis Publications.
Harding, D. W. (1972), *The Iron Age in the Upper Thames Basin*, Oxford, Clarendon Press.
——(1974), *The Iron Age in Lowland Britain*, London, Routledge and Kegan Paul.
——ed. (1976a), *Hillforts. Later Prehistoric Earthworks in Britain and Ireland*, London, Academic Press.
——(1976b), 'Blewburton Hill, Berkshire: Re-excavation and Re-appraisal', in Harding, D. W. (ed.), 1976a, 133–46.
——(1979), *Celts in Conflict: Hillfort Studies 1927–77*, Edinburgh, University of Edinburgh Department of Archaeology Occasional Paper No. 3.
——(ed.) (1982), *Later Prehistoric Settlement in South-East Scotland*, Edinburgh, University of Edinburgh, Department of Archaeology Occasional Paper, No. 8.
——(1984), 'The Function and Classification of Brochs and Duns', in Miket, R. and Burgess, C. (eds), 1984: 206–20.
——(1987), *Excavations in Oxfordshire, 1964–66*, University of Edinburgh Department of Archaeology Occasional Paper No. 15.
——(1997), 'Forts, brochs, duns and crannogs: Iron Age settlements in Argyll', in Ritchie, J. N. G. (ed.), 1997: 118–40.
——(2004a), *The Iron Age in Northern Britain: Celts and Romans, Natives and Invaders*, Abingdon, Routledge.

Harding, D. W. (2004b), 'Dunagoil, Bute, reinstated', *TBNHS*, 26: 1–19.
——(2007), *The Archaeology of Celtic Art*, Abingdon, Routledge.
——(2009), *The Iron Age Round-house: Later Prehistoric Building in Britain and Beyond*, Oxford, Oxford University Press.
——Blake, I. M. and Reynolds, P. J. (1993), *An Iron Age Settlement in Dorset: Excavation and Reconstruction*, Edinburgh, University of Edinburgh Department of Archaeology Monograph Series 1.
——and Gillies, W. (2005), 'Introduction: Archaeology and Celticity', in Gillies, W. and Harding, D. W. (eds), 2005: 1–14.
Härke, H. (1979), *Settlement Types and Patterns in the West Hallstatt Province*, Oxford, BAR International Series, 57.
Hart, J. and Brumbach, H. (2003), 'The Death of Owasco', *AAnt*, 68: 737–52.
Hartley, B. (1957), 'The Wandlebury Iron Age hill fort excavations of 1955–6', *PCAS*, 50: 1–28.
Hartnell, B. (1991), 'Recent Air Survey Results from Navan', *Emania*, 8: 1–9.
Haselgrove, C. (1995), 'Late Iron Age society in Britain and north-west Europe: structural transformation or superficial change?' in Arnold, B. and Blair Gibson, D. (eds), 1995: 81–7.
——(2000), 'The character of oppida in Iron Age Britain', in Guichard, V. *et al.*, 2000: 103–10.
——(2009), *The Traprain Law Environs Project, Fieldwork and Excavations 2000–2004*, Edinburgh, Society of Antiquaries of Scotland.
——Lowther, P. and Turnbull, P. (1990), 'Stanwick, North Yorkshire, Part 3: Excavations on earthworks sites 1981–86', *Arch. J.*, 147: 37–90.
——and Millett, M., (1997), 'Verulamion reconsidered', in Gwilt, A. and Haselgrove, C. (eds), 1997: 282–96.
——and Moore, T. (eds), (2007a), *The Later Iron Age in Britain and beyond*, Oxford, Oxbow Books.
—— ——(2007b), 'New narratives of the Later Iron Age', in Haselgrove, C. and Moore, T. (eds), 2007a: 1–15.
——and Pope, R. (eds) (2007), *The Earlier Iron Age in Britain and the near Continent*, Oxford, Oxbow Books.
——Turnbull, P. and Fitts, R. (1990), 'Stanwick, North Yorkshire, Part 1: Recent research and previous archaeological investigation', *Arch. J.*, 147: 1–15.
Hawkes, C. F. C. (1939), 'Excavations at Quarley Hill, 1938', *HFC*, XIV: 136–94.
——(1940), 'An iron torc from Spettisbury Rings, Dorset', *Arch. J.*, 97: 112–14.
——(1947), 'Britons, Romans and Saxons round Salisbury and in Cranborne Chase', *Arch. J.*, 104: 27–81.
——(1954), 'Archaeological theory and method: some suggestions from the Old World', *AAnth*, 56: 155–68.
——(1958), 'Escavações no Castro de Sabrosa (Abril de 1958)', *Revista de Guimarães*, 68, 3–4: 445–53.
——(1971), 'Fence, Wall, Dump, from Troy to Hod', in Hill, D. and Jesson, M. (eds), 1971: 5–18.
——(1976a), 'St Catharine's Hill, Winchester: the Report of 1930 Re-assessed', in Harding, D. W. (ed.), 1976a: 59–75.
——(1976b), 'Foreword and Summary', in Matthews, 1976: i–xiii.

——(1984), 'The castro culture of the peninsular North-West: fact and inference', in Blagg, T. F. C. et al. (eds), 1984: 187–203.

——and Crummy, P. (1995), *Colchester Archaeological Report 11: Camulodunum 2*, Colchester, Colchester Archaeological Trust/English Heritage.

——and Hull, M. R. (1947), *Camulodunum, First Report on the Excavations at Colchester 1930–1939*, London, SAL Research Report 14.

——Myres, J. N. L. and Stevens, C. G. (1930), *St Catharine's Hill, Winchester*, Winchester, Hampshire Field Club and Archaeological Society.

Hedges, R. and Salter, C. (1979), 'Source determination of iron currency bars through the analysis of slag inclusions', *Archaeometry*, 21: 616–75.

Heidenreich, C. (1978), 'Huron', in Trigger, B. (ed.), 1978a: 368–88.

Heider, K. (1979), *Grand Valley Dani: Peaceful Warriors*, New York, Holt, Reinhart and Winston.

Hencken, H. O'Neill (1938), *Cahercommaun, a stone fort in County Clare*, Dublin, Royal Society of Antiquaries of Ireland.

Hencken, T. C. (1938), 'The Excavation of the Iron Age Camp on Bredon Hill, Gloucestershire, 1935–1937', *Arch.J.*, 95: 1–111.

Henderson, G. and Henderson, I. (2004), *The Art of the Picts*, London, Thames and Hudson.

Hermann, F.-R. and Frey, O.-H. (1996), *Die Keltenfürsten vom Glauberg*, Wiesbaden, Archäologische Denkmäler in Hessen, 128/129.

Hey, G., Bayliss, A. and Boyle, A. (1999), 'Iron Age inhumation burials at Yarnton, Oxfordshire', *Antiquity*, 73: 551–62.

Hill, D. and Jesson, M. (eds) (1971), *The Iron Age and its Hill-forts, Papers presented to Sir Mortimer Wheeler*, Southampton, University of Southampton Department of Archaeology.

Hill, J. D. (1989), 'Rethinking the Iron Age', *SAR*, 6: 16–24.

——(1995a), *Ritual and Rubbish in the Iron Age of Wessex*, Oxford, BAR British Series 242.

——(1995b), 'How should we understand Iron Age societies and hillforts? A contextual study from Southern Britain', in Hill, J. D. and Cumberpatch, C. G. (eds), 1995: 45–66.

——(1996), 'Hill-forts and the Iron Age of Wessex', in Champion, T. C. and Collis, J. R. (eds), 1996: 95–116.

——and Cumberpatch, C. G. (eds) (1995), *Different Iron Ages; studies on the Iron Age in temperate Europe*, Oxford, BAR International Series, 602.

Hill, P. (1982a), 'Broxmouth Hill-fort excavations, 1977–78: an interim report', in Harding, D. W. (ed.), 1982: 141–88.

——(1982b), 'Settlement and chronology,' in Harding, D. W. (ed.), 1982: 4–43.

Hingley, R. (1980), 'Excavations by R. A. Rutland on an Iron Age Site at Wittenham Clumps', *BAJ*, 70, 1979–80: 21–55.

Hingley, R. (1990), 'Iron Age "currency bars": the archaeological and social context', *Arch.J*, 147: 91–117.

——Moore, H., Triscott, J. and Wilson, G. (1997), 'The excavation of two later Iron Age fortified homesteads at Aldclune, Blair Atholl, Perth & Kinross', *PSAS*, 127: 407–66.

Hogg, A. H. A. (1960), 'Garn Boduan and Tre'r Ceiri. Excavations at two Caernarvonshire Hill-forts', *Arch.J.*, 117: 1–39.
——(1971), 'Some Applications of Surface Fieldwork', in Hill, D. and Jesson, M. (eds), 1971: 105–25.
——(1972), 'Hill-forts in the coastal area of Wales', in Thomas, C. (ed.), 1972: 11–23.
——(1975), *Hill-Forts of Britain*, London, Hart-Davis, MacGibbon.
Holl, A. (1996), 'Genesis of central Chadic polities', in Pwiti, G. and Soper, R. (eds), 1996: 581–91.
Hooper, B. (1984), 'Anatomical considerations', in Cunliffe, B. W., 1984b: 463–73.
Hope-Taylor, B. (1980), 'Balbridie ... and Doon Hill', *CA*, 72: 18–19.
Hopewell, D. (1992), 'Tre'r Ceiri', *Archaeology in Wales*, 1992: 57.
——(1993), 'Tre'r Ceiri', *Archaeology in Wales*, 1993: 49–50.
——(1998), 'Tre'r Ceiri', *Archaeology in Wales*, 1998: 98.
Hughes, H. (1907), 'Report on the Excavations carried out at Tre'r Ceiri in 1906', *Arch. Camb.*, 7, 1–2: 38–62.
Hull, R. (1976), *African cities and towns before the European conquest*, New York, Norton.
Hunter, F. (1996), 'Recent Roman Iron Age finds from Fife and Tayside', *TFAJ*, 2: 113–25.
——(2009), 'Traprain Law and the Roman world', in Hanson, W. (ed.), 2009: 225–40.
IGS 1966. Map of Iron Age Monuments in Northern Britain drawn by I. G. Scott in Rivet, A. L. F. (ed.), 1966.
Ingrem, C. (2003), 'The Regional Context of the Animal Bones from Uffington Sites', in Miles, D. *et al.*, 2003: 283–5.
Jackson, D. (1974), 'Two new pit alignments and a hoard of currency bars from Northamptonshire', *NA*, 9: 13–45.
Jackson, K. H. (1964), *The Oldest Irish Tradition, A Window on the Iron Age*, Cambridge, Cambridge University Press.
Jackson, R. and Potter, T. (1996), *Excavations at Stonea, Cambridgeshire, 1980–85*, London, British Museum Press.
Jacobsthal, P. (1944), *Early Celtic Art*, 2 vols, Oxford, Clarendon Press.
James, S. (1999), *The Atlantic Celts, Ancient Population or Modern Invention*, London, British Museum.
——(2007), 'A bloodless past: the pacification of the Early Iron Age', in Haselgrove, C. and Pope, R. (eds), 2007: 160–73.
Jantzen, D., Brinker, U., Orschiedt, J., Heinemeier, J., Piek, J., Hauenstein, K., Krüger, J., Lidke, G., Lübke, H., Lampe, R., Lorenz, S., Schult, M. and Terberger, T. (2011), 'A Bronze Age battlefield? Weapons and trauma in the Tollense Valley, north-eastern Germany', *Antiquity*, 85: 417–33.
Jobey, G. (1962), 'An Iron Age homestead at West Brandon, Durham', *AA4*, 40: 1–34.
——(1971), 'Excavations at Brough Law and Ingram Hill', *AA4*, 49: 71–93.
——(1978), 'Burnswark Hill', *TDGNHAS*, 53: 57–105.
——and Tait, J. (1966), 'Excavations on palisaded settlements and cairnfields at Alnham, Northumberland', *AA4*, 44: 5–48.
Joffroy, R. (1960), *L'Oppidum de Vix et la Civilisation Hallstattienne Finale dans l'Est de la France*, Paris, Société Les Belles Lettres.

Johnston, S. and Wailes, B. (2007), *Dún Ailinne: Excavations at an Irish Royal Site, 1968–1975*, Philadelphia, University of Pennsylvania Museum of Archaeology and Anthropology.

Johnstone, C. (2004), *A Biometric Study of Equids in the Roman World*, unpublished Ph.D. thesis, University of York, York.

Jones, A. (2010), 'Misplaced monuments? A review of ceremony and monumentality in first millennium cal BC Cornwall', *OJA*, 29: 203–28.

Jones, E. (2006), 'Using viewshed analysis to explore settlement choice: a case study of the Onondaga Iroquois', *AAnt*, 71, 2006: 523–38.

Jones, M. U. and Bond, D. (1980), 'Later Bronze Age Settlement at Mucking, Essex', in Barrett, J. and Bradley, R. (eds), 1980: 471–82.

Kabát, J. (1955), 'Otomanská osada v Barci u Košic', *Arch. Roz.*, 7: 594–600; 611–13.

Karl, R. (2008), 'Random Coincidences Or: the return of the *Celtic* to Iron Age Britain', *PPS*, 74: 69–78.

Karl, R. and Butler, H. (2009), *Moel y Gaer, Llanbedr Dyffryn, Clywd, Excavations, Summer 2009, Preliminary Report*, Bangor, Bangor University/Universität Wien.

Kastelic, J. (1965), *Situla Art, Ceremonial Bronzes of Ancient Europe*, London, Thames and Hudson.

Keeley, L. (1996), *War before Civilization*, Oxford, Oxford University Press.

Kenyon, K. M. (1942), 'Excavations on the Wrekin, Shropshire, 1939', *Arch. J.*, 99: 99–109.

—— (1953), 'Excavations at Sutton Walls, Herefordshire, 1948–51', *Arch. J.*, 110: 1–87.

Keppie, L. (2009), 'Burnswark Hill: native space and Roman invaders', in Hanson, W. (ed.), 2009: 241–52.

Kimmig, W. (1969), 'Zum Problem späthallstättischer Adelsitze', in Otto, K.-H. and Hermann, J. (eds), 1969: 95–113.

—— (1992), *Die 'Wasserburg Buchau' eine spätbronzeitliche Siedlung*, Stuttgart, Theiss.

King, A. (1987), 'The Ingleborough Hillfort, North Yorkshire', *Bulletin of the Prehistoric Research Section*, Yorkshire Archaeological Society, Leeds, no page numbers.

Kirk-Greene, A. H. M. (ed.), (1962), *Barth's Travels in Nigeria: Extracts from the Journal of Heinrich Barth's Travels in Nigeria, 1850–1855*, London, Oxford University Press.

Klindt-Jensen, O. (1961), *Gundestrup Kedelen*, Copenhagen, National Museum.

Krämer, W. and Schubert, F. (1970), *Die Ausgrabungen in Manching 1955–1961 Einführung und Fundstellenübersicht*, Wiesbaden, Franz Steiner.

Kresten, P., Kero, L. and Chyssler, J. (1993), 'Geology of the vitrified hill-fort Broborg in Uppland, Sweden', *Geologiska Föreningen I Stockholm Förhandlingar*, 115: 13–24.

Kristiansen, K. (1984), 'Krieger und Häuptlinge in der Bronzezeit Dänemarks. Ein Beitrag zur Geschichte des bronzezeitlichen Schwertes', *JRGZM*, 31: 187–208.

—— (1999), 'The emergence of warrior aristocracies in later European prehistory and their long-term history', in Carman, J. and Harding, A. (eds), 1999: 175–90.

Kurz, S. (2000), *Die Heuneburg-Aussensiedlung: Befunde und Funde*, Stuttgart, Theiss.

Laing, L. (1999), 'The Pictish Symbols at Trusty's Hill, Anwoth, Kirkcudbrightshire', *PASJ*, 14: 10–12.

Laing, L. and Longley, D. (2006), *The Mote of Mark, a Dark Age Hillfort in South-West Scotland*, Oxford, Oxbow Books.

Lamb, R. G. (1980), *Iron Age Promontory Forts in the Northern Isles*, Oxford, BAR British Series 79.

Lambrick, G. and Allen, T. (2004), *Gravelly Guy, Stanton Harcourt, Oxfordshire: the development of a prehistoric and Romano-British community*, Oxford, Oxford Archaeology Thames Valley Landscape Monographs 21.

——and Robinson, M. (2009), *The Thames through Time. The Archaeology of the Gravel Terraces of the Upper and Middle Thames. The Thames Valley in Late Prehistory: 1500BC–AD50*, Oxford, Oxford Archaeology, Thames Valley Landscapes Monograph No 29.

Lane, A. and Campbell, E. (2000), *Dunadd, An Early Dalriadic Capital*, Oxford, Oxbow Books.

Lane-Fox, A. (1869), *Examination of the Hill Forts of Sussex with an account of Excavations at Cissbury and Highdown*, London, Nichols and Sons.

——(1870), 'On the threatened destruction of the British earthworks near Dorchester, Oxfordshire', *JESL*, NS 2: 412–15.

Laver, P. (1927), 'The excavation of a tumulus at Lexden, Colchester', *Archaeologia*, 76: 241–54.

Law, R. G. and Green, R. C. (1972), 'An economic interpretation of Taniwha *Pā*, Lower Waikato, New Zealand (N52/1)', *Mankind*, 8: 255–69.

Leeds, E. T. (1927), 'Excavations at Chun Castle in Penwith, Cornwall', *Archaeologia*, 76: 205–40.

——(1931), 'Excavations at Chun Castle, in Penwith, Cornwall: second report', *Archaeologia*, 81: 33–42.

Lejars, Th. (1994), *Gournay III: Les fourreax d'épée: le sanctuaire de Gournay-sur-Aronde et l'armement des Celtes de la Tène*, Paris, Éditions Errance.

Liddell, D. M. (1930), 'Report on the excavations at Hembury Fort, Devon, 1930', *PDAES*, 1: 39–63.

——(1931), 'Report on the excavations at Hembury Fort, Devon, second season, 1931', *PDAES*, 1: 90–120.

——(1932), 'Report on the excavations at Hembury Fort, Devon, third season, 1932', *PDAES*, 1: 162–90.

——(1935), 'Report on the excavations at Hembury Fort, Devon, 1934–5', *PDAES*, 2: 135–75.

Limbert, D. (1996), 'Irish Ringforts: a review of their Origins', *Arch. J.*, 153: 243–89.

Lock, G. (2011), 'Hillforts, Emotional Metaphors, and the Good Life: a Response to Armit', *PPS*, 77: 355–62.

Lock, G., Gosden, C. and Daly, P. (2005), *Segsbury Camp. Excavations in 1996 and 1997 at an Iron Age hillfort on the Oxfordshire Ridgeway*, Oxford, Oxford University School of Archaeology Monograph 61.

Lorrio, A. J., (1997), *Los Celtíberos*, Alicante, Universidad de Alicante/Universidad Complutense de Madrid.

Louis, M., Taffanel, O. and Taffanel, J. (1955), (1958), (1960), *Le Premier Âge du Fer Languedocien, pt. 1 Les habitats, pt. 2 Les nécropoles à incinération, pt. 3 Les tumulus, Conclusions*, Montpellier, Bordighera.

Lucas, A. T. (1989), *Cattle in Ancient Ireland*, Kilkenny, Boethius Press.
Luke, Y. (2011), 'Rethinking Ingleborough', <http://www.hillfortstudygroup.org.uk/news>
Lynn, C. (1977), 'Trial excavations at the King's Stables, Tray Townland, County Armagh', *UJA*, 40: 42–62.
——(1983), 'Some "early" ring-forts and crannogs', *JIA*, I: 47–58.
——(2000), 'Navan Fort Site C excavations, June 1999', *Emania*, 18: 5–16.
——(2002), 'Navan Fort Site C excavations May 2000', *Emania*, 19: 5–18.
Macinnes, L. (1984), 'Brochs and the Roman occupation of lowland Scotland', *PSAS*, 114: 235–50.
Mack, A. (1997), *Field Guide to the Pictish Symbol Stones*, Balgavies, Pinkfoot Press.
MacKie, E. W. (1965), 'The origin and development of the broch and wheelhouse building cultures of the Scottish Iron Age', *PPS*, 31: 93–146.
——(1976), 'The vitrified forts of Scotland', in Harding, D. W. (ed.), 1976a: 205–35.
Malim, T. (1992), *Stonea Camp, Wimblington, An Iron Age Fort in the Fens: Interim Report*, Cambridge, Cambridge County Council Report no 71.
Mallory, J. P. (1988), 'Trial excavations at Haughey's Fort', *Emania*, 4: 5–20.
——(1991), 'Excavations at Haughey's Fort 1989–90', *Emania*, 8: 10–26.
——(1995), 'Haughey's Fort and the Navan complex in the Late Bronze Age', in Waddell, J. and Twohig, E. S. (eds), 1995: 73–85.
——(1997), '*Emain Macha* and Navan Fort', in Waterman, D. and Lynn, C., 1997: 197–208.
——(2000), 'Excavations of the Navan Ditch', *Emania*, 18: 21–36.
——Moore, D. G. and Canning, L. J. (1996), 'Excavations at Haughey's Fort 1991 and 1995', *Emania*, 14: 5–20.
——and Stockman, G. (eds) (1994), *Ulidia: Proceedings of the First International Conference on the Ulster Cycle of Tales*, Belfast, December Publications.
Malone, P. M. (1993), *The Skulking Way of War. Technology and Tactics among the New England Indians*, Baltimore, Johns Hopkins University Press.
Manby, T. G. (1980), 'Bronze Age settlement in eastern Yorkshire', in Barrett, J. and Bradley, R. (eds), 1980: 307–70.
——(ed.) (1988), *Archaeology in Eastern Yorkshire: Essays in Honour of T. C. M. Brewster*, Sheffield, University of Sheffield Department of Archaeology.
——(2007), 'Continuity of Monumental Traditions into the Late Bronze Age? Henges to Ring-forts, and Shrines', in Burgess, C. *et al.* (eds), 2007: 403–24.
Mangin, M. (ed.), (1994), *La Sidérurgie ancienne de l'est de la France dans son context européen*, Besançon, UISPP.
Manning, W. (1985), *Catalogue of the Romano-British Iron Tools, Fittings and Weapons in the British Museum*, London, BM Publications.
Marshall, D. (1964), 'Report on excavations at Little Dunagoil', *TBNHS*, 16: 1–69.
Martin-Atkins, A. (1904), *Kingston Lisle: a fragmentary history of an old Berkshire seat and its associations*, Bristol, privately printed.
Matthews, C. L. (1976), *Occupation Sites on a Chiltern Ridge*, Oxford, BAR, 29.
Maxfield, V. (1989), 'Conquest and aftermath', in Todd, M. (ed.), 1989: 19–30.

McCarthy, M. (2002), 'Rheged: an Early Historic kingdom near the Solway', *PSAS*, 132: 357–82.

McCone, K. (1990/2000), *Pagan past and Christian present in early Irish Literature*, Maynooth, National University of Ireland Department of Old Irish.

McCormick, F. (2009), 'Ritual feasting in Iron Age Ireland', in Cooney, G. *et al.* (eds), 2009: 405–12.

McIntosh, S. and McIntosh, R. (1980), *Prehistoric investigations in the region of Jenné, Mali*, Cambridge, Cambridge University Press.

——— (1993), 'Cities without citadels: understanding urban origins along the middle Niger', in Shaw, T. *et al.* (eds), 1993: 622–41.

McKinlay, J. R. (1971), 'Waioneke 1968–69', *NZAAL*, 14, 3: 86–91.

McMillan, J. (2001), Unpublished MA dissertation, University of Edinburgh Department of Archaeology.

Mercer, R. (1986), *Hambledon Hill Fieldwork and Excavation Project, The Hillfort Spur, 1986 Interim Report*, Edinburgh, Edinburgh University Department of Archaeology.

——(1988), 'Hambledon Hill, Dorset, England', in C. Burgess *et al.* (eds), 1988: 89–106.

——(1999), 'The origins of warfare in the British Isles', in Carman, J. and Harding, A. (eds), 1999: 143–57.

——(2002), 'Review Article: *From the Ground Up: The Publication of Archaeological Projects. A User needs Survey* by S. Jones, A. MacSween, S. Jeffrey, R. Morris and M. Heyworth, *Cadbury Castle, Somerset. The Early Medieval Archaeology* by L. Alcock, S. J. Stevenson and C. Musson, *Cadbury Castle, Somerset. The Later Prehistoric and Early Historic Archaeology* by J. C. Barrett, P. W. M. Freeman and A. Woodward', *Ant. J.*, 82: 358–65.

——(2006), 'The first known enclosures in southern Britain: their nature, function and role, in space and time', in Harding, A. *et al.* (eds), 2006: 69–75.

——and Healy, F. (2008), *Hambledon Hill, Dorset, England: excavation and survey of a Neolithic monument complex and its surrounding landscape*, London, English Heritage.

——and Tipping, R. (1994), 'The prehistory of soil erosion in the Northern and Eastern Cheviot Hills, Anglo-Scottish Borders', in Foster, S. and Smout, T. C. (eds), 1994: 1–25.

Mighall, T. and Chambers, F. (1997), 'Early ironworking and its impact on the environment: palaeoecological evidence from Bryn y Castell hillfort, Snowdonia, North Wales', *PPS*, 63: 199–219.

Miket, R. and Burgess, C. (eds) (1984), *Between and Beyond the Walls: Essays on the Prehistory and History of North Britain in Honour of George Jobey*, Edinburgh, John Donald.

Miles, D., Palmer, S., Lock, G., Gosden, C. and Cromarty, A. M. (2003), *Uffington White Horse and its Landscape. Investigations at White Horse Hill, Uffington, 1989–95, and Tower Hill, Ashbury, 1993–4*, Oxford, Oxford Archaeology Thames Valley Landscapes Monograph No. 18.

Millett, M. (1990), *The Romanization of Britain, An Essay in Archaeological Interpretation*, Cambridge, Cambridge University Press.

Mills, S. (2004), 'Alloa, A Bronze Age woman and an Iron Age warrior', *CA*, 191: 486–9.

Mohen, J.-P. and Bailloud, G. (1987), *La Vie Quotidienne: Les Fouilles du Fort-Harrouard*, Paris, Picard.

Moody, H. (1970), *The walls and gates of Kano City*, Lagos, Nigerian Department of Antiquities.

Mordant, C. and Richard, A. (eds) (1992), *L'habitat et l'occupation du sol à l'Âge du Bronze en Europe*, Paris, Éditions du Comité des travaux Historique et Scientifique.

Moret, P. (1991), 'Les fortifications de l'Age du Fer dans la Meseta espagnole: origine et diffusion des techniques de construction', *MCV*, 27, 1: 5–42.

Mowbray, C. (1936), 'Excavation at the Ness of Burgi, Shetland', *PSAS*, 70, 1935–6: 381–6.

Müller-Wille, M. and Vierck, H. (1971), *Pferdegrab und Pferdeopfer im frühen Mittelalter*, Amersfort, Berichten van de Rijksdienst voor het Oudheidkundig Bodemonderzoek, 20–1.

Murphy, K. (2001), 'A Prehistoric Field System and Related Monuments on St David's Head and Carn Llidi, Pembrokeshire', *PPS*, 67: 85–99.

Musson, C. (1991), *The Breiddin Hillfort. A later prehistoric settlement in the Welsh Marches*, London, CBA Research Report No 76.

Mytum, H. and Webster, C. J. (1989), 'A survey of the Iron Age enclosure and *chevaux-de-frise* at Carn Alw, Dyfed', *PPS*, 55: 263–6.

Nash, D. (1987), *Coinage in the Celtic World*, London, Seaby.

Needham, S. (1992), 'The structure of settlement and ritual in the Late Bronze Age in south-east Britain', in Mordant, C. and Richard, A. (eds), 1992: 49–69.

——and Ambers, J. (1994), 'Redating Rams Hill and reconsidering Bronze Age enclosure,' *PPS*, 60: 225–44.

Neustupný, E. (ed.), (1998a), *Space in Prehistoric Bohemia*, Prague, Prague Archaeological Institute/Czech Academy of Sciences.

——(1998b), 'Structures and events: the theoretical basis of spatial archaeology', in Neustupný, E. (ed.), 1998a: 9–44.

——(2006), 'Enclosures and fortifications in Central Europe', in Harding, A. *et al.* (eds), 2006: 1–4.

Newman, C. (1993a), 'Sleeping in Elysium', *AI*, 7, 3: 20–3.

——(1993b), 'The show's not over until the fat lady sings', *AI*, 7, 4: 8–9.

——(1995), 'Tara Project. The Tara Survey', *Discovery Programme Reports 2*, Dublin, Royal Irish Academy: 62–7.

Nicholson, R. and Dockrill, S. (eds) (1998), *Old Scatness Broch, Shetland: Retrospect and Prospect*, Bradford, University of Bradford/Shetland Amenity Trust/NABO.

Nisbet, H. (1996), 'Craigmarloch hillfort, Kilmalcolm', in Alexander, D. (ed.), 1996a: 43–58.

Nowakowski, J. and Quinnell, H. (2011), *Trevelgue Head, Cornwall: the importance of C. K. Croft Andrew's 1939 excavations for prehistoric and Roman Cornwall*, Truro, Cornwall Council.

Ó Corráin, D. (ed.), (1981), *Irish Antiquity. Essays and Studies presented to Professor M. J. O'Kelly*, Cork, Tower Books.

Ó Floinn, R. (1999), 'The date of some metalwork from Cahercommaun reassessed', in Cotter, 1999: 73–9.

O'Neil, B. H. St J. (1934), 'Excavations at Titterstone Clee Hill Camp, Shropshire, 1932', *Ant. J.*, 14: 13–32.

O'Neil, B. H. St J. (1942), 'Excavations at Ffridd Faldwyn Camp, Montgomery, 1937–39', *Arch. Camb.*, 97, 1: 1–57.
OS (1962), *Map of Southern Britain in the Iron Age*, Chessington, Ordnance Survey.
Oswald, A. (1997), 'A doorway on the past: practical and mystic concerns in the orientation of roundhouse doorways', in Gwilt, A. and Haselgrove, C., 1997: 87–95.
Oswald, A., Ainsworth, S. and Pearson, T. (2006), *Hillforts. Prehistoric Strongholds of Northumberland National Park*, Swindon, English Heritage.
——Dyer, C. and Barber, M. (2001), *The Creation of Monuments, Neolithic Causewayed Enclosures in the British Isles*, Swindon, English Heritage.
——and Pearson, T. (2005), 'Yeavering Bell Hillfort', in Frodsham, P. and O'Brien, C. (eds), 2005: 98–126.
Otto, K.-H. and Hermann, J. (eds) (1969), *Siedlung, Burg und Stadt: Studien zur ihren Anfängen: Festschrift für Paul Grimm*, Berlin, Deutsche Akademie der Wissenschaften.
Owen, O. (1992), 'Eildon Hill North', in Rideout, J. *et al.*, 1992: 73–120.
Parfitt, K. (1995), *Iron Age Burials from Mill Hill, Deal*, London, British Museum Press.
Payne, A., Corney, M. and Cunliffe, B. (2006), *The Wessex Hillforts Project. Extensive survey of hillfort interiors in central southern England*, London, English Heritage.
Pearson, T. and Topping, P. (2002), 'Rethinking the Carrock Fell enclosure', in Varndell, G. and Topping, P. (eds), 2002: 121–7.
Peltenburg, E. (1982), 'Excavations at Balloch Hill, Argyll', *PSAS*, 112: 142–214.
Piggott, C. M. (1948), 'Excavations at Hownam Rings, Roxburghshire, 1948', *PSAS*, 82, 1947–8: 193–225.
——(1949), 'The Iron Age settlement at Hayhope Knowe, Roxburghshire: excavations 1949', *PSAS*, 83, 1948–9: 45–67.
——(1950), 'The excavations at Bonchester Hill, 1950', *PSAS*, 84, 1949–50: 113–36.
——and Piggott, S. (1940), 'Excavations at Rams Hill, Uffington, Berkshire', *Ant. J.*, 20: 465–80.
Piggott, S. (1931), 'Ladle Hill', *Antiquity*, 4: 474–85.
——(1958a), 'Native economies and the Roman occupation of North Britain', in Richmond, I. A. (ed.), 1958: 1–27.
——(1958b), 'Excavations at Braidwood Fort, Midlothian and Craig's quarry, Dirleton, East Lothian', *PSAS*, 91, 1957–8: 61–77.
——(1985), *William Stukeley, an eighteenth-century antiquary*, London, Thames and Hudson.
Pitt-Rivers, A. H. L. F. (1887), *Excavations in Cranborne Chase, near Rushmore, on the borders of Dorset and Wilts*, Vol. I, printed privately.
——(1888), *Excavations in Cranborne Chase near Rushmore, on the borders of Dorset and Wilts 1880–1888*, Vol. II, printed privately.
——(1898), *Excavations in Cranborne Chase, near Rushmore, on the borders of Dorset and Wilts, 1893–1896*, Vol. IV, printed privately.
Podborský, V. and Kovárník, J. (2006), 'Neolithic and post-Neolithic enclosures in Moravia in their central European context', in Harding, A. *et al.* (eds), 2006: 44–68.
Poole, C. (1984), 'Objects of baked clay', in Cunliffe, B., 1984b: 398–406.
——(2000), 'Slingshot', in Barrett, J. *et al.*, 2000: 247.

Powell, A. and Clark, K. M. (1996), *Exploitation of domestic animals in the Iron Age at Rooksdown*, professional report, University of Southampton Centre for Human Economy and Ecology.

Powlesland, D. (1988), 'Staple Howe and its Landscape', in Manby, T. (ed.), 1988: 101–7.

Pwiti, G. and Soper, R. (eds) (1996), *Aspects of African Archaeology: papers from the 10th Congress of the PanAfrican Association for Prehistory and Related Studies*, Harare, University of Zimbabwe Press.

Queiroga, F. (2003), *War and Castros, new approaches to the northwestern Portugese Iron Age*, Oxford, BAR International Series, 1198.

Radford, C. A. R. (1940), 'Review of *Cahercommaun: a stone fort in County Clare*', *Ant. J.*, 20: 128.

——(1951), 'Report on the excavations at Castle Dore', *JRIC*, NS 1: Appendix: 1–119.

Raftery, B. (1972), 'Irish Hill-forts', in Thomas, C. (ed.), 1972: 37–58.

——(1976), 'Rathgall and Irish Hillfort Problems', in Harding, D. W. (ed.), 1976a: 339–57.

——(1981), 'Iron Age Burials in Ireland', in Ó Corráin, D. (ed.), 1981: 173–204.

——(1984), *La Tène in Ireland: problems of origin and chronology*, Marburg, Veröffentlichung des Vorgeschichtlichen Seminars Marburg, Sonderband 2.

——(1994), *Pagan Celtic Ireland. The Enigma of the Irish Iron Age*, London, Thames and Hudson.

Raftery, J. (1942), 'Knocknalappa crannog, Co. Clare', *NMAJ*, 3: 53–72.

Rahtz, P., Woodward, A., Burrow, I., Everton, A., Watts, L., Leach, P, Hirst, S., Fowler, P. and Gardner, K. (1992), *Cadbury Congresbury 1968–73. A late/post-Roman hilltop settlement in Somerset*, Oxford, BAR British Series, 223.

Ralston, I. (1980), 'The Green Castle and the promontory forts of North-East Scotland', *SAF*, 10: 27–40.

——(1986), 'The Yorkshire Television vitrified wall experiment at East Tullos, City of Aberdeen District', *PSAS*, 116: 17–40.

——(1987), 'Portknockie: promontory forts and Pictish settlement in the North-East', in Small, A. (ed.), 1987: 15–26.

——(2004), *The Hill-Forts of Pictland since 'The Problem of the Picts'*, Rosemarkie, Groam House Museum.

——(2006), *Celtic Fortifications*, Stroud, Tempus.

——and Armit, I. (1997), 'The Early Historic Period: An Archaeological Perspective', in Edwards, K. and Ralston, I. (eds), 1997: 217–40.

——and Smith, J. S. (1983), 'High altitude settlement on Ben Griam Beg, Sutherland', *PSAS*, 113: 636–8.

RCAHMS (1946), *Twelfth Report with an Inventory of the Ancient Monuments of Orkney & Shetland*, Edinburgh, HMSO.

——(1956), *An Inventory of the Ancient and Historical Monuments of Roxburghshire*, Edinburgh, HMSO.

——(1967), *Peeblesshire: an Inventory of the Ancient Monuments*, Edinburgh, HMSO.

——(1971), *Argyll: An Inventory of the Ancient Monuments, Vol. 1, Kintyre*, Edinburgh, HMSO.

——(1974), *Argyll: An Inventory of the Ancient Monuments, Vol. 2, Lorn*, Edinburgh, HMSO.

RCAHMS (1978), *Lanarkshire, An Inventory of the Prehistoric and Roman Monuments*, Edinburgh, HMSO.
——(1988), *Argyll: An Inventory of the Monuments, Vol. 6, Mid Argyll and Cowal, Prehistoric and Early Historic Monuments*, Edinburgh, HMSO.
——(1994), *South-East Perth, an archaeological landscape*, Edinburgh, HMSO.
——(1997), *Eastern Dumfriesshire: an archaeological landscape*, Edinburgh, HMSO.
RCAHMWM (1956), *An Inventory of the Ancient Monuments in Caernarvonshire, Volume I: East*, London, HMSO.
——(1960), *An Inventory of the Ancient Monuments in Caernarvonshire, Volume II: Central*, London, HMSO.
——(1964), *An Inventory of the Ancient Monuments in Caernarvonshire, Volume III: West*, London, HMSO.
RCHM(Eng) (1970), *An Inventory of Historical Monuments in the County of Dorset, Vol. Three, Central Dorset Part 1*, Edinburgh, HMSO.
Redfern, R. (2011), 'A Re-appraisal of the Evidence for Violence in the Late Iron Age Human Remains from Maiden Castle Hillfort, Dorset, England', *PPS*, 77: 111–38.
Renfrew, C. (1973), *Before Civilization: the radiocarbon revolution and prehistoric Europe*, London, Jonathan Cape.
Reynolds, N. (1980), 'Dark Age Timber Halls and the Background to Excavation at Balbridie,' *SAF*, 10: 41–60.
Reynolds, P. J. (1974), 'Experimental Iron Age storage pits', *PPS*, 40: 118–31.
——(1993), 'Experimental Reconstruction', in Harding, D. W. *et al.*, 1993: 93–113.
Rhodes, P. (1948), 'A Prehistoric and Roman Site at Wittenham Clumps, Berks', *Oxoniensia*, 13: 18–31.
Richardson, K. M. (1940), 'Excavations at Poundbury, Dorchester, Dorset, 1939', *Ant. J.*, 20: 429–48.
Richmond, I. A. (1925), *Huddersfield in Roman Times*, Huddersfield, Tolson Memorial Museum.
——ed. (1958), *Roman and Native in North Britain*, Edinburgh/London, Nelson.
——(1968), *Hod Hill Volume 2: Excavations carried out between 1951 and 1958*, London, BM Trustees.
Rideout, J. S. (1992), 'The Dunion, Roxburgh, Borders', in Rideout, J. S. *et al.*, 1992: 73–119.
——Owen, O. A. and Halpin, E. (1992), *Hillforts of Southern Scotland*, Edinburgh, Historic Scotland/AOC Ltd.
Riek, G. (1962), *Der Hohmichele. Ein Fürstengrabhügel der späten Hallstattzeit bei der Heuneburg*, RGF Bd 25, Berlin, de Gruyter.
Ritchie, A. (1970), 'Palisaded Sites in North Britain: Their Context and Affinities', *SAF*, 2: 48–67.
——(1989), *The Picts*, Edinburgh, HMSO/Historic Scotland.
Ritchie, J. N. G. (1969), 'Shields in north Britain in the Iron Age', *SAF*, 1: 31–40.
——(ed.) (1997), *The Archaeology of Argyll*, Edinburgh, Edinburgh University Press.
Rivet, A. L. F. (1961), 'Some of the Problems of Hill-Forts', in Frere, S. S. (ed.), 1961: 29–34.
——(1966), *The Iron Age in Northern Britain*, Edinburgh, Edinburgh University Press.
——(1971), 'Hill-forts in Action', in Hill, D. and Jesson, M. (eds), 1971: 189–202.

Robertson-MacKay, R. (1977), 'The defences of the Iron Age hillfort at Winklebury, Basingstoke, Hampshire', *PPS*, 43: 131–54.

Roche, H. (2002), 'Excavations at Ráith na Ríg, Tara, Co. Meath, 1997', *Discovery Programme Reports 6*, Dublin, Royal Irish Academy: 19–82.

Rodwell, W. (1976), 'Coinage, Oppida and the rise of Belgic power in south-eastern Britain', in Cunliffe, B. and Rowley, T. (eds), 1976: 181–366.

Ross, C. R. (2011), *'Tribal Territories' from the Humber to the Tyne. An analysis of artefactual and settlement patterning in the Late Iron Age and Early Roman Periods*, Oxford, BAR British Series, 540.

Roy, W. (1793), *Military Antiquities of the Romans in Britain*, London, SAL.

Rudling, D. (2001), 'Chanctonbury Ring revisited: the excavations of 1988–91', *SxAC*, 139: 75–121.

Rynne, E. (1991), 'Dún Aengusa—Daingean nó Teampall?' *AI*, 5: 19–21.

——(1992), 'Dún Aengus and some similar Celtic ceremonial sites', in Bernelle, A. (ed.), 1992: 196–207.

Savory, H. N. (1960), 'Excavations at Dinas Emrys, Beddgelert, Caernarvonshire, 1954–56', *Arch. Camb.*, 109: 13–77.

——(1971), *Excavations at Dinorben, 1965–9*, Cardiff, National Museum of Wales.

——(1976), 'Welsh hillforts: a reappraisal of recent research', in Harding, D. W. (ed.), 1976a: 237–92.

Schindler, R. (1977), *Die Altburg von Bundenbach, eine befestigte Höhensiedlung des 2./1. Jahrhunderts v. Chr. Im Hunsrück*, Mainz, von Zabern.

Schmidt, M. (1996), 'Pā Excavation in New Zealand: A History and Review', nzarchaeology.org/elecpublications/

Scott, B. and Cleere, H. (eds) (1984), *The Crafts of the Blacksmith*, Belfast, Ulster Museum.

Sharples, N. (1991a), *Maiden Castle. Excavations and field survey, 1985-6*, London, English Heritage Archaeological Report 19.

——(1991b), *Maiden Castle*, London, Batsford/English Heritage.

——(1991c), 'Warfare in Iron Age Wessex', *SAR*, 8: 79–89.

——(2010), *Social Relations in Later Prehistory: Wessex in the First Millennium BC*, Oxford, Oxford University Press.

——(2011), Review of Haselgrove, 2009, www.prehistoricsociety.org/publications/reviews, October 2011.

Shaw, T., Sinclair, P., Andah, B. and Okpoko, A. (eds) (1993), *The archaeology of Africa: food, metals and towns*, London and New York, Routledge.

Shawcross, W. (1968), 'The Ngaroto site', *NZAAN*, 11: 2–29.

——(1976), 'Kauri Point Swamp: the ethnographic interpretation of a prehistoric site', in Sieveking, G. *et al.* (eds), 1976: 277–305.

Sieveking, G., Longworth, I. and Wilson, K. (eds) (1976), *Problems in economic and social archaeology*, London, Duckworth.

Sievers, S. (2003), *Manching—Die Keltenstadt*, Stuttgart, Konrad Theiss.

Simpson, D. (1969), 'Excavations at Kaimes Hillfort Midlothian', *GAJ*, 1: 7–28.

——(1989), 'Neolithic Navan?' *Emania*, 6: 31–3.

Small, A. (1969), 'Burghead', *SAF*, 1: 61–8.

Small, A. (ed.) (1987), *The Picts. A New Look at Old Problems*, Dundee, Dundee University/Dundee City Council.
Smith, B. B. and Banks, I. (eds) (2002), *In the Shadow of the Brochs: the Iron Age in Scotland*, Stroud, Tempus.
Smith, I. F. (1965), *Windmill Hill and Avebury: excavations by Alexander Keiller, 1925–1939*, Oxford, Clarendon Press.
Smith, K. (1977), 'The Excavation of Winklebury Camp, Basingstoke, Hampshire', *PPS*, 43: 31–129.
Smith, R. (1989), *Warfare and Diplomacy in Pre-Colonial West Africa*, 2nd edition, Madison, University of Wisconsin Press.
Smout, T. C. (ed.), (1993), *Scotland since Prehistory: Natural change and human impact*, Aberdeen, Scottish Cultural Press.
Snow, D. (1994), *The Iroquois*, Oxford, Blackwell.
Soper, R. and Darling, P. (1980), 'The Walls of Oyo Ile', *WAJA*, 10/11, 1980/81: 61–81.
Spratt, D. and Burgess, C. B. (eds) (1985), *Upland Settlement in Britain: The Second Millennium BC and After*, Oxford, BAR British Series, 143.
Stanford, S. C. (1971), 'Credenhill Camp, Herefordshire: An Iron Age Hill-Fort Capital', *Arch. J.*, 127: 82–129.
——(1974), *Croft Ambrey*, Hereford, privately printed.
——(1981), *Midsummer Hill, an Iron Age hillfort on the Malverns*, Hereford, privately printed.
——(1984), 'The Wrekin Hillfort Excavations 1973', *Arch. J.*, 141: 61–90.
Stead, I. M. (1965), *The La Tène Cultures of Eastern Yorkshire*, York, Yorkshire Philosophical Society.
——(1968), 'An Iron Age hill-fort at Grimthorpe, Yorkshire, England', *PPS*, 34: 148–90.
——(1979), *The Arras Culture*, York, Yorkshire Philosophical Society.
——(1991), *Iron Age Cemeteries in East Yorkshire*, London, English Heritage/British Museum.
——(2006), *British Iron Age Swords and Scabbards*, London, British Museum Press.
Stevenson, R. B. K. (1949a), 'Braidwood Fort, Midlothian: the exploration of two huts', *PSAS*, 83, 1948–9: 1–11.
——(1949b), 'The nuclear fort at Dalmahoy, Midlothian, and other Dark Age capitals', *PSAS*, 83, 1948–9: 186–98.
Stoertz, C. (1997), *Ancient Landscapes of the Yorkshire Wolds: Aerial photographic transcription and analysis*, Swindon, RCHM(Eng).
Stopford, J. (1987), 'Danebury: an alternative view', *SAR*, 4, 2: 70–5.
Stout, M. (1997), *The Irish Ringfort*, Dublin, Four Courts Press.
Stukeley, W. (1724), *Itinerarium curiosum, Or, An Account of the antiquitys and remarkable curiositys in nature or art, observ'd in travels thro' Great Brittan*, London, printed for the Author.
Sutton, D, Furey, L. and Marshall, Y. (2003), *The Archaeology of Pouerua*, Auckland, Auckland University Press.
Thomas, C. (1956), 'Evidence for post-Roman occupation of Chun Castle, Cornwall', *Ant. J.*, 36: 75–8.

——(1960), 'Excavations at Trusty's Hill, Anwoth, Kirkcudbright, 1960', *TDGNHAS*, 38, 1959–60: 58–70.
——(1969), 'Are These the Walls of Camelot?', *Antiquity*, 43: 27–30.
——(ed.) (1972), *The Iron Age in the Irish Sea Province*, London, CBA Research Report 9.
Thomas, N. (2005), *Conderton Camp, Worcestershire: a small Middle Iron Age Hillfort on Bredon Hill*, York, CBA Research Report 143.
Thomas, R. (1997), 'Land, Kinship Relations and the Rise of Enclosed Settlements in First Millennium BC Britain', *OJA*, 16, 2: 211–18.
Thompson, R., Hart, J., Brumbach, H. and Lusteck, R. (2004), 'Phytolith evidence for twentieth century BP maize in northern Iroquoia', *Northeast Anthropology*, 68: 25–40.
Tite, M. (1967), 'The Magnetic Survey', in Avery *et al.*, 1967: 296–300.
Toase, S. (2008), 'The pairing of hillforts: conflict, complementary, coincidence or complex?' in Davis, O. *et al.* (eds), 2008: 21–30.
Točik, A. (1981), *Nitriansky Hrádok—Zámeček, bronzezeitliche befestigte Ansiedlung der Mad'arovce-Kultur*, Materialia Archaeologica Slovaca, 1. Nitra: Archeologický Ústav Slovenskej Akadémie Vied.
——(1994), 'Poznámky k problematike opevneného sídliska otomanskej kultúry v Barci pri Košiciach,' *Študijné Zvesti*, 30: 59–65.
Todd, M. (1984a), 'Excavations at Hembury (Devon), 1980–83: a summary report', *Ant. J.*, 64: 251–68.
——(1984b), 'The early Roman phase at Maiden Castle', *Britannia*, 15: 254–5.
——(1989), *Research on Roman Britain*, London, Britannia Monograph 11.
Torke, W. (1990), 'Abschlussbericht zu den Ausgrabungen in der "Siedlung Forschner" und Ergebnisse der Bauholzuntersuchung', *BRGK*, 71: 52–7.
Tracy, J. (ed.), (2000), *City Walls: the urban enceinte in global perspective*, New York, Cambridge University Press.
Trigger, B. (ed.), (1978a), *Handbook of North American Indians, Volume 15 Northeast*, Washington, Smithsonian Institute.
——(1978b), 'Early Iroqoian Contacts with Europeans', in Trigger, B. (ed.), 1978a: 344–56.
——and Pendergast, J. (1978), 'Saint Lawrence Iroquoians', in Trigger, B. (ed.), 1978a: 357–67.
Tuck, J. (1978), 'Northern Iroquoian Prehistory', in Trigger, B. (ed.), 1978a: 322–33.
Turner, V. and Dockrill, S. (2005), 'Continuity or Change: Exploring the Potential', in Turner, V. *et al.* (eds), 2005: 172–9.
——Dockrill, S., Nicholson, R. and Bond, J. (eds), (2005), *Tall Stories? 2 Millennia of Brochs*, Lerwick, Shetland Amenity Trust.
van de Noort, R., Chapman, H. and Collis, J. (2007), *Sutton Common. The Excavation of an Iron Age 'marsh fort'*, York, CBA Research Report 154.
van Endert, D. (1987), *Das Osttor des Oppidums von Manching*, Ausgrabungen von Manching Bd. 10, Stuttgart, Steiner.
Varley, W. J. (1935), 'Maiden Castle, Bickerton. Preliminary excavations, 1934', *AAAL*, 22, 1–2: 97–110.
——(1936), 'Further excavations at Maiden Castle, Bickerton, 1935', *AAAL*, 23, 3–4: 110–12.

Varley, W. J. (1976), A summary of the excavations at Castle Hill, Almondbury, 1939–72', in Harding, D. W. (ed.), 1976a: 119–32.
Varndell, G. and Topping, P. (eds) (2002), *Enclosures in Neolithic Europe*, Oxford, Oxbow Books.
Venclovà, N. (1993), 'Celtic shrines in central Europe: a sceptical approach', *OJA*, 12, 1: 55–86.
Waddell, J. and Twohig, E. S. (1995), *Ireland in the Bronze Age*, Dublin, Stationery Office.
Waddington, C. (2011), 'Massacre at Fin Cop: new evidence of an Iron Age hillfort at war', *CA*, 255: 20–7.
——(forthcoming), 'Excavations at Fin Cop, Derbyshire: an Iron Age Hillfort at War', *Arch. J.*, forthcoming.
Wailes, B. (1976), 'Dún Ailinne: an Interim Report', in Harding, D. W. (ed.), 1976a: 319–38.
——(1988), 'Some comments on method and interpretation', in Gibson, D. B. and Geselowitz, M. (eds), 1988: 219–28.
Wainwright, F. T. (ed.) (1955), *The Problem of the Picts*, Edinburgh, Nelson.
Wainwright, G. (1969), 'The excavations at Balksbury Camp, Andover, Hants', *HFC*, 26: 21–55.
——(1971), 'Excavations at Tower Point, St Brides, Pembrokeshire', *Arch. Camb.*, 120: 84–90.
——(1979), *Gussage All Saints: An Iron Age Settlement in Dorset*, London, HMSO.
——and Davies, S. (1995), *Balksbury Camp. Excavations in 1973 and 1981*, London, English Heritage Report 4.
Ward-Perkins, J. B. (1944), 'Excavations on the Iron Age hillfort of Oldbury, near Ightham, Kent', *Archaeologia*, 90: 127–76.
Warner, R. (2000), 'Keeping out the Otherworld: the Internal Ditch at Navan and other Iron Age "Hengiform" Enclosures', *Emania*, 18: 39–44.
Warrick, G. (2000), 'The Precontact Iroquoian Occupation of Southern Ontario', *JWP*, 14: 415–66.
——(2008), *A Population History of the Huron-Petun, AD 500–1650*, Cambridge, Cambridge University Press.
Waterbolk, H. T. (1977), 'Walled enclosures of the Iron Age in the North of the Netherlands', *Palaeohistoria*, 19: 97–172.
Waterman, D. and Lynn, C. (1997), *Excavations at Navan Fort 1961–71*, Belfast, The Stationery Office.
Weber, K. (2002), *Die Rätsel der Kelten vom Glauberg*, Stuttgart, Theiss.
Webster, G. (1958), 'The Roman Military Advance under Ostorius Scapula', *Arch. J.*, 115: 49–98.
Welfare, H., Topping, P., Blood, K. and Ramm, H., (1990), 'Stanwick, North Yorkshire, Part 2: A summary description of the earthworks', *Arch. J.*, 147: 16–36.
Wells, P. (1984), *Farms, Villages and Cities. Commerce and Urban Origins in Late Prehistoric Europe*, New York, Cornell University Press.
——(1993), *Settlement, Economy, and Cultural Change at the End of the European Iron Age. Excavations at Kelheim, Bavaria, 1987–1991*, Ann Arbor, International Monographs in Prehistory, Arch. Ser. 6.

Wendling, H. (2011), Presentation to 14th International Congress of Celtic Studies, Maynooth, August, 2011.

Westropp, T. (1910a), 'A study of the fort of Dun Aengusa in Inishmore, Aran Isles, Galway Bay: its plan, growth, and records', *PRIA*, 28, Section C, No. I: 1–46.

—— (1910b), 'A study of the early forts and stone huts in Inishmore, Aran Isles, Galway Bay', *PRIA*, 28, Section C, No. II: 174–201.

Wheeler, R. E. M. (1943), *Maiden Castle, Dorset*, Oxford, SAL Research Report 12.

—— (1953), 'An Early Iron Age 'Beach-Head' at Lulworth, Dorset,' *Ant. J.*, 33: 1–13.

—— (1954), *The Stanwick Fortifications, North Riding of Yorkshire*, Oxford, SAL Research Report 17, Oxford University Press.

Wheeler, R. E. M. and Richardson, K. M., (1957), *Hillforts of Northern France*, Oxford, SAL Research Report 19, Oxford University Press.

—— and Wheeler, T. V. (1932), *Report on the Excavation of the Prehistoric, Roman and Post-Roman Site in Lydney Park, Gloucestershire*, Oxford, SAL Research Report 9, Oxford University Press.

—— —— (1936), *Verulamium, A Belgic and two Roman Cities*, Oxford, SAL Research Report 11, Oxford University Press.

Whimster, R. (1981), *Burial Practices in Iron Age Britain: A Discussion and Gazetteer of the Evidence c. 700 BC–AD43*, Oxford, BAR British Series, 90.

—— (1989), *The Emerging Past: Air Photography and the Buried Landscape*, London, RCHM(Eng).

Whitley, M. (1943), 'Excavations at Chalbury Camp, Dorset, 1939', *Ant. J.*, 23: 98–121.

Whittle, A., Healy, F. and Bayliss, A. (2011), *Gathering Time: Dating the Early Neolithic Enclosures of Southern Britain and Ireland*, Oxford, Oxbow Books.

Willett, F. (1967), *Ife in the history of West African sculpture*, London, Thames and Hudson.

Wilson, A. E. (1938), 'Excavations in the Ramparts and Gateway of the Caburn, August–October 1937', *SxAC*, 79: 169–94.

Wilson, C. (1981), 'Burials within settlements in southern Britain during the pre-Roman Iron Age', *BLUIA*, 18: 127–69.

Wilson, D. (1851), *Archaeology and Prehistoric Annals of Scotland*, Edinburgh, Constable.

Woodward, A. and Hill, J. D. (2000), 'Synthesis', in Barrett, J. *et al.*, 2000: 114–16.

—— and Leach, P. (1993), *The Uley Shrines. Excavation of a ritual complex on West Hill, Uley, Gloucestershire, 1977–9*, London, English Heritage/British Museum.

Woolf, G. (1993), 'Rethinking the oppida', *OJA*, 12: 223–34.

Yeates, S. (2008), *The tribe of witches. The religion of the Dobunni and the Hwicce*, Oxford, Oxbow Books.

Young, H. W. (1891), 'Notes on the Ramparts of Burghead, as revealed by Recent Excavations', *PSAS*, 25, 1890–91: 435–47.

—— (1893), 'Notes on further Excavations at Burghead', *PSAS*, 27, 1892–93: 86–91.

Index

Abbotstone, Essex 133
Abercromby, Lord 29
Aberlemno, Angus 198, 294
Abernethy, Castle Law, Perthshire 67–9
Abingdon, Oxfordshire (Berkshire) 135
Adomnán 245
Aduatuci 70
Áedán 244
Aedui, Aeduan 285
Aethelfrith 244
Agricola 234
agriculture, arable 144, 202
   cereal cultivation 123, 144, 206, 267, 281
   cord-rig 9, 92–3, 98–9, 201–2
   horticulture 250, 252–3, 258, 261
   recessional cultivation 267
   shifting 257, 259–60
   slash-and-burn 257, 263
   see also animal husbandry *and* pastoralism
Aidan, bishop 244
air photography 6, 42, 92, 107, 113, 120, 124–5, 126
Aitchison, N. 240–1
Aitken, Martin 93
Akerman, J. Y. 183
Alcock, Leslie 42, 100, 160, 163–4, 165, 167, 168, 169, 170, 181, 202, 207, 243–5
Aldclune, Perthshire 174
Alesia, Côte d'Or 23, 36, 193, 195, 231, 232
Alexander, D. 87
Alfred's Castle, Oxfordshire (Berkshire) 159
All Cannings Cross, Wiltshire 174
Allcroft, Hadrian 1, 29, 35
alliances 83, 130, 196, 238, 260–1, 267, 268, 277, 282, 289
Alloa, Clackmannanshire 193
Almondbury, Castle Hill, Yorkshire 67, 83, 238
Altburg von Bundenbach, Hunsrück 104, 204
Alt Clut, *see* Dumbarton Rock
amphorae, *see* pottery
Anderson, Joseph 144, 188–9
animal husbandry 22, 98, 123, 133, 144, 202, 251, 263, 267, 277, 278, 281
Arbory Hill, Lanarkshire 76
archery, archers 43, 152–3, 193–4, 195, 198
Archwood Hill, Dumfriesshire 16
Arkush, E. 196
Armit, I. 148, 257, 270

Arras culture, Yorkshire 6, 192, 210, 213, 215, 286, 291
   see also cemeteries
arrowheads, 246
   bone 194
   fire-hardened hardwood 194
   iron 193
   leaf-shaped 152, 154
   Roman 180
art, La Tène 197
   'Pictish' 198
   situla 197
Athenaeus 196
Atlantic roundhouses, *see* brochs
Atrebates, Atrebatic 159, 236, 237, 275–6, 277
Aubrey, John 30
Avaricum (Bourges, Cher) 67, 207, 230, 232–3
Avebury 30
Avery, Michael 57, 59, 63, 66, 73, 75, 77, 81, 179–80, 183, 186, 288
Aylesford-Welwyn, *see* cemeteries

Bailiehill, Dumfriesshire 127–30
Balksbury, Hampshire 91, 111–12, 159
Ballykinvarga, Co. Clare 190
Bamburgh, Northumberland 243, 244
Banks, Joseph 250, 252
Bann, R., Co. Antrim 193, 287
Barbary Castle, Wiltshire 276
Barca, Slovakia 154
Baring-Gould, Rev. S. 35
Barrett, J. 164
Barth, Heinrich 265
bastions 26, 84, 101, 187, 191, 206
Batavii 239
Battersea shield 20, 193, 287
Battlesbury Camp, Wiltshire 91, 114, 115–6, 123, 214
Beacon Hill, Hampshire 94, 110–11, 278
Bede 168, 242–5
Belgae, Belgic Gaul 73, 168, 182, 231–2, 237
Bell, E. W. 87
Bell, Richard 128
Bellwood, P. 252, 253, 254
Ben Griam Beg, Sutherland 96
Benin, West Africa 262, 263, 267
berm 11, 58, 59, 69, 72, 140
Bersu, Gerhard 36, 102, 281
Bevan, B. 141

Bibracte 36; *see also* Mont Beuvray
Bigbury, Kent 233–4
Bindon Hill, Dorset 57, 177
Birch, J. 260
Biskupin, Poland 6, 22–3, 77, 155
bivallation 11, 17, 53, 76, 206; *see also* multivallation
Black Meldon, Peeblesshire 98
Blewburton Hill, Oxfordshire (Berkshire) 38, 57, 60–2, 65, 73, 78–9, 81, 156, 192, 212–13, 232, 282
blockhouses 25, 86, 145, 147, 219, 272
boar imagery 223
Bonchester Hill, Roxburghshire 165–6
Borgou 266
Boudicca, Boudiccan revolt 132, 159, 180, 182, 235, 238
boundaries/ 'boundedness' 7–8, 134, 135, 142
Boussa, Nigeria 266
bow, *see* archery
Bradley, R. J. 216
Braidwood, Midlothian 98
Brandon Camp, Herefordshire 158, 185
Braughing, Hertfordshire 138
Bredon Hill, Worcestershire 182–3, 232
Breiddin, Powys 17, 38, 106, 156, 159
Bridei 245
Brigantes 43, 138, 238
Brigantia 168
Brightwell, Oxfordshire (Berkshire) 114
briquetage 203
Briteiros, citânia de, Guimarães, Portugal 36, 279
Broborg, Uppland 190
brochs 11, 21, 64, 86, 144–9, 162, 169, 173, 270
broch architecture 86, 147
bronze-working 163, 166, 167
brooches 162, 183, 270
  Aesica 160
  Aucissa 158
  dolphin 158
  dragonesque 162
  La Tène 2 184
  penannular 166, 174
  trumpet 162
Brough Law, Northumberland 18–19, 31, 70
Brown, I. 202, 218
Broxmouth, East Lothian 13, 15, 39, 75, 116, 125, 187–8, 208–9
Brude mac Bile 245
Bruford, A. 241
Brunaux, J-L. 246
brushwood 55, 61, 63
Bryant, S. 134
Bryn y Castell, Merionethshire 225
Burghead, Morayshire 32, 67, 171–2
  bull carvings 172

Burgi Geos, Shetland 218–19
burial 20, 28, 30, 40, 46, 101, 134, 143, 154, 157, 178, 179–85, 199, 206, 208–17, 226, 252, 256, 262, 270, 274, 280, 283, 284, 285, 286, 287, 291
  animal 212–13, 214, 215, 222, 283
    horse 213, 282
  barrow, Bronze Age 111, 116, 152
    Neolithic long 119, 152, 154, 216, 223, 274, 275
  cist 209
  chariot-/cart- 138, 143, 213, 286
  cremation 117, 157, 286
  ditch 211–13, 214–15
  'doctor's' 286
  foundation 211–12
  four-wheeled wagon 213
  fragmentary 153, 214, 215, 283
  neo-natal and infant 211, 212
  late La Tène cremation 138, 222, 285, 286
  pit- 183, 184, 208, 210–11, 214, 215, 216, 222, 259, 283
  Scythian 213
  skulls 211
  'warrior's' 192, 286
  see also cemeteries
Burland, Shetland 145–6
Burnswark, Dumfriesshire 34, 160–1
Burton Fleming, Yorkshire 142
Bury Hill, Hampshire 94, 120

Caburn, Sussex 61, 277–8
Cadbury Castle, Somerset 11, 17, 21, 30, 31, 32, 48–9, 53, 62, 63–4, 77, 83, 93, 111, 119, 158, 163, 164–5, 180, 181–2, 183, 185, 194, 198, 211, 221, 222, 228, 275, 284, 290
Cadbury Congresbury, Somerset 165
Cademuir, Peeblesshire 95–6, 190
Caesar, G. Julius 36, 41, 67, 70, 73, 131, 133, 152, 168, 185, 193, 195, 197, 207, 213, 223–4, 228–37, 239, 240, 241, 243, 246, 247, 261, 276, 281, 285, 287
Cahercommaun, Co. Clare 173–4
cairns, cairnfields 96, 101, 202, 217–18, 273
  see also burial, cemeteries
Caledonii, Caledonians 239
Caligula 132
Calleva Atrebatum 134
  see also Silchester
Camden, William 30, 31
Camp Tops, Morebattle, Roxburghshire 96–7, 201
Camulodunum (Colchester), Essex 130, 131–3, 138, 159, 289
  Garrison site 133

Gosbecks 131, 132, 159
Lexden 131, 132, 286
Sheepen 131, 159
Stanway 132, 286
Camulodunum (Ptolemy) 238
Cannae, battle of 195
Caractacus 238
Carn Alw, Pembrokeshire 191
Carn Fadrun, Caernarvonshire 96, 100–102, 113
carnyx 197
Carrock Fell, Cumbria 217–18
Cartier, Jacques 259
Cartimandua 43, 138, 228, 238
Cassington Mill, Oxfordshire 212
Cassius Dio 132, 239
Cassivellaunus 234, 235–7, 281, 282
Castell Caer Seion, Caernarvonshire; *see* Conway Mountain
Castle Dore, Cornwall 162–3
Castle O'er, Dumfriesshire 127–30, 161
castros, castro culture 9, 36, 279
Caterthuns, Angus 34–5
  Brown 76–7
Catuvellauni 135, 237
cauldrons 183, 197
causewayed enclosures 14, 119, 153–4, 155, 156, 184, 274
'causewayed' forts 76, 140
cavalry 190–3, 197, 198, 235–6, 239
Cayla de Mailhac, Aude 116
Celts 228
  'Celtic' fields 31
  Celtiberians 36, 191, 197
  Celtic languages 46
  Celto-Ligurians 94
  'Celtic paradigm' 180–20, 46
cemeteries 6, 116, 178, 208, 291
  Arras 192, 210, 213, 215, 286, 291
  Aylesford-Welwyn 210, 215, 291
  Durotrigian 209, 210
  Hallstatt 20
  La Tène 20, 204
  square-ditched barrow 6, 11, 141, 143, 215, 270
  war 40, 158, 179–85
  see also burial
Cenimagni 237
central places 17–18, 25, 44, 45, 113, 120–1, 170, 203, 277, 291
Chadwick, Sonia (Hawkes) 115
Chalbury Camp, Dorset 64, 68, 110–11, 216, 278
Challis, Aidan 67
Chalmers, George 34–5
'champion's portion' 196, 240, 272, 289
Champlain, Samuel de 259–60

Chanctonbury, Sussex 223
chariots 234–6, 239, 240
  chariot-burials, *see* burial
Chatto Craig, Hownam, Roxburghshire 171
Cherbury Camp, Oxfordshire (Berkshire) 74
Chesters, Drem, East Lothian 126, 177
chevaux-de-frise 71, 155, 190–2, 219
Chichester dykes, Sussex 130, 138
Childe, V. Gordon 10, 67, 86, 144, 168, 189, 280
Christison, David 1, 29, 34–5, 188, 191
Chun Castle, Cornwall 162
Cicero, Marcus Tullius 285
circumvallation 231
Cissbury, Sussex 277
'citadel forts' 169–71
Clapperton, Captain Hugh 265–6
Clarke, David 43–4
Clatchard Craig, Fife 166
Claudius 285
Clickhimin, Shetland 86, 145, 147
clients, clientship 130, 145, 148, 167, 240, 285
cliff-castles 233
Clonmacnoise torc, *see* Knock
Clonoura, Co. Tipperary 239
Close-Brooks, J. 221
Cnoc an Duin, Ross-shire 87
coins, coinage 131, 135
  Iron Age 46, 109, 192, 235, 285
  minting 131, 134
  Roman 30–1, 159, 161, 164, 222
Cold Kitchen Hill, Wiltshire 223
Collingwood, R. G. 217, 228
Collins, A. E. P. 213
Collis, J. R. 44, 45
Columba 245
Commius 135, 236, 237
Conderton Camp, Worcestershire 93, 98
Condé-sur-Suippes, Aisne 131
Connah, G. 5, 266–7
contours, contour forts 1, 10, 15, 16–17, 58, 250
Conway Mountain, Caernarvonshire 70, 100, 102, 195
Cook, James 250, 252
cooking sheds 254
cord rig; *see* agriculture
Cotter, C. 174
counterscarp; *see* ramparts
Cowen, J. D. 192
craft specialisation 131, 138, 262, 263, 280
Craigmarlock, Renfrewshire 188
Craik Moor, Morebattle, Roxburghshire 55–6
crannogs 168, 252, 253, 290
Crawcwellt West, Merionethshire 225
Crawford, O. G. S. 12, 110, 119, 135
Credenhill Camp, Herefordshire 104

Creeveroe, Co. Armagh 273
Crew, P. 224
Crickley Hill, Gloucestershire 16, 17, 21, 24–5, 38, 47, 61, 63, 64, 65–6, 67, 69, 74, 77, 78–80, 84, 89, 104, 105, 152, 154, 186–7, 252
Croft Ambrey, Herefordshire 77, 78, 102–4, 106, 187
Cunliffe, Sir Barrington 9, 25–7, 44, 72, 73, 113, 120, 121, 123, 130, 142, 185, 203, 206, 208, 210, 211, 216, 221, 275, 276–7, 280
Cunnington, Mrs Maud 115, 159, 212, 214
Cunobelinus 132, 159
currency bars 183, 203, 223–5
Curwen, E. C. 153

Dalmahoy, Midlothian 169
Dál Riata 168, 244
Dalsetter, Shetland 145
Danebury, Hampshire 14, 21, 25–7, 38, 44–6, 47, 48, 50, 59, 73, 75, 81, 84–5, 103, 110, 112–13, 119, 120–3, 124, 130, 153, 186, 192, 193, 194, 195, 203, 204, 206, 207, 208, 210, 211, 216–17, 221–2, 224–5, 275, 276, 277, 278, 283, 284, 287
    Danebury Environs Programme 44, 50, 113, 119, 120–3, 124
Dani, New Guinea 196
Datchet, Berkshire 193
Davidson, J. 252
Déchelette, Joseph 36
Deganwy, Caernarvonshire 163
Degsastan 244
'developed' hillforts 7, 13, 15, 16, 17, 40, 111, 123, 142, 203, 208, 256, 261, 275, 276–8, 279, 289
Devil's Dyke, Hertfordshire 133
Devil's Dyke, Sussex 277
Devil's Hill, Yorkshire 142
Diepeveen-Jansen, M. 121, 270
diffusionism 12, 41, 43
Dinas Emrys, Caernarvonshire 163
Dinas Powys, Glamorgan 163
Dinorben, Clwyd 25–6, 57, 81, 83, 105, 159
Diodorus Siculus 196–7, 228, 240
ditches, function of 5, 11, 14, 27, 42, 53–4, 58, 61, 69, 72–3, 74–5, 78, 87, 106–7, 109, 121, 153, 156, 184–5, 206, 210, 211, 212–13, 214–15, 224, 231, 263, 292
   internal 106, 109, 129, 139–40, 265
   quarry– 11, 14, 24–5, 54, 58, 88, 212, 265
   see also causewayed enclosures *and* linear earthworks
Diviciacus (of Aedui) 285
Dixon, Philip 38, 187

Dobunni 135, 224, 276
Dockrill, S. 144
Doon Hill, East Lothian 54
Dreva, Peeblesshire 190
Drewett, P. 216, 251
Driffield Wold, Nafferton, Yorkshire 142
droveways 142
druids 29, 30, 238, 240–1, 285, 286
Dryburn Bridge, East Lothian 125
dual ownership 17
du Fresne, M-J. M. 252
Duggleby Howe, Yorkshire 142
Dumbarton Rock, Clyde 169, 243
Dumnorix (of Aedui) 285
Dumyat, Stirlingshire 171
dun 70, 168, 172, 173, 175
   -enclosures 11, 169
   -houses 144
Dun A' Chrannag, Knapdale, Argyll 170
Dunadd, Argyll 29, 35, 166, 167, 169, 170, 244, 290
Dun Aengus, Inishmore 47, 70–2, 157, 173, 190, 219–21
Dunagoil, Bute 189
   Little Dunagoil 170
Dún Ailinne, Co. Kildare 72, 106, 107, 108, 109, 284
Dun Dubh Cathair, Inishmore 190
Dundurn, Perthshire 169, 170, 171, 244
Dun Fhinn, Argyll 168
Dunion, Roxburghshire 170
Dunkeld, King's Seat, Perthshire 170
Dùn Mac Sniachan, Benderloch, Argyll 87
Dunnichen Hill, Angus 245
Dunnideer, Aberdeenshire 87
Dunragit, Galloway 168
Dunsinane, Perthshire 34
Durden, Henry 183, 184
Durnovaria (Dorchester, Dorset) 158
Durotriges, Durotrigian 110, 158, 179, 224, 275–6, 277, 279
Dyke Hills, Dorchester-on-Thames, Oxfordshire 16, 135–6

Earle, Augustus 254
Ecgfrith 243, 245
Eddisbury, Cheshire 47
Eildon Hills, Roxburghshire 273
   Eildon Hill North 95, 99–100, 156, 201, 278–9, 289
Ellison, A. 216, 251
Els Vilars, Arbeca 191
Emain Macha 240–1
   see also Navan fort
entrances, structure and use of 5, 75–83, 84–5, 89, 111, 113, 121, 139–40, 152–3, 156,

177, 179–80, 181–5, 186, 187–8, 256–7, 258, 264–5, 268, 271, 272, 280, 283
  barbican 81, 84–5
  bridges 78–81, 84, 187, 206
  dual or twin portal 81–3, 84–5, 283
  fighting platforms 58, 82, 251–2, 265
  gatehouses 78, 81, 84, 86, 206, 272
  guard chambers 25–6, 77, 81, 82, 83, 102, 105, 182, 186, 206, 265, 276
  hornwork 84–5, 121, 194
  lack of 17, 55, 86–7
  sentry posts 77, 81, 83, 194
  stone-lined 24, 64, 78, 81, 181, 186, 232
  timber-lined 78, 81, 155, 187
  twin carriageway 64, 78, 81, 83
Entremont, Aix-en-Provence 84, 94
Eogan, George 47
Eppillus 235
excarnation 22, 185, 214, 215–17, 283–4
Eye Water, Berwickshire 17–18

Feachem, Richard 54, 95, 125, 170–1
Fécamp, Seine Inférieure 73
Ffridd Faldwyn, Montgomery, Powys 57, 78, 81, 103, 104, 106, 187
fields, field systems, field boundaries 8, 98–9, 110, 120–1, 130, 132–3, 204, 258, 265
  see also agriculture
Figsbury, Wiltshire 120, 121
Finavon, Angus 86–7
Fin Cop, Derbyshire 184, 272
Fitzpatrick, E. 173
Flimston Bay, Pembrokeshire 221
Flodden, Northumberland 141
Foel Trigarn, Pembrokeshire 35, 113, 152, 273–4
Fojut, N. 144, 145, 148
Forde-Johnston, J. 9, 15, 17, 75
Forgandenny, Castle Law, Perthshire 67, 87
Forschner, Baden-Württemberg 154
Fort Harrouard, Eure-et-Loir 155
fosterage 240
four-posters 6, 21–2, 102–6, 112, 113, 115, 116, 121, 187, 204–5, 216, 217, 221, 251–2, 276, 278, 281, 284
  see also grain storage
Fox, Lady Aileen 250, 252, 253–4, 256
Fox, Sir Cyril 9, 276
Fraser, J. 245
Frere, S. S. 238
Frilford, Oxfordshire (Berkshire) 223
Fürstengräber 37, 116, 286
Fürstensitze 37, 116, 121, 170, 203, 284

Garn Boduan, Caernarvonshire 100, 102, 171, 195
gates, structure and use 75, 77–81, 84, 152, 182, 185–7, 231–2, 245

Gauls, Galli 228–33, 237, 240, 241, 285
  'Gallic' forts 10, 67, 189
geophysical survey 42, 93–4, 98, 104, 106, 109, 111, 114, 284, 291
Gergovia, (plateau de Merdogne, Puy-de-Dôme, Auvergne) 36, 229
Germans, Germani 229–30
Gibbs Hill, Dumfriesshire 55–7
Giessübel-Talhau, Baden-Württemberg 116
Gildas 165
Gilmour, Simon 101
glass 163, 167, 169, 263, 290
Glastonbury, Somerset 43–4, 174, 195
Glauberg, Hesse 284
Gob Eirer, Lewis 147
Goldberg, Baden-Württemberg 36
Gondole, Auvergne 213
Gosbecks, Colchester, Essex; *see* Camulodunum
Gosden, C. 275
Gournay-sur-Aronde, Oise 134, 246
grain storage, granaries 21–22, 102, 104, 105, 123, 216–17, 222
Grant, A. 123
Gravelly Guy, Oxfordshire 204, 282
Great Chesters, Northumberland 160
Greenlands, Rudston, Yorkshire 142
Greenwell, Canon William 33
Gretton, Northamptonshire 224
'grey literature' 50
Grimes, W. F. 221
Grimthorpe, Yorkshire 38, 58, 59, 142, 143, 251
Groube, L. 250
guard chambers, *see* entrances
Guilbert, G. 105, 108, 207–8
Gundestrup, Denmark 197
Gurnard's Head, Cornwall 70
Gussage All Saints, Dorset 212, 225

Hadrian's Wall 31, 160
Halliday, S. 57, 95–6
Hallstatt, Austria 197
  period, culture 37, 46, 94, 116, 121, 170, 192, 203, 213, 284, 286
  types 192, 387
Hambledon Hill, Dorset 13, 16, 17, 92, 110, 119, 152, 153–4, 216, 260, 274, 276, 279
Ham Hill, Somerset 51, 159, 185, 207, 212, 224, 271
Hamilton, J. R. C. 145
Hamilton, S. 277
Hamilton-Dyer, S. 222
Hannibal 195
Harbison, P. 191
Harding, Anthony 141, 155, 156
Hardy, Thomas 7

Harehope, Peeblesshire 54
Härke, H. 121
Harting Beacon, Sussex 278
Haselgrove, C. 18, 124, 125, 134, 135
Haughey, Charles 47
Haughey's fort, Co. Armagh 47, 107–8, 157, 273
Hausa 5, 265
Hawkes, Christopher 1, 28, 33, 36, 38, 44–5, 119, 120, 133, 227
Hayhope Knowe, Roxburghshire 55, 87, 96–7, 201–2
head-hunting 260, 261–2
hearths 21, 83, 93, 94, 104, 105, 174, 224, 254, 259, 286
Heathrow, Caesar's Camp, Middlesex 221
 temple 221
Heidengraben bei Grabenstetten, Baden-Württemberg 207
Heidenreich, C. 259
Helsby, Cheshire 47
Helvetii 189
Hembury, Devon 39, 57, 153, 158, 185
Hencken, H. O'N. 174
Hencken, T. C. (Mrs) 182
henge monuments 16, 58, 139
Hengistbury Head, Dorset (Hampshire) 39
Heuneburg, Baden-Württemberg 25, 37, 116, 206
hierarchy, settlement, structural 169–70, 206–7, 243, 267, 287
 see also social structure
High Knowes, Alnham, Northumberland 21, 54–5
Hill, J. D. 18, 227, 240, 278, 283
Hill, Peter 39
hill-slope forts 15, 16
Hingley, R. 114–5, 224
hoards 138, 158, 162, 287
 currency bar 223–4
 sling-stone 82–3, 192, 194–5
Hochdorf, Eberdingen, Baden-Württemberg 286
Hochelaga, Montreal Island 259
Hod Hill, Dorset 11, 12, 16, 17, 58, 63, 73, 84–5, 110, 121, 158, 185, 211–12, 216, 224, 260, 276, 279
Hogg, A. H. A. 44, 100–102, 218, 233
Hog Island, Shetland 146–7
Hohmichele, Baden-Württemberg 37, 193
Holl, A. 267
Hollingbury, Sussex 57, 59
horses 199, 213, 282
 -bits 192
 breeding
 paired draught 192, 240
Horsley, John 31

horticulture; *see* agriculture
hostages 261
Houbie, Shetland 145
Houghton Down, Hampshire 121
houses, cellular 100–102
 figure-of-eight 106, 108
 rectangular 100, 102–4, 105, 131, 134, 154, 172, 204, 254, 259, 285
 round 8, 20–1, 24, 25, 46, 96, 110, 113, 121, 127, 133, 134, 143, 217, 254, 278, 279, 282
 chief's, elite 17, 21, 110, 144, 254, 259
 platforms 95–6, 99–100, 105, 110–11, 113
 post-ring 21, 105, 112, 116, 140
 ring-ditch 21, 96, 98, 128, 202
 ring-groove 95, 96, 98, 112, 127, 133, 157
 stake-wall 21, 104, 105, 108, 111, 112, 217
 stone-built 35, 38, 39, 70, 100–102, 218
 'Votadinian' 39
 wheelhouses 148
 see also brochs *and* dun–houses
Hownam Law, Roxburghshire 92, 95–6, 201, 279
Hownam Rings, Roxburghshire 38–9
 Hownam model 38–9, 251
Hull, M. R. 133
Hull, R. 279
Hunsrucken, Bavaria 284
Hunter, F. 124, 161
Huron 257–62
Hutchinson, William 31
Hut Knowe, Hownam, Roxburghshire 8, 98–9
huts, hut-circles *see* houses

Ida 243
Ife, Nigeria 262, 263
inauguration sites 145, 177, 241, 282
Ingleborough, Yorkshire 69–70, 96, 218, 273
'invasion hypothesis' 19, 44, 177
Inveresk, East Lothian 162
iron working 16, 163, 223, 224–5
Iroquois, Iroquoia 257–62, 277
Ivinghoe Beacon, Buckinghamshire 38

Jackson, Kenneth 20, 240–2
James, S. 19, 20, 178
Jenné-jeno, Mali 266–7
Jobey, George 31, 70, 102
Joffroy, R. 284

Kae Heughs, Barney Mains, East Lothian 126–7
Kaimes Hill, Midlothian 190
Kagoro 265
Kano, Nigeria 265–6, 267
Karl, R. 242

Kauri Point, Tauranga Harbour, North Island 251, 256
Kebbi 265
Keiller, A. 153
Kelheim, Bavaria 225
  -type rampart, *see* ramparts
Kenyon, Dame Kathleen 52, 212, 227
Kildonan, Argyll 70, 168
Kimmig, Wolfgang 37
King, A. 70
King's Barrow, Yorkshire 213
King's Stables, Navan, Co. Armagh 107–8, 157
kinship 17, 89, 148, 263
Kirkburn, Yorkshire 286
Knock, Co. Roscommon 287
Knocknalappa, Co. Clare 158
Knock Scalbert, Kintyre, Argyll 78
Knowes, East Lothian 125
Knowth, Co. Meath 47
Krämer, Werner 37
Kristiansen, K. 192–3, 196
kumara 250

'ladder settlements' 143
Ladle Hill, Hampshire 87–8
Laing, L. 170
Lamb, R. 147
lances, lance-heads, lancers 192–3, 197, 198, 199
Landberg, Fair Isle 147
Lane–Fox, Col. A. H. 33
  see also Pitt-Rivers
Lausitz culture 154–5
La Tène culture 192, 203, 240, 284
Leach, P. 222
Le Camp d'Artus, Huelgoat, Finistère 233
Leckhampton, Gloucestershire 61, 64, 83, 187, 190
Leeds, E. T. 162
Le Petit Celland, Manche 233
Lexden, Colchester, Essex; *see* Camulodunum
Leyland, John 30
Liddington Castle, Wiltshire 75, 276
Limbert, D. 173
linear earthworks 128–9, 130, 142–3
  village 142–3
Little Dunagoil; *see* Dunagoil
Little Wittenham, Castle Hill, Oxfordshire 78, 91, 114–5, 123, 155–6, 210, 214
Little Woodbury, Wiltshire 21, 22, 36, 102
  see also 'Woodbury economy'
Livy 195
Loch of Huxter, Shetland 86, 147
Lock, G. 19, 178, 275
Lorrio, A. J. 191
Loughnashade, Co. Armagh 107–8, 157
Lukis, Rev. W. C. 35

Lydney, Gloucestershire 223
Lynn, C. 106, 108

MacKie, E. W. 145, 147, 189
MacLauchlan, Henry 31
Madmarston Camp, Oxfordshire 93, 224
Maeatae 239
Maiden Bower, Bedfordshire 184, 212
Maiden Castle, Bickerton, Cheshire 64
Maiden Castle, Dorset 7, 12, 13, 14, 22, 24, 27, 30, 39–42, 44, 46, 48, 51, 59–60, 63, 64, 72, 73, 75, 81–3, 84–5, 93, 119, 121, 151, 158, 179–80, 184, 185, 194–5, 207, 208–10, 211, 222, 274, 275, 279, 283
Mallory, J. P. 109, 157, 242
Maltby, M. 222
Mam Tor, Derbyshire 17, 96, 156
Manby, T. 140
Manching, Bavaria 37, 78, 89, 94, 131, 134, 207, 225, 280, 284–5, 288
Mandubracius 236
Mangakaware, Waikato, North Island 252, 253, 254, 256
Manley, J. 277
Manning, W. 183
Marsden, Samuel 253
Marshall, Dorothy 170
Martin-Atkins, Edwin 33
Martin Down, Wiltshire 33
Martinsell, Wiltshire 17
Meare, Somerset 195
Melsonby, Yorkshire 138
Meon Hill, Warwickshire 224
Mercer, R. 14, 18–19, 48, 96, 110, 153
Mercury Bay, Coromandel Peninsula, North Island 252
metalworking, metallurgy 6–7, 43, 109, 157, 163–4, 263
metrology 25, 89
Midsummer Hill, Herefordshire 17, 78, 83, 103, 104
Mill Hill, Deal, Kent 192, 213, 286
Moat Knowe, Buchtrig, Roxburghshire 170
Moel Fenlli, Clwyd 202
Moel Hiraddug, Clwyd 25–6, 83, 105–6, 202
Moel y Gaer, Llanbedr, Clwyd 189
Moel y Gaer, Rhosesmor, Clwyd 21, 38, 57, 63, 64–5, 67, 89, 104–5, 106, 207–8
Monasterevin, Co. Kildare 242
Mons Graupius 239
Mont Beuvray, Burgundy 24, 36, 131, 233, 288
Mont Lassois, Burgundy 284
Moody, H. 266
Mooghaun, Co. Clare 47, 158, 173
Moore, T. 18
Moredun, Moncrieffe Hill, Perthshire 170

Moret, P. 191
Mortonhall, Edinburgh 192
Mote of Mark, Dumfriesshire 163–4, 167–8
Mount Roskill, Auckland 251
Mount Wellington, Auckland 251
Mucking North, Essex 139
Mucking South, Essex 139, 140
multivallation 7, 11–13, 15, 38, 41, 53, 75, 111, 177, 194, 199, 206, 251, 288
 see also bivallation
murus Gallicus; see ramparts

Napoleon III 35–6
Navan fort, Co. Armagh 47, 106–8, 109, 157, 241, 242, 273, 284
Nechtansmere, battle of 198, 245
Nennius 163, 245
Nervii 231
Ness of Burgi, Shetland 86, 147
Nettlebank Copse, Hampshire 121
Neustupný, E. 27–8, 196
'New Archaeology' 43–4
Newhall Hill, Dumfriesshire 17
Ngaroto, Waikato, North Island 253
Nicholas, J. L. 253
Niederneundorf, Brandenburg 155
Nitriansky Hrádok, Slovakia 154
Northumberland, Duke of 31
North Oxfordshire Grim's Ditch 135, 137, 138
Noviodunum 73, 231
'nuclear' forts 101, 169–71, 287, 288
Numantia, Soria, Spain 36, 197

oblong forts 16–17, 86–7
Oengas, son of Fergus 244
Ó Floinn, R. 174
Ogbury, Wiltshire 30
Oldbury, Kent 73
open/unenclosed settlement 6, 39, 98, 99, 122–3, 124, 204, 256, 267, 276, 278
oppida 14, 39, 94, 125, 130–8, 207, 208, 213, 225, 230, 233, 234, 275, 279, 284, 285, 288
 enclosed 130
 minor 95
 nuclear 130, 133–5
 terrain, territorial 1, 8, 130, 131–3, 135–6, 159, 170, 207, 234
Ordovices 238
Ó Ríordáin, Sean P. 109, 172
Orton Meadows, Northamptonshire 224
Ostorius Scapula, Publius 238
Oswald, A. 17, 140
Otakanini, South Kaipara Harbour, North Island 251
Over Rig, Dumfriesshire 129
Oyo-Ile, Nigeria 263–5, 267

pā 250–7
 marsh, swamp 250, 252
'pacification of the past' 18–20, 46, 177–8
Paeroa, Bay of Islands, North Island 252
palisades, palisaded settlements 1, 9, 38, 53, 54–7, 73, 98, 105, 108, 109, 121, 124, 142, 151, 154, 155, 188, 192, 202, 243, 251, 252, 256, 257–62, 265, 268
 double 54–5, 56–7, 155, 188, 258
 embanked 54, 57
 triple 258
pastoralism, pastoralists 22, 100, 101, 229–30
 see also animal husbandry
Paulinus, G. Suetonius 180, 238
Pearson, T. 17
Peketa, Kaikoura, North Island 252
Penda 244
Pendergast, J. 259
Penycloddiau, Clwyd 202
Pen-y-Gaer, Llanbedr-y-Cennin, Caernarvonshire 191
peripheral places, hillforts as 17, 120
Petillius Cerialis 42
Pfostenschlitzmauer, see ramparts
'Picts' 243, 244–5
 'Pictish' sculpture 192, 198, 245
Piggott, Mrs C. M. 38, 55, 251
Piggott, Stuart 22, 30, 87, 155, 229
Pimperne, Dorset 21, 193, 214–15
pit, pits 22, 33, 46, 93, 94, 104, 110–11, 112, 113, 115, 116, 117, 142, 194, 204, 210, 217, 259, 276, 278, 281
 -alignments 126, 142, 192, 224
 -burials, see burials
 iron-working- 157
 post-pits 78–9, 81, 112, 156, 186
 storage- 21, 22, 98, 104, 113, 121, 254, 259, 278, 281
Pitchbury, Essex 131
Pitt–Rivers, Gen. A. L. F. 29, 33–4, 135
plateau forts 15, 16
'polyfocal settlements' 134
Portknockie, Green Castle, Banffshire 67, 164, 172
Posidonius 196, 229
pottery 37, 44, 290
 amphorae 135, 138, 163, 164
 Atrebatic 277
 bead-rim 41
 Durotrigian 277
 D-ware 163
 E-ware 163, 165, 166, 167, 169
 Gallo-Belgic 135
 Late Bronze Age 107
 Neolithic 10–7
 post-Deverel-Rimbury 139

Roman 101, 102
  samian 135, 138, 158, 161
  'saucepan' 121
  south-western 203
Pouerua, Pakarata, North Island 251, 256
Poundbury, Dorset 63, 68
promontory forts 9, 11, 12, 15, 16, 33, 3537, 67, 144, 146–9, 151, 171–2, 218–19, 221, 223, 250, 273
Ptolemy 238
publication 47–50

Quarley Hill, Hampshire 38, 44–5, 119–21, 130
quarry ditches; *see* ditches
'quern replacement' 102
querns 101, 160
  rotary 174
  saddle 102, 174

Radford, C. A. R. 162, 174
Raffin, Co. Meath 242
Raftery, Barry 116, 157, 174, 242
Rahoy, Argyll 168
Rainsborough Camp, Northamptonshire 63, 65–6, 77, 79, 83, 89, 93, 186, 213, 272
Ráith na Ríg; *see* Tara
Ralston, I. 87, 191
ramparts, breastwork 58, 73, 84, 152
  counterscarp 11, 14, 73, 211, 212
  buttressing 59, 70, 72
  dump or *glacis* 15, 24, 53, 63, 69, 72–3, 74, 89, 108, 112, 140, 147, 155, 163, 198, 212, 231, 265, 288
    timber-faced- 59, 63
    stone-faced- 68, 70
  fighting/watch towers 231, 251–2, 258, 265
  gang construction 25, 65, 84, 87–8
  internal divisions, 'casemate construction' 63, 65, 69–70
  iron nails/spikes 24, 67, 164, 171–2, 225, 233, 288
  Kelheim type 288
  median wall faces 70
  mud-brick construction 25, 206, 265, 266
  parapet 24, 58, 65, 72, 89, 206
  'professional'/specialist architects/engineers 25, 83, 89
  stepped/tiered revetment, 'back terracing' 65–7, 69, 70–2, 89
  wall-rampart 15, 53, 58, 69, 72, 74, 288
    hollow timber-framed wall 55, 57
    murus duplex 19, 31, 70, 191
    murus Gallicus 24, 64, 66–7, 89, 171, 225, 232–3, 288
    Pfostenschlitzmauer 62, 63–4
    timber-reveted timber-framed wall 22–4, 33, 38, 53, 55, 58–63, 112, 154, 155, 166, 198, 272, 288
    stone-reveted timber-framed wall 38, 63–8, 75, 164, 171, 172, 189, 198, 288
    stone wall without timber frame 68–72
  wide-spaced 14
Rams Hill, Berkshire 73, 78, 155–6
Ranachan Hill, Kintyre, Argyll 70, 77–8
Ranscombe Camp, Sussex 61
Rath of the Synods, *see* Tara
Rathgall, Co. Wicklow 116–7, 123, 157
raths 33
Remi 231
Renfrew, Colin 43
Reynolds, Peter 21, 98
Rhee, Netherlands 204
Rheged, kingdom of 168
Richie Ferry, Lanarkshire 98
Richmond, Sir Ian 110, 158, 211
ridge forts 16, 250
ringforts 11, 168, 171, 172–3, 242
ring-works 17, 107, 139–41, 142, 143, 145, 147, 250
Ritchie, J. N. G. 239
Rivet, A. L. F. 232
rondels 16
Rooksdown, Andover, Hampshire 282
Rotherley, Wiltshire 33, 212
roundhouses, *see* houses
rounds, Cornish 17
Roy, Gen. William 32, 34, 128, 171
Rubers Law, Roxburghshire 166
Rubh an Dunain, Skye 147
Rutland, R. 114
Rynne, Etienne 219–20

Sabrosa, Guimarães, Portugal 36
Salmondsbury, Gloucestershire 224
salt 203–4
samian ware, *see* pottery
Santa Luzia, citânia de, Viana do Castelo, Portugal 279
Sarmento, Martins 36
Savory, H. N. 83
Scatness, Shetland 86, 147
Schulten, Adolf 36
'scooped' settlements 38, 125
Scowther Knowe, Roxburghshire 98
Scratchbury, Wiltshire 16, 116, 214
seasonal occupation 21, 95, 96, 100, 102, 111, 160, 161, 201–2, 204, 217, 218, 253–4, 256, 281
Segsbury Camp, Oxfordshire (Berkshire) 276
Selgovae 95
shale, Kimmeridge 203

Sharples, N. 14, 41, 125, 179, 180, 194
Sheepen, Colchester, Essex; *see* Camulodunum
shields 20, 182, 193, 198, 199, 231–2, 239, 286, 287, 289
shrines, sacred sites 6, 8, 22, 113, 134, 165, 185, 217, 221–3, 238, 255–6, 284
Sidbury Hill, Wiltshire 121
siege, siege-works 17, 36, 72, 179, 230, 231, 244, 247, 265–6
Silchester, Hampshire 130, 134–5, 138, 276, 289
single combat; *see* warfare
situla art; *see* art
slaves, slavery 25, 229, 244, 266, 268
sling, slingstones, slingers 12, 31, 41, 73, 83, 84, 102, 153, 192, 193, 194–5, 198, 232, 246
 see also stoning
Smith, R. 267
social structure 18–20, 25–7, 45–6, 120, 144, 148, 167, 172, 177, 206, 230, 237–8, 240, 242, 253, 261, 263, 267, 285–7, 289
souterrains 22, 174
South Lodge, Wiltshire 33
spears, spearheads 179, 182, 183, 192–3, 195, 197, 198, 199, 253
Spetisbury, Dorset 183–4
Spišský Štvrtok, Slovakia 154
Springfield Lyons, Essex 76, 140
Sròn an Dùin, Berneray (Barra Head) 147–8
St Albans, Hertfordshire; *see* Verulamium
St Blane's, Bute 170
St Catharine's Hill, Winchester, Hampshire 25–6, 81, 119, 121, 186, 277
St David's Head, Pembrokeshire 8, 15, 35
St Joseph, J. K. 13
Standingstone, East Lothian 125
Standlake, Oxfordshire 33
 scabbard 287
Stanford, Stanley 78, 102, 104
Stanish, C. 196
Stanton Harcourt, Linch Hill, Oxfordshire 135
Stanway, Colchester, Essex; *see* Camulodunum
Stanwick, Yorkshire 30, 33, 39, 42–3, 68, 74, 136, 138, 207, 228, 238, 239
 'Stanwick economy' 229, 270
Staple Howe, Yorkshire 54, 142
Stead, I. 38, 213
Steinbichel, Bavaria 284
Stephen (Eddius Stephanus) 243–4
Stevenson, R. B. K. 169–70

Stična, Slovenia 116
Stirling torcs 287
Stockbridge Down, Hampshire 120
Stone, Stephen 33
Stonea Camp, Cambridgeshire 10, 238
Stonehenge 30, 43
stoning 73, 193–5, 198, 232, 258
 see also sling
storage 21–2, 98, 104, 105, 113, 121–2, 123, 144, 201, 203, 204–6, 216, 217, 225, 250, 254–5, 256, 259, 268, 276, 278, 280–1, 291
 see also pits *and* grain storage
Stout, M. 173
Strabo 19, 195, 228, 229, 240, 281
stratigraphy 33, 35, 36, 42, 44, 48, 60, 78, 112, 145, 156, 157, 164, 173, 174–5, 179, 211–12
Stukeley, William 29, 30–1, 32, 221
Suddern Farm, Hampshire 121
Suessiones 73, 231
Suetonius 39, 184, 207
Sundhope Kip, Hownam, Roxburghshire 98, 201
Surame, Nigeria 265
Sutton, D. 253
Sutton Common, South Yorkshire 205–6
Sutton Walls, Herefordshire 180, 181, 183, 211
swords 20, 183, 192–3, 195, 196, 198, 199, 239, 286

Tacitus 42, 138, 182, 228, 230, 235, 238–9
Tamshiel Rig, Southdean, Roxburghshire 8, 126
Taniwha, Te Kauwhata, North Island 254–5
Taplow Court, Buckinghamshire 57, 73, 155, 191
Tap o' Noth, Aberdeenshire 87, 96, 273
Tara, Co. Meath
 Mound of the Hostages 47, 109
 Ráith na Ríg 47, 107, 109, 284
 Rath of the Synods 47
Tasciovanus 134
Tate, George 31
Te Awanga, Hawke Bay, North Island 251, 254
Te Kauwhata, Waikato, North Island 254
Telamon 234
temples, Romano-Celtic 27, 41, 133, 159, 164, 221, 222–3
testudo 231–2, 238
Thomas, Charles 162
Thwing, Paddock Hill, Yorkshire 139–40, 141, 142, 143
Tidbury Rings, Hampshire 159
Tincomarus 135
Tintagel, Cornwall 165, 174
Tipping, R. 96
Tisbury, Castle Ditches, Wiltshire 111

Tite, Michael 93
Titterstone Clee, Shropshire 83
Todd, M. 158, 180
Tollense valley, Mecklenburg 178
Torberry, Sussex 277
torcs 160, 183, 197, 287
'tortoise'; see *testudo*
Tower Point, Pembrokeshire 70
towns, town planning 6, 40, 42, 44, 95, 98, 100, 106, 110, 131, 207–8, 262, 267, 279, 280
   see also urbanization
trackways 87, 130, 132, 134, 142–3, 191, 202
transhumance 98, 202
   see also seasonal occupation
Traprain Law, East Lothian 15, 36, 51, 95, 124–6, 156, 161–2, 289
   Traprain Law Environs Project 124–6
Tregeare Rounds, Cornwall 16
Tre'r Ceiri, Caernarvonshire 35, 70, 96, 100, 101, 102, 159–60, 195, 207, 273
Trevelgue Head, Cornwall 16, 221
Trigger, B. 259
Trinovantes 133, 237
Trundle, Sussex 119, 277
Trusty's Hill, Anwoth, Dumfriesshire 170
Tungrii 239
Turin Hill, Angus 245

Uffington, Oxfordshire (Berkshire)
   Castle 33, 46, 59, 74–5, 274–5, 276, 278
   Dragon Hill 275
   White Horse 275, 278, 282
Uley Bury, Gloucestershire 17
Ulster Cycle 20, 240–2, 246
unenclosed settlement; *see* open settlement
unenclosed platform settlement 96
'unfinished' hillforts 14, 87–8
univallation, univallate earthworks 7, 11, 38, 53
urbanization 43, 95, 110, 131, 134, 135, 138, 207–8, 262–3, 266–8, 279–80, 284, 289
Urnfield culture 151, 155, 192, 289

valley forts 250
Venclovà, N. 221
Veneti 39, 41, 233
Venutius 43, 138, 228, 238
Vercingetorix 36, 193, 232
Verulamium, Hertfordshire 130, 133–4
   Beech Bottom Dyke 133–4
   Devil's Dyke 133
   Gorhambury 134
   Prae Wood 134
Vespasian 39, 179, 180, 207, 275
Villeneuve-Saint-Germain, Aisne 131

vitrified fort, vitrification 34, 67, 87, 186, 187, 188–90, 198, 272
Vix, Burgundy 286
Votadini, Votadinian 39, 95, 125, 162
votive deposits 20
Vries, Netherlands 204

Wailes, B. 240
Wainwright, G. J. 70
Waioneke, Kaipara Harbour, North Island 256
Walbury, Berkshire 94
Wandlebury, Cambridgeshire 63
war cemeteries *see* cemeteries
warfare 17, 18–20, 41, 155, 178–9, 192, 194, 230, 234–6, 239, 240, 245, 246, 247, 249, 252, 260, 261–2, 267, 272, 291
   'ritualized' 178, 196–9, 246
   single combat 196–7, 240, 246, 272, 289
   'warrior panoply' 199
   see also chariots
Warner, R. 109
'Wasserburg' Buchau, Baden-Württemberg 154
Waterbolk, H. T. 204
Waterman, D. 47
water supply, sources, springs 8, 17, 101, 111, 117, 142
Wells, P. 225
Welwyn, Hertfordshire 286
West Brandon, Co. Durham 54
Westhampnett, Sussex 222
Wetwang Slack, Yorkshire 143
Wheathampstead, Hertfordshire 130, 133–4
Wheeler, Sir Mortimer 12, 33, 39–42, 44, 47, 48, 50, 52, 59, 73, 84, 133–4, 138, 158–9, 177, 179–80, 194, 207, 210, 211, 212, 228, 233, 238, 279
wheelhouses, *see* houses
White Meldon, Peebleshire 95–6
Whittingehame Tower, East Lothian 125
Wilbury Hill, Hertfordshire 31, 212
Wilson, A. E. 61
Wilson, Daniel 29, 34–5
Windmill Hill, Wiltshire 153
Windy Dido, Hampshire 120
wine 204
   see also pottery *amphorae*
Winkelbury, Wiltshire 33
Winklebury, Hampshire 91, 112
Witham, Lincolnshire, shield 20, 193, 287
   sword 193, 287
Wittnauer Horn, Aargau, Switzerland 36–7, 155
Woden Law, Roxburghshire 92–3, 98
'Woodbury economy' 230
Woodcuts, Dorset 33

Woodeaton, Oxfordshire 223
woodland management 24, 54, 63, 89
Woodward, A. 222
Woolbury, Hampshire 120, 121
Woolf, G. 14, 138
Woolley, Sir Leonard 227
Worlebury, Somerset 70
Worthy Down, Hampshire 121
Wrekin, Shropshire 83
Wyche Rocks, Malvern, Worcestershire 224

Yarnbury Castle, Wiltshire 121, 159, 212
Yarnton, Oxfordshire 211
Yeavering Bell, Northumberland 17, 21, 31, 95, 201, 279
Yoruba 5, 207, 263, 265, 267, 272
Young, H. W. 171

Zeijen, Netherlands 204–5
'zoning' 104, 105–6, 110, 112, 113, 131, 134, 135, 201, 207–8, 280